L. RON HUBBARD HAS EVOLVED INTO ONE OF the most controversial names of the new millennium. Somewhere between the castigation from his critics and the fervent praise of his followers existed a real man with a real mission. What this mission was, however, is debated with as much vehemence as the praises and castigations.

L. RON HUBBARD — THE TAO OF INSANITY delves deeply into the occult underpinnings of this man and his mission to reveal deeper insights into the matrix that he operated in that put him at the center of so much intrigue that surrounded key players in the military industrial complex such as Robert Heinlein, Jack Parsons, and Marjorie Cameron.

WITH HIS ROLE IN THE BABALON WORKING L. Ron Hubbard found himself as a participant in what has been heralded as the most ambitious occult ritual of the last century or perhaps even the last millennium: an attempt to deliver a Moon Child that would assuage the oppression and terror that has been ever-present in Mankind's history for millennia. While this clearly did not work, it can also be viewed as when the first Apollo mission failed with the astronauts being burnt to a crisp on the launching pad. The errors were studied and fixed, and after several more exploratory missions, Mankind was able to land on the Moon. You are invited to explore the depths of this magical process and the various factors involved. As history always repeats itself, this book sets the stage for the future with a new perspective.

L. RON HUBBARD
THE TAO OF INSANITY

BY PETER MOON

SkyBooks
NEW YORK

L. Ron Hubbard — The Tao of Insanity
Copyright © 2020 by Peter Moon

Cover art by Creative Circle Inc.
Typography by Creative Circle Inc.
Published by: Sky Books
              Box 769
              Westbury, New York 11590
              email: *skybooks@yahoo.com*
              website: www.skybooksusa.com
              www.digitalmontauk.com

Printed and bound in the United States of America. All rights reserved. No part of this book may be reproduced in any form or by any electronic or mechanical means including information storage and retrieval systems without permission in writing from the publisher. Certain quotations are included within the text by right of fair use as allowed for in copyright law.

Library of Congress Cataloging-in-Publication Data

Moon, Peter
    L. Ron Hubbard — The Tao of Insanity
        288 pages
        ISBN 978-09631889-7-7
1. Body, Mind, Spirit: Occultism 2. Body, Mind, Spirit: General
Library of Congress Control Number 2019953449

*This book is dedicated to the
untapped potential within you*

OTHER TITLES FROM SKY BOOKS

by Preston Nichols and Peter Moon
The Montauk Project: Experiments in Time
Montauk Revisited: Adventures in Synchronicity
Pyramids of Montauk: Explorations in Consciousness
Encounter in the Pleiades: An Inside Look at UFOs
The Music of Time

by Peter Moon
The Black Sun: Montauk's Nazi-Tibetan Connection
Synchronicity and the Seventh Seal
The Montauk Book of the Dead
The Montauk Book of the Living
Spandau Mystery
The White Bat

by Joseph Matheny with Peter Moon
Ong's Hat: The Beginning

by Stewart Swerdlow
Montauk: The Alien Connection
The Healer's Handbook: A Journey Into Hyperspace

by Alexandra Bruce
The Philadelphia Experiment Murder:
Parallel Universes and the Physics of Insanity

by Wade Gordon
The Brookhaven Connection

by Radu Cinamar with Peter Moon
Tranyslvanian Sunrise
Tranyslvanian Moonrise
Mystery of Egypt — The First Tunnel
The Secret Parchment
Forgotten Genesis

CONTENTS

INTRODUCTION — by Peter Moon..........9
CHAPTER ONE — The Funny Farm..........19
CHAPTER TWO — The Wrestler..........27
CHAPTER THREE — Insanity..........31
CHAPTER FOUR — Fishing..........43
CHAPTER FIVE — Sympathetic Magic(k)..........47
CHAPTER SIX — The Postulate..........53
CHAPTER SEVEN — Word Power, Mind Language..........59
CHAPTER EIGHT — Typhon..........75
CHAPTER NINE — Sympathy for the Devil..........79
CHAPTER TEN — Baphomet..........85
CHAPTER ELEVEN — Everything is Permissable..........95
CHAPTER TWELVE — Excalibur..........113
CHAPTER THIRTEEN — The Agent..........124
CHAPTER FOURTEEN — Lookout Mountain..........127
CHAPTER FIFTEEN — The Anchluss..........139
CHAPTER SIXTEEN — The Abyss..........147
CHAPTER SEVENTEEN — Dianetics and Karma..........157
CHAPTER EIGHTEEN — Blueprint to Heaven..........165
CHAPTER NINETEEN — Eclipse of the Soul..........177
CHAPTER TWENTY — Under the Moonlight..........185

CHAPTER TWENTY-ONE — City of the Pyramids............195
CHAPTER TWENTY-TWO — Qualifications......................203
CHAPTER TWENTY-THREE — On the Radar....................211
CHAPTER TWENTY-FOUR — White Noise.......................219
CHAPTER TWENTY-FIVE — The Aftermath.....................227
CHAPTER TWENTY-SIX — Meta-synch.............................231
CHAPTER TWENTY-SEVEN — Meta-chess.......................237
CHAPTER TWENTY-EIGHT — The Time Reactor.............241
CHAPTER TWENTY-NINE — Interpol................................249
CHAPTER THIRTY — Mae Day..251
CHAPTER THIRTY-ONE — Holy Holocaust, Batman!......253
CHAPTER THIRTY-TWO — Analysis...................................257
CHAPTER THIRTY-THREE — Conclusion..........................267
EPILOGUE — by Peter Moon...269
APPENDIX A — The Tree of Life...273
APPENDIX B — The Book of the Law..................................277
APPENDIX C — The Philadelphia Experiment..................279

Introduction

Do we need one more book on L. Ron Hubbard? Many books have already been written about him and there is a plethora of websites about this very controversial man and his work. Justly or not, most of these judge him harshly. There are some, but far fewer in number, that laud him and his work. I do not think there is a man in modern times who has been subject to more vitriolic derision than L. Ron Hubbard. Even characters like Saddam Hussein and Osama bin Laden, who are considered to be contemptible characters by most Americans, do not elicit the vitriol that the mention of Hubbard's name can produce. Not even the mention of Adolph Hitler, Joseph Stalin nor Charles Manson stir up so much emotion. The reason for this is that such nefarious characters are not only out of action, most people have them pigeon-holed into a comfortable corner of their mind. People in the West generally recognize such characters to be psychopaths. According to their own assessments, this is all that most people consider they need to know. When it comes to L. Ron Hubbard, however, there are still unresolved issues which have manifested in society and have been publicized ad nauseam.

Multitudes of people have made public censures as well as experienced absolute horrors as a result of their involvement in L. Ron Hubbard's most notable creation: Scientology. There are countless accusations, sometimes accompanied with varying degrees of evidence, of extortion, hypnotism, deliberate scamming, false promises, forced disconnection from families, and intimidating surveillance and harassment of adversaries, the latter of which include former Scientologists. There have also been instances of infiltration of private and government offices. What is the saddest aspect of all of these horrors, however, are the number of ruined lives that have been precipitated by people's involvement with the legacy of L. Ron Hubbard.

Despite the many attempts to portray the man, his character, and his legacy, there has been a renewed and continuous feeding frenzy by the media in recent times whenever his name or his philosophy, Scientology, is mentioned. As I write these words, this fascination by the media, as well as the general public, has grown to rather astounding proportions. L. Ron Hubbard and Scientology have become such buzz words that virtually any mention of them will make people stop and take notice. No matter how much he or his adherents are exposed or decried, the feeding frenzy does not quit. As time rolls on, the subject becomes more magnified. Even if it is unfortunate, it is understandable that the media's innate nature is to sensationalize the topic and get ratings. Above and beyond sensationalism, however, there has also been an increasing and genuine desire by members of the media to try and gain a better understanding of this controversial and often very zany subject.

In the spirit of creating a better understanding of this man, it is my intention to capture and share key essential aspects of L. Ron Hubbard that have, for the most part, been overlooked or under emphasized. I do consider myself qualified in this endeavor because I used to work in his personal office aboard his ship, the *Apollo*. It was my duty to be awake when he was awake and to serve in whatever capacity I was asked. I had access to all sorts of information that rank and file crew members, let alone Scientology staff or public, were never allowed or even in a position to see and therefore think about. During that time, I signed a long term non-disclosure agreement not to discuss certain information that was considered to be key or confidential. As this has now expired, I am at liberty to discuss certain aspects I have not mentioned before in my previous writings on the subject. In addition to these confidential matters, there were a host of experiences and vantage points I occupied that should provide a clearer understanding of L. Ron Hubbard and why he, his philosophy, and his legacy continue to fascinate and captivate people.

It is important to point out at the outset of this work that it is not my intention to castigate Hubbard nor to laud him. Instead, I am going to approach this subject in a different way than others have. Instead of trying to write a strictly biographical portrayal or attempting to explain the entirety of his work, which I consider to be a virtually impossible task, it is my intention to reduce the matter to its lowest common denominator: power. Whether you like Hubbard or not, no one is going to deny that he generated a tremendous amount of personal and organizational power. More than anything else, it is Hubbard's seizure of or rise to power that has left so many people baffled and wondering. If he were just a questionable self-help guru that wrote a best seller, no one would care. It is the fact that he has had so many adherents and created such a powerful and intimidating organization that makes people take notice and sometimes gives them cause for apprehension or deep concern. The many reports of ruined lives augment the horror that the words *Scientology* or *L. Ron Hubbard* can conjure up in people's minds.

There are a lot of opinions as well as hard data with regard to Hubbard's powerful influence over people. Known as a skilled hypnotist, there are many who think that his exotic and extravagant use of this skill enabled him to attract and cultivate such a formidable organization of zealots. There is no question that Hubbard did more than dabble in the occult and had a hypnotic effect upon his followers. This hypnotic effect has been extended to the media and general public as well because they cannot get enough of this man and his creation: Scientology. Why is this so? These are the factors which I will examine and explain, to the best of my current ability, in this book.

INTRODUCTION

Underlying Hubbard's most well known legacy, the Church of Scientology (including the many offshoots which have splintered from it), there is an occult matrix. Although some aspects of this occult matrix have either been alluded to, directly pointed out or acknowledged, it is not well understood by the general public nor even the authors who have "exposed" it. Some of this matrix consists of policies, technical procedures and directives that are mysterious only because they are unfamiliar to outsiders. There is also a deep energetic imprint that all of these policies and technical procedures are based upon, and this has to do with the mind of L. Ron Hubbard. They all derived from his mind. In this book, I will also attempt to give you insight into Hubbard's own mind. There are many opinions as to what was in his mind as well as data that gives insight as to what he was thinking at a particular time. While it is an impossible task to assess the exact contents of a person's mind, I will try to reduce my examination to the lowest common denominator.

If we are going to consider the makeup of one particular individual's mind, it is advisable to first consult the dictionary which states that the mind possesses at least three primary characteristics. First and foremost, the mind refers to recollection or memory. Second, it represents the element or complex of elements in an individual that feels, perceives, thinks, wills, and especially reasons. This refers to the conscious mental events and capabilities as well as the organized conscious and unconscious adaptive mental activity of an organism. Third, it refers to the determination, intention or desire of an organism. As a mind is evaluated, particularly in human terms, by how intelligent it is, it is also advisable to consult the definition of *intelligence*. In the dictionary, *intelligence* is the skilled use of reason as well as the ability to learn, understand or to deal with new or trying situations. It is also the ability to apply knowledge to manipulate one's environment or to think abstractly as measured by objective criteria. Both of these definitions suggest that Hubbard was highly intelligent if only by reason of his manipulation of people and circumstances. In his own writings, Hubbard explicitly stated that intelligence does not determine whether a person is good or evil. That, he said, has everything to do with motive. It is not my intent in this book to suggest to you that Hubbard was either good or bad but rather to point out that he was both powerful and intelligent.

All intelligence is based upon input of information. In an individual human being this has everything to do with one's physical perception but also the flow of communication within one's environment and one's access to it. In a more exotic sense, it would also apply to that which could be considered psychic perception. While people might argue about Hubbard's own paranormal abilities, there is no question that he knew enough about it so as to exploit it to an extent that was unprecedented. This, in turn, suggests that he enjoyed a degree of paranormal perception and most likely one that greatly exceeded your run-of-the-mill psychic intuitive. He did claim to have worked as a swami on Hollywood Boulevard while studying the human mind. In this book, I will also examine in more depth the paranormal aspects of Hubbard and his religion but primarily from the perspective of power. People are often attracted to Scientology because of its paranormal claims. Whether you believe those or not, the fact that one man could create an industry around it is very compelling to those on the outside looking in. They might not want any of the "Kool-Aid", but they are certainly interested in how he made it.

From my own experience as a result of working in his personal office, I can give you further insight into his character by telling you something that I have not yet seen in print. It is a fact that Hubbard personally believed that he was the true author of the *The Prince*, a classic book on politics by Niccolò Machiavelli. In his own handwriting, Hubbard stated in an inter-office memo in response to someone who had sent him either a copy or excerpt of this work, "This is my work! Machiavelli stole it from me". I am paraphrasing the exact quotation from memory, but it is true. Hubbard believed that he was Lorenzo de Medici. As I recall, this inter-office memo was written by him so that one of his staff could give the sender of the book a written reply in the form of a letter. A comment such as this by Hubbard was not intended to go into the reply. The fact that Hubbard thought he was de Medici and so deeply identified with *The Prince* has been under-reported, if at all reported, and has consequently gone unnoticed by many critics of Hubbard as well as other prying eyes. *The Prince* is considered to be one of the first major treatises of political philosophy in the West, and all major schools of political science are based upon its tenets. Its most famous tenet is "the end justifies the means".

If you consider that all Western political science is admittedly based upon the tenets in *The Prince*, it tells you that all politicians, and I am talking about the highest level of power politics, are playing by rules the walk-about citizen could never play by without getting himself arrested. In other words, those at the top of the food chain do not play fair. Why? Because they do not have to. Morals are for commoners, and the elite have an entitlement of exemption. When they do get in trouble, courts routinely dismiss the charges or obfuscate the issue, unless one of the elite has been chosen as a scapegoat by his brethren. To understand Hubbard, you must understand that he viewed the world this way. He definitely saw himself as something more than an average walk-about citizen, and he was playing a game of power. Whether accepted as one of the boys or not, he was playing in their sphere and by the laws of political science. Keep in mind that he identified with these laws to the point where he said that he wrote them. This does not mean that he wrote them or that he did not write them, but it tells you that they were a part of his soul-matrix and a definite part of his modus-operandi. In trying to understand Hubbard, it is important to understand that most citizens of this planet do not have the emotional composition to act like Machiavelli, at least not to the point that Hubbard and various politicians have. Only a small minority are able to get away with acting this way. Others aspire to do this and try but are not successful. For the most part, regular people are like Munchkins from the *Wizard of Oz*. Hubbard identified with the Wizard. He could also act like the Wicked Witch when he wanted to and sic the flying monkeys on his adversaries.

I cannot tell you that Hubbard was Lorenzo de Medici or any of the other famous figures he claimed to be. It is quite obvious that he deeply resonated with certain famous figures. He identified with powerful and famous people. Whether his claims are true or not, it is rare that such a claimant can apply the laws of his alleged former self to the point where he can either intimidate or awe an entire civilization, or at least a significant portion of it. Hubbard has indeed accomplished that in my opinion. That is why people keep talking about him.

Earlier, I mentioned that intelligence is based upon the input of information. As this applies to the human mind, so does it apply to political institutions. When we consider the spectrum of power politics, input and output of information becomes very shady in that it is always subject to regulation. He who controls the input and output of information is in a position to sway politics. This principle is always above and beyond the regulation of constitutions. Those who seek power likewise seek to control the information flow, and they also seek to remain undetected in this respect. They may or may not have a public profile. In this respect, intelligence and power go hand-in-hand. When we consider the Machiavellian mind-set, it is easy to understand that those who play power politics use or control intelligence agencies. It is therefore no wonder to realize that L. Ron Hubbard had his own personal intelligence agency, known as the Guardian's Office, that was larger than those of most countries.

I feel it is important to mention at this point that ordinary human beings, and this includes most Scientologists and ex-Scientologists, are very naive when it comes to the subjects of intelligence agencies. This includes many who think they are in the know about this subject. I have witnessed many pissing contests between people who like to argue about Hubbard's role in Naval Intelligence. While it is an undisputed fact that Hubbard served in the Office of Intelligence for the U.S. Navy, people often argue about how deep his service really went. Some like to minimize his import in this regard, insisting that he could not possibly have been of any importance to the Office of Naval Intelligence. What I would like to point out in this regard is that intelligence agencies serve those in the corridors of power. Sometimes, and not infrequently, the information they possess is so valuable that they are able to control and influence politics in ways that are unseen by the general public. Hubbard's acumen for power reveals that if he was not deeply schooled in intelligence tactics, he certainly exceeded the capacity of most agents — by leaps and bounds. While people will continue to argue or debate whether he was a big player or tiny player, it is a readily observable fact that his use of intelligence techniques went far beyond that of the average intelligence officer in that he created his own personal intelligence agency. Once again, I am referring to that which he called the Guardian's Office.

Although Hubbard clearly achieved a remarkable amount of undisputed success in terms of either influencing or controlling other people's minds, there are serious professionals who believe that Hubbard suffered from a psychiatric disorder. While this might be true, Hubbard had far more insight into the human condition than those who might analyze him. His insight into the human mind is evident in the comments of Dr. Margaret Singer, an esteemed clinical psychologist who frequently testified in courts as an expert on mind control and cults. She was most famous for her defense of Patty Hearst. In an interview with a former and displaced Executive Director of Scientology International, Dr. Singer stated that Hubbard's techniques were not only more sophisticated than those used in North Korea and Communist China but that he took the "art of control and persuasion" to an entirely new level. In other words, she held the opinion that Hubbard brought the art of mind control to a never-before-seen state. To this highly revered establishment authority, Hubbard surpassed everyone and that included the Nazis, the Communists, Madison Avenue advertising, and every professional who was familiar with every form of mind control that had existed on Earth up until that point. That is a rather stunning endorsement of Hubbard's insight into the human mind, albeit by someone he would have considered an adversary. So, for those who think that Hubbard had no qualifications as a student of the mind due to no college degree or the like, keep in mind that there is no psychiatrist or psychologist in the world who would be capable of influencing people the way he could or did. He was outside of the system and operating more like a comet rather than a planet with an ordinary and routine orbit.

When you couple a knowledge of military intelligence techniques with extraordinary human intelligence and unrivaled insight into the human mind (at the very least in terms of manipulation and persuasion), you have considerable power that is well beyond the thought processes of ordinary humans and that includes the tried and true professionals of the civilization. The Machiavellian aspects of his character give everything a cunning overlay suggesting this power was not only formidable but dangerous. As so many people have proclaimed themselves to be victims of L. Ron Hubbard and Scientology, one could readily assume, and quite correctly, that this power was dangerous. If it is indeed so dangerous, one would expect humans to want to do all they can to control and contain it so that negative things do not repeat themselves. Such power frightens and excites people. It is the core of what attracts the media to this too often discussed subject. While it is often discussed and written about, the core element of his power and where it comes from is neglected, even if it is recognized to a limited extent. Even where it is recognized, it is not well understood and this is because it was designed to be this way. I am referring to his connections to the world of the occult. Although these connections have been publicized ad nauseam, they are generally sensationalized either by reporters or bloggers who are either limited in knowledge or experience with these difficult to understand and booby-trapped subjects. Accordingly, there is a rush to judgment and to simply say that Hubbard was either evil or consumed by evil. Such appellations, however, usually play second fiddle to the judgment that he was just plain nuts. People read a certain amount of information, some of which is false and some of which is true, and are comfortable making a judgment. The problem with such data and judgments, however, is that neither quell the public's fascination with the subject nor the ill effects that are attributed to the legacy of this man.

As I have had the opportunity to acquire several unique vantage points with regard to both his private and occult persona, I will do my best to help people better understand the phenomena that this highly controversial and sensational man unleashed upon the world. As I said already, however, the key point I will be approaching the subject from is that of the proposition of power. When you begin to examine the inner corridors of power, let alone occupy them, you find that power politics intertwines with intelligence agencies (including some that you have never heard of), secret societies, the military, and even occult forces that are sometimes completely unknown to all of the various players in whatever drama is at hand. Anyone who exercises significant power in the world is going to be involved in struggles and/or associations with all of the above. L. Ron Hubbard was no exception. How deep he was involved in any of these factors is a very hotly debated topic on the internet, and many have chosen to judge him as an incompetent wannabe. I would suggest, however, that if you choose to study and judge him in this regard that you measure him by the fulcrum of power that he exercised. In my estimation, it will give you the greatest possible insight into his mind. On a positive note, I hope that whatever understanding I can convey to you on this subject will enable you to empower yourself as well as give you an immunization from the negative effects attributed to Scientology and L. Ron Hubbard as well as occult operations in general.

Before I begin the actual narrative of this book, I would also like to send out a word of caution to those who might seek to do everything possible in their power to not only bury this man and his legacy but to remove his name or any mention of it from consciousness itself. It is a principle of nature that when you bury life, it will rise from the grave. The more you bury

Hubbard, the more power you give him and what he represented. If you do not believe me, I advise you to study the psychological archetypes of Pluto and Scorpio, both of which fit hand-in-glove with the archetype of power. One of the characteristics of power is that it can lead to obsession. Hubbard was indeed obsessed, and while he might not like that characterization, I do not think he would disagree with me if I delineated my views with more acceptable words. What I choose to point out here, however, is that many people are obsessed with the subject of L. Ron Hubbard. They are reacting to his power and this becomes an obsession in itself. If one is either agile or wise enough, it is far easier and more beneficial to leave the subject alone.

With regard to Hubbard's legacy, in general, I think it is wise to heed the rather profound statement of his former magical partner, Jack Parsons, who said that you cannot begin to understand the legacy of a human life until 100-150 years after the death of a person. It is only after fifty years, he said, that you begin to get even an inkling of what their legacy might be.

Many ex-Scientologists and people who feel that either themselves or others have been victimized by L. Ron Hubbard and/or Scientology are too often in a reactionary mode that is sometimes akin to Post Traumatic Stress Disorder. While this is understandable, and many have a genuine need to abreact, it is best to seek out a relaxed frame of mind before seriously contemplating the entire subject and its full implications. I would advise such people to put as much distance between yourself and the subject as possible and to seek out enjoyment rather than to wrestle with issues that might possibly be obsessive in nature. However, if such people are not too reactionary and are capable of controlling their emotions to some degree, it is my hope that this book might help them better understand what they were dealing with and thus enable a reconciliation with their own life drama.

It is also advisable if not absolutely necessary to approach this subject with a QUIET MIND and refrain from POISON TONGUE. Poison tongue does not necessarily just refer to verbalization. If you are saying or hearing venomous words in your own mind, your mind is being affected by past inputs that are reactionary in nature. Such will lead you to irrational conclusions.

When I was personally involved with it, I never thought of Scientology as an unpleasant subject. I would be quick to add, however, that by its very nature, it purposely caused you to look at the unpleasant "cobwebs" in your own mind as well as the negative or dismal aspects of existence in general.

It is important to remind everyone that Hubbard's seminal work, published in 1950, was titled *Dianetics: The Modern Science of Mental Health*. Originally, it was said that the word *Dianetics* derived from the Greek words *dia* + *nous* which mean "through the mind". Later, this was altered for legal reasons to state that it meant "through the soul". It is noteworthy to point out, however, that the very word *sanity* itself is derived from the Latin word *sanus* that was in turn based upon the Greek word *dianetik*. Different Greek individuals have confirmed for me that *dianetik* is a Greek word for sanity. My point here is that if Hubbard had called his work *Sanity: The Modern Science of Mental Health*, he would not only have triggered a lot of public relations and legal problems, he would have given his subject a rather odious tenor. Anyway you look at it, Hubbard was tackling a very uncomfortable subject and was exploiting people's ignorance and lack of experience with it. Insanity is a subject that most people feel they are either unqualified to think about, have no desire to pursue or just no reason to even contemplate.

While I am not claiming to be an expert on the subject of insanity (which might be enough to get you locked up in a society where the insane are often said to be running the asylum), I will share what insights I have from working with Hubbard, studying his life and writings, and the subsequent fallout that has resulted. Do keep in mind that Hubbard was trying to teach us to deal with insanity and to, quite literally, make the insane sane. Scientology and insanity go hand-in-hand. If you worked in Scientology, you heard the terms "insane" and "insanity" frequently and far more often than you ever would in the regular world. Wherever the word *Scientology* is heard, insanity is just around the corner. Even in the best of times, all Scientologists or ex-Scientologists would agree with this. I do not think Hubbard himself nor his critics would disagree with me either.

I have used the words *Tao of Insanity* in the title of this book for a very specific reason. *Tao* is a Chinese word which cannot be defined by its very definition. Commonly identified as "the way", Taoists will tell you that all duality, including the concepts of yin and yang, derive from the Tao. As everything derives from the Tao, that would also include the manifestation of sanity and insanity. As those who cultivate and practice the Tao seek harmony, this approach puts a perspective on insanity that can give you an advantage when dealing with the subject.

Everyone has a ratio of insanity to sanity in their daily lives. Hopefully, the insanity you have to deal with is nothing much more than an incorrect billing that you have received from a utility company or on a credit card purchase. These can usually be resolved without too much trouble, but one can, of course, have much more insanity to deal with in life than an insane billing. The key in dealing with any kind of insane or chaotic behavior in your life is to find what harmony you can in dealing with it. One needs to optimize the ratio of sanity to insanity in their lives.

This principle is akin to the way ancient Taoists are taught to deal with their body. There is an optimum ratio between tension and relaxation in the human body. One does certain exercises to flex the body but also to release the tension. When an optimum ratio is achieved, it is called "the song". It is all about harmony. Accordingly, I invite you to apply this general principle in dealing with such a formidable subject as Scientology can be at times. There are many things you might find astonishingly useful in Scientology. On the other hand, and I would be surprised if you did not, you might find other things that are either unwieldy and utterly anathemic to your regular state of mind. Some things might also be downright insane.

At the outset, it is important to tell you that I am not a Scientologist nor do I practice independent Scientology. Although I was involved in the organization for over a decade, sometimes at the higher levels, I left the organization in 1983 and never returned. That does not mean that I deem everything that I discovered in Dianetics and Scientology to be useless, but I long ago ceased to think in the specialized language of "Scientologese".

Before I begin the narrative of this book, it should be said that this work is not intended to be autobiographical. I will only give anecdotes from my own life to the degree I feel it is necessary to enhance the quality or credibility of my observations, particularly in regard to them being tied to actual experience. In 2005, before most of the current obsession with Scientology had fulminated (circa 2010-2013), I released an autobiographical account of my life, including an extensive account of my adventures with L. Ron Hubbard, in a work entitled *The Montauk Book of the Dead*. I realize that there will be a considerable amount of people who read the book you now have in your hands who are not aware that I am already an author of over a dozen books. *The Montauk Book of the Dead* was not written to either expose or describe Scientology. It was written to explain to my regular audience the unique path that I followed in my life and how this path enabled me to arrive at a destination whereby I would write about certain esoteric subjects, most of which is centered around the physics of time. That is another story.

The last thing I want to let you know before you begin reading this book is that I never personally incurred the wrath of L. Ron Hubbard. There are different reasons for this, and I will explain them in the context of this work, but this has enabled me to remain calm and objective on the subject. I do not have an axe to grind. I am also aware that there are countless expressions of people who have received what they term to be abusive behavior from the personage of L. Ron Hubbard, his agents or his legacy. It is not my prerogative to deny these people their experiences nor to suggest that they did not occur. I cannot answer to what other people have experienced or endured. It is my hope that this book not only enables such people to heal or reconcile their own predicaments but that it gives deeper insight to all.

The depths of infinity are here to be explored.

Peter Moon
Long Island, New York
February 14, 2016

— CHAPTER ONE —

The Funny Farm

"Madness in great ones must not unwatched go."
William Shakespeare — Hamlet

According to a historical anecdote, a professor at George Washington University once told a rather astonishing story to the president of the university during an evening dinner. The professor mentioned that one of his students, Lafayette Ronald Hubbard, had gone missing. He claimed to have found this student at the nearby St. Elizabeth's Mental Hospital where he was wearing a straightjacket and confined in a padded cell. Kicking and screaming, Hubbard was claiming he was Jesus Christ.

Before we attempt to evaluate the potential accuracy and implications of this anecdote, it is important to make it very clear that there are a lot of people who might have an agenda for making such a claim. Besides discrediting Hubbard for whatever reason, there are also those who would somehow feel relieved or vindicated, even if only for a short while, if it could be proven or even reasonably established that L. Ron Hubbard was certifiably insane.

This story found its way to the internet by way of Arnie Lerma, a former Scientologist and member of L. Ron Hubbard's Sea Organizaton (referred to as the Sea Org). Although Arnie would be considered a hostile witness in a court of law with regard to the subject of L. Ron Hubbard or Scientology, this does not mean that his story is inaccurate. According to him, it came to him as a result of having known the son of the former president of George Washington University. Arnie's competence in electronics led to him installing a sound system in a restaurant in Arlington, Virginia. The man who owned the restaurant subsequently read about Arnie's wars with Scientology, contacted him, and told him the above story. The professor who originated the information in question was a psychologist named Mossell (phonetic spelling). If we take the story at face value, Arnie could have made up a much better and more detailed story if he was trying to serve an agenda.

While I cannot tell you the precise truth of this situation, my intuition and investigation skills tell me that it should not be dismissed. If one treats it as a hypothetical truth, it reveals a rather interesting and expository connection between Hubbard and the world of insanity. There is no question that Hubbard has at least one thing in common with certain insane people and that is the ability to access tremendous power. In the case of some insane people, they are known to possess virtually insurmountable physical strength when they are worked up. While Hubbard was not known to be insurmountably physically strong in this respect, he was certainly rather formidable from a mental standpoint in that his will was known to overcome or command large numbers of people. The insane are also known to be very willful at times. If they are intelligent and cunning, they can be all the more challenging to deal with. While it might be arguable to compare physical strength with mental strength in terms of insanity, I think it is a fair comparison. Both Joseph Stalin and Adolph Hitler are considered to be insane, and they exerted an extreme mental power over their people. All force is not physical.

In this chapter, I am going to examine Hubbard's connection to St. Elizabeth's Mental Hospital, a place which he admittedly frequented, and how it fits into a logical paradigm which helps explain some of the tremendous power and influence he exerted over others. First, however, we will examine his first ostensible link to St. Elizabeth's.

Hubbard attributes his early interest in the human mind to Commander Snake Thompson, a neurosurgeon and medical officer of the U.S. Navy whose real name was Joseph Cheesman Thompson. Thompson was part of ONI, the Office of Naval Intelligence, and served as a spy in pre-World War I Japan with Consuelo Andrew Seoane, an in-law of L. Ron Hubbard's family. Seoane was a deep operative in the ONI. Thompson was later sent to Vienna by the U.S. Navy to study psychoanalysis directly under Sigmund Freud. According to Hubbard's own words, it was Thompson who stuck his nose into books on the human mind while visiting the Library of Congress.

In order that you get an idea of the powerful controversy that L. Ron Hubbard could and can still generate, it is important to point out that Hubbard's claim to knowing Commander Thompson was at one time virulently refuted. Long before the internet became a household device, Hubbard's adversaries denied his association with Commander Thompson by asserting, with very passionate if not absolutely convincing rhetoric, that there were no records of the man. In other words, they stated that Thompson did not exist and Hubbard was just making up his past history. The Church of Scientology, however, responded with equal suspicion, making claims that Thompson existed and "proving" it by citing their discovery of a relative in an old phone book whom they had called to confirm his existence. This was clearly a rhetorical war by each side hoping to realize some sort of imagined "gain" by convincing others of their own particular opinions in this matter. All of these rhetorical claims took a back seat with the advent of the internet whereupon it was evidenced beyond any shadow of a doubt that Commander Thompson did indeed exist. While Hubbard's precise relationship with this man will always be questioned by some, it is obvious that the two men knew each other and probably quite well. The exact nature of their relationship, however, is perhaps not as significant as the virulence with which both sides argued the point; and I use this as only one example with regard to Hubbard's history. Some of it is vague and some of it is not accurate. What stands out, however, more than any of the inaccuracies, is the virulence by which different factions seek to either negate of promote various claims about his history as well as the relative validity of his brain children: Dianetics and Scientology. Emotional opinions and tactics cloud both his adversaries and his proponents. Hubbard had power. No one will deny that. Thousands if not millions have either chosen or felt compelled to struggle psychologically with the legacy of that power if only to reconcile their experiences in their own minds. When someone becomes virulent, on either side of the issue, it is an exercise of emotional hostility that is seeking to either quell another or the expressed point of view of another. Such a reaction is an attempt to neutralize the potential power that an opposing viewpoint might represent. The most obvious reason for people reacting to Hubbard's power in a negative way is that it either threatens them or might possibly disempower them or perhaps others. In their own way, they are either reacting to Hubbard's power or playing off of it.

Although Hubbard passed away in January of 1986 at the age of 74, the legacy of his power is very much alive to the degree that people are contentious about his legacy and fight over the prospects of it. He is the only author in history to have his work preserved in titanium vaults, duplicated on numerous continents, so as to preserve it in case of apocalyptic type events.

So it is that Hubbard's first claim to learning about the human mind is immersed in extreme controversy. It is easy to find such controversy swirling around most every key point in his life. We know that Hubbard was able to exert considerable power over the minds of others or at least to persuade them in a powerful way. Such controversy is a symptom of power. If Hubbard was just milk toast, no one would care. The question for many, however, becomes, "Was this the power of a calculating and cunning individual who had been encouraged if not trained by an ONI officer or an insane man who had once been in a straightjacket at St. Elizabeth's?"

If we examine Commander Snake Thompson's known history a little further, we discover that he was raised in Japan by missionary parents in the wake of Commodore Matthew Perry's forced "commercial invasion" of Japan. Fluent in Japanese, Thompson was known as a renaissance man who immersed himself in Asian culture and could read Sanskrit as well.

Although it is neither well understood nor appreciated — as well as not being the subject of this current work — the hostilely enforced trade upon Japan by the United States was not only the historical precursor to World War II, it was at the behest of railroad barons who wanted to build a trans-Siberian railroad whose line would extend from Moscow across Siberia, down to the Korean Peninsula and across the very narrow straight to Japan. Although the exact religious denomination of Thompson's parents is unknown, the traditional first imperative of economic Western invasion of a foreign culture is to send Christian missionaries into an area. Besides Thompson's history as a deep cover spy in pre-World War I Japan, his life situation groomed him to be an asset of the highest order for the Office of Naval Intelligence and whatever agenda the latter might have had for serving Western economic interests.*

Hubbard is said to have met Thompson while on a cruise from Seattle to the East Coast. The two had a lot of time to spend together, and it is quite likely that Hubbard's claimed familiarity and knowledge of Asian culture was in no small part the result of his acquaintance with Thompson. Hubbard also supplemented this knowledge with his own visitations to the Orient.

In addition to being a neurosurgeon and a colorful character in the ONI, Commander Thompson was also a close colleague of William Alanson White, an American neurologist and eminent American psychiatrist of his day who was a professor at George Washington University at the same time that he was also the superintendent of nearby Saint Elizabeth's Mental Hospital.

As Hubbard attended both a prep school in the area as well as George Washington University, it provided a window of opportunity for him to have continued his friendship with Thompson but also to form the special relationship he claimed to have had with White, a man he credits for helping him discover Dianetics and Scientology.

Through his friendship with Thompson, Hubbard said that he was able to attend so many lectures given at Naval hospitals that he was able to become generally conversant with psychoanalysis as it had been exported from Austria by Freud. To understand the context in which L. Ron Hubbard came of age with regard to his studies of the human mind, it is import to understand that it occurred not only with the key players involved at St. Elizabeth's but on the grounds of the facility itself. St. Elizabeth's was actually a colloquial name for what was originally designated as the Government Hospital for the Insane. It was established in 1855 as the first federally funded institute for the insane with the military also using it for the care of their mentally ill personnel.

It found another use during and immediately after the Civil War. Wounded soldiers were admitted who had no place else to be hospitalized. When the soldiers wrote home, they did not want to say they were staying at the Government Hospital for the Insane, so they began to refer to it as St. Elizabeth's although that was not the official name until 1916. All of these wounded soldiers were suffering extreme trauma which we now refer to as PTSD or Post Traumatic Stress Disorder. In some way, shape or form, L. Ron Hubbard found himself attending a university that served, in conjunction with St. Elizabeth's, as a historical focal point for treating those who suffered PTSD.

When I first examined all of these connections, I could not help but wonder if Hubbard had indeed ended up in a straight jacket by reason of being subjected to shock treatments in this environment. Doing a little research,

---

* The English word *tycoon*, by which Perry was referred to by the Japanese (as he represented imperialists whom they deeply resented), derives from the Japanese word *taikun*, meaning *shogun*.

I soon found out that William White was a vigorous and vocal opponent of any type of shock therapy. If such did happen, it is not likely that it came from White nor from Thompson who was a staunch ally of the former and most definitely was not a fan of such therapy. Shock treatment, imported from Europe, did not really become prevalent until Hubbard left Washington.

There were, however, two famous lobotomists in the environment. These were James W. Watts, a neurosurgeon and a member of the faculty of George Washington University Hospital. The other was Walter Freeman, a neurologist and psychiatrist who was the head of the neurology department at George Washington University. Together, both of these men performed the infamous lobotomy on Rosemary Kennedy, ruining her life. Freeman was not even a surgeon and had the reputation of a butcher. While White was an opponent of both shock treatment and lobotomies, I do not think there is anyone who demonstrated themselves to be a more vocal critic of these two "therapies" other than L. Ron Hubbard. Lobotomies were not a common practice at either George Washington University nor St. Elizabeth's until White had passed away and Hubbard was long gone.

Circumstances do not suggest that Hubbard's alleged straightjacket incident was the result of either shock treatment or a lobotomy. It is possible, however, if we want to speculate, that he might have been the subject of exploratory surgery by his neurosurgeon friend, Dr. Thompson. The only reason I suggest this possibility is because of Hubbard's own vague references in his taped lectures to having been on an operating table and experiencing "out of the body" phenomena. His time at George Washington University and St. Elizabeth's would present a window of opportunity for such.

As Freud was an advocate of drug use in psychoanalysis, it is also quite possible that Hubbard was subjected to some sort of drug therapy at the behest of Dr. Thompson. He was certainly not shy about using drugs in his later life. An accidental overdose or a deliberately induced overdose could be the explanation for the alleged straightjacket incident. If it did indeed occur, it was quite possibly a temporary reaction to an experiment that did not work out so well. Mega doses and extreme conditioning are long-honored techniques when it comes to disciplining and conditioning the mind, body, and soul. They have been used in the martial arts and religion throughout history. In and of itself, the field of psychology was relatively new as Hubbard came of age. Prior to that, however, the subject of psychology had its own niche in religion, martial arts, and also politics. We may never know the truth about the colorful anecdote of the straightjacket, but in such an environment, especially as a somewhat naive student, Hubbard would have been a prime candidate for avant-garde experimentation.

When we put all the available facts and stories together, it paints a picture that L. Ron Hubbard was exposed to the country's leading practitioners in the field of psychoanalysis and psychiatry. When you consider his later life, there is no question that his familiarity with these subjects was so great that it spawned his future vocation as the founder of an institution which was based largely upon techniques concerned with mental therapy. Hubbard always spoke of Commander Thompson with high regard as a mentor and inspiration. In my estimation, based upon all that I have read as well as my own inside personal exposure to Hubbard, he would have been directly schooled in Freudian therapy and would also have served as a therapist in some capacity, if only as a "student". Hubbard would have received a certain amount of psychoanalysis as well. In his later life, Hubbard would emphatically advocate that it was vital to sit on both sides of the desk.

It was during this period that Hubbard attended George Washington University. Detractors have always pointed out with great feverishness that he got poor grades, and they particularly like to cite that he failed a class in "Atomic and Molecular Phenomena", the first class of its kind in a subject that is now known as Nuclear Physics. In his own writings, the aforementioned Arnie Lerma (who we can thank for bringing us the colorful story of Hubbard in a straightjacket) astutely points out that it is rather difficult to get such poor grades IF you are at least attending the classes. He suggests that Hubbard might have indeed been spending most of his time elsewhere, the most likely location being St. Elizabeth's.

Hubbard most definitely had an arguably healthy contempt for what might be called "learned men" which would refer to those with diplomas who were neither doers nor achievers. While there are many brilliant people who have university degrees and have been actual achievers, there are also those who hide behind a diploma and are neither distinguished nor particularly brilliant. Whether you agree with this or not is beside the point. Hubbard most definitely was not enamored of such people. If he was not an early mover and shaker within the cutting edge community of Freudian psychology in America, he was certainly privy to the major player who was; and by extension, to Thompson's other connections in the world of psychiatry and mental health. As much as was possible, Hubbard was learning from the horse's mouth; and such first-hand experience was just not available at George Washington University nor any other university of the time. His forays into learning about the human mind under live laboratory-like circumstances would have made his psychology class seem like milk-toast. Although he has been virulently attacked throughout the years for not having a degree of any kind, it never seemed to bother him. He was not the type to capitulate to the mores of a society that he considered was lacking in knowledge to the point where it did not really educate people in an honest manner. Once again, you do not have to agree but do understand that this was his view. He most definitely did not fit in with the typical mind-set of common students, none of whom would have been inclined nor capable of creating an organizational movement such as Dianetics and Scientology. Hubbard's lack of a degree is really an irrelevant matter with regard to his own efforts as it would not have satisfied nor deterred his detractors.

While we can argue about how peripheral Hubbard's involvement might have been with movers and shakers such as Dr. Thompson and Dr. White and their role in the premier American institution for dealing with insanity, we can also make a case that he was learning about and possibly, if not likely, engaged in techniques and information that were state-of-the-art for that time period. When you throw in Snake Thompson's connections to the Office of Naval Intelligence, it opens the door to other potentials as well.

After White died and Thompson relocated to San Francisco, St. Elizabeth's was taken over by Dr. Winfred Overholser and shock treatment became prevalent if not the order of the day. Dr. White would never allow it. By this time, Hubbard was making a living primarily by writing pulp fiction. The old guard that resisted shock therapy and lobotomy was now long gone from St. Elizabeth's. Overholser spoke fluent German and eventually became a part of the Office of Strategic Services when Colonel Wild Bill Donovan enlisted his support for studying Nazi methods of interrogation through drugs; in particular, mescaline. He became known as the Chairman of the "Truth Drug Committee" of the OSS. Overholser was also used to recruit Nazi scientists for repatriation as a part of Project Paperclip. In the early fifties, in his book *Science of Survival*, Hubbard became the first person to expose the operations of the "Truth Drug Committee" when he wrote about Pain-Drug-Hypnosis whereby a subject would be induced with pain and drugs to influence their behavior.

One of Overholser's close colleagues was Dr. Webb Haymaker who also spoke German and recruited for Project Paperclip. Together, they recruited Dr. Hubertus Strughold, a Nazi scientist who was in charge of human experimentation at Dachau but eventually assumed high-ranking medical positions with both the U.S. Air Force and NASA, whereupon he became known as "The Father of Space Medicine". Overholser, Haymaker, and Strughold were all responsible for experiments using radiation to affect brain centers. Strughold eventually suffered public dishonor because of his Nazi history that included the death of human beings by reason of his experiments.

In the 1990s, George Washington University became a focal point for investigation with regard to radiation experiments conducted upon human beings. Although the findings produced many instances of inhumane experimentation, the investigation was said to be a whitewash with regard to the actual circumstances. It should also be noted that Hubbard has been cited as having been a victim of such experimentation. Proof of such, however, is not going to be forthcoming by the very nature of the matter at hand.

Besides absorbing Nazi research, St. Elizabeth's Hospital, under the direct stewardship of Overholser, became a laboratory for projects such as MK-ULTRA, CHATTER, BLUEBIRD, AND ARTICHOKE.

In his later years, Hubbard would become adversarial with the institution of psychiatry; and this was especially in concert with his former mentors although Hubbard's position was vehement and extreme to the point of being fanatical. His old stomping grounds had been taken over by secret projects that were not in the public interest and served an agenda that is highly questionable by any reasonable standards. In the 1960s, he hired private investigators and based upon their information made an intelligence hypothesis that the World Bank was behind various attacks on Scientology and that these were instigated by Mary Appleby, the Secretary of the National Association of Mental Health in England, her uncle being Otto Niemeyer of the World Bank. Niemeyer, according to independent sources, facilitated the laundering of gold from Czechoslovakia to the benefit of the Nazis.

According to another independent source (*Mind Control, World Control* by Jim Keith), The British National Association for Mental Health was the brainchild of Lord Montagu Norman, the Governor of the Bank of England who was prone to mental problems and hospitalizations. He had been a strong supporter of Hitler prior to World War II. Montagu essentially renamed the National Council of Mental Hygiene, which had pushed eugenics before the war, and called it the British National Association for Mental Health or NAMH. The officers of the NAMH were all Nazi sympathizers and included Richard Austen Butler, the Earl of Feversham, Priscilla Reyntiens Worsthorne Norman, and Niemeyer.

While all of the above information might set the table for considerable drama to be played out, this is not my purpose. I am only trying to give you a genuine view of how Hubbard viewed the world, and that includes his opponents, whether real or imagined. While he was fervent, if not fanatical, in his convictions, he was also not alone when it came to the assessment of his chosen opponents. Had he not elected to embark upon a mission of personal power, however, none of the above drama would have played out to the degree it did in his own life. It was his own choices that led to the drama.

While this book will embrace certain aspects of global intrigue, it will primarily be from the reference point of Hubbard's mind and how it affected him and his followers. It is not my job to convince you that there is a world conspiracy that seeks to control the world through psychiatry. For those of you who do want to take this into conspiratorial realms, however, there is a great irony at work here and that has to do with what became of St. Elizabeth's hospital. Only a small percentage of the records were retained by the National Archives before the building was razed and the very land where the hospital had stood eventually became the Office of Homeland Security.

THE WRESTLER

"I have cast fire upon the world, and see, I am guarding it until it blazes."
Jesus of Nazareth — The Gospel of St. Thomas

In the previous chapter, I painted a picture that L. Ron Hubbard trafficked with the major players in the field of mental health in a rather unique and intense manner that provided him an opportunity to grasp an understanding of the human mind in a way that few others of his time would have. His mentors, Dr. William Alanson White and Dr. John "Snake" Thompson, were both indisputably key assets of the United States Government and the military. Were these just chance connections he made or circumstances set up by fate for the players in a bigger game? Whatever the relative truth of these matters is, Hubbard's later years would demonstrate an exceptional ability to deeply influence the minds of thousands, if not millions, of different individuals.

The words I have used to paint this picture are based upon data that I have taken at face value and believe to be reasonably accurate with regard to available historical resources. The straightjacket incident is admittedly sketchy, but there is no reason to dismiss it either. Even if it is not exactly true, the anecdote is an ironic metaphor for Hubbard's life and self-assigned mission. He was not only juxtaposed at the crossroads of insanity and its various therapies, he himself had a Messiah Complex, and please note that this is not a pejorative term. By definition, a Messiah Complex is a state of mind in which an individual holds a belief that he is, or is destined to become, a savior. In his own mind, as well as that of several others, he was indeed a messiah; and, more specifically, the Maitreya, the second coming of the Buddha who would achieve complete enlightenment for the world. In his own mind, Hubbard struggled with the idea of healing the world by "clearing the planet", a term he used frequently and sincerely with regard to clearing the mind of every individual on Earth.

The picture of Hubbard in a straightjacket provides us with another apropos irony when we consider that the most conventional definition of the word *Israel* means "to wrestle or struggle with God". This definition comes from a passage in the *Old Testament* where Jacob wrestled with what appeared to be a man who would not reveal his own name. When the unidentified man could not overcome Jacob, he gave Jacob the name of *Israel* as someone who had struggled with God. The reader is left with the conclusion that the unidentified man was God Himself or perhaps an angel. This is a very apropos analogy with Hubbard because Jacob, after his successful struggle, was given a mission to build a bridge between Earth and heaven, a task that Hubbard also sought except that he chose to use different semantics. Jacob's bridge was known as Jacob's Ladder. The analogy, however, does not end there.

In 1990, a movie by the name of *Jacob's Ladder* was released. It was about a soldier whose whole unit suffered from post traumatic stress disorder as well as some form of Pain-Drug-Hypnosis. The theme of the movie is perhaps most aptly manifest when the protagonist, Jacob Singer, emerges from the hospital with his friend, Louis, who quotes the 14th century Christian mystic Meister Eckhart:

> "The only thing that burns in Hell is the part of you that won't let go of life, your memories, your attachments. They burn them all away. But they're not punishing you," he said. "They're freeing your soul. So, if you're frightened of dying and ... you're holding on, you'll see devils tearing your life away. But if you've made your peace, then the devils are really angels, freeing you from the earth."

As the movie ends, Jacob is actually dying and the potpourri of various incidents and story lines invite one to think that his life, with all of its drugs and PTSD phenomena, is rushing before him prior to his final moment. He dies in peace, finally figuring out what happened to him and how he got there.

We do not know what Hubbard's final moments were like inside of his own psyche; but just as he wrestled with insanity during his own life so have his former followers and humanity at large been put into a position where they have had to wrestle with the subjects of L. Ron Hubbard and Scientology, if not insanity itself.

Buddhism not only teaches non-attachment, it teaches one to have a healthy ratio between non-attachment and attachment. Many people who identify themselves as either ex-Scientologists or recovering Scientologists are still very much attached to the subject of Scientology. As Hubbard left all of his works behind in multiple titanium vaults, he is still very much attached to this earth-bound world, at least by these particular theological standards.

Based upon the success and general public acclaim of his early efforts, Hubbard knew enough about the mind and business to have created a very prosperous but comparatively modest upper middle class life for himself. This would have been easy for him. In fact, it would have been too easy. He literally had a mission to share what he knew with the world and to save it. This is a mind-set that is well beyond a normal citizen who, when they think in such grandiose terms, do not usually think of themselves as the protagonist.

Hubbard did not just seek a bigger stage, he sought the biggest one that could be imagined. He was not only at the crossroads of insanity but sought the crossroads of the deity itself; and, in particular, where those two factors (insanity and the deity) interfaced. This is not much different from the quote above where "the devils are really angels, freeing you from the earth" except that it is not quite so simple, particularly if you find yourself being punished in a manner that devils are "tearing your life away". Many, if not most people who abandoned Scientology, did so for the very reason that their life was being torn away. Did this make them feel free? Perhaps; and, in many cases, yes; but for some, it is like emerging from having been in a lock-box for a decade or more. This is a lot different than jumping off of the highest mountain and flying a hang-glider into a relative paradise. Some of us chose to do the latter while others remained attached for whatever reason they deemed suitable or by reason of not understanding that they were subjected to an indoctrination of which they were not fully clued-in on in the first place.

For those who knew Hubbard or had the experience to listen to him on a relatively familiar basis, he was sincerely concerned about the plight of humanity and he cultivated this type of thinking in his subordinates; and he was also scoping things out and making plans from a vantage point that most human beings do not even think about. There is therefore a huge chasm in how this man's mind worked in comparison with an every day human being who is just managing to survive an ordinary existence. Hubbard's realm was also a region where the demons could literally tear your heart away if you were to walk into the path of his fire. If you understood Hubbard and where he was coming from, he was not too difficult to deal with. If you did not, however, you could become vulnerable to having your life torn away. There is an infamous story of a small child who got loose on Hubbard's ship, the *Apollo*, and found his way to the telex machine where he chewed up an important telex. Hubbard was furious that anything or anyone might impede his mission by compromising his international communication lines and the kid was placed in the chain locker. This sent a message to the whole crew not to mess with what he considered to be most sacred: his communication lines.

Stories of the chain locker and the like send absolute chills into people reading or hearing about this some forty plus years after the fact. Although I was on his ship and served in his personal office, I never heard about this until most of the general public did. He did not use the chain locker for such when I was aboard, and the crew I knew told me it was a practice long since abandoned and that the majority of it was attributable to Baron Barez, the ship's Master at Arms during the early days of the Sea Org. Many people have tales of absolute horror with regard to their interactions with Hubbard. I, however, am not one of them. Just as everyone has different experiences in life, so did everyone have their own different experiences with Hubbard.

Was he a devil who was really an angel freeing you from the Earth as per above? Personally, I do not know, but it would depend upon your own personal psychological attachments. Anyone experiencing severe emotional upheaval or the phenomena of having their life torn away has psychological issues that have far more to do with themselves than any external source, and this applies whether it is Hubbard or not.

Most human beings are psychologically attached to all sorts of data, ideas, and habit patterns. Many of these, if not most, are completely incorrect if not insanely dangerous. This is just a fact of life. This ranges from how to eat for optimum nutrition, how to grow crops, how to care for children, how to breathe, how to exercise, how to treat other people, how to overcome your own ignorance, and how to spend one's time. It is also common for people to attach themselves to a philosophy of life or a particular person that is not in their overall best interests There are many more examples.

When we consider the aforementioned quote from Meister Eckhart, it is important to realize that Hubbard is a devil to some and an angel to others. He could identify with either. On the one hand, he refers to Aleister Crowley, a man he identifies as the Beast 666, as his good friend. On the other hand, he formulates a code for Scientology counselors, called the Auditor's Code, that he deems to be nearly Christ-like. Hubbard believed that the mind, and the subconscious in particular, contained opposite memes or archetypes within it that sometimes competed with each other in terms of swaying a person's consciousness in one direction or the other. Resolving these various dichotomies, which could be quite numerous in any given individual, would result in a cleared mind. Outsiders have a challenging time understanding his own personal views and insights on dichotomies and so did many of his insiders. This, however, was just one aspect of his mind.

It is common for those who do not understand Hubbard either to disrespect him or to label him as just a very crazy person. He was, however, not "just another crazy person". He wielded power that influenced multitudes of people. There are also those who will continue to rail against him no matter what, as if to bring him down to a level that they can understand. At his best, Hubbard incited you to stretch your boundaries of what you thought you could accomplish. At his worst, he caused you to stretch further still or perhaps to recoil in fear, resentment or with some other negative emotion. It was, however, the power he exerted that made this possible; and that power had everything to do with the mind.

What I have offered in this chapter is just one piece of insight into his mind. It is my own insight; and it is not based upon anything from the internet but rather on my own experience. I have included a theological undertone because you cannot have a comprehensive or foundational understanding of what this man was about without it.

A learned man once told me that the word *Israel* means to wrestle with God on the highest level. Whether Hubbard was wrestling on the highest level is an arguable point for many, but he certainly was wrestling. He drew quite an audience, too.

INSANITY

"A neurotic is a man who builds a castle in the air. A psychotic is the man who lives in it. A psychiatrist is the man who collects the rent."
— Jerome Lawrence, Playwright

Before I more deeply address the key topics of power and occultism, particularly as the latter relates to the former, I am going to address the subject of insanity, primarily within the lens of my own experience with the subject.

The dictionary defines insanity as the state of being seriously mentally ill or madness. It also refers to extreme foolishness or irrationality. While this might seem self-explanatory, it becomes obvious very quickly that mental illness can only be defined according to an arguably arbitrary standard. In other words, an individual can only be judged to suffer from insanity if there is an authority who makes a judgement. This begs the question: Who or what is a valid authority that can make such a determination? Before we examine this question, however, I would like to point out and emphasize that insanity comes under the heading of or is subordinate to the act of determining. In other words, one is making up their mind or others are making up their minds about someone else. It boils down to choices. Another way to look at it is that it is up to a mind or minds, individually or collectively, to determine that another mind or part of itself is dysfunctional.

England's Lunacy Act of 1878 provided for the appointment of a Master of Lunacy whose job it was not only to determine the mental functionality of individuals but also to sequester their assets and provide for their care and treatment. While this Lunacy Act was ostensibly authorized to provide more humane care for the mentally afflicted, it also provided the opportunity for the seizing of assets. There are other cultural and political implications to the Lunacy Act which we will not consider at this time, but it is certainly a reasonable judgment, at least on the surface, to make the insane pay for their care if they cannot care for themselves.

While the history of England is replete with intrigue, abuse, and torture as it relates to the intertwining of religion and power politics, it seems to pale in comparison to the Spanish Inquisition which set an earlier precedent with regard to the seizing of assets. Instead of the word *insanity*, however, the Inquisition used different semantics and determined that certain mental views, particularly when expounded, were heresy. In other words, they were establishing and enforcing a social norm where it came down to what thoughts were allowable. The Inquisition was well known for targeting certain wealthy individuals and then finding justifications as to why such could or might be considered to be heretics, the end result being the forfeiture of their assets to the Inquisition. So, while it is obvious to everyone that there are some people who are mentally dysfunctional to the point where they require some form of extreme care, it must also be recognized that the adjudication of what is insane can be utilized as a powerful tool of a political regime. Note that we have the words *adjudication, insane, powerful,* and *political* snugly and appropriately fitting together into the same sentence.

With regards to your own personal self, it is important to point out that the last sentence can be used with great advantage by an individual if they can apply it to their own circumstances. If you can recognize or adjudicate what is insane in your own mind or environment, including the thoughts and verbal projections of others, you are much more powerful to politically maneuver people and situations for your own benefit. It also teaches you who to stay away from. We all experience some degree of insanity in life if only by reason of our juxtaposition to the toxic environment that has been unleashed by the so-called civilization of this world. It behooves us to understand it.

I would also suggest, in addition to the dictionary and clinical definitions of insanity, that the severely mentally handicapped be viewed as symptoms of a toxic environment and/or situation(s). The word *toxic* derives from *poison* which in turn derives from *potion* which brings us back to the realm of occult magic. While I did not include either the words *occult* or *magic* in the aforementioned sentence, they would fit in nicely as well. Biologically, poison is generally determined to be too much of a substance in a particular cellular environment that is beyond a certain tolerance level. Any substance can potentially be a poison, but it is the ratio that determines whether or not it is poison to the host. Earlier, I spoke of one balancing the ratio between sanity and insanity in their lives. It is not much different.

In the introduction to this book, I urged readers not to indulge in "POISON TONGUE" as it is far better for the individual to address the toxicity itself rather than to imbibe it and have it reflected in their speech. I also suggested that readers approach the subject with "QUIET MIND" so as to calmly assess the data being presented. Accordingly, I will now present my own first exposures to insanity, at least as far as literature was concerned. I will later return to the poison theme for the implications it presents are enormous.

The first time I read about any form of clinical insanity was in a book entitled *Fear Strikes Out,* by Jimmy Piersall, an autobiographical account of a professional baseball player. The book was made into a movie of the same name starring Karl Malden as his oppressive "stage-father" who acted more like a pushy drill sergeant than a loving father so as to ensure his son would become a successful baseball player. Piersall was a speedy and excellent center fielder who played next to Ted Williams for the Boston Red Sox. Although successful, he played and lived under the constant fear of failure and not meeting up to his father's expectations. In the process, Piersall developed a very edgy personality which precipitated fights with opposing players. Whatever he resented about his father, he took out on other players. Finally, he had a nervous breakdown and was hospitalized under the direction of the Red Sox. Piersall described getting relief from shock treatments. I specifically remember him writing in the book that he remembered waking up to the face of a doctor who looked just like Desi Arnaz. His recent memory, however, was wiped out. While the treatment seemed to help him as far as distancing him from his neurosis, at least for the time being, he had paid the price of memory loss. Piersall's mental problems later manifested again, and he was traded and released, later ending up with the Los Angeles Angels where he seemed to mature and settle out, eventually becoming a baseball executive and then a successful baseball announcer.

It was not until I would become involved in Scientology that I would hear any mention of shock treatment being used brutally and/or having extreme negative effects upon an individual. Although I did not know it at the time, my paternal grandmother had received shock treatments during the 1950s. At a family reunion, I learned from my cousin that my grandmother had become inordinately depressed when her two sons had grown up and left the home. She apparently felt quite purposeless. Going to a doctor, they recommended and administered shock treatment. Learning this, I could now see why she would sometimes appear very distant or "out to lunch" as she became older.

My next encounter with insanity through a literary lens was a reading assignment given to all of my tenth grade English class: *I Never Promised You a Rose Garden* by Joanne Greenberg. This book is about a teenage girl's struggle with mental illness wherein the protagonist creates an imaginary world that she can escape into in order to cope with trauma revolving around the surgical removal of a tumor from her urethra. Her imaginary world contains characters or entities that are at first very friendly but eventually become controlling. This was a semi-fictional book where mental illness was depicted as parts of the mind breaking off and creating independent control centers which interacted with her as if they were gods or independent characters. One can easily infer that the mind breaking off into parts precipitates the opportunity for an actual entity, spirit, or demon to occupy the intimate space or thoughts of the individual. The bottom line with this book is that the individual had lost the ability to control the thoughts and processes within her own mind.

It was the following year, in the eleventh grade, that I would experience my next literary encounter with insanity. It was Ken Kesey's critically hailed *One Flew Over the Cuckoo's Nest*. In Northern California, where I grew up during my high school years, Kesey was a celebrity but more so for his sponsoring of the "Acid Tests" where his team would pass out tabs of LSD as the newly formed Grateful Dead would perform in a completely spontaneous manner that would play off the synergy of the audience and their psychedelic experiences. Kesey became known as the instigator or father of the hippie movement, particularly on the West Coast. Timothy Leary is sometimes recognized as Kesey's East Coast counterpart, but the two were very different and only became truly acquainted in later life when the hippie era became nostalgic and idealized.

Kesey was a farm-boy athlete and All-American type with conservative inklings until he got involved with LSD while taking part in a graduate fellowship program at Stanford University. The LSD was administered to him as part of a program he had volunteered for at the nearby Menlo Park Veteran's Hospital, a facility where he also worked the night shift as a guard. It was during this time, while under the influence of LSD, that he composed *One Flew Over the Cuckoo's Nest*. While this book gives you an insider's arm-chair analysis of the psychiatric conditions to be found in a mental hospital, the theme and drama of the book is concerned with the insanity of society itself, a system which is structured with the potential, if not the obsessed predisposition, to destroy one's individuality and replace it with a conformist mind-set. While the financial success of *Cuckoo's Nest* spawned financial freedom for Kesey, it also gave him the opportunity to gather like-minded individuals in creating a social community based upon the very philosophy of rebellion against the aforementioned system, a system which became identified as the Establishment during the 1960s but was referred to as the Combine in *Cuckoo's Nest*. The Combine essentially sucks the life out of humanity and humane impulses by using technology and pharmacology to make individuals submissive via social control. The acme of this is the horrific use of shock treatment applied to the most extreme or rebellious cases.

The LSD experiments Kesey was involved in were financed and supervised under the umbrella of the Government's MK-ULTRA program. In the age of conspiracy culture, many have tried to depict Kesey as a stooge at best or a duplicitous agent with regard to MK-ULTRA. It is not that simple nor is that accurate. Kesey was not only a man of the times, he was a creative personality who helped create the times, for better or for worse. MK-ULTRA and their ilk are not quite as clever as people sometimes think, but their influence should not be underestimated either. LSD was used to pacify people and make them more controllable, but it had the opposite effect and the drug had to be outlawed. The same agencies that facilitated LSD in the first place deliberately took it off the black market. Instead, they would offer the youths only watered down hallucinogenics and mix them with other drugs or offer other substances that were less potent and generally more destructive to the body and/or habit forming. The Government did not want people taking LSD unless it was under their direct supervision. As for Kesey, he ended up as an outlaw and became a fugitive from justice over marijuana possession, a relatively serious crime during that time period. Kesey's ultimate prank idea to "stick it to the Man" was to announce his appearance at an auditorium in San Francisco even though he was a fugitive. When the police and Feds (who were also on his case) came into arrest him, he would exit through a door to the roof where his best friend, Ken Babbs, would be waiting for him in a helicopter to fly him away. Things did not work out so well, and he ended up being pursued in a car whereupon he tried to run away but gave up and was apprehended, eventually spending about five months in prison. Kesey was an inspiration to many of us who were growing up in Northern California and primarily for his anti-establishment and anti-conformist thinking which was also put into action.

In those days, there was a saying that was not only proliferated on the youth grapevine, it was also deeply believed: "Don't trust anyone over thirty." This statement typified the rebellion of established views and traditions. Some or many of you reading this might not be able to easily imagine how seemingly contradictory for the times it was that "us youths" could accept the writings and persona of L. Ron Hubbard, a man who was in his fifties at the time and was most definitely considered to be "old" by our standard. Nowadays, there is a greater understanding and teamwork between youths and adults, much of it centering around economic interdependence. In those days, when everyone over thirty was suspect, we marveled over the fact that we were paying attention and giving credence to an old man! The fact that Hubbard was anti-establishment and that his ideas were radical not only made him somewhat appealing, it was symptomatic of the times. To the degree that his ideas actually worked, it made him all the more acceptable.

So it was that my exposure to the subject of insanity, via literature, paved the way towards my experiences in Scientology, a subject which has its own views and definitions of insanity. Although I am not going to rely on Scientology definitions in this book, I will share some of them, all of which are important to understanding L. Ron Hubbard and his own mind-set. His chosen definition for insanity was not so bad. It is the opposite of sanity, a word which he defined as the ability to recognize differences, similarities and identities. This particular definition is absolutely relevant with regard to understanding the subtleties involved with L. Ron Hubbard and Scientology but also with respect to the occult matrix behind them. There are many shades of gray, and it is not wise to adjudicate something as either good, bad, black or white. People generally have a tendency to paint over subjects with a broad brush that is more consistent with their own judgments and adopted belief stream than the subject itself. It is not that their judgments are always incorrect. Sometimes they are very correct, if only with respect to themselves and their own life purpose. What I would point out, however, is that anyone painting a subject with a "broad brush" is acting in the capacity of an artist.

He or she is creating his or her own view with the "paint". And, by the way, L. Ron Hubbard was quite a "painter", and not only that, he had a knack for getting people to look at his "paintings" and pay a lot of money for them. All of this makes him a rather unique example of the quote by Jerome Lawrence at the beginning of this chapter. Hubbard not only collected the rent, he created the castle and lived in it. This is not unlike authors in general. Each and everyone of them create their own castle, often live in it; and if they are lucky, they are able to collect some rent. Hubbard's work, viewed positively or negatively, gets a lot of attention because his creations were powerful and potent. Keep in mind that the word *potent* is intrinsically related to the words *potion* and *poison*.

Earlier, I explained that the word *toxic* derives from *poison*. The environment of the Combine as depicted in *Cuckoo's Nest* is most decidedly toxic, but it must also be recognized that this toxicity is also one of the biggest challenges in our environment in current times. The issue in *Cuckoo's Nest* is very applicable to the experiences of many people who entered and left Scientology. They were given a potion or antidote that was designed and/or purported to clear the individual's mental issues as well as those of society. People joined and continued on with Scientology because the antidote was demonstrably workable, at least to a marked degree. At some point, the organization — and this is a potential within any organization — began to emulate the Combine by sucking the life out of them, using whatever techniques were at its disposal to make individuals submissive via social control. Instead of shock treatment, the individual would become subjected to various forms of extreme punishments.

I personally watched the Scientology movement wholeheartedly embrace the Combine. There was no mistaking it. Each person who remained in the movement made their own individual choice to remain; but for far too many, it took extreme "poisoning" to get them to the point where they realized they were making decisions that were not in their own best interest. Instead, they were letting their fate be determined by others.

But what about L. Ron Hubbard? He is the subject of this book. Was he insane like many have asserted? Was he a rebel against or an agent of the Combine? Whatever conclusions we might arrive at, he had most certainly thrust himself into a maelstrom of events and circumstances that can best be described as a battle ground between various factions seeking to influence or control Mankind as well as its evolution or devolution.

To address the first question of whether or not Hubbard was insane, I think it is fair to say that we all have moments when our analytical functions are compromised. It is always a matter of degree. But we are really referring to the capacity to function in a society without having to be consistently monitored so that others are not harmed. Hubbard was consistently monitored by various authorities, and there are many that will tell you that either he or his techniques were very harmful. These facts will also beg some to assert that he was able to evade detection or official incarceration by his ability to hide behind laws or otherwise utilize such to his own advantage. It is also relevant to point out in such an argument that one of the prime characteristics of a sociopathic personality is to be an artist at avoiding detection. Although Hubbard appears to have shared certain characteristics of a sociopath at various times, it is my personal opinion that adjudicating him to be relegated to such a designation is the metaphorical painting of a simple brush stroke that renders a myopic piece of art. It is very tempting for people who have been frustrated by Scientology or Hubbard to make such a proclamation. In my opinion, it is far wiser to suspend judgment and view the bigger paradigm because there is actually much more involved in the life, work and legacy of this very complex man. One hundred years from now, everything about him will be viewed differently. Whether that is laudatory, condemnatory or whether it fits our own personal prejudices or intuitions is irrelevant.

What is extremely relevant to point out with regard to Hubbard is that he placed himself into a position where he not only could evade the consequences of any critical, judicial or psychiatric pronouncements made upon himself but that he placed himself in a position where he could make his own pronouncements and adjudicate who was sane, insane, and all of the varying degrees in between. He was very happy to discard the system that society inflicts upon all of us, and create his own system, all to his own advantage. Before you jump to any easy conclusions, it is vital to realize that such cannot be accomplished without a formidable degree of power. Thus, power becomes the underlying fundamental principle by which one can adjudicate sanity. None of this, however, ensures or means that the adjudicating power is sane in itself. It does suggest, however, that power is a very important factor with regard to the survival of an individual as well as life as a whole. Hubbard was able to use his knowledge and judgments about insanity in such a way that he acquired considerable assets. While this understandably turns people off, it is also in keeping with the long standing tradition on this planet. He who holds the power makes determinations.

As the relationship between power and insanity is critical, I will subsequently make a further assessment of power as it applies to the individual and the whole. Right now, I will address the second question with regard to whether or not L. Ron Hubbard was a rebel or an agent of the Combine. He most definitely was aware of the Combine although he had different names for it, and he did rebel against it. His knowledge and life experience, however, placed him in a position where he could take advantage of it. There is also another more subtle factor at work in this equation that is easy to overlook. That has to do with the fact that we as individuals are all agents of the Combine.

It is only a matter of degree as it is nearly impossible to avoid. For example, virtually all consumers in the modern world are buying and using or eating products that are produced either by slave labor or virtual slave labor. With the way that the economic chain works in this world, this is unavoidable unless you live in a completely self-sustaining environment. It is an onerous task to list everything you consume and trace its origins. In other words, our very survival is enhanced or made possible by those at the bottom rung of the economic commerce chain. This aspect of our existence should not be ignored even if we cannot reach complete purity of consciousness with regard to these matters. My point here is not to make you feel guilty but rather to illustrate the paradigm of survival whereby "only the strong survive" or that "the strong survive on the back of the weak". Recognizing and believing this paradigm, one of L. Ron Hubbard's most basic philosophic precepts was that the common denominator of existence is SURVIVAL. He called this the dynamic principles of existence. This concept can be viewed as rather brutal, but there is also a considerable amount of pragmatic truth in this.

When you view the world through this paradigm, the Combine is part of our existence and our juxtaposition with it is too often a predicament we need to deal with in regard to our own personal survival. It is a continuous threat to destroying our humanity and individuality. Whether or not we are a part of the Combine has to do with degree. The bottom line in this scenario is that your inclinations to conform are what bind you to the Combine.

Survival can be viewed as a maelstrom of chaotic building blocks streaming through space, any of which could destroy us like a comet. If we are lucky, we have a family or family-like unit of building blocks that surround us and protect us not only from the ordinary chaotic maelstrom but from various "rock fighters" in the sky who would want to break us or our "family" apart for whatever reason. In such an environment, the criteria for what determines sanity becomes more and more relative. It all depends upon how you view the world. None of that matters, however, unless you, your "family" or the so-called "good" powers of the universe have the ability to maintain themselves and remain stable in the context of "SURVIVAL". So it is that survival, power, and sanity are inextricably intertwined. This includes the microcosm of how these factors function in our own personal lives.

I think it is very safe to say that the most sincere definition of insanity can be summed up as a somewhat arbitrary but also clear-cut determination made with regard to how we function and fit in with our environment. If you consider the building block analogy above, something or someone is agreeably insane when they do not fit in with a specific schematic of blocks. In other words, it is like the analogy of a round peg in a square hole. The so-called Combine is really just a part of the environment that we have to cope with until, if we think idealistically, we can overcome it.

It should be pointed out that the idea of the Combine is somewhat similar to various concepts that have appeared in religious philosophy, but I am using the Combine herein because it is how I grew up to view the world but also because it expresses a very suitable modern analogy for summarizing the dehumanizing influences extant in our current culture.

While Hubbard's early explorations of the human mind were under the direction of Commander Thompson, he certainly had no inhibitions about going off in his own direction. While people profusely criticize his credentials or off-the-cuff manner when it came to research, there is no question that Hubbard continuously and persistently engaged in exploration of the human mind in others as well as his own. As was said earlier, he was working outside the box of most practitioners in the field of psychology, most of whom possessed a mentality wherein they primarily stood in line to get their diploma. Hubbard sought no such permission. He would eventually issue his own diplomas. While this rankles many people, it might serve best to give you an analogy.

Most of you have heard of Tarzan of the Apes, the legendary character created by Edgar Rice Burroughs, who could not only literally beat the crap out of the animals (this is what happens in the actual book), he could communicate with them on an intimate level, usually from the position of a dominance he had established. Tarzan had a familiarity with the jungle and its creatures that would extend far beyond that of any European explorer. In such a scenario, the academic zoologists could come in and record every fact and feature they could compile about the jungle and its animals; but in the end, this could never amount to more than a watered-down fraction of the experiential knowledge someone like Tarzan would possess.

Coming from Montana, Hubbard was more like a bronco buster when he explored the mind than someone who was going to tamely record and categorize observations in a laborious and tepid manner. But it is not completely fair to categorize him in this way. He did categorize things, but he did it to his own tune and in his own verbiage. But, no matter what anyone says, he spent tens of thousands of hours exploring the mind. There are few who have done such; and further still, there are far fewer who have gotten others to do it. But all of this is just to give you context. He was bronco busting in the area of insanity. He fell off the bronco a few times, too.

There were many different angles of approach that Hubbard used to understand and treat insanity. One of these was his theory that the mind consists of numerous goals that are related to genetic memories and/or life experience. He also believed in and developed processes that were purposefully designed to discover, uncover or recover such goals, particularly major goals that had been submerged. Finding one's goal could not only ignite powerful emotions in an individual, it could give them a passion for life that would enable them to thrive upon their own internal impetus to fulfill their inherent purpose in life. Such goals are at the core of everyone's mind. Now, this concept can viewed very simplistically. For example, a man who wanted to be an artist his whole life was forced by circumstances to become a construction worker and is consequently very unhappy. Suppose his boss is a compassionate individual, maybe even a Scientology auditor, who sits down with him in an effort to find out why he's not happy. When the boss finds out that the worker is really frustrated over his artistic impulses being nullified, he acknowledges the man's failed goals but also directs him on a new path to fulfill such. It might be putting him in a new job where his artistic impulses can shine, like redesigning classic houses or the like. Maybe he can learn architecture or just start attending an art class at night. Although such a solution requires some compassion and cooperation by the people in his environment, the whole situation is relatively simple. This sort of resolution is, however, antithetical to a culture which is known for people not living their dreams, working for "the man" and having to cope just to survive. In our society, there are too few who are so lucky as to live their dream.

According to Hubbard, however, the subject of goals is not as simple as I have presented above, and this has to do with the prospect that the Combine, or whatever name you want to call it, sucks the life out of human beings and their individuality. Goals are therefore not only nullified but buried, and they are buried beneath a series of complex events which include traumas. If you also add the prospect that individuals have lived a series of lives wherein they had different goals, each life being subject to the dehumanizing effects of the "Combine", a human being can be viewed to be buried beneath a matrix of submerged goals that might be compared to a hornets nest that would like to explode but cannot because it is surrounded with toxic clay. And if you do not embrace the prospect of earlier lives, you cannot dismiss the prospect that the genes of human beings carry all sorts of buried experiences within them. Further, the nature of genetics teaches us that genes are common to a species and share various experiences without even cross-breeding. All of this gives life the potential to be buried in a quagmire of crisscrossing goals, none of which were accomplished yet might hold some push and pull somewhere in the individual's own psyche. When exacerbated, total madness is in the offing.

Does all of this convince you that L. Ron Hubbard actually explored the corridors of insanity?

What is presented here is only a summary of a fraction of his work in this regard through my own personal lens of interpretation. If you were to look at the tomes he wrote on this subject, it might not be quite so clear to you. I have summarized what I have so as to be as expository as possible in as simple a way as possible. There is, however, yet more complexity involved in this paradigm of how insanity can manifest.

These buried goals are often in contradiction to each other. For example, a person might find that he has memories buried within him of having been a Nazi who shared a goal to annihilate Jews. Buried deeper beneath this, you might find that he had a memory of once having been a devout Jew who practiced his religion diligently. His ideal to be a good Jew, however, might have been annihilated as a result of being persecuted by the Inquisition. This made him give up any idea of wanting to be a Jew with his subconscious wanting to avoid anything Jewish; and further, adopting the survival maxim that Jews were dangerous. Buried beneath this, he might find a memory of having been a Christian who was persecuted for his Christian goals, thus convincing his subconscious to adopt a Jewish persona. And so it goes. Hubbard's explorations revealed that people had many memories buried deep within them of having been a multitude of different identities; and further, identities that opposed each other. The stronger and more intense the opposition is, the more is the emotional charge that has been deposited deep within the psyche of an individual. Areas of such charge could be exhibited to be quite explosive. When discharged, however, it could bring quite an amazing amount of emotional relief to a person.

So, it is not necessarily enough that you simply find a person's goal in this life, rehabilitate it and send him on his way. While that might work and sometimes could, finding a person's goal might also result in stirring up a series of such past oppositions and might drive him a bit mad. In other words, his discovered goal just might be a reaction to other circumstances rather than a genuine goal of the actual human being concerned. And even if it is a genuine goal — and this might well be the case — anyone is still subject to having many other unfinished goals in his memory banks, all or many of them in opposition to each other.

It should be pointed out that none of this was considered easy business in Scientology. In fact, all of these goals and oppositions were considered to be buried beneath layers upon layers of either traumatic or disjointed experiences that were fed by mental mechanisms based upon reactions to the oppositions suffered. So, it was not prudent to just go digging for goals. One would first have to uncover layer upon layer of trauma first, none of which was necessarily easy, and each layer was considered to have its own peculiarities.

Now, I cannot stress enough that what I am telling you is the tip of the iceberg and a simplification of procedures and circumstances. But again, my purpose is to give you some insight into what was inside of Hubbard's mind and how and why he approached things the way he did.

While I realize that some of you might be fascinated by the prospect of what has been presented here and might even want to dig into your own mind, there are others who might understandably look at this with contempt, disinterest, or with merely the proposition that such deeply buried issues, whether real or imagined, have nothing to do with them. Life is challenging enough without having to take on the hidden layers of the unconscious, particularly when it originates from such a controversial character. For others, however, this controversy stirs interest.

What I do want to reiterate in regards to this aspect of goal-hunting, however, is to be cautious about painting a brush stroke over this and dismissing it. As I continue the narrative in this book, I will attempt to give a more coherent and cohesive explanation of the various factors at work in the mind and legacy of L. Ron Hubbard.

Life is an evolutionary process. As it evolves, it faces different dynamics and adapts accordingly. The principle of change is inherent in life. This applies equally to an individual. If you cannot change your mind from time to time, you are not going to evolve.

While the forgoing is not all I have to offer on the subject, I first wanted to give a general reference point with regard to the subject of insanity itself and also a bit of an inside look at how Hubbard viewed it. With regards to the subject of Scientology and Hubbard himself, there is another point to make in regards to his view regarding goals and how they play into the human mind. While there are always exceptions, most people who experienced Scientology were not able to shake loose of this paradigm. In other words, their goals in Scientology, which were often to become an Operating Thetan* free from a human body and with full perception independent of the physical senses, became relegated to the category of more failed goals in the aforementioned paradigm of buried goals. Ex-Scientologists and Ex-Sea Org** members often become virulent critics, vociferously opposing that which they espoused and dedicated decades of their life towards. Even Hubbard himself, in the last days of his life, voiced that he had failed. While I will have more to say on this subject later on, this suggests that Hubbard could not escape the paradigm he had mapped out. I liken this to the jungle, particularly the Amazon, which has a reputation for consuming that which enters it.

My best advice to everyone is to stand back and look. Do not judge, just look. We can all ask if Hubbard was insane or if the paradigm he presented was sane or valid. Once again, it is a matter of degree and how things fit.

My own experiences tell me that most people were not suited to dig as deeply as Hubbard chose to or as he encouraged others to do. People who were or are not psychologically capable of doing such digging also have a tendency to be vulnerable to being misled. This is not much different than climbing Mount Everest or swimming the English Channel. Few are suited to do it. It all boils down to one question: How deep do you want to dig?

---

* In Scientology, the word *thetan* is synonomous with spirit. An Operating Thetan refers to a spirit who can operate without a body. The are many levels of Operating Thetan.

** The Sea Org or Sea Organization is a fraternal body that manages of Scientology.

FISHING

"If you bring forth what is within you, what you bring forth will save you. If you do not bring forth what is within you, what you do not bring forth will destroy you."
— Jesus of Nazareth, Gospel of Thomas

If you want to reach beyond a superficial and reactionary cognizance of L. Ron Hubbard, it behooves you to first acquire a basic familiarity of the occult. For millennia, occult knowledge has been passed down to aspirants in a manner that is sometimes very pompous through a series of grades or initiations. Modern Freemasonry is only one latter day example. In most cases, those who pass down such knowledge exert or enforce a certain amount of control or influence over the aspirant.

Thanks to my own experiences, personal involvement with and instruction from L. Ron Hubbard, it is my hope that I can give you some laser insight into these matters without yourself having to suffer or endure such indoctrination. It is important to point out, however, that while occult organizations are often corrupt and cause chaos and misfortune in society, their structure is sometimes if not often based upon occult truths or principles that are either betrayed by or are not reflected in the individual members and officers.

There is no better way that I can think of to introduce people to the occult, and especially as it applies to Scientology and L. Ron Hubbard, than through the concept or mythical archetype of Neptune, known as Poseiden to the Greeks, the god or ruler of the ocean. Recognized as the King of Atlantis, Neptune had the power to literally swallow up that fabled city and also spit it back up, each occurrence thereof happening in its own time and over as long a time period as deemed relevant. So, when you think of the ocean and all it represents, think of Neptune as the ruling principle that you pay homage to.

Neptune's identification with the sea has everything to do with the fact that most of what is contained in the ocean remains hidden. And although the ocean has a finite quantity, it has an infinite quality, particularly with regard to what might manifest when you are in its realm. There is no limit to the varying conditions of the sea, and it is a place where creatures, objects and events seem to pop out of nowhere and often at irregular intervals.

Neptune is often said to represent the hidden unconscious or, more accurately, all consciousness which remains hidden to us. When you penetrate any aspect of the unconscious, you are in the realm of Neptune and anything and everything it is said to rule or represent. L. Ron Hubbard himself and his brainchild, Dianetics and Scientology, were all based upon the prospect of digging, probing and penetrating the unconscious and bringing aspects of it into the conscious mind. It is no more complex than that. The more you dig, the more becomes viewable. Try fishing on an actual boat in the open sea for a week if you do not believe me.

According to Hubbard himself, the most useful and/or highly prized aspect of such digging was the counseling process he referred to as auditing. Auditing is a lot like fishing, particularly deep sea fishing. When you fish, you throw out chum or bait to attract bigger fish. Sometimes you get a nibble and you will feel the fish on the end of your line before it goes away. Sometimes the fish will bite hard and you will have a real life struggle to pull it aboard.

Besides big fish and little fish, there was another aspect at work that can be likened to cod fishing which is a notch below regular deep sea fishing. Cod not only frequent the sea floor, but they do so at a depth which is far below regular deep sea fishing. Cod will often be found at a depth thousands of feet beneath the ocean's surface. Even when they are only as deep as two hundred feet, there is a particular phenomena that occurs when you pull up a cod fish. Due to the change in pressure, the cod fish will suffer an internal explosion, one manifestation of which is the eyes popping out. The point here is that when you pull up a very deep fish, it looks very different than it did at the ocean's bottom. Besides that factor, it is well known that the deeper you go into the ocean, the stranger and stranger is the sea life. My point here is that Scientology auditing occasionally involved people digging up very strange phenomena; and further, the descriptions of the metaphorical "fish" that was hooked might be less than accurate. Hubbard himself was no exception to if not the rule with regard to digging up strange phenomena which could be construed to have come from a very deep level.

When you dig into the mind with auditing, it is like casting a line into the water to see if you get any bites. This is usually done with a series of questions or a list of words or phrases that are designed to get a "bite". The so-called "bite" manifests through a galvanic or skin response.

A cult of mystery has been built up around the galvanic skin response meter or e-meter as it is known in Scientology, but this mystery was never perpetrated in Scientology nor by Scientologists but rather by its critics who are most often inept at understanding the actual process involved and are generally more often preoccupied with seizing an opportunity to expose or criticize, always at the expense of viewing and comprehending the bigger picture. This is to be expected.

There is a whole body of data and experience concerning galvanic skin response and its association with life energy. The Chinese call it chi and Wilhelm Reich referred to it as orgone. Carl Jung even used a galvanic response meter. There is also a more exotic angle to this subject known as Quantum Skin Tantra which was featured in a book I published entitled *Ong's Hat: The*

Beginning. The article on such is also available on the internet. My point here is that the relationship between life force and skin is a much deeper subject than the casual critic might suspect. Readers are encouraged to study up on their own, particularly if they are having trouble understanding it.

In Scientology procedures, the only real proof you need with regards to your own experience and/or that of others is whether you can get a "fish" to "bite" with regard to the "hidden unconscious". For example, one might get a galvanic skin response on a word or phrase associated with "anger". As you probe deeper into this subject, you get more and more galvanic skin responses accompanied by deeper and deeper issues being vocalized and re-experienced or "abreacted" by the person being counseled. The proof is right there in the observation of the person going through the experience. It is very obvious.

The auditor or counselor has essentially TRIGGERED an issue. The more it is viewed, re-experienced, or re-visited, the more it is said to discharge or dissipate. At some point, the anger, angst or whatever response was triggered will be VANQUISHED. For all practical purposes, it will disappear, all of which is generally accompanied by a feeling of relief or great relief. But, you might ask, relief from what?

The answer is encysted and/or embedded pieces of the unconscious that were not only previously hidden to the individual but were indeed possessed of potential energy, susceptible to being triggered, that was harmful to the person concerned and could also make him or her feel bad at the very least.

When I tell you that auditing is like fishing, there are also days when the fish do not bite. Sometimes you have to go to different waters. There are also different sizes of fish. Sometimes you get a big one which is accompanied by getting a lot of relief. Sometimes it is only a small one with a little relief.

Another reason auditing is like fishing is that if you go out on a fishing boat, not everyone on it catches the same fish. Sometimes a lot of people catch the same type of fish and sometimes they do not. It depends upon a lot of factors and there are a lot of variations of this theme. Sometimes you or someone else will catch a very strange fish that only the captain or an old salt can identify. These are comparable to some very weird aspects in the human mind that sometimes come to the surface in various human beings.

A fisherman also has to study and deal with changes in the weather, currents and seasonal migration periods. No less important is the maintenance and safety of his boat. Without a platform, you cannot do any fishing. Scientology had a lot of issues with people trying to sink the boat or questioning their right to have a boat. Whether you like or agree with Scientology or not, no one can do much fishing without a boat. Pier fishing works to an extent, but you do not get big fish by such.

While I have extolled the virtues of "deep sea fishing" herein, there is also a great danger. That has to do with pursuing the "great white whale" which is an allusion to the novel *Moby Dick* wherein Captain Ahab obsesses about capturing the great white whale named Moby Dick that once bit off his leg. He not only goes down to his grave in pursuit of this whale, he takes the entire crew and ship with him, save for Ishmael, who tells the story. In other words, one can subordinate one's life to the process of auditing to the point where you consume yourself like a snake eating its tail and you have no boat anymore upon which to fish. A fisherman fishes to either feed his family or village or to sell at a profit so that he can increase his capacity to fish, explore or whatever.

There is also Hemingway's story of *The Old Man and the Sea* where the protagonist catches a huge marlin, but it is so big, he cannot fit it in his boat. Instead, he ties it to his small boat; but on his journey home, where he will show off his prize fish, sharks consume the carcass and leave him with nothing but the skeleton. In this story, the humble fisherman has pursued a fish that is out of his league. It would require a bigger boat, a lot more resource, and a more complex life that would undermine the tranquility of his rather simple and peaceful life. Pursuing the big fish was a waste of his time; but then again, a lesson learned.

There are many people who might argue that Hubbard was chasing a great white whale and that his followers went to the metaphorical deep sea grave right along with him. Perhaps this is so, but there is also the biblical story of Jonah who was spit back out by the giant fish who had previously consumed him. In that story, Jonah was chosen by God to warn the huge population of Ninevah to repent. At this writing, Hubbard has pretty much been swallowed up by his many critics. While there are some who expect him to return to this world, I would only suggest that some or much of what he had to offer might someday resurface in some capacity so that it can be used positively in society. I will touch more on this aspect later.

The metaphor of the ocean and deep sea fishing is directly applicable to what Hubbard was digging up in his mind or that of others. If you choose to look yet deeper into this analogy, you will find that the allusion to the archetypal Neptune is far more precise than you might have imagined. In both cabala and astrology, two subjects which are inextricably intertwined, Neptune represents dreams, illusions, imagination and idealism. On the flip side, Neptune also represents delusion, addiction, guilt, self-sacrifice, escapism and the lost self. Whether or not you give any credence to either cabala or astrology, you can clearly see all of these factors in Scientology.

In this chapter, I have sought to explain and demonstrate for you how auditing worked. It was also how Hubbard thought and worked. I have, however, decided not to indulge you with his specific systems and procedures. While these are not completely irrelevant, they are far too cumbersome to discuss here; and more importantly, they are subordinate to the process of "fishing" I have described herein.

SYMPATHETIC MAGIC(K)

"Wherever sympathetic magic occurs in its pure unadulterated form, it is assumed that in nature one event follows another necessarily and invariably without the intervention of any spiritual or personal agency. Thus its fundamental conception is identical with that of modern science; underlying the whole system is a faith, implicit but real and firm, in the order and uniformity of nature."
— Dr. J. G. Frazer, *The Golden Bough*

The above quotation, which is extracted from Aleister Crowley's *Magick, Theory and Practice*, gives you the idea that magic is or should be as sober a subject as science itself. If you read his book, Crowley will give you the same idea. In either case, however, the challenge for either the practitioner or the character witnessing himself in this paradigm, is that our ordinary instruments of perception do not avail us of the entire processes of nature. Much of it remains hidden and is therefore referred to as the occult. If we are going to understand the fullness of nature, let alone become a competent practitioner of sympathetic magic, we are going to have to supercede the ordinary. This idea, in and of itself, is a major stumbling block to anyone trying to truly understand the occultism behind L. Ron Hubbard. I will attempt to overcome this to whatever degree is possible by giving an idea of what sympathetic magic is, what it implies, and its place in the mind and modus operandi of Hubbard.

The world of occult magic or magick is all based upon sympathies. The first step is therefore to understand that the word *sympathy* means "to feel together"; and in its origins, *sympathy* often referred to a common or universal feeling in the community. When we embrace the entirety of nature as the above quotation might inspire us to do, we are encouraged to think that the entirety of existence might be imbibed with feeling or be based entirely upon feeling in and of itself. The word *feel* basically means to have a conscious perception of a sensory experience. Here is the so-called "observer" from the paradigm of relativistic physics. There is no observer if there is no conscious perception. In this way, the observer-based universe is completely dependent upon the concept of feeling.

All people who write or opine on the subject of L. Ron Hubbard are writing as a result of their feelings. Many pretend or try to be "objective" in this endeavor. On the other hand, some address the subject as if they were either discussing the subject of vomit or trying to deal with their own. This negativity has to do with toxicity. If one experiences too much data or energy so as to overwhelm or disturb their mental equilibrium, it causes their system to reject the subject in a violent manner or one that suggests an outright expression of hostility. The subject of occult magick is similarly barbed.

When you look at the way magic is presented by Frazer in the previous quote, it encourages us to paint a very aesthetic picture and wax poetic about nature and its mysterious processes. We have the potential for idealism and nature intertwining in the highest of aspects. All of this is the complete opposite of what we are dealing with when we consider the likes of Aleister Crowley and the negative offshoots associated with L. Ron Hubbard.

When we consider nature, we have to take stock of the fact that it is possessed of polarity, referred to as yin and yang in the East, and this includes the paradigm of evil. Here is a quote from the *Tao Te Ching*:

"Give evil nothing to oppose and it will disappear by itself."

This tells us that it is wise to avoid fighting with what we consider to be evil. That does not mean that we take no action to protect ourselves or others, but that we do not stand in front of our enemy with our fist shaking. That only tells your opponent that he should be wary of you and tips them off to your intentions.

I would therefore suggest to you that your first lesson with regard to sympathetic magic would be to consider the position and perspective of your opponent. In other words, have some sympathy for what they might think, particularly in regards to your situation with or juxtaposition to them. If you foster a perception in their minds that you are dangerous, they now have a motive to harm you. If you appear docile, impotent or inconsequential, they will put their attention on other things. Whatever you might do to protect yourself should be as far away from their perception as possible.

What this means is that you want to have some feeling for your opponent. When we consider the macrocosm, we want to have some feeling or consideration for the bigger or more potent instances of evil in the universe. We do not have to obsess about it, but we have to recognize that it exists.

When we consider the macrocosm, it is important to consider that ancient man was in a world surrounded by stars. After doing his toil during the day, the evenings were for contemplation and speculation. The very word *consideration* literally means "with the stars". While the moon and the sun had the most obvious influence on their ecosystem, ancient man also noticed correspondences or similarities between certain placements of the stars and planets and how these related to the various animals and plants in their environment. Farmers would use the horn of a cow, fill it with herbs and bury it. They would sometimes mix it with water and make a sympathetic or homeopathic style tincture to increase the fertility of crops. Each of these herbs, procedures and the horn itself would have a correspondence to the stars and planets. All of this "superstition" was measured by actual success. Over time, a virtual library of data was collected on what worked. The *Farmer's Almanac* of today is only a slight trace of ancient knowledge that farmers used to swear by. An assault on the traditional farmer has been under way for well over a century. If you want a more practical reference frame to work from in modern times, you can look into the subject of biodynamics. It is an obscure but very potent means to increase the life component in organic farming or gardening.

The correspondences between the heavens and the Earth did not end with farming. There were classifications and records on how various life forms corresponded with various other factors, including internal organs, disease and whatever else might be imagined. Some of these can be found in ancient alchemical texts. The stars and planets became an index with regard to understanding these various correspondences. All of this has to do with sympathy or sympathies. When you hear banal examples of a witch using bat wings in a potion, it is really based upon ancient observations of how a bat might correspond to other factors which one is trying to influence. All of the correspondences in the ingredients of potions can be very complex, but they are theoretically based upon ancient knowledge of such. How well they have been categorized in various traditions that have been handed down and how successful they are is another question entirely. That depends upon the validity of the knowledge as well as the skill of the practitioner.

None of this, however, is meant to serve as an enticement for you to practice sympathetic magic as has been described herein. It is to demonstrate that is a deep subject that has roots that go back into antiquity. At its core, it is based upon feeling. If you are in a room surrounded by rabbits, you will most definitely have a different feeling than if you were in a room full of reptiles. A room full of felines will again be different. You get the idea.

Sympathy is basic to magic because it is basic to LIFE. It requires energy in motion; and these two words, *energy* and *motion*, make up the word *emotion* or *E-MOTION*. Life forms require a series and congregation of emotions in order to live together in continuance. All of this is ordained and coordinated by a will to survive. Life organisms are generally subordinate to a will. The obvious question here is "Who's will?" The answer is *your* will as well as those other wills to which one is accountable.

Magic is an exercise to attract and repel sympathies. You can see this in crowd control as well as public relations. Attracting and repelling sympathies is also a major factor in the art of war. You can create emotions in a crowd or population. You can also simulate emotions and amplify such with electronics. Whoever has control of broadcast media controls sympathies and this bridges us into the subject of power.

There is a word that was frequently used in Scientology and that was *affinity*, a synonym for *sympathy* which was, however, not a word unique to

Scientology. It is part of the regular English language lexicon. When you break it down phonetically, you find the concept of "finity" or "finite" at work and this suggests a finite section of space. When we examine the concept of sympathy further, through its synonym *feeling* — the original concept introduced at the beginning of this chapter — we can trace the general derivation of how words like *finite* and *affinity* came into being.

First, break down the word *feel* to *fe + el* and consider the full implication of the roots. The root phoneme or word *el* often refers to either "first" or "God" while *fe* or even the word *feel* itself refers to *feline* or *cat*. Although it will not necessarily be readily noticed by most, the words *cat* and *at* are homonyms when the *c* is silent.* The word "at" designates distance and this implies space and, more specifically, the space between two things. We now have a *finite* space and also the potential for *affinity*, all as a result of this designation of space. The closer something is, the more of a "feel" you have for it and the more familiarity. Without space, there is no affinity nor concept of affinity. Hubbard realized this and offered it as the building block of the universe. When you have space, you have the potential for "to and from" which is conceptualized as communication, said communication being based upon the perception of and through at least two points in space. Also inherent in this construct is permanence or lasting quality of the designated space which is defined (both in and out of Scientology) as reality.

So it is that *feeling, affinity,* and *sympathy* go hand-in-hand.

Hubbard has often been accused of creating Scientology as a tool to effect mass hypnosis. He would have told you that society and human beings in general were already suffering from hypnosis long before he came along. More to the point in all of this, however, is that people who think of Scientology as hypnosis do not really understand the subject. Hypnosis was derived from Mesmerism, and you can find this in the history books. Franz Anton Mesmer, the founder of Mesmerism, was a skilled practitioner and advocate of animal magnetism. Here we have the principles of attraction and repulsion. Like Hubbard, Mesmer was a controversial figure who attracted much derision with reports of scandal. More significantly, and this will be missed by many in the West, the phenomena that Mesmerism was manifesting was really an instance of what is known in the East as Chi, a word which means "breath, spirit or life". It is not uncommon to see such phenomena produced by practitioners of Chi Gong (which means "breath work"), but

---

* Ancient peoples regarded the cat as the most holy of all concepts, and we see this in the Hebrew's most holy expression *kadoish* which derives from or compares to *kadis*, the Nubian word for "cat". This is why Leo was chosen by the ancients as the most exalted of the signs of the zodiac. More important to this narrative, however, is that ancients or others would not necessarily pronounce the phoneme we use as a hard letter *c*, instead expressing it with silence. The French word for cat is *chat*. This would be pronounced "at" in Hebrew where the *ch* is silent as in the word *Chanukah*, commonly pronounced in English as *Hanukkah*.

it is also important to note that such a powerful tool is subject to misuse. In the days of Mesmer, just as in the days of Hubbard, it is interesting that you had people divide themselves into separate camps as to whether or not such phenomena, and that included the potential for such if not the phenomena itself, was fake or real. Dianetics and Scientology were designed to break people out of the so-called hypnotic trance of life that is akin to what Hindus referred to as samsara, the endless wheel of life. Any technique which can do this, however, is a double edged sword which can be used in the opposite direction. When it is, Scientology can serve as hypnotism.

Scientology is all based upon sympathetic ideas. Many of these included considerations with regard to the human body. For example, Scientologists, as a result of the writings and teachings of L. Ron Hubbard, will readily divide the world into two camps: those who think they are bodies and those who think they are spirits occupying bodies. This, however, is not an idea unique to Scientology. There is an age old war between the two factions. Aside from that proposition, the Catholic Church emphasizes other sympathetic factors with an agenda of their own, all of which has to do with your eternity as well as the well-being of your immortal soul. Right or wrong, their intention is to steer your behavior through emotions. Protestant religions have their own sympathies with regard to the *Bible* which are at odds with the Catholic Church. Different factions have different views.

What is particularly fascinating and most relevant in these "wars" or disputes of spirituality or the prospect of reincarnation is that all of the different sides are within the framework of sympathetic magic. The naysayer of spirituality is exercising a particular sympathy that is based upon his will, decisions and attitudes concerning such. The person who is open to spirituality is likewise exercising a sympathy based upon his will, decisions and attitudes. As the subject of sympathetic magic embraces nature, it embraces all viewpoints. Further, it has the capacity to use opposing viewpoints so as to thwart the opposite. Nature can switch sides. The field of literature, both fiction and non-fiction, is filled with anecdotes of the unfortunate man who learned a lesson due to his lack of regard for the virtues of spirituality. Likewise, there are also anecdotes where people believed in spirituality to the detriment of their own human condition, particularly when their belief was delusory and not based upon any tangible reality.

The answer to all of these varying viewpoints is balance or equilibrium. Though they might seem wrong or are just plain wrong, opposing viewpoints have their place and usefulness in the matrix of creation. Keep in mind that true nature is the genuine backdrop of sympathetic magic. The problem with sympathetic magic is the same problem that occurs in life. At some point, the will of a particular individual or a group of individuals becomes dominant and out of equilibrium with the rest of the environment. This produces a reaction, a counter-reaction, and a cacophony of events results. Eventually, there will be an effort to balance and either create or return to a state of equilibrium. Life has a tendency if not an outright program to seek out balance. Whatever life is doing, it is sooner or later going to come to a state of equilibrium.

When we consider sympathy and feelings and the tendency of life to "seek", we are clearly in the realm of DNA. Recognized as the catalyst that enables matter to be animated, DNA is the result of a series of choices or bifurcations. It not only applies to humans but to other creatures and life forms as well. There is an undeniable sympathy between yourself and all of life. More to the point is that there are all sorts of sympathies in your DNA that you are not necessarily aware of; and more importantly, the very construct of DNA contains sympathies that cross-reference each other.

DNA is, quite literally, the first computer, at least as far as ordinary life forms are concerned. It stores memory and responds to sensory data, and it does so in an organized fashion that is continuously predisposed to changing its responses. Man-made computers are the result of DNA-based creatures so it is quite significant to point out that computers are an extension of life and not necessarily an anathema to life. Everything that has been generated is based upon feeling.

There is a lot more that can be said about sympathetic magic. What is included here is to serve as a primer as well as a background context for the rest of the content in this book. We will return to the theme of sympathetic magic form time to time as we continue.

— CHAPTER SIX —

THE POSTULATE

> *"I regard consciousness as fundamental. I regard matter as derivative from consciousness. We cannot get behind consciousness. Everything that we talk about, everything that we regard as existing, postulates consciousness."*
> — Max Planck

Each and every human being is a virtual postulate machine. By that, I mean that everyone is either continuously engaged in making postulates or is relying upon postulates he or she has made in the past while continuing to live under the direction of such. This applies whether or not you are a scientist, an occult magician or a Scientologist. I have made the preceding comment because the word *postulate* is common to science, occult magick and Scientology. It is also part and parcel to the human experience.

For those who became or become involved in Scientology on virtually any level, you either heard or will repeatedly hear the word *postulate* on a daily basis. Although this is a common Scientology word with its own specific definition, it does not really stray significantly from the common English usage of the word. Let us begin with the regular dictionary definition.

> **postulate** *verb* 1. to ask, demand, or claim. 2. to claim or assume the existence or truth of, especially as a basis for reasoning or arguing. 3. to assume without proof, or as self-evident; take for granted. 4. *Mathematics, Logic* to assume as a postulate.
>
> **postulate** *noun* 5. something taken as self-evident or assumed without proof as a basis for reasoning. 6. *Mathematics, Logic* a proposition that requires no proof, being self-evident, or that is for a specific purpose assumed true, and that is used in the proof of other propositions; axiom. 7. a fundamental principle. 8. a necessary condition; prerequisite.

Before we go into the occult or magical aspects of a postulate, it is important to recognize that there are two types of postulates or axioms in math or science. The first is a postulate that is clearly self-evident. It is referred to as a logical axiom. The other, called a non-logical axiom, might ultimately be true or not true, but it is used as a basic foundation upon which to build a logical pattern or argument. One example of a non-logical axiom in mathematics is the square root of negative *1* ($\sqrt{-1}$) which is designated as an imaginary number or *i*. This is used in equations and is demonstrably workable although the actuality of such is not tangible in a normal sense. While a non-logical axiom can be useful to scientists or investigators in the process of discovery, it can also be used to manipulate data or circumstances. The same applies to magicians who can use a postulate in alignment with truth or in order to manipulate. Many people live their lives based upon non-logical axioms.

There is yet another aspect to the use of postulates in either science, the occult or pragmatic human situations and that has to do with exactitude. You see this frequently in mathematics or in drafting where approximations of a measured distance will satisfy a particular equation or situation. As an example, the Great Pyramid was built with a remarkable knowledge of angles and precise geometry. In the end, however, this magnificent work of architecture will suffer from inexactitude if you get down to the microscopic level. The following quotation sums up the "Rules of Thumb" concerning a postulate, "Thumb" being a play on words for an anonymous source:

Rules of Thumb

> **Thumb's First Postulate:** *It is better to use a crude approximation and know the truth, plus or minus 10 percent, than demand an exact solution and know nothing at all.*
> **Thumb's Second Postulate:** *An easily understood, workable falsehood is more useful than a complex incomprehensible truth.*

Hubbard's entire methodology was susceptible to these so-called "Rules of Thumb", and I do not mean this in a disparaging sense. He would say that you had to be more right than wrong in order to be credible. In his case, he found it most expedient to take a quick measure based upon observation and previous experience and make a postulate. It would be judged based upon its relative workability. This was a pattern he used to figure things out.

In Scientology, the idea of a postulate was pretty much the basis of everything. If something happened, it was colloquially accepted that it happened because you postulated it. While such was often either seemingly or demonstrably true, such an idea could often be over-used or become corny. The ultimate idea behind this, however, is that thought is senior to matter. This, of course, is an idea that is not unique to Scientology.

For the purposes of the magical arts, Crowley very clearly emphasized that "ALL" conforms to the postulate. In other words, it is an a priori condition or determination that precipitates a new condition or a series of circumstances. This is where the idea of a human mind being a virtual postulate machine fits in. People are making up their minds about everything all the time, continually casting assessments or judgments upon the data or circumstances that are before them. Sometimes, these judgments concern existential matters such as religion, life or death. Many times, if not almost always, people make postulates on such matters based upon the authoritative figures in their lives whether it be parents, clergy or otherwise. It is common in our society for people to let others do their thinking for them, particularly when it comes to areas that are either unfamiliar to most or that require a certain degree of expertise. If one is neither intelligent nor circumspect with regard to their own postulates, they can be severely short-changed by life. You see this readily in people who adopt bad or negative attitudes which is accompanied by a lower quality of life when it comes to health and social conditions.

On a human level, whether it be positive, negative, in the context of occult magick, Scientology or just regular life, it is self-evident that current circumstances (either yours or "ours" collectively) in the HERE-NOW zone of reality (whatever reality you happen to be in) are the result of a myriad of decisions or postulates. Where you began to participate in this stream of postulates is another question entirely. In this respect, postulates and, in particular, what might be termed original or a priori postulates, are contextualized by deferring to nature which includes the prospect of deity.

Although Scientology recognized deity as a phenomena, it never officially embraced it with respect to its spiritual techniques. Nevertheless, its various definitions of a postulate do not escape the prospect or role of a deity. The official Scientology definition of a postulate is as follows:

> **postulate** *noun* **1.** a self-created truth would be simply the consideration generated by self. Well, we just borrow the word which is in seldom used in the English language, we call that postulate. And we mean by postulate, self-created truth. He posts something. He puts something up and that's what a postulate is. **2.** a postulate is, of course, that thing which is a directed desire or order, or inhibition, or enforcement, on the part of the individual in the form of an idea. **3.** that self-determined thought which starts, stops or changes past, present or future efforts. **4.** (a postulate) is actually a prediction.
>
> **postulate** *verb* **1.** In Scientology, the word postulate means to cause a thinkingness or consideration. It is a specially applied word and is defined as causative thinkingness. **2.** to conclude, decide or resolve a problem or to set a pattern for the future or to nullify a pattern of the past. **3.** to generate or "thunk" a concept. A postulate infers conditions and actions rather than just plain thinks. It has a dynamic connotation.

If you refer to the above definition you will find that the word *decide* is used as a synonym for *postulate*. The word *decide* is very illustrative of what takes place in the process of a postulate whether it be contextualized by Scientology or not. *Decide* is closely related phonetically to the word *dice* in English as well as the words *diez*, and *Dios* in Spanish. *Dice* suggests the random casting of fate while *diez* means "ten", a number recognized as being related to *Dios* (the divinity or God). It is within this context that we are encouraged to consider where we either consciously or unconsciously entered the stream of postulates that resulted in our own existence.

Anyone who is conscious of their own postulates will readily find a comfort zone with regard to the power of their own postulates. It is quite easy for most people to decide or make a postulate that they will get up and go to the refrigerator. Some postulates, such as going out and getting a new job, might be require considerably more effort to perform but are still in the range of ordinary human activity. More lofty postulates, such as winning an Academy Award or obtaining millions of dollars, are definitely in the range of human capability but might be more challenging to achieve. As one moves into the esoteric areas of life, however, postulates take on a new dimension. People who explore such can often find that one's postulates sometimes manifest mysteriously. In such cases, however, one is going to eventually reach a condition where one's postulates or so-called magical acumen hits up against a fixed or solid paradigm where things do not manifest so easily and sometimes not at all. In such cases, one is encountering a realm, such as the physical universe, where the postulates of other determinisms hold more sway than a simple idea of your own. Whether or not one views this realm as indicative of an existential crisis is a personal choice in regards to the attitude one will adopt. It is, however, indicative of an area of existential juxtaposition where one's postulates have to come to terms with the postulates of other determinisms.

Every person who grows up in this world faces the postulates that have been presented to themselves in this regard. Most of those in the West are faced with the postulates of those who advocate the *Bible* as well as the postulates of those who wrote it, compiled it and inspired it. Some people make their own postulate to accept the postulates of those who came before them while others make their postulates so as to question such. Any arguments or convictions about such, however, are all subordinate to the postulate(s) one makes. This is the same sort of pattern that take places in virtually any human activity. One makes a postulate and then mentally seeks to corroborate, validate or enforce the prospect that one's original postulate(s) is/are correct.

Whether or not we agree with the *Bible* or the way it is interpreted and enforced upon the population, it becomes obvious to anyone that postulates have a great deal to do with authority and power. There is no question that postulates are imbedded into the laws of the universe itself. We see this readily in the laws of physics, gravity being the most obvious. The universe has its own claim to authority and power that we are subject to. Whether or not we want to attribute this to a deity or not is dependent upon our postulates, but the postulates behind such a paradigm are something we will have to contend or deal with.

When we consider the realm of authority and power, we are either in or approaching the realm of magic and the occult. People typically study the occult or magic in order to obtain power that they either do not have or could not otherwise acquire, at least in their own minds. Postulates are therefore the woof and warp of what they work with.

According to both Crowley and Hubbard, the postulate is the senior mechanism. Most serious magicians, however, seek to enforce their postulates with words and letters which are known as *grammar* which is archaically known as *grimoire*. The subject of grimoires is complex and is deeply tied into the roots of both the political and celestial hierarchies in play with regard to life on Earth. People who study such are inclined to get lost and to miss the forest from the trees.

Crowley gives a clue with regard to how to study magick and use postulates in his seminal work *Magick in Theory and Practice* when he tells you to align with nature. Nature, of course, manifests in myriad ways and is an aspect of life that defies definition. Behind nature is the Tao. While people can easily attribute the properties of the ultimate postulate to Tao (i.e. all postulates originate from and are subordinate to the Tao), this is not totally accurate. Tao, by its own definition, is not definable. This aspect, however, should put some perspective on the paradigm of magick. Although magick can be very powerful, it is subordinate to nature which is subordinate to Tao.

There is another aspect of the postulate that is not only apropos to the Scientology experience but also to those who explore the realm of the metaphysical. This has to do with the experience of your postulates being in rhythm with your experience. There are times when we can do no wrong. Athletes refer to this as being in the zone. This area is akin to what is referred to as "when the particle becomes a wave" which refers to the concept in physics of a particle (usually of light) being identified as a wave or an aspect of a wave being identifiable as a particle. It is, quite literally, the realm where physical matter can potentially become pure energy. The reverse of this (when a wave of energy collapses and becomes identifiable as physical reality) is known as a collapsed wave. While many people have experienced varying degrees of this, it represents a very powerful state of mind, if one can master it.

In the next chapter, we will explore the relationship between the postulate and power; and, in particular, how it relates to the phenomena surrounding L. Ron Hubbard and Scientology.

— CHAPTER SEVEN —

WORD POWER, MIND LANGUAGE

*"Small wonder that spell means both a story told,
and a formula of power over living men."*
— J.R.R. Tolkien, On Fairy Stories

In order to give you an understanding of the occult matrix underlying the methodology of L. Ron Hubbard, I have thus far attempted to give you a pragmatic understanding of two instruments that are key to the practice of magick: sympathetic resonance (or affinity) and postulates. Both of these are manifested through a third component: *grimoire*, the French word for grammar or "words and letters". We can use the words *grimoire* and *grammar* interchangeably if we choose.

Grammar consists of words and letters. In common usage, this refers to simple language and literature, but the origins of "grimoire" has far more to do with magick and with specific reference to executing one's will. I will touch more deeply on the association between traditional magick and grammar in a subsequent chapter, but for now, I want to focus on words.

A word is a series of letters or glyphs that make up a unit which also is meant to represent sounds or, more precisely, physiological expressions that manifest as iterations associated with the gullet. Although words are associated with sounds and the gullet and are clearly modified by the emotions and physiological temperament* of the organism, they have a much deeper root that initially manifests through the lower or gestative region of the anatomy, the latter of which the Hindus refer to as the root chakra. What is important here is that the words that we hear and iterate are received and translated through our whole being. This often goes unnoticed, particularly by the filters which relegate most people to an approximate ten per cent usage of their brain capacity. Thus it is that the words you hear and iterate (whether it be from television, a friend or whatever) have a more profound effect than most people would be apt to recognize.

It is ironic that, in my attempt to describe the relevance of words and grammar with regard to magick and the occult matrix beneath Scientology, I have stumbled upon the realm that synchronizes with Hubbard's theories about an engram, a word which refers to a command phrase that affects the entire organism on an unconscious basis. It is important to understand the word *engram* if you want to understand how Hubbard thought although his

---

* The word *temperament* is used here in the sense and context of Old Physiology where it refers to "the combination of the four cardinal humors from alchemy, the relative proportions of which were supposed to determine physical and mental constitution".

particular definition is not necessarily what I am trying to emphasize in this chapter. The regular English (medical) usage of the word *engram* signifies, according to the *Oxford Dictionary*, "a hypothetical change in neural tissue postulated in order to account for persistence of memory." The original term *engram* is credited to have originated in 1904 with a German scholar, Richard Semon, who defined it as a "stimulus impression" which could be reactivated by the recurrence of "the energetic conditions which ruled at the generation of the engram." The most interesting aspect of the word *engram*, however, at least with regard to this narrative about magick, is the etymology from the *Oxford Dictionary* stating that it was coined in German from the Greek *en*, meaning "within" and *gramma*, referring to grammar or a letter of the alphabet. The very idea of an engram or stimulus upon an organism is embedded with the idea of a letter or a series of letters (a word or spell, as in the word *grimoire*) impinging upon a life form. A word, of course, represents a concept or idea.

With regard to a stimulus upon a cell, it is important to point out that in the human realm such stimuli can be readily placed into two categories: 1) that which the organism is aware of and 2) that which the organism is not aware of, including any sensory input occurring during a period of where consciousness is either reduced or completely subdued by reason of an accident. Besides ordinary sensory data, the input of words or grammar will have a substantial impact upon a person's consciousness. You can witness this yourself by watching the effect that advertising has. While media advertising is communicated to people in a manner that they are aware of, it also has a more insidious way of permeating one's awareness more than one might like.

When it comes to the input of data when our ordinary awareness is deprived, we are in a no-man's land. This realm, however, is subject to the power of words and grammar; that is to say, spells. When a magician or witch invokes spirits and uses bat wings, herbs or the like, it is based upon the idea that such elements will have a calculated impact upon the mind/brain complex.

While it is both challenging and dubious to list every conceivable permutation of possible causes and effects with regard to magical operations that affect the unconscious realm, it can be viewed very simply. Ordinary humans are only aware of a small percentage of the cognitive processes and that includes their sensory input. All of that latent or "dead" gray matter is indeed active; and further, it is additionally under the influence of factors that an individual is generally unaware of. This is the realm of the occult and while it might be tempting to some to either relegate this either to the idea of bat wings or some other jocular and derogatory reference, there is a mysterious process at work underlying all of this and it has to do with nature; and more specifically, DNA.

DNA is all based upon sensory input that responds according to environmental stimuli, all of which is processed according to different reference points within it, all based upon previous experience. Although DNA was unknown to scientists until the 20th Century, it was not unknown to those who were privy to the most occult doctrines of yesteryear. Although this sounds more intriguing and mysterious than it should, the idea that such data might be known is not really surprising if we examine the issue with common logic. The processes by which information is processed in the organism is based upon nature, all of which is enabling the organism to survive. There is, however, a bigger picture at work. The organism is not only trying to survive for itself, it is also attempting to create in reference to the species it belongs to. Beyond that, there are other organisms and species which are competing for survival in a larger theater. All of these life forms, however, are all interwoven and subject to a higher or more basic function which is the concept of life itself. The common denominator of life is DNA and with particular reference to the function that it represents.

With reference to magical doctrines and words of power and grammar, it requires no leap of the imagination at all to realize and understand that the patterns of DNA processing have been deeply imbedded within our own organisms and their antecedents forever; and further, that if such is the case, any categorization of such, if it is at all reasonably or approximately accurate, should not surprise us as being either mysterious or occult. Unfortunately, however, such data has been manipulated so as to make it seem very occult, mysterious and inaccessible.

All magical grammar is based upon correspondences with DNA. In order to explain this as clearly and simply as I can, it is first necessary to evaluate the underlying principle upon which such a conclusion is based.

Throughout history, there have been various traditions which serviced the general needs of the people. Beyond that, however, there were traditions which served and honored the needs of life itself. In certain cultures, these were identified as mystery schools which were based upon the patterns and traditions of life. By and of themselves, these mystery schools appear to have equally mysterious origins as well. The factor of mystery, however, is not much different than going out into nature at spring time and witnessing all the unknown and virtually invisible processes at work. Life, as it evolves, follows a prescribed course of indoctrination that allows for an infinitude of variables so as to make it more suitable or adaptable to the circumstances it has to deal with. In other words, life follows a template which is stored in the DNA and responds accordingly to environmental stimuli. The concept of such a fluid pattern has often been referred to as the Tree of Life. Although the processes represented by the Tree of Life are not fixed, different cultures have featured systems of thought with accompanying diagrams featuring fixed symbols for the purpose of either explaining or getting others to understand such a concept. One of the more popular renditions in today's culture is the

Kabbalah, Cabala or Qabala. The *K* is for the Jewish tradition while the *C* is for the Christian version and the *Q* for the Islamic. Each of these versions have a different slant or perception of the schematic of life.*

Earlier, I stated that to understand the patterns of DNA processing, any categorizations of such should be "reasonably accurate". While no two-dimensional rendition is going to be too precise, all we can expect is a model that will help us understand the Tree itself. While there are many omissions in virtually all cabalistic doctrines, even the most error-filled renditions can give us at least a basic grasp of how the Tree works. For example, each designated reference point or line in a Tree of Life diagram represents a station of life with a particular series of impulses and characteristics. Such characteristics, over time, have been rendered with different archetypal expressions, the Greek gods and goddesses being the most familiar to us. What is important, however, is not the reality or unreality of the gods or goddesses but rather the characteristics and general nature of what they are meant to represent. In the course of evolution, such archetypes, however crudely analyzed and applied, tell us a tale with regard to DNA processing.

For example, you can witness various renditions of DNA, either in the plant or animal kingdom, that are more representative of the aspects of Venus or beauty than are others. Some might be more representative of the aspects of Mars or warrior energy than others. This applies equally to all of the other archetypal deity aspects that are rendered in a Tree of Life diagram. It is as if each reference point or archetypal realm represented in the Tree is a "stopping off point" for life as it responds to stimuli by recording that which has occurred and then integrating what characteristics it can from that particular station of life. As life evolves, it then moves on to its next reference point or station, integrating what is appropriate or simply passing and maintaining or fortifying the extant genetic structure.

While this is a completely logical explanation, the precise details are challenging to categorize for obvious reasons. Nevertheless, different schematics of the Tree of Life have been utilized for millennia, generally reserved to a priestly class. More relevant to the power of words and grammar in this narrative, each station in the Tree has been assigned different sounds, sometimes identified with words of power, there being the idea that certain combinations of letters or sounds will have a certain type of impact upon life. The most obvious example is giving an order or request to another person who then complies with your wish. With regard to magic, however, we are talking about a much more subtle form of influence that is not typically realized. In other words, there is an entire science or art dedicated to the prospect that life can be influenced and directed though a secret or otherwise inaccessible

---

* In the event that you are unfamiliar with either the Tree of Life or Cabala, I have included a simple primer on the subject in Appendix A.

language which is really just a series of sounds. It is all based upon the precept that if you do A, B, C, and D, you will get a specific result called E. It is not the subject of this book to go into such details, but there are entire languages dedicated to creating such effects. One of the more popularly recognized of such languages is Enochian, sometimes referred to as the language of the angels, which is identified with what might be referred to as the creation zone. Although this language has its own syntax and grammar, you will not learn about it in schools or universities. There are also indigenous forms of such communication which work upon the same principles. While all of this invites endless speculation, it is a problematic area for ordinary human beings to indulge themselves in and for various reasons.

While it is impossible to even attempt even a cursory analysis and description of such in this book, it is important to recognize that the language of occult magick is a subject that is and always has been taken very seriously by certain factions. What is most relevant in this book is that L. Ron Hubbard was subjected to such language by reason of his own involvement in the occult; and further, that such language was used to create certain intended effects. To what degree it affected him has to remain speculative, but it is a very important factor with regard to his life and how it manifested. It must not be cast aside nor overlooked when trying to assess his life and its impact upon the world. I will touch on more details later. Right now, I am simply laying a foundation with regard to the occult principles that underlie the entire paradigm presented by Scientology.

Referring back to the principle that all words and letters represent concepts, do realize that a concept is the essence of a word and all that really matters in the equation. If the concept is either understood or communicated, the words or letters used are relatively irrelevant. As per the laws of both magick and Scientology, postulates are senior. A postulate is also a concept. In other words, if a clear postulate is made, certain machinations will manifest so as to facilitate the creation of the postulate. You do not have to concern yourself about the words. Things will fall into place automatically. Words and grammar, however, should be neither underestimated nor neglected.

Differentiated from but not altogether separated from the magical aspects of words is the field of semantics, a field of study which is very important when it comes to the realm of power. The word *semantics* is defined as follows:

> **semantics** *adjective* 1. (Linguistics) of or relating to meaning or arising from distinctions between the meanings of different words or symbols
> 2. (Philosophy) of or relating to semantics
> [derivation from Greek *sēmantikos* having significance, from *sēmainein* to signify, from *sēma* a sign]

Although semantics and rhetoric have been studied rigorously in universities for a very long time, these subjects are either abused or misunderstood by a large percentage of the population. More importantly, they have everything to do with power. Semantics allow you to steer or control certain situations, particularly when you define the terms in your own words or convey communication in such a manner as to narrow the definition of a particular word or series of words. There is also the idea of *newspeak* from George Orwell's novel *1984* where you can change the meaning of a word in order to control the thoughts of a population or group of people. You can obliterate certain concepts by literally changing the meaning of words or omitting certain definitions either from dictionaries or common popular usage.

L. Ron Hubbard has frequently been accused of creating his own language so as to confuse and manipulate people to conform with his wishes. It is true that Hubbard created his own language, and he referred to it as Scientologese. His openly stated reason for such was that the subjects of psychology and psychiatry did not have adequate terms to discuss the phenomena he was encountering and addressing with his counselling techniques. People can get very heated on this aspect and insist it was done for hypnotic reasons in order to control. While I readily understand how people arrive at such conclusions and why they get so animated about it, I find this proposition to be a result of their own ignorance. Ignorance, in and of itself, can make you predisposed to all sorts of manipulation, all of which begins with your thinking processes.

Hubbard was a strong if not obsessive advocate of a process he called word clearing. This was a procedure wherein a person would look up all possible and relevant words they did not understand. This even involved digging for words that you thought you understood but did not. The stated purpose was to rehabilitate your education and to enable you to actually recognize what you were thinking and saying as you used different words.

Many if not most of the people in the Scientology movement had a tendency to adopt and use words that they did not really understand. Sometimes, they really did understand them but their comprehension would be overrun by political factors which would make their true understandings irrelevant. All of this resulted in a "group think" which was not only divergent from whatever was being taught, it perpetrated all sorts of falsehoods. These would be adopted by people as living truths which were not truths at all.

I am well aware that there are thousands upon thousands of people who are recovering from their experiences in Scientology. While I was well aware that such people were on a dubious path when I left in 1983, I am astonished by how severely messed up many became and continue to be to this day. I cannot answer for their experiences, but I know why I did not suffer such and also why I made a virtually seamless transition into the regular world. It had everything to do with understanding the words I read.

When you understand a word, it resonates through your entire physiological structure in a way that is neither mysterious nor puzzling. It has no mysterious or unknown power over you. This applies to sentences, laws and any written form of communication. This principle was particularly applicable in a Scientology environment which could be quite toxic to your own determinism if you did not properly understand the words being used. In my own experience, I found that when people sought to use words or laws against myself or others in a negative manner, and I am referring to Scientology policies, they could be easily outmaneuvered. The reason for this is that when people seek to act in a manner that is against you or anyone else for that manner, they are usually not only acting in a manner that is incorrect or just morally deficient, it is a result of them not understanding the policy in question; and, in particular, its contextual application. People would often do crazy things and blame it either on the policy or technical applications. My answer to this is that when one finds themselves in a position where they are confronting illogic and the potential of engaging in behavior or actions that are either destructive to oneself or others, it is vital to recognize that you are suffering from either your own or someone else's severe misunderstandings of life. This applies particularly in the event that you feel predisposed to indulge in the questionable behavior. These principles also apply to ordinary application of civil law.

While understanding words and their meanings is very helpful in regular life, this does not necessarily help you with magical words or grammar that either have no apparent meanings or lost meanings. There is, however, a solution that can be employed and this has everything to do with the field of semantics. While the subject of semantics is often thought to be about words, it is really about signs, sigils and their significance. Words, while very powerful and important, are inclusive of a bigger picture. Above and beyond language, life has its own way of communicating. Native Americans often see significance of great import when certain animals appear in their day to day life. In other words, you need to become familiar with the jungle of your own life and learn about the different "animals", "plants" and territory you live in. Reading people's intent and body language is also a skill that will supercede the power of words. This is particularly applicable when a person is telling you one thing and they mean something else. A person who is sharp will be able to tell if the person is lying. On the other hand, there are people who will be suspicious of a person telling the truth because they cannot recognize the truth in themselves. All of this tells us that we not only need to pay attention to words but the actual intentions behind them; and further, the vectors and momentum of nature. Finally and most important, if you do not understand words or concepts, you are predisposed to being controlled by them and thus can become a slave to the thoughts of others or even your own.

With regard to being controlled by words, I will now return to the concept of an engram, both with regard to the concept set forth in the dictionary as well as Hubbard's application of it. This concept is the entire basis of what Dianetics is based upon; and Dianetics, of course, is the forerunner and foundational aspect of Scientology.

The idea of an engram, as defined, is a postulate. It is, in fact, the idea that perceived sounds have a stimulus-response effect upon an organism. In the realm of Dianetics, one being counseled was simply trying to find the words and ultimately, the postulates, that were affecting his mind in a negative or unconscious manner. While this approach had a workability to the point where it excited thousands upon thousands of people, it is not exactly the same as the postulates and grammar of magic. This does not mean that one engaging in Dianetic therapy was restricted from grasping or engaging the tentacles of magical grammar or associated postulates, but it is important to note that there are certain aspects of such which are virtually hard-wired into the anatomy of the mind-brain-body complex that would make either penetration or revelation of such rather challenging. Hubbard himself, as well as many if not most Scientologists, were or are aware of the idea that one can attack the unconscious or restricted portions of the mind by approaching it through various techniques. Nevertheless, an ignorance or lack of familiarity makes the proposition extremely challenging if not virtually impossible.

To put it bluntly, all of the wonderful propositions, hopes and dreams that either could be or might be accomplished by Hubbard's techniques, or even similar techniques, are susceptible to being held hostage by occult factors that are not recognized. In this regard, it is important to take note of the fact that Hubbard was a steward or carrier of occult energy, and it was a very powerful occult energy. His associations with Jack Parsons and Aleister Crowley alone brand him as a complete wild card when it comes to occult matters. This will be examined later on, but right now, I am only trying to establish that Hubbard used words and taught people to use them in order to recover their own memories and postulates. He was, however, subject to words and powers of a more deeper order. This is not, by the way, a criticism but rather a fact, and it will be well demonstrated as we continue.

Let me now direct you back to the quotation by Tolkien at the beginning of this chapter where it states that a spell is not only a story told but a formula of power over living men. Keep in mind that a spell is nothing more than a combination of words and letters. This not only applies to the writings of Hubbard but to the iterations of a leader of any kind; and with particular regard to their usage in politics. Words tell stories, and the stories are only significant and influential if people pay attention to them. If they are paid attention to, they can direct a nation. Whether such stories or words are positive or negative is another matter entirely.

The writings which have the most powerful influence over Mankind in our current culture are the texts of the three primary Abrahamic religions: the *Old Testament* and *Talmud* of the Hebrews, the *New Testament* of the Christians, and the *Koran* of Islam. These dictate the thoughts, minds, and behavior of billions of people. Many if not most of these followers are ignorant of the fact that each of these texts are based upon a hidden tradition of either Kabbalah, Cabala or Qabala as was alluded to earlier. These hidden traditions dictate the hierarchy of the aforesaid religions. Even if one chooses to view the Abrahamic religions with a jaundiced eye, such texts are only a reflection of the Tree of Life itself. If the doctrines are bent or faulty, then so is the Tree or at least that limb that we find ourselves stuck on or preoccupied with. Whether we choose to define the Tree as either God or Life, we are facing the proposition of a concept that rules and dictates the creatures of creation.

Although Hubbard studied the Cabala and mentions it in his work, he had his own particular schematic or "Tree" but it was not like any of the examples you are likely to be familiar with and certainly not the ones mentioned herein. I will go into that "Tree" at the appropriate time; but for now, it is important to relay something Hubbard once said to his personal communicator who, I believe, was his butler at the time.

> "Life is more important than Scientology. People think its the other way around, but it's not."

This quote was told to me by his former personal communicator who I used to work under in the Personal Office of L. Ron Hubbard. While this did not surprise me at the time I heard it, nor would it have surprised me at any time during my Scientology years, I would readily agree with Hubbard that most Scientologists would reverse the priority.

What is important is that Hubbard recognized that life itself was a commodity that had to be adhered to and that this concept completely superceded any religious of philosophical system, scheme or tradition that one might put before it. Whether he applied this intelligently or not is a different issue. The crux of this, however, is that Hubbard devised his own system or "Tree" and that is what he lived by. While this will be addressed in detail later on, it should be recognized that whatever words or concepts he ascribed to his version of the "Tree" or anyone else describes in their versions, it is life itself that is the senior proposition, not the schematic. Many people stayed in Scientology diligently or slavishly, subscribing to the system. They only got the hell out when life began to hit them in such a violent or dramatic way that they realized there was no other path. This is something on the order of people sitting on the beach with a prescribed meditation that teaches you to handle everything that might come up in your life. When a tidal wave appears on the horizon, you get up and run for high ground. In a metaphorical sense, you can expect there will be some who will diligently stick to the meditation and be numb to the fact that they will be consumed by the wave.

A tidal wave represents power; and a power that is relentless and unforgiving to those who do not heed its destructive potential. It is devastating to those who stand in its path. Scientology, in and of itself, was and is just a body of data, but there was and is an occult current associated with it that is not unlike a tidal wave: relentless and unforgiving.

In this chapter, I have attempted to augment your understanding of the power of words and their relationship to occult magic. In the scenario of the tidal wave, however, we are not talking about anything but a pure force. Words and grammar might well be associated with it; but we can only ask, what words and grammar? If I could answer that question in a simple sentence or two, that would be that, and there would be no point in taking this any further. All we know, however, is that such a force represents nature. Hurricanes, another component of nature which represents a force as equally destructive as tidal waves, are particularly known for being associated with occult energies. While the words associated with such might be obscure or unknown, we can only recognize that such a force is something we can learn about if only by recognizing it and its associated components.

But now, from this vantage point, we are moving beyond the reference frame of word power and mind language. We are moving into the world of FORCE and POWER.

CHAPTER EIGHT

TYPHON

*"All you are is a fart in a hurricane, kid;
now read about the Real Power!"*
— *L. Ron Hubbard (spoken to L. Ron Hubbard, Jr.),
L. Ron Hubbard: Madman or Messiah?*

While Hubbard is portrayed or thought of as a beneficent hero to some and a mentally imbalanced exploiter of men's hopes and fears by others, both factions would readily agree that he had or utilized considerable power. It is this element of power and his relationship to it that is a fundamental thesis of this book. As the title of the book also deals with the subject of insanity, the relationship between sanity and power is also of keen interest and relevancy in these matters.

If an insane person has no power, he is of little relevance to his environment and is not considered dangerous. If such a person does have power, there is no telling what calamity might ensue. The reverse can be said for a sane person. If he has no power, his sanity will have no relevancy. If he has great power, it can be of great benefit to many. Any way you look at it, power is an important keystone in the construct of civilization and human life.

All of Hubbard's power was a direct result of his forays into psychotherapy and the heralding of his discoveries and the potentials he postulated. He painted an inspiring picture which was not only designed to capture the hopes and dreams of the human mind, it did and still does capture such. All of this is based upon the proposition that you yourself are far more capable than you might have otherwise dreamed of by reason of the limitations society has deliberately or not deliberately placed upon consciousness in general.

With regard to Hubbard, his power can be divided into at least two aspects: political power and occult power. While the two are not necessarily mutually exclusive of each other, they were most certainly two different reference frames from which he operated. While you cannot absolutely divide them from each other and their intermingling is fascinating, it is easiest to approach them, at least initially, as two separate reference frames.

I will begin by relaying what is perhaps the most lurid, foreboding and sensationalistic example of his power, from which the above quotation at the beginning of this chapter is extracted. I will preface this, however, by relating a story relevant to the subject at hand.

In 1971, unlike many of my fellow students in Scientology, I took occasion to investigate the *Reader's Guide* in the library in order to search out all the articles that had been written about Scientology, Dianetics, and or

L. Ron Hubbard. This was well before I joined the Sea Organization and when I was just a beginning student in the movement. There were vindictive claims about Hubbard by Sara Northrup, his second wife, and also by L. Ron Hubbard Jr., both of whom claimed outrageous and abusive behavior on his part. While I do not remember them too well, the accusations were over-the-top with regard to what you might hear from a typical estranged family member or ex-spouse. One article claimed he had kidnapped his own daughter, and while this sounds so horrible, any legal expert will tell you that you cannot kidnap your own daughter, especially when you have custody within the eyes of the law. One writer also seemed rather preoccupied with portraying Hubbard as an extravagantly gauche self-styled aristocrat by stating that he would have a Coca-Cola delivered to him every afternoon by a butler on a silver tray. (His butler, by the way, never remembered such.)

Like many of the articles I read in magazines at that time period, these were particularly biased, but they indicated a disturbance in Hubbard's life stream that was atypical. When I brought them up to my supervisors in Scientology, they simply told me to judge them (meaning themselves and the Church in general) by what results I could get from applying the techniques I was learning in Dianetics and Scientology. As I got better and more familiar with these techniques, the legacies of Sara Northrup and L. Ron Hubbard Jr. became irrelevant. There was, however, no question that these family members either were or felt badly burned by their experiences with L. Ron Hubbard. The more I learned about Scientology and the nature of my own mind as well as that of others, the more I understood how people could misfire when it came to dealing with these subjects that were preoccupied with probing the most sensitive areas of the human mind. In my experience, I have found that the human mind is loaded with very many sensitive triggers which can be likened to land mines on a battlefield. When you step on one, it literally blows the thinking and behavioral aspects of a person into chaos, sometimes resulting in personal catastrophe. While some people can address these sensitive triggers and take it all in stride, there are many who cannot.

These observations concerning sensitive triggers, by the way, do not just include my experience with Scientologists but also with people in the occult world as well as ordinary humans trying to understand difficult subjects.

With regard to my own experiences with the techniques of Dianetics and Scientology, which were extremely positive, I recognized that my deep appreciation for the subject was not necessarily matched by the family of L. Ron Hubbard. Aboard the *Apollo*, the Hubbard family were there by reason of circumstance and not by reason of choice. They seemed to have comparatively little interest in or lack of appreciation for the mechanics of these subjects and their potential. While I would not say they were dismissive, they most certainly did not exhibit any zeal with regard to these matters.

Consequently, I never took them too seriously. This aspect, however, should not be too surprising, at least if you consider that Hubbard was a virtuoso in any sense of the word. The talent of a great athlete, musician or inventor does not necessarily transfer to their children.

L. Ron Hubbard Jr. did not appear again on my radar screen to any significant extent until I began to work in the Personal Office of LRH. LRH Jr. had become quite an albatross, and I could not have avoided learning about him if I had wanted to. I learned of his long history of being paid by the press for giving lurid stories about his father. He would then publicly recant them with a signed affidavit in return for big money he received from the Church of Scientology. This was in the six figure category as I recall. It was very profitable for him to speak out. He would frequently if not always pander to the highest bidder. While this behavior pattern defeats his credibility in terms of being any sort of reliable legal witness, the entire set of circumstances speaks for itself. Interpreting it, however, can be more than a little challenging.

I do recall, from time to time, being briefed upon what had transpired between LRH and his son, at least in terms of correspondence. Keep in mind, it was deemed important by my superiors, including LRH himself, that I should know exactly how LRH felt and thought about things and exactly what he had to say about them. After all, I was trained to be his eyes and ears. After one of these public dust-ups had been settled and Nibs (this was the nickname of LRH Jr. and was what everyone referred to him as whether he was in good graces or bad graces) was back in the fold so to speak, I recall that Hubbard had sent a special message to the person preparing a letter of reconciliation. A paraphrase of this message, which was to be included as a post script to the original letter, was, "Tell Nibs that Mary Sue and I still love him." For his own part, Nibs would write to LRH and tell him about his grandchildren and how he used the tech (this refers to applications of Dianetics and Scientology) on them. In other words, despite his contradictory behavior, Nibs still found value with regard to the techniques of Dianetics and Scientology.

As controversial or out of tune this correspondence might have been, it had absolutely no effect upon me with regard to my daily toil or my involvement with Dianetics and Scientology itself. It is not unlike being a ball player and reading about the manager's family difficulties that have nothing to do with the ball game itself.

I only learned about the quotation at the beginning of this chapter when I ran across the book *L. Ron Hubbard: Madman or Messiah?* by Bent Corydon and L. Ron Hubbard Jr. That book was a whole earful and gave me a vantage point on Hubbard that I had never experienced before.

This quotation about being a fart in a hurricane was, according to Nibs, the result of a discussion with his father who had told him he required more help and needed him for backup. After telling Nibs he did not have much horsepower, Nibs responded by telling him that he was doing OK. This, however, unleashed a torrent of fury as LRH was said to have slammed his hand down on a set of occult magic books that were on the table, stating the following:

> "You snot-nosed kid. You don't know your ass from a hole in the ground! All you are is a fart in a hurricane, kid; now read about the Real Power!"

The real power referred to the books on the table which, per Nibs, were as follows: *The Book of the Law, The Sacred Magic of Abre-Melin,* and *The Sex Magick of the Ninth Degree.*[*] Nibs then pulls out all the stops and portrays his father as the most obsessed and crazed man you might ever want to imagine:

> "The books and contents to be kept forever secret, he says. To reveal them will cause you instant insanity: rip your mind apart; destroy you."

While we will never be able to verify that Nibs is telling the exact truth due to his contradictory behavior, it is hard to imagine why he would lie in this particular way about this particular type of information. For myself, as I read this passage, it was as if the universe had opened up a pathway. Poetically, I would liken this pathway as a vortex into time, but in actual fact, it was a pathway to understanding the occult matrix that was always lurking beneath the foundation of Dianetics and Scientology.

When we talk about instant insanity, ripping the mind apart and destruction of the individual, it is highly relevant to harken back to the words of Margaret Singer, the clinical therapist who frequently testified in court on behalf of mind control victims and stated that Hubbard's techniques were not only more sophisticated than those used in North Korea and Communist China but that he took the "art of control and persuasion" to an entirely new level.

In Nibs' lurid description of his father, he further quoted him as saying:

> "Secrets, techniques and powers I alone have conquered and harnessed. I alone have refined, improved on, applied my engineering principles to. Science and logic. The keys! My keys to the doorway of the Magick; my magick! The power! Not Scientology power! My power! The real powers of Solomon."

Whether or not this dialogue is precise, it is consistent with the wake Hubbard has left behind him. When we combine it with the earlier allegation,

---
[*] The subject matter of these books will be addressed in a subsequent chapter.

that he was once in straight jacket at St. Elizabeth's mental hospital, claiming he was Jesus Christ, it presents a picture of a person who was completely out of his mind. If we assume the premise that these allegations are either true, reasonably accurate or even somewhat accurate, it presents something of a riddle with regard to how he could assert so much control as well as manage such a large and dynamic movement as Scientology. In this respect, I want you to keep in mind that Hubbard was intelligent, creative, and prolific. He also believed that he had tapped a reservoir that contained all of the answers that had ever puzzled the mind of humanity. It can easily be deduced that his propensity to be creative as a writer played off of his own experiences and forays into the occult. The most reasonable assessment I can make of all this information is that he identified very deeply with the magical texts he had become familiar with.

While this report by Nibs is a completely different look at Hubbard than what I experienced in my personal adventures, there is a familiar thread and common denominator between the two divergent views and that is Ron's personal preoccupation with power. I can easily imagine him having said such things and also doing it in a very private manner.

According to Nibs, LRH had prefaced the entire diatribe by stating that he was going to outlive the whole damned world. This indicated, at least at that particular time, that LRH had an indomitable will to survive.

In order to present a contextual understanding of what took place at that particular time, and especially what it represents to the fallout that has occurred with regard to Hubbard and his movement, it is important to focus upon the forceful aspect of nature. The aforesaid scenario presents a picture that Hubbard either aligned himself with or was himself an intimidating force. Whether or not this indomitable force is viewed as positive or negative, it was an inescapable part of the Scientology experience, and it exhibited itself more strongly the closer you got to Hubbard's own personal lair.

In referring back to the quotation about the hurricane, and whether you believe it is authentic or not, there is no question that Hubbard frequently identified himself with such a force, and his connections to occult magick cannot be denied as they are too abundant. They are, however, not well understood. With regard to the hurricane analogy itself, Nibs was not the only one who found himself to be a fart in a hurricane. There are many accounts of people who, correctly or incorrectly, have felt that they were either directly or indirectly victimized by what Hubbard unleashed upon the world.

In the context of ordinary religion, such victims are equatable to those who have been damned, a word which is phonetically and etymologically not much different than *doom*. Both words connote judgment, condemnation, ruination and law. Whether such victims are somehow responsible, by reason of the law of karma or whatever, is an age-old riddle that has occupied the minds of men for millennia. When a hurricane or tidal wave wipes out an entire village or beach front, why does it reach some and not others? All that matters, at least when we are dealing with the torrents of occult magick — whether they are associated with natural forces or not — is that if we choose to become educated in such matters, we will not be inclined to be adversely affected by such phenomena. It is for this reason I am writing this book. I cannot overstate how little these subjects are understood, and this includes many of the people who write about them.

With regard to victims of Scientology, there is another element which is important to take stock of and that is the process of calculation. People who got involved over their heads suffered as result of their own miscalculation. In other words, they were at the wrong place at the wrong time. More often than not, however, they were an active participant in the calculation or thinking process that placed them in the situation. When someone discovers that they have been thinking incorrectly for years upon years, it frequently causes them to either emotionally cave in or go into an abject denial. Any such miscalculation, however, is very worthy of forgiveness when you consider the nature of what they were dealing with.

The specific characteristics embodied by L. Ron Hubbard's persona as has been depicted in the aforesaid scenario are not foreign to either serious students or practitioners of occult magick. Such characteristics would be viewed as representing what is referred to as the Typhonian Current, a name which is borrowed from the god Typhon from Greek mythology. While the word *Typhon* is synonymous with a typhoon or hurricane, it represents the most deadly creature in Greek mythology, a monster with hundreds of snake heads emerging from its shoulders. Typhon was identified as terrible, outrageous and lawless. Amongst the hundreds of snakes with burning heads was a fearful dragon with multiple flickering tongues and fire flashing from under the brow of his eyes. From the various heads, unspeakable sounds were made that the gods could not understand. When they could be understood at all, they were the sounds of ungovernable fury. There are various descriptions of Typhon, and it is significant to point out that it appears that the Beast of Revelation in the *Bible* was adopted from this archetypal model.

While the identification with the Beast is very important, particularly as we examine the magical or occult current upon which L. Ron Hubbard operated, it is also significant, if not more so, that the Typhonian Current, as well as the god himself, represents what the Hindus describe as kundalini, an ancient term which, in my opinion, has never been well understood in juxtaposition to L. Ron Hubbard and Scientology.

Kundalini refers to a reservoir of primordial energy or "coiled" power that rests at the base of the spine. When it is unleashed, either recklessly or by patient cultivation, it rises through the spine like a snake ascending a pole and metaphorically explodes through the head. It is not unlike a tidal wave because it washes out that which was before it and gives the person experiencing it an entirely new viewpoint of consciousness. It is often associated with facilitating higher consciousness and is identified with facilitating inspiration, genius and paranormal abilities. Despite this, it is sometimes associated with loss of equilibrium and states of mental imbalance. As an experience, the idea of kundalini or the experiences associated with it were not recognized by common psychotherapists until the last few decades. Today, while not all therapists are aware of it, there are a significant amount who are and will treat it in the context of the general experiences associated with Hinduism. Kundalini, however, is also commonly associated with mental illness. This does not mean that practitioners view kundalini as something that makes you crazy. It only means that they sometimes run into people who had a kundalini experience that they could not cope with and are thus seeking professional help. There are plenty of people who are able to take the experience in stride and integrate it as best they can into their lives.

If you study the early publications of Dianetics and Scientology, you will learn that Hubbard often referred to the experiences of preclears "going up the pole". In other words, they had experienced an abrupt or dramatic change of consciousness. This was often accompanied by people experiencing that they had left their body, sometimes looking down from the ceiling or even feeling stuck to it. As a result, processes (a series of instructions or commands given to a preclear) were developed to disentangle one from such an experience, which is to say, enable one to integrate their experience to the point where they could consciously return to their regular environment.

Despite this rather obvious association, it is not my imperative to do a comparative analysis between kundalini as recognized by the ancient Hindus and the various phenomena encountered by Scientologists undergoing therapy. There is no question that Hubbard would have been familiar with the most basic tenets of this phenomena, and I say that by reason of his association with Commander Snake Thompson, the Navy psychiatrist who influenced Hubbard and was also very familiar with the Hindu religion. Hubbard, whether mentored on this point by Thompson or not, took a very different approach than the ancients did with regard to awakening the so-called fire snake.

What is more important, at least at this point in my narrative, is that Hubbard himself was possessed of this primordial energy. It was a part of his personality and the primordial energy or power that he had accumulated would sometimes be unleashed in a manner that would overwhelm his rivals or even the people who had chosen to huddle under his umbrella.

Although Hubbard can be categorized as a "son of the snake" so to speak, it is misguided to point a finger at him and call him the devil or to judge him as unabashedly evil. These aspects were only a part of his entire personality, and such judgments only dehumanize him as well as the one who casts judgment upon him. He could also be quite affable and humanitarian at times. What is more important is to recognize that the primordial aspects or Typhonian Current that ran through him or that he exhibited was a characteristic of his personality and, in particular, that part of his personality which facilitated his identification with power.

Hubbard kindled ideas and hopes of super-human abilities that inspired countless thousands if not millions to reach beyond conventional horizons and aspire to be far more than they ever thought possible. In this respect, he was following a tradition that was not new to this Earth. Meeting the aspirations of such goals, however, has always been considered a rarefied act of specialized attainment that is unobtainable by the common man. For better or worse, Hubbard tried to make his system both accessible and workable for the common man. His relative success in this endeavor is not so relevant in this narrative, but there is a key point of reference with regard to why the path of the fire snake is so daunting.

The ancient Egyptians recognized the path of the fire snake or kundalini. Initiates were indoctrinated in at least two mystery schools in order to obtain enlightenment from such. One was the school of the Left Eye of Horus and the other was the Right Eye of Horus. The Left Eye, which corresponds to the right hemisphere of the brain, concerned the so-called non-linear aspects of consciousness which include creativity and intuition. The Right Eye, corresponding to the left hemisphere, concerned linear or logical thinking. When one had obtained proficiency in both, the fire snake was said to uncoil and make its way up the spine, eventually reaching an exaltation in the pineal gland which would correspond physiologically with the emergence of an isotope of gold (also sometimes known as white gold or manna) out of the forehead, often identified as the third eye. This idealized state was not only the goal of alchemy, it represented the epitome of what represents Mankind's greatest hopes: reconciliation with God or the Creator. The Egyptians, however, were well aware of the daunting aspects of the primordial energies of the fire snake. Accordingly, they had a doctrine that the cat was the antidote to the serpent. The cat represented felicity and love and if these energies were not present, the fire snake would unleash in the most unpredictable and reckless manner imaginable. The snake could, however, be tamed by the power and energies of the cat, also identified as Leo. This gave rise to the stories of Jesus ben Pandera (son of the panther) mentioned in the Talmud and elsewhere.

Early Christianity was an attempt to induce such a doctrine of unconditional felicity and love into a tyrannical environment that, like Typhon himself, was indeed terrible, outrageous and lawless. Without even casting judgment upon Christianity as authentic or not, it was as if either the mystery schools or Creation itself had attempted to tame the primordial aspects of consciousness with a doctrine of love that would facilitate the ascension of Mankind to an ultimate reconciliation with the Divine.

All of this makes a lot more sense if you view it though the process of DNA whereby the primordial aspects of the gestation of life evolve in their own complex ways so as to reach out in an effort to return to their own original place of reference, like the ouroboros (snake eating its tail). When we have life accelerated to the point where we have a full blown drama such as that depicted in the *New Testament*, we not only have a piece of literature that has commanded the minds of billions, we have a statement of myriad components of DNA expressing themselves, telling a story of life seeking to return to the Creator; and perhaps more to the point, the challenge and obstacles in the way of such.

So it is that the doctrinal objectives of magick and the more "sanitized" versions of Christianity are not as different as one might think. Various interpretations, however, often myopic, work to polarize different factions so as to continue the drama and reinforce the frustration of such a goal. While Christianity, Occult Magick and Scientology all use different semantics to describe their goals, the final objective contains a common thread and that has to do with immersing oneself in a God-like state or at least one that has considerably transcended that of the ordinary human being.

L. Ron Hubbard most definitely saw himself as a human being who had reached beyond the pole so to speak and was trying to save Mankind. Whether you believe he was delusional or not in this respect, the task at hand, whether by him or anyone else, is incredibly daunting to say the least. He was well aware of the odds; and with his own self-styled engineering mind-set, he sought to solve the problem. How he sought to solve it and the specific mind-set he employed will be delineated later.

When you look at the dilemma of consciousness as I have just laid out, it suggests that perhaps Nibs Hubbard and abused Scientologists are not the only farts in the hurricane. All of us could be identified as being in the same boat or perhaps being designated as something more solid. The Egyptians' answer to this dilemma, at least in part, was symbolized by the scarab or dung beetle who would roll dung into balls to use as food but also as a structure or virtual womb in which to lay eggs and provide their larvae with sustenance. As the scarab beetle has wings, it was also seen as a creature who could fly to the heavens and was viewed as representing birth and death.

L. Ron Hubbard and Scientology inspired a lot of people and they continue to do so. There is certainly nothing wrong with dreaming of and fulfilling your highest potential. One cannot escape, however, the fall from grace suffered by that movement as well as the fall from grace that has been endemic to humanity and commented upon by so many religions. The concept of the scarab, however, gives everyone hope and teaches the lesson that we can use the rejections and toxic matter of the past to rebuild our destiny and create children that can fly to the heavens.

We will next have a look at Hubbard's identification with one of the most prominent dung beetles of all time.

SYMPATHY FOR THE DEVIL

"Be as shrewd as the serpent but as gentle as the dove."
— *Jesus of Nazareth, Matthew 10:16* *

The dung beetle referred to in the previous chapter is none other than Aleister Crowley, the man who self-styled himself as the Beast 666 and was very content to be recognized under that moniker. We do not need the assertions of L. Ron Hubbard's disenfranchised son, however, to either believe or recognize that LRH deeply identified with Crowley. The following is a word for word quotation from *The Philadelphia Doctorate Course, Lecture 18, "Conditions of Space-Time-Energy"* (1952) in Hubbard's own words:

> "The magical cults of the 8th, 9th, 10th, 11th and 12th centuries in the Middle East were fascinating. The only modern work that has anything to do with them is a trifle wild in spots, but is a fascinating work in itself, and that's the work of Aleister Crowley — the late Aleister Crowley — my very good friend."

The Philadelphia Doctorate Course lectures, including the above passage, have pretty much always been available to any Scientologist who wanted to hear them. Like much of the data in his tapes, however, this passage was largely overlooked and forgotten because it was not a part of any regular curriculum. Although most Scientologists never hear of it while they are in Scientology, it has nevertheless created a rather mammoth stir with ex-Scientologists and the general public who are often shocked, dismayed, disgusted or repelled to learn that Hubbard would refer to Aleister Crowley, the man who called himself the Beast 666, as his very good friend.

It is important to add that if any practicing Scientologist were to hear the above quotation or stumble across it for any reason, they would most likely be non-plused in the extreme due to the fact that it is just not a part of the modus operandi of Scientology processing, i.e. therapy. It either does not fit in or does not seem to fit in. People who have become disaffected from this therapy or who have an axe to grind, however, will figuratively jump up and down and say something on the order of, "See! He's aligned with the devil!"

The world of Scientologists who are engaged in the disciplines of their religion, whether they are applying what they have learned competently or not, is a completely different one from those who are outside the movement;

---

* This verse has also endured other translations such as "Be wise as snakes and as innocent as doves." or "Be shrewd as the snake and harmless as the dove."

and in particular, with regard to its criticism. There is, however, a third world in this scenario and that is the world of occult magick.

The propensity of journalists and others to point at the Crowley-Hubbard connection in the aforesaid manner is indicative of a sophomoric approach if not a dismissive ignorance of the fundamental nature of occult magick, a subject which is far mor intricate and substantial than those who are unfamiliar with it might suspect. The deeper you go into it, you find that it is based much more upon scholarship than it is mumbo-jumbo. The deeper you go into the scholarship, however, you will be beset by codes and ciphers that, if you are clever and lucky enough decipher them, just might enable you to discover that regular scholarship, at least as it is promulgated in universities, is based upon mumbo-jumbo. I am not being sarcastic in this regard. It is an extremely challenging area to negotiate, and the difficulties encountered are echoed in the concept of the fire snake mentioned in the previous chapter. The topography, including the codes and ciphers, is booby-trapped in such a manner that as you proceed to access certain areas of occult knowledge, you will frequently find the primordial powers of the fire snake either breathing down your neck or standing in your way so as to prevent you from learning and perhaps doing much worse. It is not like studying texts in school and listening to lectures and simply passing a test. I should add that this dilemma of life that I have conjured up for you is not just about hidden knowledge but about the power, hidden power or alleged power that accompanies it. The fire snake neither yields its power nor allows access to it easily. It has always been said that you have to prove your worth or pass the test or standard of initiation.

Navigating the occult can be likened to playing a pinball game where you insert quarters with a ball emerging only to encounter obstacles representing the fire snake which is there at every turn to devour your ball and shoot it down a hole into oblivion. The key to succeeding at pinball is familiarity with the nature of the game, the nuances of the platform itself and how and when to manipulate the controls. The more quarters you put in, the more familiar you become and more eligible you are to win the prize which is generally just a free game or more. The prize with magick, however, is much different and it has everything to do with the predisposition and will of the player. Many are attracted to magical power, and this can lead to serious problems. Ultimately, winning at occult pinball, if you are able to do it, leaves you looking at your true self. This is enough to trigger someone into madness. For others, it is like coming home to your true nature and being at peace with it.

We can also liken Scientology to a pinball game. There are all sorts of bright lights that blink with fascinating twists and turns that move the ball in magical ways. This analogy, however, is likened to a pinball game located in a bar in the *Twilight Zone*. The person is fascinated by all of the colored lights and sounds and whistles that are emitted from the machine. He keeps putting in quarters based upon either hope or encouragement by reason of his relative successes in playing the game. After a while, he loses perspective and just plays the game by reason of habit or addiction. At some point, he runs out of quarters which represent his life force or wherewithal. The owner of the bar then pushes him out on the street where he collapses and lies with all of the others who have failed at the game. Amidst scattered bodies on the street, Rod Serling* then comes out and says something on the order of:

> "John Doe, another middle class kid from a nice family whose hopes and dreams were caught up in a contraption of amusement. What Joe did not realize is that a pinball game is like any game, and it follows the never ending and ever-repeating patterns of life. Like any game, if you do not keep your eye on the path and lose your bearings, you'll end up in...the twilight zone."

To continue this analogy, let us imagine that the following week, there is a sequel to the show. Serling is now seen standing in front of the same bar, but you can now see the signage featuring its name which is the *93 Club*.**

> "Here is the *93 Club*, a bar that looks like any bar but with a pinball game that is not like any other pinball game. The many who have lost the game with blinking lights, the game called Scientology, you see scattered in the streets, breathing their last breaths, but here is Jane Doe, a woman whose dubious fortune was to win the game; but what did she find? A transformation of the playing platform with new art work and words and instead of Scientology, the theme was Thelema, the Greek word for will and the motto of the Great Beast himself, Aleister Crowley. Not unlike Scientology, most of the players fail miserably at Thelema; but instead of being thrown out on the street, they are carried to the back alley where they lay dying amongst the refuse."

---

* Rod Serling was a pivotal character on television during the 1960s, serving as the announcer and creator of *The Twilight Zone* as well as the writer of many of its episodes. Extremely popular and now iconic, the *Twilight Zone* featured science fiction and fantasy plots with the characters always facing some sort of moral or existential dilemma.

** The number 93 is numerologically equivalent to the Greek word *thelema* which means "will" and is the central focus of Aleister Crowley's teaching which is "Do What Thou Wilt Shalt be the Whole of the Law". Followers of Thelema, known as Thelemites, will sometimes greet each other with high fives, exclaiming "93!"

In this episode, Jane lights up the board when she flips a ball up a ramp that has "Babalon" written on it and it lands into a bull's eye that says "Scarlet Woman". As bells and whistles go off in celebration, the mast of the pinball game turns into a mirror and Jane sees herself as the Mother of All Harlots and begins to take on all the men of the bar which wears her out physically, morally and about any other way you might imagine. She is exhausted and spent as the bar owner removes her to the alley. Rod Serling then reappears, this time in the alley amidst other bodies prostate in refuse.

> "Another tragedy of Thelema. Jane, a woman who saw in herself the potential to be the ultimate facilitator of the greatest prospect for humanity: the birth of a moon child, a savior of Mankind that would enable reconciliation with the Creator. She saw the potential in every man she saw and did what she could to actualize it, but as has always been the case, it came to naught and here she is, in the scrap heap known as the twilight zone."

The analogy of the pinball games leaves us with a daunting landscape but also one that is not much different from that which lies before humanity. This particular analogy of Jane Doe concerns one of the books mentioned in the previous chapter by Nibs: *The Sexual Magick of the 9th Degree*. This refers to the 9th Degree initiation of the O.T.O. or Ordo Templi Orientis, the magical society once headed by Aleister Crowley, the entire purpose of which is to create a moon child, a term that is not well understood.

A moon child is commonly thought to be a super being that would embody all of the characteristics of salvation. Although this is a fair enough definition, it is open to interpretation on many levels. While some of the interpretations might prove to be more insightful than others, all of them pale in the prospect of a birth that would serve as a catalyst to the reconciliation of all humanity with the Divinity.

I will now introduce another quotation that Nibs attributes to his father in the same diatribe.

> "Sex by will, Love by will -- no caring and no sharing -- no feelings ... Sex is the route to power. Scarlet women! They are the secret to the doorway. Use and consume. Feast. Drink the power through them. Waste and discard them."

When Nibs asks him what he means by scarlet, Hubbard answers.

> "Yes, scarlet: the blood of their bodies; the blood of their souls."

Now this might sound rather grisly to you; and it most certainly is within the context of what might be termed ordinary civilized behavior. Occult magick, however, is neither concerned with civilized behavior nor the restrictions it places upon the evolution of Man. Genetic evolution, like occult magick, is relentless with regard to achieving its objective. If you begin to view the bigger picture, within the context of the ouroboros, it is as if the Creator itself is using a relentless process to find reconciliation. It it the primordial energy at work, just as has been previously explained with regard to mystery schools.

When LRH refers to the blood of their bodies and souls, it serves as a direct analogy to the menses as well as the soul of each individual woman who carries the primordial programs of evolution within her own DNA. While none of this is meant to excuse or justify what appears to be the reckless attitude and personality of L. Ron Hubbard, it serves to explain his mind-set. It also suggests that he was possessed, at least in a sense, by either a genetic program deeply embedded within his own DNA or by a strong hypnotic-like influence or fascination with such a principle. In my opinion, it was a primordial imperative within his own genetic construct that he was able to cultivate and amplify by reason of the associations he sought out in his own life. This is where the principle of magical sympathy kicks in.

Hubbard was empathic. To empathize is generally thought to be a condition or quality whereby one is sensitive to the feelings of others. Originally, it meant to project yourself into a work of art and literally sense it to the point where you become it, to the best of your perceptions. The word has also come to refer to the characteristic of projecting yourself into a person so as to feel their emotions, etc. With regard to Hubbard, he would have, to some degree, cultivated at least some of this inclination by reason of working with others in the capacity of psychotherapy. As a matter of fact, administering Dianetics and Scientology processes on individuals day in and day out puts you in circumstances where you develop an empathy for people in general. He would be no exception. If you observed him or chronicled his behavior in any way, you would learn that he was particularly empathic. For example, he was known to hang around with people or read books and walk away as if he was the person or the book. While he might or might not assert such, he could take on the characteristics of either and also blur the line of where his own knowledge was acquired from a specific source. This was not so much a characteristic of trying to obscure where he got his information but rather the fact that he would become so absorbed in whatever he read or whoever he talked to that distinguishing himself from the information was less important (to him) than the information itself. We see this particularly in the case of his relationship with the work and persona of Aleister Crowley.

There is no question that Hubbard immersed himself in Crowley's work. If we believe even a thread of that which has been put forth by Nibs, we know that it was endemic to his personality. He was indeed the magic of Crowley and identified himself as such, not just as a student. It should therefore not be a surprise that he would identify himself as his very good friend.

If you study the routine history of Aleister Crowley and L. Ron Hubbard, you can quite readily determine that the two never met. This becomes even more clear to the casual observer if you read this passage from Crowley's letter to Karl Germer:

> "Apparently Parsons or Hubbard or somebody is producing a moonchild. I get fairly frantic when I contemplate the idiocy of these louts."

Virtually everyone in magical and academic circles interprets this as a no-brainer that Crowley was suspect of Hubbard and that the two had nothing in common save for perhaps an interest in Jack Parsons' money. There is, however, information that has come to light suggesting this might not be the case. This will be addressed later in the book.

What is significant to emphasize at this juncture is that Hubbard's empathic nature propelled him to absorb Crowley's magick like a sponge and literally become it. It was part and parcel of his personality where it either remained dormant or was activated in accordance with the relevancy of the various moments and circumstances of life.

In this chapter, I have sought to induce an amplified understanding of the very nature and potential of Hubbard's association with Aleister Crowley, the Great Beast. The true nature of what this association represents, at least in terms of its historical geo-political implications, cannot be truly appreciated, however, unless we begin to understand the aforesaid cults of the 8th to 12th centuries. We will examine this subject in the next chapter.

— CHAPTER TEN —

BAPHOMET

"After one look at this planet any visitor from outer space would say 'I want to see the manager.'"
— William S. Burroughs

Although the quotation from that last chapter linking Hubbard to Crowley is broadly recognized, virtually no emphasis has been placed upon LRH's blatant reference to the magical cults of the Middle East. I will focus on that aspect in this chapter as well as how it influenced both Hubbard and Crowley. First, however, I will give some perspective on the context in which Hubbard was referring to all of this in that specific lecture.

In *The Philadelphia Doctorate Course, Lecture #18,* entitled *"Conditions of Space-Time-Energy"*, LRH was talking about the initial conditions of a human spirit and how one was originally outside of this universe and had descended into it, not unlike a crashed landing, but subsequently found themselves in a reverse position, thinking they were either a part of physical matter itself or trapped inside of it, looking up instead of down. Further, Hubbard viewed all of these circumstances to be inherently subordinate to a spirit's own personal intention which can be successfully executed at will if one is so free or unconditioned so as to be unencumbered by either physical incarnation or other potential entrapments that the physical realm can allure one with. It was in this context that he was talking about the cults of the Middle Ages that were based upon ritual magick with specific causes creating corresponding effects. Like Crowley, and perhaps even more so, Hubbard always believed that the postulate was senior to any mechanical conditions. Nevertheless, both men had immersed themselves in the energetic signatures of ritual magick to the degree that their respective legacies cannot be separated from it save for perhaps a collective "absolution" of the human condition designed to result in a corresponding reconciliation with Divinity itself. Whatever you might think of either of these individuals, both were professionally and privately concerned with the theme of universal salvation. How they went about trying to facilitate it is another prospect entirely.

At this juncture, I am going to introduce you to a perspective on the Middle Eastern cults previously alluded to; and more particularly, how it played/plays into the occult current associated with both L. Ron Hubbard and Aleister Crowley. The best I can do in this work is to give a brief overview of this history, but that is all that is really necessary. As it is written, history is only an approximation of what happened that is based upon isolated events that have written by similarly isolated or uniquely designated (by themselves or otherwise) scribes whose predispositions or possible agendas remain unknown. Regardless of such myopia, however, history always tells us about or alludes to underlying currents or streams of consciousness that were cascading through civilization at that time. Sometimes such history also points to or even gives reasonably involved accounts of such occult influences or currents.

The magical cults of the 8th to 12th Centuries that Hubbard alluded to were the Islamic sects that surfaced with the legacy of the Prophet of Islam in the 8th Century and had receded with the dissolution of Hassan Sabbah's Assassin stronghold at Mount Alamut in 1256.

As the West has been culturally dominated by Christianity for hundreds upon hundreds of years, it is challenging for both Europeans and especially Americans to acquire either an unbiased or accurately informed assessment of Islam. This has been further aggravated by British Imperialism which deliberately created the word *Sufi*, often considered to be the more mystical faction of the Islamic faith, in order to divide and conquer Muslims.

Islam is a faith where all practitioners, regardless of their particular sect, practice both an inner or esoteric discipline as well as an outer worship. While these practices might vary, they are all taken very seriously; and it is neither fair nor accurate to consider that those who are designated as Sufis by the outside world are above, better or more in tune with the mystical aspects of religion than are any of the other sects. To understand the true mystical aspect of Islam; and with particular regard to its influence upon Western Magick, you have to consider the entire paradigm of the religion.

Whatever the case with the different sects might be, all of Islam in popular tradition is the result of revelations received by the Prophet Muhammad in the Cave of Hira in 610 A.D. These were originally written down and became the *Koran* according to Muslim tradition. There are at least two ways to evaluate what happened. First, one can assume that things pretty much happened, more or less, the way history and Islam have recorded them. In other words, we are taking the historical writings at face value. Second is that the historical and religious writings of the early Islamic years, including the most scrutinized esoteric doctrines of the time period, were concoctions of mysterious people operating behind the scenes. In other words, there was a secret cabal that was aligned with the old mystery school doctrines and was reinventing them anew so as to conform to the times. I choose to address this history with an approach that will neither deny nor wholeheartedly embrace either perspective. The purpose is to be as objective as possible.

Whether you believe it or not, Islam is based upon the proposition that there was a character called Muhammad whose experiences were so profound and inspirational that it ignited a dramatic change in the culture of the Arabian peninsula and resulted in a unification of tribes that the region had not known for at least thousands of years. Further, that this ruthless warrior culture, as it grew in strength, eventually created a Golden Age of Islam where learning and education were cultivated in a manner that was never witnessed under the stewardship of either Judaism or Christianity. While Islam always had its fundamentalist factions, its tolerance was far over-the-top compared to its ancestor religions. Whatever you want to say about Islam, however, positive or negative, it was always directed by a territorial imperative that concerned power and, if necessary, the quelling of or even the eradication of its adversaries. Christianity and Judaism also contain this characteristic which is nothing more than the primordial imperative to survive.

Previously, I delineated the primordial aspects of DNA in an effort to explain that life in general, no matter what form it takes, is indeed an expression of the collective Tree of Life itself, or at least an arm or leg thereof. Once again, the primordial aspects of consciousness are likened to the ouroboros and the head of the snake finding itself. Thus, it does not matter so much if the reported experiences of the Prophet are true with reference to whatever system of belief or objective analysis you might want to apply to the situation. What is obvious is that Muhammad, as has been described, either experienced an opening of a previously unfamiliar part of his mind that allowed a communication with the Archangel Gabriel to take place, or that something of a similar nature occurred or was concocted by reason of intense inspiration. In either case, a dynamic movement or imperative was generated that subjugated a large part of the world. As a matter of fact, Islam is said to have at least 1.6 billion adherents and is cited as the world's fastest growing religion and is projected to overtake Christianity in the coming years as the world's largest religion. I, however, am not attempting here to sell you on Islam nor take a position on it. What is important in this narrative is that the entire movement is all based upon a territorial imperative (survival) that is further based upon revelations received that are tied to the primordial aspects of consciousness.

While all of the cults of this time period inspired the European alchemy that was to follow in its wake, it will be most relevant to focus on the Assassin cult of Hassan Sabbah whose lineage traces back to the Ismailis of Egypt.

A thousand years ago in Cairo, the Ismailis ran one of the most successful and abundant mystery schools in the modern era. They were renown for their teaching and educational accomplishments. Under the political intrigue of the day, they were deposed and a different faction of Islam ruled in Egypt. The Ismailis went underground after that and have retained a base in Cairo which still exists to this day. Although their roots have remained as an underground movement, they received their most public notoriety in the 11th Century when a Persian by the name of Hassan Sabbah reinvigorated the movement and established a remote outpost at Mount Alamut in Iran. Although he is often referred to as the Grand Master of the Assassins or the Old Man of the Mountain, he was only known in his own time as "the Master". He is an actual historical character who Marco Polo commented upon during his travels. Popular legends have him drugging young men and transporting them to a "garden of delights" in order to convince them that they were in heaven. By such stimulus-response conditioning, advocates believed that they would reach paradise if they followed the will of the master.

Hassan Sabbah was one of the most influential and pervasive people of his time and used assassination as the most expedient political tool of the day. Despite great odds, he subordinated the entire area of the planet in which he lived. According to a legend with much historical merit, he convinced an approaching Christian army to leave him alone by merely giving a hand signal to one of his devotees who was perched over a high drop. Upon receiving the signal, the man willingly jumped to his death upon the craggy rocks below. Whatever the reason or the motivation, Hassan Sabbah had mastered men's minds through the principles of devotion and sudden death.

In retrospect and with regard to Margaret Singer's comments that Hubbard took the level of mind control to a new level, we have to consider that Hassan Sabbah was a reasonable if not highly superior comparative.* While Hubbard did not use assassins, the frenetic and zealous loyalty he cultivated in others demonstrated a mastery of people's hearts and minds that did indeed rival that of Hassan Sabbah. Hubbard, however, did not use pleasure gardens or sex maidens. He did not need to. His understanding of the human mind and the motivations of people was enough for him to create his own empire. With regard to the occult current, however, he was tapping into and motivating people's primordial energy which included their primordial hopes and dreams to either be god-like or to reach their ultimate potential.

To put all of this into context, we have to bring into perspective the relationship between Aleister Crowley, Hassan Sabbah and Muhammad, all of which centers around the enigmatic deity recognized as Baphomet, the very name which Crowley identified himself as by reason of his title as the Outer Head of the OTO or Ordo Templi Orientis.

The name *Baphomet*, which has often been thought to be a corruption or transliteration of *Muhammad* or *Mohamet*, first achieved popular historical recognition during the trials and torture of the Knights Templar who confessed to dialoguing with or kissing a severed head with that name. While the stories and legends of the relationship between Baphomet and the Knights Templar go far deeper, it is most significant to know that the Templars themselves were

---

* Hubbard gave a lecture on September 17, 1951 entitled *Black Dianetics* that exposed the use of PDH or Pain-Drug-Hypnosis and discussed the techniques of Hassan Sabbah and the Assassin cult. He stated that the knowledge of Dianetics could be used to take over entire governments and that up to about 1948 only "Black Dianetics" was in use (by governments or similarly related control groups). Prior to that time period, such knowledge of the mind was seldom if ever used positively used for therapy. For all of his complexity, Hubbard deserves credit for being the first one to broadly disseminate the Government's use of PDH.

initiated by Hassan Sabbah and the Assassin cult. This is regular history, and the initiation took place within or below what were considered to be the ruins of Solomon's Temple in Jerusalem. This area is not only highly significant, it is a highly charged cross-roads of all types of events which blend history with legend. Most importantly, it gives us a fulcrum to understand the occult currents at work in this scenario.

This area is identified today as the Dome of the Rock, in reference to being the rock where Muhammad flew to heaven on Al-Burak, a pale horse of a baroque nature. The word *baroque* is derived from Al-Burak, a name which also is identified as being connected to the word *rock*. The rock itself beneath the dome is believed to be where Adam was born as well as the exact rock upon which Abraham began to sacrifice his son. It was also the rock slept upon by Jacob (who wrestled with an angel — from which the name *Israel* was said to be derived) when Jacob's Ladder manifested before him. Recognized as a locale where heaven meets earth, it was where Solomon built his temple.

You will seldom find a physical location that is so emotionally charged and ripe with intrigue by reason of so many diverse and intersecting stories surrounding it, all of which are hard-wired into the politics of the present time. The oldest name of the location is Mount Moriah, a name which is related to *mor, morte* and *muert*, all referring to death. This is most appropriate because it is indicative of what might be considered the most expository if not fascinating aspect of the entire complex; and that is the fact that beneath this very rock is a chamber that is known as the Well of the Souls. Although the well area is partially filled in with dirt, it is known to hide a much deeper conduit or cavity. It is also known that the area beneath the Dome of the Rock is loaded with tunnels and caverns which include waterways. It is, however, the Well of Souls that is representative of the occult history of power that is associated with this geographical complex.

Ancient peoples viewed the world very differently, and much of it had to do with their dead ancestors. The idea of a well of souls is not unique to Jerusalem but its legends, myths and stories have been rather regulated to fit within the parameters of the Abrahamic paradigm. So, in order that you might better appreciate how the ancients viewed such matters in general, I will present a comparative and that has to do with a similar well of souls in Rome, perhaps dating back to the Etruscan Empire.

Prior to the Roman Empire as well as during its heyday, a well of souls could be found beneath the "lapis manalis" in the Forum. *Lapis* means stone and *manalis* was named after the goddess Mana and her male consort Mantua. Together, they presided over the ancestral well of souls which included the entire panorama of dead spirits. Ghosts came under the domain of Mana. Once a year, people would pay homage to the Goddess Mana or Mania (also sometimes identified as Amana) as she was known and from which the adjective *manic* was derived (from the wanton behavior that is associated with so many Roman holidays). This annual celebration surrounding the Roman well of souls was known as Pandemonium. In this context, the word *mana* means "mother of all". *

Today, *mania* refers to a state of relative madness or excitement. Originally, these features were more socially acceptable in society and conduits were made for manic expression. Manic behavior was also revered as being divinely inspired. If you choose, you can even view a manic episode as the frenzy of an old dead ancestor trying to express itself through the DNA. There is no question that such an environment as Pandemonium is going to give all latent characteristics embedded within DNA an opportunity to express themselves and perhaps even reproduce. Patriarchal religions such as the Abrahamic ones impose much more regulation with regard to breeding.

It is fascinating if not ironic that unregulated breeding and the regulation of such share an interesting juxtaposition at the Dome of the Rock. All of it has to do with postulates and sympathetic magic that is inextricably tied to the three Abrahamic religions, all of which are wrapped up to this very day in the drama surrounding the associated legacy and legends of King Solomon or Sulaiyman whose temple is believed to have been built and destroyed over this rock.

Per the *Old Testament,* Solomon had thousands of women at his disposal, both wives and concubines, indicating he had virtually no restrictions with regard to whom he might copulate with or what progeny he might conceive. This is particularly important, at least with reference to the biblical scribes, because they stated that the Messiah (Jesus) would come from the stem of Jesse (Solomon's grandfather). Solomon's potential for or predisposition to extreme promiscuity, particularly from the reference point of the King of Israel, can be viewed as the impetus for an extreme breeding program that was indiscriminate in its attempt to deliver the deliverer. This was a man who, per the *Old Testament,* had the wisdom by which to literally control the realm of both demons and angels. The magical texts and legends which arose out of this legacy, including those of Freemasonry, are not only all concerned with this locale but the power that it represents. Controlling angels and demons is something that not even Lucifer could accomplish. So it is and was that the hope for such power might be accomplished through Solomon's offspring.

---

* The word *mana* or *manna* was also defined as the food of and from the gods as is the word *pan* when we consider that it means "bread" in Spanish (*panem* is the word for bread in Latin) and is sanctified as the body of God/Jesus in the Holy Eucharist. The most exalted aspirations concerning the use of manna can also be found in the Egyptian religion where it is associated with black powder that be transmuted into monatomic white gold. This subject is discussed in full in the book *The Black Sun: Montauk's Nazi-Tibetan Connection* (by Peter Moon) and further ramifications are covered in *The Montauk Book of the Living* (by Peter Moon).

Now, I want you to imagine for a minute that whether by design or accident that you were fated to acquire just a portion of such power. It does not require much imagination at all to think that if you were to consider such, you might, if only for an instant, indulge yourself in some manic feeling. Such power taps into all sort of wishes, primordial ones especially, that would dictate different behavior patterns for your own life. This sort of phenomena was indeed precisely what L. Ron Hubbard cavorted with whether if only as a fiction writer or as the leader of a dynamic movement. While he might not have been able to control all demons or angels, he could certainly have his moments of power where he was either exerting power over such or thought he was. He certainly could influence the lives of countless people.

Although Aleister Crowley never had anywhere near the popular following of Hubbard, he was much more involved with energies and aspects of the more subtle or hidden realms. You can make of that what you want, but it most definitely relates to his own involvement with that other so-called "Steward of the Rock" which is known as Baphomet.

Legends portray Baphomet as a severed head that served as an oracle that was representative of King Solomon's power. The function of this oracle and how to manifest it was the secret imparted by Hassan Sabbah to the Knights Templar beneath the very Dome of the Rock. In such a paradigm, we are no longer dealing with something that is necessarily tangible in the way you would think of a computer. Like so many mysteries, it is deliberately embedded in stealth. The only tangible connection you can make to it is the power itself. This can be obtained simply by perceiving it or just recognizing whatever you might feel about it in your own mind. If only by psychology, this mystery has captured if not subdued the minds of Western man. The secret societies that deeply influence the world pay homage to this mystery. To what degree they believe in or dialogue with Baphomet or a similarly structured entity is another question entirely, but the social and political preoccupation with it cannot be denied.

The behavior of man is dictated by the psychology of man, and the psychology of man is determined by its relationship and experience with archetypes which are merely an intellectualization of expressions that are within the DNA of individuals. And so it is, by whatever reasons, these various nexus points within the genetic construct of man have found a grander nexus point which is nothing more than a projection and sympathetic resonance generated by the former. An attempt to codify this aggrandized nexus point (Baphomet), deemed to be outside of the human structure but controlling it, was accomplished by Alphonse Constant in 1856 who expressed his own cultivated understanding of Baphomet in illustrated form (see next page).

Constant is a pivotal character in this stream of consciousness but not for reasons that are generally well known to either the public nor even occultists.

BAPHOMET AS DEPICTED BY ELIPHAS LEVI IN 1856

Under the name Eliphas Levi, he mistranslated the Enochian rituals that were later to become the foundation of the magic of the Hermetic Order of the Golden Dawn, the secret society that is regarded as the most influential with respect to Western occultism. It is believed he did this purposely. This, however, is not the only reason he is cited as a pivotal character. As he died several months before the birth of Aleister Crowley on October 12, 1875, Crowley identified Levi as being none other than his previous incarnation. In this respect, Crowley was very much like Hubbard in that he could empathize or project himself into another persona or set of circumstances and absorb it like a sponge. By the time Crowley had learned about Levi, he had already found an identification with the Beast (666) by reason of his mother discovering him having sex with the maid and referring to him as such. This is another example of sympathetic magic. While it is easy to dismiss Crowley's projected identifications with such personas as either wishful thinking or the product of a deranged mind, you will garnish much more understanding by viewing it from the perspective that there was an actual occult current running through the man's spirit-body-mind complex or DNA that was either predisposed to such identifications or mandating them. Whether he liked it or not, the occult current of Baphomet, tracing back to the history of the Knights Templar, was in his blood.

Previously, I had given you more than a clue that the purpose of the Ninth Degree of the Ordo Templi Orientis or OTO is to create a moon child, a being that would reconcile the Divine with its creation. As my own narrative will enfold, you will see how clearly this program is hard-wired into the mind-set of Western civilization. The primordial purpose of any of these deities that have arisen through history, at least on some level, is for the so-called snake head of the ouroboros to find reconciliation with itself. The paradigm we are presented with, however, is the head of Medusa with several snakes and none of the various programs seeming to work so well. Nevertheless, this primal impulse continues at a rampant rate, not unlike the millions of sperm cells that seek to find an egg so as to unite with and fertilize. It is therefore much wiser to view Aleister Crowley as someone whose psychological predisposition, by reason of his own genetic construct, was to create a moon child at all costs. In other words, his rather crazy and unrelenting passion to have sex with most anyone was driven by such a territorial imperative, the original purpose of which was an effort to accomplish the above. This paradigm also gives more perspective on Freud's preoccupation with sex. Diagnosing people by reason of their various sexual frustrations and repressions is indeed understandable, but this perspective affords us a much broader view. Everyone, biologically speaking, is hard-wired so as to want to get in on the act.

Although he was a member of Golden Dawn, Crowley never made the mistake of using the Enochian rituals prescribed by Eliphas Levi, giving reason to believe that he might have been in on the joke as well as adding fuel to the fire that he might have been Levi. In any case, Crowley demonstrated himself to be in a rather deep sympathetic rapport Levi as well as the latter's most well known icon: the illustration of Baphomet. After understandably coming into conflict with the Golden Dawn, Crowley went off on his own, eventually transmitting his seminal work, *The Book of the Law*.* I will go into *The Book of the Law* in greater detail at another point, but it is important at this juncture to highlight its mandate, "Do What Thou Wilt Shalt Be the Whole of the Law". Besides this maxim, the book itself was concerned with rampant lust and a virtually unbridled sexual appetite. It was, however, dictated by what Crowley referred to as a praetor human intelligence. (In other words, a primordial intelligence as has previously been expounded upon). It was only after this work; in fact, a few years after it was written, that Crowley was introduced to and initiated into the OTO by Theodore Reuss, a German who

---

* *The Book of the Law* is one of the three books referred to by Nibs Hubbard in the previous chapter with regard to being kept secret. Once again, Nibs had quoted his father as saying, "The books and contents to be kept forever secret...to reveal them will cause you instant insanity: rip your mind apart; destroy you."

was involved in many secret societies that ranged from the Rosicrucians to Adam Weishaupt's Bavarian Illuminati. Of most significance in this stream of consciousness, however, was Reuss's purpose in creating the OTO (with Karl Kellner) which was "to work the various rites of high-grade Masonry". While there have been all sorts of sensational "exposés" to reveal the "true secrets" of the Freemasons in both books and by the media, they all miss the mark, at least in regards to what I am about to share here.

While most people consider the billion year contract that Sea Org members sign to be utterly ludicrous, society in general, and particularly the media, are too seldom outraged nor too vocal when it comes to the sacred oaths taken by members of Freemasonry which include accepting the punishment of death for revealing secrets and also the commitment to kill others for such. Although many members of Freemasonry do not realize it, their entire society is a landscape for a secret breeding program. When you reach a certain level in Freemasonry, you might be called upon by the "management" to perform a certain duty that might very well include copulation with a person of the opposite sex towards the purpose of having a child who will serve some purpose that is unknown to yourself. This would be completely outside the parameters of any extant marriage or relationship you might have in your regular life. It is also meant to be kept very secret. You are led to assume that all necessary arrangements will be taken care of for the child, and it is not necessarily your business to be involved further. It depends upon the agenda at hand. While you can speculate to your heart's content about what these children might be used for, perhaps serving as a blood sacrifice or even to be groomed as a future politician, this is not really the point, nor is it my intent to malign the dubious nature of Freemasonry in and of itself. My point is that Freemasonry is a highly complicated and organized structure that is run by a primordial imperative, the primary one of which is to create the *Luna Puer Maximus* (Moon Child Maximus). There are countless agendas within the complex structure of Freemasonry, some being incredibly mundane. Some members are not considered suitable candidates for creating progeny in alignment with the aforesaid agenda. Each performs according to their own ability to contribute. Further, it is my objective to provide you with an understanding that Freemasonry is not so much ruled by a global elite but rather a nexus of desires and agendas that manifests itself within its own reference frame that is either akin to or precisely what has been defined as Baphomet.

The entire picture is much more involved; and while there is considerably more that can be shared, you have now been introduced to the "management" of the planet as has been referred to by William Burroughs in the quotation at the beginning of this chapter. For now, we will examine an attempt to undermine the management and how L. Ron Hubbard fits in, ever so snugly.

EVERYTHING IS PERMISSIBLE

> *"Scientology can do more in ten hours than psychoanalysis can do in ten years."*
> — William S. Burroughs

William Burroughs is often referred to as the father of the Beat Generation, a name inspired by key literary personalities of the Fifties who in turn inspired the counter-culture of the Sixties. The most prominent names associated with this group, besides Burroughs, were Alan Ginsberg, Jack Kerouac, and Neal Cassady, the latter having bridged his influence with direct participation in the early hippie contingent fostered by Ken Kesey. Although not a charismatic character, Burroughs was considered a father figure to this group because he was older and more experienced. Perhaps oddly, and despite being a heroin addict, he outlived them all.

Burroughs and his brethren readily recognized the wounds of society and communicated what they saw, making them open wounds that everyone could see. The deeper they looked, they traced the wounds back to the very circumstances and conditions of creation. Allen Ginsberg's pivotally famous poem *Howl* was inspired during a stay in a psychiatric hospital where he witnessed the bottom rung of how bad things could be, not only for himself but for others. Dedicating *Howl* to his cell mate, who just happened to be the nephew of a publisher, turned out to be the bridge to a heralded literary career for Ginsburg which enabled Burroughs to be published as well. *Howl* is a deeply cutting poem which illustrates man as a living breathing beast juxtaposed against Moloch and the evil machinations of a reactive entity which seeks to mechanize, nullify, and ultimately destroy the best part of us (that which breathes and lives).

William Burroughs crossed a very strange line as a human being when he tried to emulate the famed archer William Tell, the latter being legendary for having shot an arrow as to split an apple while it rested on his son's head. Burroughs, who used a highball glass for an apple and a gun instead of a bow and arrow, shot and killed his wife while under the stupor of alcohol. The death having taken place in Mexico, Burroughs bribed various witnesses to testify on his behalf; but when his Mexican lawyer had to skip town for his own misgivings, Burroughs fled the country and was convicted of culpable homicide, eventually receiving a two-year suspended sentence in absentia.

Burroughs saw the killing of his wife as a pivotal catalyst with regard to his writing career, indicating that it would not have manifested without that tragic event that catapulted Burroughs into the arena of public consciousness to be let loose on the world. In a very strange way, the line that Burroughs crossed led him to the crossroads of Hassan Sabbah's lair, but not in the physical sense. Burroughs, who had pursued his desires for drugs and homosexuality in Morocco, subsequently found himself to be a frequent patron of a restaurant in Tangier called *One Thousand and One Nights*. The proprietor of the restaurant, a surrealistic artist named Brion Gysin, who happened to harbor a lifetime fascination with Hassan Sabbah's assassin cult, was to eventually collaborate with Burroughs in an exploration of the legacy and influence of Hassan Sabbah, all of which centered around the maxim, "Nothing is true. Everything is permitted." This collaboration, however, was facilitated by an equally pivotal character whose very strange life is not only a reflection of Baphomet itself but also links and catalyzes various occult currents ranging from Huna magic of the Hawaiian Islands to Dianetics and the CIA inspired LSD movement of the Fifties and Sixties. There were plenty of other interesting stops along the way as well. I am referring to John Starr Cooke, an early "star" in the Dianetics movement.

Almost as soon as *Dianetics: The Modern Science of Mental Health* was released, Cooke's wife, Millen, flew to New York without his knowledge and began to indulge herself in Dianetics. Cooke immediately drove back east and became a very competent and sought after practitioner of Dianetic techniques. While in New York, he met Mary Oser, the wife of Peter Oser, a great-grandson of John D. Rockefeller who found it difficult to function by reason of his great wealth. As the Osers lived in Switzerland, Cooke moved there with them. Peter became an ardent if not blind follower of Cooke. His wife soon left him, proceeding to marry Cooke.

Cooke was already extremely wealthy by reason of his own family, a missionary family that industrialized the Hawaiian Islands. It was there that Cooke was exposed to Huna, integrating it into his own persona to the point where you could say that there was an admixture of the two. Cooke travelled throughout the world seeking spiritual guidance, even using a Ouija board to direct his quests. No matter how you size Cooke up, he comes off as both a very improbable and roguish character while maintaining a somewhat likeable if not laughable quality.

To give you a realistic scope of how Cooke walked into the life of Burroughs and Gysin, you have to visualize Tangier* of the early 1950s for what it was: an international city that cultivated decadence, cut-throat profiteers, and espionage informants and double-agents who were there to garnish whatever advantage might be obtainable. Although Gysin's restaurant, *One Thousand*

---

* Tangier, which rests directly opposite the Rock of Gibraltar, is legendary for its reputation as a smuggling haven and safe house for international spying activities, ranging at least from the 19th Century through the Cold War. Officially designated as an international city in 1923, Tangier attracted foreign capital due to its political neutrality and commercial liberty. It was also a frequent port of call of L. Ron Hubbard's yacht *Apollo* in the early seventies.

and One Nights, was founded by reason of his passion to provide a venue for the Joujouka musicians,* it was also a magnet for any curious or vigilant eyeballs that frequented the fabled city.

So it was that Cooke, knowing damn well who Gysin was, came in with his wife and approached him directly. Coincidentally, Burroughs just happened to be standing by when Cooke was said to have uttered the following.

"Guess where we came from and guess who we are?"

Whatever you want to make of that question, it bespeaks the nature of a man who is wrapped up in mysticism, but also a man who likes to be ostentatious as if to mockingly taunt the object of his fancy, or perhaps, what he considers to be his prey. While Cooke credited the Ouija board as the instigator of his interest in Gysin, it is also true that Gysin was on the ropes financially at this particular time. Cooke invested heavily in the restaurant and was single-handedly responsible for keeping this den of rogues alive and functioning. This invites reasonable speculation that one or more agencies wanted to keep the place alive to keep a beat on their prey. Cooke's subsequent extensive involvement as a sponsor of the LSD counter-culture has led many to label him as a CIA asset. As Cooke's family was also heavily involved in Theosophy, however, I choose to view him as a member of a wealthy elite who used spiritualism and the CIA as assets, not the other way around. To keep on point, however, I want to remind you of the thesis from the end of the previous chapter which alluded to the prospect that the global elite is run by "a nexus of desires and agendas that manifests itself within its own reference frame that is either akin to or precisely what has been defined as Baphomet". Anyway you look at it, Cooke was an assortment of very strange odds and ends that was being directed by a primordial aspect. As we probe this aspect more deeply, it will indeed lead us back to the occult current of Baphomet.

During this time period, L. Ron Hubbard had been in London and is said to have visited Tangier and asked Cooke for financial help. The two knew each other from the earliest days of Dianetics and Hubbard knew Cooke was far from poor. I tend to believe this story might well be true as Hubbard once approached Jack Parsons for financial help, years after they had done their magical workings.** Cooke's refusal was understandable, but it might have cost him dearly as you will soon learn. He has, however, been given credit for suggesting to Hubbard that he form his organization as a religion. I have also heard that other sources

---

* Gysin referred to Joujouka music as "the Rites of Pan under the ragged cloak of Islam."

** During the 1950s, Hubbard was trying to recover from the financial collapse of Dianetics which had climaxed with the scandals surrounding the dissolution of his marriage to Sarah Northrup. The data about Hubbard approaching Parsons for financing was supplied to me by George Frey, Parson's close friend. The conversation between the two former partners occurred not too long before Parson's death and was well after the Babalon Working and the dissolution of Allied Enterprises (a joint partnership between Hubbard and Parsons) . According to George Frey, Parsons referred to Hubbard as a science fiction writer who ripped off people.

suggested the same to Hubbard who did eventually return to the United States and incorporate the Church of Scientology in 1954.

Of greater relevancy to our story is that Cooke, who was expert in the techniques of early Dianetics, gave Brion Gysin an earful about the procedures and particularly how they related to words and their influence upon the unconscious mind. Cooke, viewing Gysin as a great talent and "natural" for Dianetics, tried to persuade him into becoming an auditor and a dynamic leader in the movement but Gysin was not interested. He did, however, take Cooke's lessons to heart with regard to words and their influence. Burroughs, however, became very interested and would later dedicate himself full time to the study of Scientology. While one cannot dismiss the obvious prospect that Dianetics and Scientology influenced so much of the so-called Burroughs phenomena, we cannot also dismiss the reverse: that Burroughs, who put his fingerprints on every major beat or hip trend, could not have helped himself from also leaving an imprint on Scientology.

The Cut-up Method

Although the collaboration of Burroughs and Gysin is legendary and is the subject of adulation bordering on worship by those who are either fans of the Beat Generation or those who seek to emulate the trendiness of it all, there is much more to appreciate than what has been already rather broadly recognized. I am referring to the so called "cut-up method" that is based upon the principle of surrealism.

As a surrealistic artist, Gysin understood the Dada movement which was a precursor of the surrealist movement which juxtaposed different subjects which came from two entirely different contexts. This would be something like the Roman army of Julius Caesar marching into the Super Bowl. It rescrambles creation. The Dada movement was created by various artists who were making a statement about the circumstances of society in regard to the first world war. They would take various cultural icons and juxtapose them so as to reposition them. It was a powerful artistic statement and only rose out of frustration with the existing system which had proven itself to be of no service to the common people. Amidst this existential crisis was the story of Tristan Tzara, a Dada poet who had caused a riot by pulling words out of a hat and composing a poem from them. So, whatever Gysin learned from Cooke with regard to the power of words, he had already studied the prerequisites, but none of this really came home to roost until years later, in 1959, after Gysin was forced to leave Tangier (when it became a part of Morocco) and followed Burroughs to the "Beat Hotel" in Paris. It was here where Gysin saw a photo collage that Burroughs was putting together and saw how a collage of words could be applied to clippings from newspapers.

The essence of the cut-up method, as alluded to above, is to overthrow the control that words have upon the human condition by descrambling them, recompiling them in a random order, and then reading the message. It was Burroughs, however, who did most of the running with this concept and used it to compose novels. It also led him back to Scientology; and his cut-ups also included that subject. After his initial cut-up success, which resulted in him communicating with either real or virtual entities which manifested through the cut-ups, Burroughs went whole hog into Scientology, attesting to Clear and even doing at least the first three levels of Operating Thetan.* Although he tried to get his fellow Beat Generation buddies involved in Scientology, he was not successful. It is reported that he even pressed Gysin at one point, not so much to get him into Scientology, but rather to help him unlock the secrets of the OT levels. This was a dead end for Burroughs; and this could not help but be the case as Gysin was never interested in Scientology and there was no common frame of reference. Burroughs was trying to unlock something even deeper than just releasing the control system that society, Moloch or Baphomet run on the living breathing human being. Inspired by Hubbard's assertions, Burroughs was attempting to discover the secret that enables a released spiritual being to manifest powers. Gysin's stated goal, "to rub out the word", was heady enough, but what did he really mean; and, once you have the word rubbed out, what do you have left?

This is a very deep existential question, and it is an issue which must not be underestimated, at least if you are going to maintain a healthy regard for the existing state of affairs in the universe.

Rubbing out the word, as Gysin put it, refers to taking out the human mind's interpretation with regard to the "original" communication of a given amount of written words. Keep in mind, one is taking a newspaper, a book, or even a paragraph and rescrambling the words and/or letters. This precipitates the proposition that one might (by picking the words or letters out of a hat) experience the feedback of every possible permutation of the words or letters. This process gives one the opportunity to see the original communication by a virtual infinitude of different vantage points. Above and beyond that, it rescrambles creation. All of this either is or has the potential for the elements of the narrative "speaking" to the reader.

Imagine doing this with the *Bible*. It brings to mind a particular quote from the *New Testament*:

> [*2 Corinthians 3:6*] "Who also hath made us able ministers of the new testament; not of the letter, but of the spirit: for the letter killeth, but the spirit giveth life."

---

* The term "Operating Thetan" is a Scientology term for an operating spirit or "thetan" who is adept at overcoming the limitations imposed on life by matter, energy, space, and time.

Rescrambling the *Bible*, in the spirit of Gysin and Burroughs, would be akin to reading scripture on acid (LSD). This particular quote teaches us that the spirit takes precedent over words because the spirit is the core of what is being communicated in the most unadulterated sense of the word. Whatever you think of the *Bible*, it is obvious that it is used as a control system to herd the consciousness and behavior of people. Rescrambling the words and letters offers the potential for you to be interacting with all the characters in that rather lengthy tome. For the individual reader, cutting up the *Bible* can or would make it come alive in a way that it never has before.

While the same process can be applied to any literary work, it can also be applied to Scientology and/or all the writings of and about L. Ron Hubbard. After all, that is the subject of this book. This concept is a very important step in attempting to understand the man and his legacy, a prospect that is very daunting to many, especially due to the fact that no matter how much he is vilified, people cannot get enough when it comes to hearing about him. L. Ron Hubbard remains a compelling and fascinating character to so many, whether they despise him or not.

To many, one of the most puzzling if not repelling of Hubbard's characteristics was that he would continuously and frequently either talk or write in such a fashion that it seemed like he was talking off the top of his head in a manner that could be viewed as unfiltered. This applied especially to what he referred to as the Whole Track, a term representing the entire track of time. To Scientologists, and especially to Hubbard, each individual is viewed to be living an eternity of lives and has been programmed to forget them by reason of implantation. Here, we are talking about a universal control system which has been around since the beginning of time which successfully seeks to keep people ignorant in order that the control system might maintain itself. This control system is no different than that described by either Kesey, Ginsberg or Burroughs, save for the fact that Hubbard exuded a much stronger current, providing a lot more details and exploiting his knowledge of the concept.

In the biggest scheme of consciousness, such a control system is an observable fact of life. Whether it is more like the aforesaid have described or whether it is more like the concept of the Beast 666 as it corresponds with the *Bible* is not as important as the fact that such a control system does exist. It is routinely mimicked by the press and other conventional aspects of society.

When Hubbard would, as he often did, make assertions and give stories about space opera or civilizations that existed on the whole track, he was in a highly creative mode. Although much of what he said would sound absolutely ludicrous to someone who was unfamiliar with his train of thought, it was usually offered to his audience in some sort of context. None of this, however, means that what he said was particularly true or untrue, but it was true to him, or at least he imagined it to be true and decreed it so.

As a writer, an individual, and as the founder of Scientology, he possessed and exhibited a very rich and colorful imagination. This is the underpinning of a creative mind and the creative process. What is important and relevant in this narrative is that all of Hubbard's seemingly off-the-cuff and off-the-wall meanderings or assertions can be viewed in the context of a cut-up. In other words, he was communicating with Creation itself. He saw bits and pieces of life in his imagination, and instead of dismissing them such as most people would do, he would pin them down and integrate what he observed into his stream of consciousness, often writing it down. In other words, he was playing with aspects of his mind that most would consider too abstract to even consider, and he tangentialized them, even if it was only to put them into a story or anecdote. While the relative value of these abstractions is questionable to so many, the fact that he was able to harness them to the point where he could generate interest, enthusiasm and money made him powerful. Burroughs, who is viewed as an iconic inspiration to fans of the Beat Generation, was not particularly powerful. While Burroughs was trying to overcome the control system, he was not trying to supplant it with a new system. Hubbard excited people because he was inspiring them and even enabling them to shed the control system, but he was replacing it with another control system.

There is, however, more at stake than just the control system. Burroughs was trying to send this control system topsy-turvy and to get at the core beneath it. When you have the core, you are no longer in the realm of ordinary matter, energy, space and time and certainly not words. Keep in mind that human beings are wedded to matter, energy, space and time via the perceptions of their mind. The cut-up process breaks this up and rescrambles it, replacing it with new perceptions or new ways of perceiving things.

When we are dealing with insanity in a human being, we are dealing with someone who cannot or chooses not to filter what is coming into his or her mind. It results in chaos. While engaging in the cut-up process certainly does introduce chaos into a structured interpretation, the goal is not to introduce chaos so as to either establish or perpetuate insanity but to get at the core. When we mention core, we are talking about the underpinnings behind the original communication. While the concept of the core is somewhat enigmatic and abstract in itself, examining the simple etymology of the word *core* gives an amazing symbolic insight into the entire subject under discussion.

> **core (n.)** early 14c., "heart or inmost part of anything" (especially an apple, pear, etc.), of uncertain origin, probably from Old French *cor, coeur* "core of fruit, heart of lettuce," literally "heart," from Latin *cor* "heart," from PIE root **kerd-* "heart."

When we consider the core of L. Ron Hubbard's brain child, Scientology, it is important to remind the reader that, from the very beginning, we have been penetrating and examining the occult current or matrix underlying it. All of the various themes and treatises in this book have thus far led us to this very crossroads, and we are not just talking about the core of Scientology but the core of ALL (the ancients described *ALL* as *Pan*). Scientology, however, fits into this matrix in a rather interesting if not notable way.

Dianetics and Scientology have excited the imaginations of millions of people. There are, of course, different degrees of excitement and experience, ranging from the shallow to the deep. While it is possible to compare experiences, there is no absolute consistency amongst them. Each and every person who experienced Scientology had their own very specific experience. While there are indeed commonalities, each individual who participated was faced with the proposition of confronting and dealing with what was inside of their own mind. More relevant to this discussion is that everyone has a different mind and a different filtering process. Therefore, if you want to do a complete cut-up of Scientology, you are required to not only include all of the materials on the subject, including the critical diatribes, but you have to take each and every experience of everyone who has every encountered the word. This is a daunting task that would best be accomplished by artificial intelligence. It would also require a filter of some sort because raw data would only be raw data. What this process would do, however, is give completely new perceptions on the subject.

When we take our focus off of the Scientology lens and look to the bigger picture, consider the story of the Tower of Babel. That was a time when all people, theoretically, spoke the same language. The word *babel* literally refers to a gateway to God and this is the etymology of *Babalon* or *Babylon*. When the builders of Babel erected their tower in order to access the wordless core and reach into the very realm of God, their communication frequencies were jammed, and all they heard from each other was "babble", a word which derived from this experience. In this context, it is very relevant to point out that the word *baffle* is not much different phonetically than *babble*, and we also have the concept of *Baphomet* to accompany it. Baphomet represents the filter of Mankind, and the word *baffle* derives from this enigmatic concept.

When we consider the Middle East magical cults of the Middle Ages, it is important to reiterate and reemphasize the role of Baphomet with regard to the initiation of the Knights Templar beneath the Dome of the Rock. These initiations, to repeat, were administered by Hassan Sabbah and his Assassin cult. The rock is where Muhammad's baroque horse, Al-Burak, departs for heaven. Al-Burak is a surreal creature that is a genuine cut-up, representing infinity. This is Muhammad's vehicle to the Infinite. Per tradition, his filtering process resulted in the *Koran*.

Sanity and insanity have everything to do with the aforementioned filtering process, all of which is akin to processing data and correlating it so as to act in concert with the environment. Any human being that represents too much chaos to the environment will be locked up by the legal system or perhaps even put in an institution for the insane. Whether the control system itself is insane or exhibits a degree of such is another issue entirely, but it is an issue that fits hand-in-hand with the legacy of Hassan Sabbah, the inspiration of Brion Gysin, whose last words he ever uttered were reported as "Nothing is true. Everything is permitted". These final words of wisdom from a man who had reached the top of the food chain in terms of political power are not only a tribute and acknowledgment to what can be termed the quantum prospect of unlimited possibilities, it is also an endorsement to indulge the concept.

Perhaps it is no coincidence that at the time Burroughs and Hubbard grew up, both Quantum Mechanics and the Surrealist Movement were emerging on the world stage. Although these are apparently very different studies, there is a commonality between the two. Both allude to the prospect of infinite possibilities. If you identify God with the Infinite, it is clear that both subjects, at the very least, represent baby steps toward the Divine.

I think it will help you better understand this point if I relay a conversation I once had with a scientist who was not only highly credentialed but also very competent. When the word *quantum* came up, he mentioned that he did not like that word, and he was referring to the fact that it is too often used sloppily, often as a catch-all term, suggesting that anything is possible. He is quite right that the word is used in such a manner, often by people who are just running unfiltered thoughts through their head without any discipline or clear thinking. There is, however, another reason not to like the word and that is due to the fact that Quantum Mechanics does open the door to the prospect that all potential realities are a part of existence. The *Many Worlds Interpretation*, also known as the *Everett-Wheeler Hypothesis*, deals with this very prospect. When when opens the door to such thinking, it is like stepping into the *Twilight Zone* and opens the door to chaos. This is baffling because it butts up against the limits of ordinary human experience.

While it might seem easy to dismiss all this as ancient history, it is important to recognize that our current political paradigm and the morality that is adopted by society is all based upon history. In fact, history can be viewed as a live current of energy, even when it is falsified. People will take scripture or any other literature attributed to be historical, quote it and feed off of it in order to establish laws, traditions and a sundry of other elements in order to create a moral climate. This also applies to occult factors which are designed by their very nature to remain invisible to the common folk.

Based upon history as well as other tangential occult factors, the power of Hassan Sabbah and his Islamic sect was centered around a mysterious reverence to Baphomet, the conscious mystery of which has been so pervasive in our culture that it, as said previously, inspired the English language word *baffle*. The influence upon our culture has been profound. There is, however, an even deeper legacy concerning the underpinnings of what this is all based upon, and this concerns the fact that the sect of Hassan Sabbah operated within the ruins of Solomon's Temple and the extensive if not magnificent control system that the character of Solomon represents.

The legends of Solomon render him as a powerful king with great wisdom but also one who had a very dark legacy laced in black magic. The stories of Solomon being able to control the jinn as well as the angels of heaven and the demons of hell have been highly revered in our culture and particularly by those seeking influence upon the minds of men and their associated power structures. The institutions of Freemasonry are all based upon this legacy. We have to keep in mind, however, that the entire process is a control system.

I wrote an entire and very lengthy book, *Synchronicity and the Seventh Seal*, which was an involved explanation, much of it in allegorical form, exposing the secret word of Freemasonry which is, in essence, the concept upon which all civilization and even the universe is based. A word, however, as we have just learned, can only be a stop-gap for what it is that one is trying to explain. This word will be explained, at least to some extent, later on in this book. To put it in a nutshell, however, and to give as much relevancy as possible at this juncture, this word is *shin*[*] in Hebrew which is actually a letter that means "tooth" in the common vernacular but has a hidden or esoteric meaning which is CHANGE and/or SPIRIT. In other words, the concept behind the word is that change is facilitated by spirit. It is this power to change via spirit is what King Solomon was said to possess.

Per tradition, Solomon's use of this principle or word was intrinsically tied to a magic ring he possessed by which he could control angels, demons or more specifically, the jinn. In this reference frame, a demon (a word which means "of mon" or "of God") is a double-headed proposition. In other words, a demon is an angel on one side and the inverse on the side, the latter being identified as a demon in the common vernacular. This double-sided "head" was previous how civilizations visually interpreted the concept of Baphomet where it was commonly depicted with a male head on one side and a female head on the reverse. The Eliphas Levi illustration is more commonly used in this day and age. In either case, it is the principle of duality that is the most relevant aspect.

---

[*] As will be explained later in this text, the Hebrew letter *shin* is the middle letter of the name *Yod-He-Shin-Vau-He* which was transliterated into *Yeshua* and then *Jesus*. The more deeply you dig into the mysteries of this legacy, you will discover that the character people identify as Jesus Christ is a mirror image reflection of a natural expression embedded within the structural functionality of DNA. How accurate that reflection is, however, is another issue entirely, based upon the filter being employed.

It was through this ring that Solomon was able to control the Jinn in order to amass great resources in order create his temple. While some will dismiss the whole proposition of the temple, whether it be viewed either as history or legend, it is an incredibly serviceable metaphor, especially if you want to understand various aspects of the occult.

The heart of Solomon's Temple, and the most ostensible reason it was created, was to house the most sacred witness to the Godhead: the Holy of Holies. Inside the Holy of Holies would rest the Ark of the Covenant, and atop it and between two ornately carved cherubs is the Mercy Seat which houses the most sacred aspect of the Hebrew religion: the shekinah, a word which means dwelling, signifying the void, or empty space of the feminine energy itself. Once a year, the High Priest goes into this forbidden area whereupon a flame manifests which is known as the Shekinah Glory, aka the Glory of the Feminine Energy. Christian cabala identifies the Shekinah Glory as Christ.

What is most relevant in this narrative is that the Shekinah Glory represents the Moon Child in its more perfect form. Here, however, we are not talking about an abortive attempt nor do we have to subscribe to the assertions or doctrines of various religions or mystery schools, even though their doctrines, sometimes flawed, are completely dedicated to the birthing of such. Whatever you want to make of Jack Parsons's Babalon Working, it was a rogue operation designed to create a Moon Child. It is important, if you want to understand his role or that of Hubbard, that you have an appreciation for the grander template. I would offer, however, that the "grand template" I have offered is not a pure reflection in and of itself. It is only a summarized account based upon various traditions and aspirations and is, as I said, a serviceable metaphor.

When one indulges in a cut-up process, they are opening a "vortex" so to speak. It is a phenomena in and of itself. In this book, we have opened the door to the stream of consciousness with regard to the very people who initiated it into our culture as a phenomenon. Further, the cultural launching of the cut-up process is wrapped up in Scientology and its founder, not unlike the Babalon Working itself. Brion Gysin's interest in and inspiration from Hassan Sabbah is also a very important part of the mix, the latter's legacy coming with it. All of these factors represent a quantum affinity or magical sympathies between the players herein as well as the legacy of Solomon's Temple and the more modern perspective of the *Many Worlds Theory*. We can readily add the legacy of John Starr Cooke because it is clear that none of this would have taken shape if it were not for his embracing of *One Thousand and One Nights* and keeping the restaurant operating. He is attached to it all in the most bizarre and significant of ways.

PELE

Cooke's exploits are legendary and are the subject of books. He went on to feed the LSD culture and make a general mess of things, but that is not so important with regard to this narrative. In the aftermath of his involvement with Gysin, he was struck with a great tragedy. Before I address that, however, I want to address how his family legacy relates to the legacy of King Solomon; and in particular, the magic ring of King Solomon which featured the inscription *PELE*, a name that is obliquely but significantly tied to the Hawaiian volcano of the same name. And when it comes to volcanoes, we must not forget that L. Ron Hubbard formatted so much of his upper levels of Scientology around the idea that all earthlings suffered from implants involved with atom bombs being exploded on volcanoes. Besides all of these various factors, I have found it necessary to address the underlying circumstances of John Starr Cooke's misfortune as well as the incomplete healing he received by a Dianetic auditor.

Cooke's family was intertwined with the invasion of the Hawaiian Islands. Before I begin discussing that history, I will add that when Europeans or their descendents begin to do most anything, whether it be science, art of the cut-up methodology, they are far too apt to discount or not recognize indigenous energies. This is aside from but related to the wanton abuse that is generally directed at indigenous cultures.

Cooke's family was directly involved with establishing the Royal School in Hawaii. This was set up originally to educate the royal family of King Kamehameha III who stewarded the Hawaiian Islands from an absolute monarchy to a "Christian Constitutional Monarchy". As missionaries, Cooke's family actually educated the royal family of the Hawaiian Islands, including their indoctrination into Christianity. As Cooke's own family heritage was so deeply imbedded into the magic of the Hawaiian Islands, it causes one to wonder who was really educating who. Were the missionaries (the Cooke family) who came to conquer and educate the Hawaiians really being conquered and educated themselves? I will share some insight into this question with regard to what I learned directly from a Hawaiian shaman.

The tradition of Huna is based upon acceptance. They will listen to the stories of Christianity and/or any other information they receive and take it into their heart. This applies to people as well. If there is not a reciprocal acceptance and respect by the party being so accepted, there can be problems. Its predisposition was all about integrating whatever experience might come their way. This sort of philosophy is the ultimate integrity because, after all, the word *integrity* has to do with being whole and that means being able to integrate or communicate thoroughly with one's environment.

Well before Cooke's ancestors "civilized" the Hawaiian Islands, there was another Cook who visited the islanders and opened them up to the West; and in particular, to the British Empire. This was the famous Captain Cook who, on his third visit to Hawaii, attempted to take the king hostage and was killed in retaliation. The kahunas subsequently disembowelled Cook's body and baked it in a special process to remove the flesh in order to preserve the bones in a special manner that would serve as religious icons.

Do you get what was happening in this scenario?

Hawaii was invaded by Cook(e)s who were likely from the same genetic source. While Captain Cook was English, John Starr Cooke's family had English origins but were Sons of the Revolution from New England. The essence of the original invader was literally "cooked" and preserved as a talisman. The circumstances created the potential if not a mandate for a dwelling place that will enable a very angry Kahena* to unleash a torrent of primordial energy upon the invaders and their progeny and/or anyone who is aligned with that energy by reason of their (DNA) predisposition.

When it comes to the raw forces of nature, no place has been more under assault than the exotically beautiful Hawaiian Islands. What appears to be a tropical paradise has become a nightmare of genetically modified foods and human biological nightmares. I say this not only based upon what you can read about but from a medical doctor who visited the island and saw many genetic nightmares that have manifested throughout a generation of children. What could be viewed as the evil invasion of a foreigner, and that includes both Captain Cook and the Cooke family, could indeed be the result of the unchecked fury by Hawaii's most vehement goddess, Pele herself, who is credited with creating the Hawaiian Islands. The irony of her name, *PELE*, with the inscription upon the magic ring of King Solomon has already been noted and should not be overlooked

Cooke claimed that he ran his life by consulting a Ouija board and that is what had brought him to Gysin in the first place. The entire set of circumstances invite us to speculate upon whether the Ouija board was running the Government or whether it was being used as a front with regard to this

---

* The term *kahena* refers to an indigenous nature spirit of Hawaii, sometimes referred to as a kahuna. If you examine the phonetics of *kahena* closely, you will see that it is virtually identical to the word *cochina* of the Native American tradition, the primary tradition of which concerns a blue cochina. *Kahena* is a word that goes back thousands of years to Central Africa and is the word for an Amazonian sorceress. This subject is covered in depth in *The Montauk Book of the Living* which refers to the source material of Egerton Sykes, a British dowser and intelligence officer who travelled throughout the world researching every historical writing he could find on the subject of Atlantis and put it into a bimonthly periodical entitled *Atlantis*. It is also relevant to point out that the most exalted word in Hebrew is *shekinah*, (derivable from *she-kahena* or *chi-kahena*) which means "dwelling" and represents the most holy spot imaginable in the Jewish faith: the space over the Mercy Seat which sits between the two Cherubs (sometimes referred to as olive trees) on the Ark of the Covenant.

specific encounter. Whatever the case might be, it appears that Cooke's either careless or reckless views of spirituality seemed to have caused him the most profound setback of his life, and I will now share what happened.

While he was in Morocco, Cooke became associated with a Sufi sect amongst whom he was regarded as "a great healer and saint". While Cooke did not identify himself as a Muslim, he made a rather severe mistake with regard to not taking his role with this sect very seriously. Whatever oaths or non verbal commitments he had made to them, he one day announced to them that he was going on his merry way and off to Algeria, exactly where the Ouija board had directed him. Making last minute preparations for his trip, he was buying his ticket when he was approached by a humble sweeper who was a part of the Islamic sect.

"Oh, you're leaving?" asked the sweeper.

"Yes, I am," replied Cooke.

"Oh, you think so?" was the sardonic reply.

After buying the ticket, Cooke went to the bank where he encountered another member of the sect who gave him a silk scarf which he put on for the first time. At the time he was receiving the scarf, a young man with whom Cook was already familiar happened to be cleaning the floor and tugged at his trousers as if to get his attention. This ended up as a double shock to Cooke's system. With regard to the scarf, he experienced the sudden sensation of being stung by a scorpion on the shoulder and tore away the scarf. Simultaneously, the tug on the trousers was accompanied by a feeling of being slugged at the base of the spine. Red marks remained on the shoulder as well as at the base of the spine. The worst part, however, is that he experienced sudden paralysis, an affliction he would suffer from for the rest of his life. To the typical Western mind, there is no logical explanation for what happened.

Cooke's first reaction was to contact L. Ron Hubbard who was in London. Whatever Cooke might have thought or said about Hubbard over the years, he viewed Dianetics as the greatest potential to fix his horrible situation. It was his only hope. Hubbard, who was invited to take on his case personally, did not take up the offer. While considerable payment would have been offered to Hubbard, I do not believe that he would have turned him down as a tit-for-tat response to Cooke's previous refusal to back Dianetics financially. Hubbard always operated with a bias towards expansion and reaching as many people as he could rather than concentrating upon one rich individual. Instead, Hubbard arranged for an Australian by the name of Jim Skelton to take on the case. Although Skelton got some positive results in reducing Cooke's pain and discomfort, he was not able to eradicate the condition. When Skelton complained that the techniques were not working, Hubbard responded by telling him he was not doing the techniques properly. While

I cannot guarantee that Cooke could have been fixed from his malady, I can tell you from my own personal experience that when things did not work with either Dianetics or Scientology, it was always a case of key steps either being omitted or improperly administered, provided that certain environmental and circumstantial controls were in place. Skelton's own mind-set and opportunism in this matter invite considerable suspicion because he ended up acquiring Cooke's wealthy wife. While it was never uncommon for an auditor, even a good one, to miss a step or two, their job was always considerably more challenging when they faced a tough case. Based upon my own experiences in dealing with very tough cases and without having the data from Cooke's auditing sessions, there are some rather obvious red flags. For example, if the circumstances with the Islamic sect were not properly addressed, there would be little hope of recovery. Cooke was neither honoring them nor was he circumspect about his own predisposition with regard to welcoming them into his life. He was already involved in phenomena way over his head by reason of his involvement with the Ouija board. It led to serious trouble for him, and this is the harsh blow back anyone can expect when one begins to invest their consciousness in dialogues with invisible entities.

None of this would have been brought to the forefront if it were not for Burroughs and his dedication to practicing the cut-up method and his attempt to communicate with the core. Nor would the magical sympathies have been recognized had I not been taught (courtesy of L. Ron Hubbard) to scrutinize the underlying factors of the failed attempt to address the malady of John Starr Cooke, a pivotal character who not only served as a catalyst for the cut-up method itself but became excessively damaged by reason of his association with the key players. These threads not only run far deeper than what I have presented thus far, they stir up many other potentials which we can refer to as either infinite possibilities or as quantum infinity. There is considerably more to the equation. This is what the cut-up phenomena fosters.

Another historical character who takes no back seat to this set of circumstances is Dr. John Dee, the court astrologer of Queen Elizabeth I, who pursuing logical scholarship to its fullest possible extent, found himself in a bizarre dialogue with angels who taught him how to build a schematic for communicating with them; and further, identified themselves as those who taught and empowered the very King Solomon we have been discussing. John Dee, who was able to wield power from behind the throne of Queen Elizabeth I, literally created the British Empire and laid down the foundations upon which all formal Western Scholarship is based. According to Dee, he actually received the ring of King Solomon as a gift from said angels, the same ones that gave him the Enochian language.

According to the writings of Dee, Archangel Michael had stated that this *PELE* ring is "that by which all of Solomon's miracles are revealed and of which philosophy dreameth". Further, the word *PELE* has been defined as "he who will work wonders". (It is interpreted as being gender specific.) But, there are also two additional letters to be found on the ring: *VL*, which has been unanimously translated to mean "hidden one".

THE HIDDEN ONE

The "Hidden One" is a very significant concept with regard to occult politics. First and foremost, it is of vital importance to point out that this concept is one of the most significant and overlooked aspects of Islam. According to the history of Shia Islam, there is a character called the "Hidden One" who traces back thousands of years. His name was Muhammad al-Mahdi, born in 869, and he assumed the Imamate when he was only five years old, following the death of his father, Hasan al-Askari. During his early years, his only contact to his followers was through four deputies. He remained hidden. This period was known as the Minor Occultation, a period which lasted sixty-nine years. Upon the death of his fourth deputy, he sent a letter to his followers declaring the beginning of a Major Occultation, meaning he would no longer be in touch with his followers. While this might sound fanciful to outsiders, it is not only a hard core belief of Shiite Muslims, it is also the core of what their mysterious politics revolve around, completely unrecognized by the media and politicians who are constantly "baffled" by Muslims.

Muhammad al-Mahdi is recognized as the Mahdi from the Koran, the ultimate savior of humankind and the final Imam of the Twelve Imams who will emerge with Isa (Jesus Christ) in order to fulfill their mission of bringing peace and justice to the world. The Twelve Imans refer to the twelve divinely ordained successors of the Prophet, the last one of which, Muhammad al-Mahdi, will save the world as per the above.

While not all Muslims believe in this tradition, it is a very powerful tradition and, most importantly, that which influences the most powerful Islamic politics of today. The intrigues of the Islamic world cannot be fathomed without a basic appreciation of these facts and what they suggest.

In my book, *The Montauk Book of the Living*, I explained that Madame Blavatsky, in *Isis Unveiled*, reported that ancient religious traditions featured an oracle who could provide divinely inspired truth. The oracle, however, would never be seen, even by his closest disciples who would number in twelve. Only one would be permitted to see the oracle and he was the "Peter" or "Pater" which meant "interpreter". This long-held tradition preceded the Twelve Apostles associated with the *New Testament* and the assignment of the name Peter to Simon the fisherman.

In the case of the Hidden One of Shia Islam, we have a circumstance that is built upon or following a tradition that is far older than the machinations of modern politics. While we cannot pin down the Hidden One by the very nature of what is being alluded to, we cannot help but see the correspondence with if not the identification with Baphomet, a word which has often been identified as a corruption of Mahomet. It prompts us to ask if Muhammad is an expression of Baphomet or vice versa. In either case, we have an identification with and correspondence to the Temple Mount and Al-Buraq, the cut-up which was a vehicle to heaven. If we hypothesize that the Hidden One is representative of the hidden control of the continuum, we have an intelligence model which explains so much of the hidden political world.

The Solomonic magic of John Dee influenced the politics of Queen Elizabeth and England which orchestrated the settling of Palestine, an action which has created so much controversy and bloodshed. All of this, however, revolves around Solomon's ring with the *VL*, emulating the Hidden One, identifiable with Baphomet, who serves, for better or for worse, as the interface between the "angels" of Creation and the earthly realm. The instruments of the interfacing are the "Keys of Solomon". Baphomet is the case officer who serves as a functionary to the physical world of 666. The physical world is referred to as 666 because we live in a carbon based universe and a carbon atom has 6 protons, 6 neutrons and 6 electrons. Thus it is that Aleister Crowley not only refers to himself as Baphomet 666 but also as the Caliph[*] or Outer Head of the Ordo Templi Orientis.

This also explains why Crowley and his successors are referred to as the Outer Head, the Inner Head referring to the Hidden One or Baphomet. You can connect the dots any way that you want, but this is the basis of world government. One can also argue whether or not Aleister Crowley was THE force or just emulating the force. It does not matter. He was most certainly in sympathy with the THE force. So are the other functionaries of Baphomet. People who pursue earthly power seek to emulate Baphomet. Whether or not they are the "real thing" is another issue. Again, it is an intelligence model with regard to understanding politics. As it is hidden, it is not so easy to pin down and deal with in a regular pragmatic context. It is meant to be that way.

SUMMARY

The cut-up method opens the door to ALL. It is unrestricted and no-holds-barred. L. Ron Hubbard emulated this lack of restriction in the way he wrote and the way he lived. Whatever you think of him, he was far more interested in the core of creation and living out his own relationship with the infinite than he was in crossing *t*'s and *i*'s in order for him or his work to fit inside the boundaries of convention. Whether we call it that or anything else,

---

[*]The word *caliph* derives from the Arabic *khalifa* or *"successor"* and is used to designate the leader of an Islamic sect.

he was also engaging in the cut-up process in his own way and interpreting everything through his own filter.

The Scientology auditing processes that he developed can also be likened to the cut-up process because they both encouraged and facilitated people embracing all sorts of considerations, ideas, strange propositions and existential circumstances that they would have never otherwise entertained. This certainly opens up the mind if nothing else. The cut-up process does the same except that there is no filter whatsoever other than the individual himself. The auditing process has an auditor and a case supervisor behind the scenes functioning as a monitor or filter with regard to what is entertained or probed. This is not meant to be a sinister control but is rather to serve as a guiding function. Perhaps the most liberating aspect of Hubbard's auditing techniques can be found in the very same upper levels of Scientology that are routinely castigated in the media and also woefully misunderstood by far too many who indulged in them. I am referring to the procedures of "solo-auditing", a term which refers to an individual functioning as one's own auditor or counselor. There is a considerable amount of freedom in this process because one is not burdened with the necessity to explain oneself so much. One simply sees and "hears" and makes notes. In other words, one becomes their own filter and can release one's bondage to other determinisms, including the entire apparatus of organized Scientology. If wisely perceived and properly administered, solo-auditing enables one to turn the control system of Scientology completely topsy-turvy. Too many people, however, either did not learn this or did not see it that way and chose to follow the directions of others that were not only not in their bests interests but not in anyone's best interests.

To filter means to move something through a device to remove unwanted particles. To audit one's mind and filter what is inside of it is the same as detoxifying it. When you open your mind to the infinite, you open the doors to the control system that seeks to reduce infinity into a controlled or regulated experience. In Greek mythology, Uranus was the god of heaven and was so uncontrolled and bothersome that his son, Chronos, the god of quantitative time and structure, castrated him and threw his testicles into the sea whereupon they manifested as the goddess Aphrodite. Chronos, however, was too structured and controlling, eating all of his children, just as time eats all of us. Chronos, in turn, had to be tricked into not eating his last child who, in turn, overthrew him. Life, any way you want to look at it, is a continual process of interaction between chaos and structure. Finding a proper harmony between these two ideas is ideal and akin to the Tao.

This chapter was designed to give you an expansive view of the environment we all operate in and that includes L. Ron Hubbard and the occult factors who have influence our world and continue to do so to this day.

— CHAPTER TWELVE —

EXCALIBUR

"No neurotic harbors thoughts of suicide which are not murderous impulses against others redirected upon himself."
— Sigmund Freud

I have been collecting "cut-ups" of L. Ron Hubbard for well over the last decade. For the purposes of this book, I have attempted to integrate them into the narrative. This process, however, was ironically interrupted by the present time environment coughing up a brand new cut-up that I could not ignore. It concerns a subject that I did not plan to address any further: the report by Arnie Lerma in Chapter One that L. Ron Hubbard was once in a straight-jacket in St. Elizabeth's mental hospital claiming he was Jesus Christ.

On March 16, 2018 Arnie Lerma shot his wife, Ginger Sugerman, in the face and then committed suicide by gunshot at his home in Sylvania, Georgia. His wife survived, but her face was badly damaged, requiring at least three surgeries. She said that Arnie had taken money from her without her consent, and she threatened to file papers and divorce him if he did not return it within 72 hours. Sugerman also stated that Arnie had suffered considerable back pain which included surgeries that did not go so well for him.

This was a tragic end to a life that was beset with strife and adversity ever since he stepped into Hubbard's line of fire and began to challenge the powerful institution of Scientology. Arnie posted information on the internet containing the secret upper levels of Scientology. He became involved in a court battle with Scientology after federal marshals and lawyers from the Church raided his home, alleging he was in possession of copyrighted documents and guilty of copyright infringement and trade secret misappropriation. Lerma eventually lost the case in 1995 and was fined $10,000.

All of this sheds a new light on his claims and causes us to revisit the proposition that Ron was in a straight-jacket, kicking and screaming and claiming that he was Jesus Christ. It is important to remember, this was originally stated to be a fourth-hand report and Arnie never claimed to have direct knowledge of the situation. Specifically, it was the report of a man whose father had heard it from a professor. It was the unidentified professor who allegedly saw a straight-jacketed Hubbard.

Arnie is far from the only ex-Scientologist or Scientologist to have committed suicide. In fact, there are whole websites dedicated to listing countless people who had done so with their experiences with Scientology allegedly being a contributive if not direct reason. In this respect, I want to remind you of the words of Margaret Singer, the clinical therapist who stated that

Hubbard's techniques were not only more sophisticated than those used in North Korea and Communist China but that he took the "art of control and persuasion" to an entirely new level. And once again, there are the words of L. Ron Hubbard Jr. who said the following:

> "The books and contents to be kept forever secret, he says. To reveal them will cause you instant insanity: rip your mind apart; destroy you."

If we accept these comments at face value, it tells us that the occult principles underlying Scientology are indeed powerful enough to rip your mind apart; and further, that L. Ron Hubbard and/or his writings had a tremendous ability to control and/or influence people. Let us, however, take this a step further and state again the other infamous quote from Nibs:

> "Secrets, techniques and powers I alone have conquered and harnessed. I alone have refined, improved on, applied my engineering principles to. Science and logic. The keys! My keys to the doorway of the Magick; my magick! The power! Not Scientology power! My power! The real powers of Solomon."

We are now talking about the powers of Solomon, and this correlates directly with what was discussed in the last chapter about Hassan Sabbah and Brion Gysin's fascination with him and the applied work of William Burroughs. I will add more on the subject of Solomon's powers in subsequent chapters, but I choose to mention the above to give context with regard to this particular narrative.

I find it noteworthy, interesting and ironic that although Hubbard has been castigated for so many suicides being associated with his work, that he does not get proportionate credit for his own claims about his seminal work entitled *Excalibur*, a book that he said contained the basis of what later became Dianetics and Scientology. More specifically, he claimed that those who initially read the manuscript went crazy or committed suicide. There are different versions of the story. Hubbard's claims of that book causing suicides or insanity are routinely mocked by critics. On the other hand, similar or identical critics are quick to blame suicides on Scientology.

According to various sources, including himself, LRH experienced a near-death state in 1938 when he was twenty-seven years old. He was having an operation when, as he stated it, his heart had stopped beating and he was "deader than a mackerel". In his own taped lectures, he said that he had exteriorized from the body without realizing that he had "kicked the bucket". While exterior, he just thought about all of the things he had not done in his life. After a while, he realized that he was experiencing the phenomenon of death. Instead of "blacking out", however, he realized there was an entire array of phenomena that was going on around him that was completely independent of the Earth-based consciousness he knew as a living human being. He also noticed that he could look down on his body and experienced that he was a spirit independent of such.

Accompanying his experiences were visuals which, according to his literary agent Forrest Ackerman, included "a fantastic great gate, elaborately carved like something you'd see in Baghdad or ancient China". As LRH moved towards the gate, he saw an "intellectual smorgasbord on which was outlined everything that had ever puzzled the mind of man". This included all ancient secrets and questions that philosophers had dealt with throughout the ages. It included the beginning of the world and the question of God. As the information came in, he absorbed it until he felt something like a long umbilical cord pulling him back. Resisting the pull, he was quoted as saying "No, no, not yet!" but he was pulled back anyway. When the ornate gate closed, he realized that he was back in his body.

LRH discussed this experience from time to time during his life so there is no reason to believe Ackerman's account is not what LRH said. In his own taped lectures, LRH gave a different view or perhaps additional angles on what happened. He stated that he could see above the street and felt sorry for himself and "decided they couldn't do this to me". As the body's heart had stopped beating, he said that he could see a bunch of interesting mechanisms in the head that restimulate a body's heartbeat. He just "took hold of them and snapped the body back to life".

When he woke up, he saw a doctor standing there with a long needle full of adrenaline. Having shoved it into the heart, the doctor claimed that he had contributed to the recovery, but LRH said the doctor had nothing to do with it.

Many critics of Hubbard and Scientology, including many ex-members, do not accept the prospect of exteriorization[*] as being anything other than a hallucination or mental delusion. This is extremely myopic because there is copious literature and studies in the last few decades on the subject of out-of-body experiences (known as OBEs) and near-death experiences (known as NDEs).

There are different accounts of the incident from various sources, but there is no doubt that this highly subjective occurrence became the focal point and defining moment of what was to be LRH's future life. He immediately wrote down everything he could fathom from the experience in an initial attempt to codify what he had discovered. His manuscript was called

---

[*] Exteriorization is a word that Hubbard coined with regard to an individual being able to leave the body and experience multiple perceptions independent of physiological senses.

Excalibur, named after the sword of King Arthur which symbolized the power of the philosopher's stone. It was in this work that he codified what he called the basic or dynamic principle of existence which was "Survive". This work included the basic template of what was later to be developed into Dianetics and Scientology.

There were a couple of things that struck LRH about his experience. One was that he was amazed at how much information people are able to accumulate without even perceiving it. As he said, "the greatest shock was to find out how much game I was playing without knowing I was playing it". Besides that, there was the way in which he exteriorized. He knew people had exteriorized from time to time during the millennia, often under hazardous and tortuous circumstances. What was so novel about his experience was not only that he had exteriorized but that he also seemed to have a complete subjective awareness on what had happened. Besides that, his experience left him with a complete text on the subject and what it was all about. The last part of the incident he experienced included a command to forget the experience, but he was able to avoid that. The very idea that he was able to remember what most people would forget is, in part, what made his future message and movement so powerful. That is at least what he thought, in addition to the consideration that he was operating with an advantage over what most people cannot see, let alone think about.

With regard to the current narrative, it is important to point out that LRH's idea about "how much information people are able to accumulate without even perceiving it" is representative of the aforementioned cut-up method. All sorts of information was bouncing around inside of his head. More relevant is that this, by his own admission, was THE defining moment in his entire life. Whether anyone agrees with it or not is beside the point. It is how he chose to define his life. He was perceiving the aforementioned "core" that William Burroughs referred to. How he filtered what he saw is another matter entirely. This direct link-up to the "core" placed him in a reference frame that was far beyond the ordinary individual. How this applies to the concept of insanity has everything to do with what was said in Chapter Three with regard to an arbiter making a determination. This, once again, has everything to do with the filtering process. Hubbard was very clearly, however, engaging in what I have termed "deep sea fishing".

You see an example of this as well as an insight into his own psychology when you consider his short story entitled *One Was Stubborn* that was released in *Astounding Science Fiction* in 1940. It concerns a man experiencing an existential meltdown with the reference points of the physical universe disintegrating and a messiah teaching that all matter is non-existent and only an idea. The protagonist, very identifiable as a projection of Hubbard himself, realizes that it has been very long since anyone has come up with an original idea that would be universally acceptable; and further, it is only by virtue of perfect communication to the masses that such acceptance can be achieved.

All of this sounds like a self-created template for Hubbard's own future, but there is another element in the story that is even more indicative of it being a window into Ron's soul. At the very end of the story, as space and time fade away and cease to exist, the protagonist realizes that the only way to save the universe is to CREATE!

To any of us who knew Hubbard, this was indeed a prime characteristic of his personality. He stated that "to create" was at the top of the scale, meaning that it was the highest functional characteristic of a human being. It is the complete opposite of being robotic or giving a programmed response.

One Was Stubborn was published just two years after his Excalibur experience, after which he was introduced to John W. Campbell, the editor of *Astounding Science Fiction*, who was the driving force behind popularizing science fiction and making it what it became. What is more relevant to this narrative is that it clearly demonstrates that Hubbard was communicating with the core, and he was doing so in a way that was heuristically guiding his own future. The story also includes a flirtation with what we could consider to be complete madness: the props of the universe disappearing.

In the end, we are left with a picture of Hubbard challenging the very control system of the universe and possessing a mind-set that he had universal answers to mysteries that had forever plagued the minds of men. Whatever you might think of him, he had a very live conduit to the "core" that not only energized his writing, but he wielded it like a sword. After all, Excalibur was the name of King Arthur's sword. It seems to be a very appropriate name for how Hubbard's would live out his future.

When we consider the bigger picture and the issue of either the potential or propensity of Scientology to trigger full blown insanity in an individual, it is important to remember that when Alan Ginsberg wrote his poem *Howl*, he was in an institution, personally witnessing the depths to which man could sink, all of it reinforced by a control system of oppression. The poem *Howl* triggered an open rebellion against the control system which included extensive legal battles which changed the mores and laws of the society. The modus operandi of the control system, however, seeks to co-opt the rebellion in such as way as to reinforce the control system.

Dianetics and Scientology offered an individual the prospect of rebelling against the control system of one's own mind. As it evolved, it thrived on the prospect of overcoming the control system of the planet. Hubbard's own understanding of the world led him to voice the opinion that his own system would be eventually co-opted.

As was said previously, anyone who was seriously involved with Scientology used the term insanity on a routine basis. You could not participate in Scientology without frequently indulging the reference point of insanity as a concept. How you personally perceived or thought about insanity is a personal issue. To the degree that one was either being audited or auditing others, one was probing deeply into the pathways of the human mind which, for the most part, was territory that was previously unexplored. Hubbard's personal excursions, for better or for worse, can be viewed in the same light.

One of the most valuable pieces of information I learned from him about insanity is that an insane person is generally operating in one of two particular modes: he is either unwilling to duplicate or unwilling to be duplicated. In the first mode, you have a person who can perceive what we consider status quo reality but denies it, asserting that he is Abraham Lincoln and needs to give the Gettysburg Address at 2:00 o'clock. Such a person sees the status quo but does not want to play that game, generally because it is too painful or that he cannot psychologically cope with it. In the second mode, we have a person who attempts to defy being comprehensible to status quo humans. This makes him mysterious or undetectable and therefore intractable and not beholden to the control system of society.

Another factor with regard to insanity, and this evolved out of Hubbard's later work, involved that it was driven by evil intentions. These could be the evil intentions buried within one's own consciousness that were either self-generated, inflicted upon oneself by others or even by simply being exposed to others executing evil upon others. A prime example of the latter is one who is subject to watching others being tortured and losing their mind in what amounts to a case of Post Traumatic Stress Disorder.

If you study the subject of magick, you will learn that the hidden pathways of the mind were mapped out centuries or millennia ago, and they are guarded by what might best be termed the denizens of the deep. An admixture of biblical history and legend will teach you that the power to navigate these pathways and to control these very denizens was contained in the ring of Solomon which, as said before, included the letters P-E-L-E.

Whether or not you believe that the *PELE* inscribed on this legendary ring had anything to do with the Hawaiian volcano of the same name, or whether or not you believe Hubbard was either consciously or subconsciously aware of this association, he intentionally had the illustration of a volcano placed upon his book *Dianetics: The Modern Science of Mental Health*. The reason he did this was because he believed it was something people would respond to by reason of what was buried in their unconscious mind.

We will now take a look at some of Ron's early history as a result of growing up in a military family. For some, it is a very controversial topic over a man who exuded considerable controversy.

THE AGENT

> *"This form of hypnotism has been a carefully guarded secret of certain military and intelligence organizations. It is a vicious war weapon and may be of more use in conquering a society than the atom bomb. Pain-drug-hypnosis is a wicked extension of narco-synthesis, the drug hypnosis used in America only during and since the last war. But pain-drug-hypnosis, due mainly to the intent of the operator, is a much more vicious procedure. The Foundation undertook some tests with regard to the effectiveness of pain-drug-hypnosis and found it so appallingly destructive to the personality..."*
> — L. Ron Hubbard, "Science of Survival"

It has not gone unnoticed by anyone who has looked into the background of L. Ron Hubbard that he was assigned to the ONI (Office of Naval Intelligence). What is most significant or at least interesting about his background in ONI is not what he actually did in this capacity but rather the amount of vehemence by which people assert their opinions on this subject. No one, however, decries the fact that he was assigned to the ONI. How deeply and in what capacity he served remains illusory.

Much of this controversy was fueled by Fletcher Prouty, a distinguished and decorated member of the military who, amongst many other duties, served as a liaison between the CIA and the Air Force. His credentials, which included working for the Joint Chiefs of Staff, are extensive.

Hired by the Church of Scientology in his later years, Prouty boldly stated that he had personally inspected L. Ron Hubbard's military files and indicated they were "sheep-dipped", a term meaning that they were falsified. Specifically, he stated that Hubbard answered to or worked directly under Vincent Astor, a close personal friend of President Franklin Roosevelt, who also served as his unofficial but very serious and potent head of intelligence. Astor's group was known as "The Room" and operated out of New York City. Like Hubbard, Astor was a yachtsman, and he sailed around and spied on the countries he visited, flying the flag of the Explorers Club as a cover. Hubbard himself was a member of the Explorers Club, a very exclusive society of which he was very proud to be a member.

Many people have taken issue with Prouty because they feel that the church hired him to further falsify Hubbard's record so as to make him appear to be a war hero when, according to their view, he really was not. What is most perplexing about the Church-Prouty connection is that they mysteriously unhired him, long before his controversial statements reached a fever pitch.

Prouty later said that his statements about Hubbard made on behalf of the Church of Scientology represented a "work for hire". This is equally vague.

Although most of the information on the internet suggests that Hubbard compulsively and routinely lied about his military history, there are some sites which show contradictions with regard to either his status or his actual service history. What I find most interesting is that critics of Hubbard are so subscribed to the proposition of military documents being accurate and infallible. The documents and the presentation thereof have far too much emotion attached to them for my preference. And with regard to people who rail against Prouty's assertions, I find it odd that the people who challenge him have a much higher regard for those who produced or presented the official documents, all of whom were clearly subordinate in rank to Prouty as well as serving a much lesser function when it comes to intelligence issues.

When presenting information of a controversial or debatable nature, it is important to address the subject of what is called framing.

> **framing** (*Psychology Dictionary*) the process of defining the context or issues that surround a problem or event in a way that serves to influence how the context or issues are seen and evaluated.

If you go through what files are available on L. Ron Hubbard with regard to his service record, you can cherry pick different items to make a case. The majority seem to pick records to frame Hubbard as an inveterate liar and blowhard who was a crackpot seeking to con the world, eventually creating his own religion. Others seek to show that he had a serious role in the intelligence service, possibly even serving the English Crown as a secret agent.

In the final analysis, I am not so sure that L. Ron Hubbard's official role in these matters is so important. If we choose to assume that he was a deep operative, any official role he might have had would have been deliberately obscured; and further, the deeper the role, the deeper the obfuscation. What is more significant, at least as far as this book is concerned, is that we are dealing with the occult matrix underlying Hubbard; so, whether or not he had an assigned role from the military, he was operating in a manner that was intended to be hidden. The fact that he thrived on the concept of mystery, selling it as both a writer of pulp fiction as well as the founder of a religion, makes it suitable that he also thrived on being mysterious himself. It very much suited his personality. All of the assertions about him, however, whether they are positive or negative or for him or against him, fit into the cut-up at hand. If we are cutting up Hubbard, we cannot ignore his military history or the multiple versions thereof.

What I would also tell you at the outset of what I have to present in this chapter is that most who write on this subject are trying to get across a point that they believe strongly, and while they frame the subject, they do not tell you they are framing the subject. As for my own agenda, I at least have the courtesy of telling you what I am trying to frame. I have no attachments to Hubbard's actual or alleged role in intelligence. My purpose is to create an intelligence model, not only profiling Hubbard as an intelligence agent but one who was either placed or found his way into a nexus of highly sensitive spheres of power where military secrets of the highest grade mixed with occultism and cutting edge science in addition to any other nefarious aspects that are associated with the military industrial complex. Only the tenor of time will give a conclusive answer. This is only an intelligence model, a tool that intelligence agencies routinely use in the course of business. An intelligence model helps ferret out the truth of an individual, a group or situation.

Perhaps the most important aspect to put forth at the beginning is that L. Ron Hubbard lived a life that defied ordinary probability. Whether he was a legitimate ONI officer doing undercover work or not, he ended up cavorting with top rocket scientists and nuclear physicists who were not only constantly under the watchful eye of the military, they represented the cutting edge of military and atomic technology. If he was not a bona fide intelligence agent during this period, he had a very unusual capacity for insinuating his way into the center of the fire and commanding people's attention.

Perhaps the most intriguing piece of evidence connecting him to the intelligence world is contained in a document that surfaced during a law suit between the Church of Scientology and Gerry Armstrong, a former Sea Org member who had served on the *Apollo* and, prior to defecting from Scientology, was assigned to work with Omar Garrison, a professional journalist who was paid by the Church to write a biography of their founder. The document in question was a personal letter to a seventeen-year-old Hubbard (aka "Red") which reads as follows (a faded copy of the actual letter is on the next page).

> British Legation
> Peking, China
> Jan. 1, 1929

Dear Red,

You'll probably hear this officially soon but I want to let you know first. You're still a Lieutenant. You've been retained in spite of all the fuss the Ambassador made. He tried to convince everyone that you also worked for the U.S.* That is the best I ever have heard. With you so blotto that you don't know one end of a gat from the other.

---

* If you consult the original document, the *U* in *"U.S."* is not so clear. I have seen it transcribed as "S.S." but the initials *"U.S."* are more consistent when you zoom in on the image.

Don't resign when you get the cable. You've time to catch the Mariana Maru if you decide quickly. Please come back up for, although you've only been gone three weeks we all feel frownish and ugly. One day of your method of carrying our business and we'll be fine again.

Giovinni never came out of it poor devil. Of course we know that you think differently. He was a damned devil, Red, but just a poor one now. I guess your face got all right. That was a damned nasty slash he gave you, but I caught one on the hand that is giving me hell. Loosen up sometime and give me the whole story.

Well, you and your perpetual "Godamn" will be back here soon teaching more wops how to use their own sword.

Pip pip!

Mac

P.S. Bring me a mestizio from Manila.

While I believe I have transcribed the original letter with a fair degree of accuracy, there is room for error. None of the potential errors are critical save for the reference to "*U.S.*" If this is correct, then "*U.S.*" clearly refers to the United States with this letter suggesting that, although he was clearly an American, he was not working for his own country but rather the English Crown. We can assume that the Ambassador alluded to is Great Britain's ambassador to China. If the "*U.S.*" is indeed an "*S.S.*", as has been suggested by another, and I do not believe that to be the case, the date of the letter is too early in history for it to suggest Germany's *S.S.* but it could, however, possibly represent the secret service of the British. In either case, he was on the radar of the Ambassador which suggests he was of considerable importance.

Ian MacBean, the author of the letter, was a British Secret Service agent representing MI6 and working at the highest levels of British Intelligence. His chummy attitude with such a young man is quite noteworthy as is his cheeky request for the underage Ron to bring him a "mestizio", the name for a woman of mixed race, in this case referring to a Chinese Filipino. These women were known for being used by sex trafficking interests as well as just ordinary prostitution. This was obviously some sort of inside joke, but it shows Ron was being treated as "one of the guys" and certainly had the respect of someone whose rank was not insignificant. He also confirms Ron's rank, but it is non-specific. Although Hubbard was registered as having performed service for the Montana National Guard from October 19-28, 1928, he was listed as a private, not a lieutenant. The date of MacBean's letter is also well before Hubbard joined the Marine Corps Reserve 20th Regiment in May of 1930, a stint which lasted until October 22, 1931. This letter suggests

```
                                           Jan. 1 1929
Dear Led,
        You'll probably hear this officially soon but I want to
let you know first. You're still a Lieutenant". You've been
retained in spite of all the fuss the ambassador made. He tried
to convince everyone that you also worked for the U.S.. That is the
best I ever have heard. With you so blotto that you don't know
one end of a gat from the other.
        Don't resign when you get the cable. You've time to
catch the Mariana Maru if you decide quickly. Please come back up
for, although you've only been gone three weeks we all feel
frownish and ugly. One day of your method of carrying on our
business and we'll all be fine again.
        Giovinni never came out of it poor devil. Of course we
know that you think differently. He was a damned devil, I'ed, but
just ... not one now. Guess your face got all right. That was
a damned nasty slash he gave you, but I caught one on the hand
that is giving me hell. Loosen up some time and give me the whole
story.
        Well, you and your perpetual "Godamn" will be back
here soon teaching more wops how to use their other words of
                                    ip pip !
P.S. Bring me a mestizio from Manila. 73c.i.
```

that his status as a lieutenant was both an irregular and secret designation, and also that it was assigned by a foreign interest. We can only speculate beyond that.

It is extremely challenging in terms of time to do an investigative study to determine if LRH was indeed a "certified and verified" spy in the British Secret Service. It is also something one will not prove. It is noteworthy if not just amazing, however, that many people need to have it explained to them in "BOLD LETTERS" that spies are not certified as, by their very nature, their roles are designed to remain hidden. This also makes them and their legacy easy to dispose of without any recoil upon their spy master(s).

If we want to fast forward on the trail of LRH's alleged spy craft, we can consult a broadly distributed interview with L. Ron Hubbard Jr. in *Penthouse* magazine that appeared in 1983 wherein Nibs stated the following:

> "Two of the people we were involved with in the late fifties in England were Errol Flynn and a man who was high up in the Labor Party at the time. My father and Errol Flynn were very similar. They were only interested in money, sex, booze, and drugs. At that time, in the late fifties, Flynn was pretty much of a burned-out hulk. But he was involved in smuggling deals with my father: gold from the Mediterranean, and some drugs --mostly cocaine. They were both just a little larger than life. I had to admire my father from one standpoint. As I've said, he was a down-and-out, broke science-fiction writer, and then he writes one book of science-fiction and convinces the world it's true. He sells it to millions of people and gets billions of dollars and everyone thinks he's some sort of deity. He was really bigger than life. Flynn was like that, too. You could say many negative things about the two of them, but they did as they pleased and lived as they pleased. It was always fun to sit there at dinner and listen to these two guys rap. Wild people. Errol Flynn was like my father also in that he would do anything for money. He would take anything to bed --boys, girls, Fifty-year-old women, ten-year-old boys, Flynn and my father had insatiable appetites. Tons of mistresses. They lived very high on the hog."

I bring up Erroll Flynn because, in the process of researching the "mestizio connection", I discovered that Flynn was a slave trader in New Guinea as a young man who had once murdered a native. Although he was brought to trial, he beat the rap. One of Flynn's biographers points out that being a slaver in a British Crown Colony was par for the course in those days as natives were all viewed as significantly inferior creatures. He stated that if you consider Flynn negligent in this regard, then so should you also consider all Englishmen of that time to be equally guilty. In such an environment of British superiority, this clearly explains how and why Hubbard acquired the term "wog" to refer to non-Scientologists. The term *wog* had already long been in use by the British for centuries. The term *wog* was an acronym for the satirical appellation *Worthy Oriental Gentleman*.

Flynn was an ardent Nazi sympathizer and according to research by Charles Higham, he was also a spy for German causes. He used his position as a movie star on location to take pictures of the air base in Hawaii before the Pearl Harbor incident, and he also did overhead shots of a base in San Diego. Both were turned over to the enemy. Flynn also volunteered his spy services to William Donovan of the OSS when he was going to Ireland.

Although Donovan turned down the request, Higham had reason to believe that, despite his known Nazi affiliations, the British accepted a similar request from Flynn. It seems he was at least a double agent and possibly more than that.* In his final years, Flynn also ended up in Cuba, working as a reporter who was also a supporter of Castro's revolution. He was already a regular in the Caribbean at that point, living in Jamaica as a neighbor of Ian Fleming, a very highly placed British intelligent agent who by that time had become famous as the author of the James Bond novels.

All the time I was in Scientology and during the time I worked in the Personal Office of LRH, I never heard a whisper of an Erroll Flynn connection. I was no stranger to the tales of Robert Heinlein and Jack Parsons, but their adventures were relatively calm compared to the recklessness of Flynn.

Nibs' interview with *Penthouse* gives an even more colorful if not alarming portrayal of his father as a rogue agent.

> Penthouse: *"And what about this Labor Party official?"*
>
> Hubbard: *"He was a double agent for the KGB and for the British intelligence agency. He was also a raging homosexual. He wanted my father to use his black-magic, soul-cracking, brainwashing techniques on young boys. He wanted these boys as his own sexual slaves. He wanted to use my father's techniques to crack people's heads open because he was very influential in and around the British government — plus he was selling information to the Russians. And so was my father."*
>
> Penthouse: *"Your father was selling information to the Soviets?"*
>
> Hubbard: *"Yes. That's where my father got the money to buy St. Hill Manor in East Grinstead, Sussex, which is the English headquarters of Scientology today."*
>
> Penthouse: *"What information did your father have to sell the Soviet government?"*
>
> Hubbard: *"He didn't do any spying himself. What he normally did was allow these strange little people to go into the offices and into his home at odd hours of the night. He told me that he was allowing the KGB to go through our files, and that he was charging £40,000 for it. This was the money he used for the purchase of St. Hill Manor."*

---

* For further information, read *Errol Flynn: The Untold Story* (1980) by Charles Higham.

If we accept Nibs' assertions at face value, it presents a situation that gives great insight into just how LRH looked at the governments of the world. In the case of the "raging homosexual" we have utter depravity at the highest level of the U.K. government. This is consistent with today's incessant reporting of pedophilia in their government, much of it surrounding the antics of Jimmy Savile. Regardless of any misgivings he might have had on his own part, Hubbard viewed world governments as utterly corrupt and not to be taken seriously as far as having the best interests of the people at heart.

This data also offers an explanation as to why the British government was so hot to kick Ron out of England. It is easy to understand that they might not like a movement like Scientology and persecute it, but if what Nibs said is true, it explains the virulence with which they pursued their target. At this point in his life, if he had been working for British intelligence in some capacity, he had clearly flown the coup, something intelligence agents often do and for various reasons, often as a result of being deserted by their spy masters. In such a scenarios, Hubbard's knowledge and connections alone would cause him to be viewed as a complete wild card who might stir up all sorts of unpredictable problems.

In all honesty, I cannot tell you whether the assertions by Nibs are true. I can tell you, however, that they do give an insight into the roguery that occurs in intelligence circles. Keep in mind what I said earlier. LRH developed his own intelligence agency that was bigger than that of most countries. It was also incredibly efficient with hordes of dedicated people working for him. If he was not a bona fide expert in intelligence, there is no way he could have produced such a formidable organization. And that was only one of the organizations he created. Known as the Guardian's Office, it was there to protect and preserve Scientology organizations.

Whatever knowledge, experience, and credentials Hubbard either did or did not have, he was viewed as a formidable player on the world stage when he attempted to take over the country of Morocco in 1972. I was a first hand witness to that, and by take over, I mean that he was attempting to set up a direct conduit to King Hassan II so that he would have a safe country to operate in as well as help the King run the country with Scientology administrative policies. There was a similar attempt with Mexico at this same time period. I should also add that his intelligence agency known as the Guardian's Office had nothing to do with these operations. They were carried out entirely by Sea Org personnel operating from the *Apollo*.

Whatever you want to make of the cut-ups I have provided, L. Ron Hubbard was familiar with the world stage, having the experience of an intelligence officer, an occultist, as well as a mind-control expert. There has never been anyone quite like him, that being at least one of the reasons why he cannot be so easily dismissed or forgotten.

LOOKOUT MOUNTAIN

*"We place no reliance on virgin or pidgeon.
Our method is science, our aim is religion."*
— Aleister Crowley

When you mix the highest levels of military intelligence with high levels of occultism, you have a recipe for mystery and intrigue, two features which L. Ron Hubbard precipitated and thrived on. To live or be around him was to find yourself in circumstances that were ripe with drama. In this chapter, I will explore how these factors make for an intriguing cut-up which gives insight into a time that regular history has overlooked or ignored.

Addressed as a serious subject, magick is outside of the boundaries of ordinary thinkers. Its usefulness and effectiveness, nevertheless, can be observed and studied. First, it will manifest as a sympathetic vibration whereby the supplicant will begin to notice associations that he previously either did not recognize or denied. I use the term *supplicant* because anyone engaging in the study or practice of magick is making an overture or evocation to powers that are outside of one's ordinary horizons. This is not the same as asking daddy for an ice cream, the boss for a raise or asking your spouse to buy you a new jacket. If you think you are only studying the subject, the very nature of the undertaking necessitates and causes you to look inside of your own mind and assess the components that make up your own identity. After all, the subject is defined as follows (by Aleister Crowley):

"Magick is the science and art of causing
change to occur in conformity with will".

Another aspect of magick is that, due to its operating in a sympathetic reference frame, it is not always precisely on the money. For example, you might make a postulate to become a movie star or even engage in a ritual in order to reinforce the postulate by engaging elemental forces. Instead of getting an offer to be part of a major film, you get a request to be in a low budget stage production sponsored by a charity group or perhaps even an offer to be in a porno movie. When one engages in the magical world, there are plenty of low vibrations and discordant frequencies that can either distract or attract you. So much of it has to do with the mirror inside of your own soul. This personal interface is the same as the previously mentioned filter connected with the cut-up method. In such an instance, one can blame the ritual, the lack of precision in the postulate, or a host of other things. One can, of course, review one's thinking and rephrase the postulate as well as the specific goal in mind. In any case, one is seeking or conversing with a power or authority that is outside the bounds of one's ordinary experience and can be considered to be outside of one's self. Although the Devil too often shows up, it does not have to be that way. The reason for the preponderance of demons or devils showing their face not only has to with what is inside the practitioner's mind, it has everything to do with the fact that one is traversing the realm of Baphomet (or the archetype thereof) who plays the role of a traffic cop, and a traffic cop who can be influenced by bribery or some sort of offering.

L. Ron Hubbard, by the way, was always very cognizant of bribery and willing to use it if the need arose. When he would go out for his motorcycle rides while on the *Apollo*, especially in Morocco, he would have the pockets of his jacket lined with at least $3,000 in negotiable currency in the event he would need to bribe his way out of a situation while riding around by himself in a foreign land. Bribery is to be expected as a due course of business in the realm of Baphomet, and that includes the politics of this planet.

For those who might recoil at the devilishness of these propositions, at least in regard to evoking outside forces, this is no different than praying for your aunt to recover from an illness or praying for your children to succeed at a particular endeavor. The only difference is the context. In either case, one is praying to an outside force. There are many complex factors at work, and it all has to do with your own frequency and what you resonate with.

I only became interested in magick as a result of reading the book *L. Ron Hubbard: Madman or Messiah?* (by Bent Corydon and L. Ron Hubbard, Jr.) which informed me that Ron was far more deeply wrapped up in magick than I had previously realized. I was familiar with many of the stories but not how much he was rooted to the subject. Having spent twelve years of my life in the Scientology movement, it behooved me to find out what was behind this man who had profoundly influenced my life, albeit in a very positive way.

Although I did not realize it at the time, and perhaps due to the extensive osmosis factor of working for Hubbard on a personal basis, I was interacting with a live magical current while reading that book and subsequently following it up by studying the works of Aleister Crowley as well as Jack Parsons. Looking back, it was very powerful and the truth of this observation is very clear to me in hindsight. While I have written about these adventures in other books, I can only touch on them in a book like this. One of these, however, never really made it into a book and this deserves some attention as it fits in with this narrative. It concerns one of the most prominent and celebrated Scientologists of the 1970s: Ingo Swann.

Ingo Swann is mostly known as the "Father of Remote Viewing" by reason of experiments he engaged in at the Stanford Research Institute. These are legendary in themselves, and I will not go into them here. There is, however, another aspect about Ingo that he was not so public about and was even quick to deny. That is the fact that he was an ardent student of magick. His gallery in Manhattan was studded with OTO people. In his later years, Ingo also denied that he was ever really a Scientologist. This is absurd, at least if you read his letters to Hubbard as I did. As Scientology has fallen into disrepute over the years, it is has been typical for people to disavow any connection to the subject. Many also change and twist their personal stories.

I bring up Ingo Swann because his presence played a pivotal role in me being able to compose the present chapter. This is in spite of the fact that, in real life, Ingo played an adversarial role with regard to my own research and was not an ally in any sense of the word. Although Ingo was not about to help me in real life, he did service me in a very interesting way via the dream state. Dreams, of course, are the epitome of a cut-up. They are a result of the mind reaching across a broad spectrum of experience and attempting to reconcile themes or issues the conscious mind has not been able to grasp. Dreams can draw from the past or future.

It was in 2005 that I had a very poignant and strange dream that made quite an impression on me. In the dream, Ingo Swann was in a class room and standing at a chalkboard. With emphatic and firm resolve, Ingo implored me to look into the connection between Ian Fleming and L. Ron Hubbard. Once he had made his point, I drifted back into the dream world, but he somehow commanded my attention and emphatically made his point once again. This dream was well before Ingo passed away.

Subsequently, I tried to find a plausible connection between L. Ron Hubbard and Ian Fleming. The only thing I came up with initially is that Hubbard was accepted into the U.S. Navy in July 1941, the very same time period when Ian Fleming came to Washington and visited Roosevelt as a member of British Naval Intelligence. This was also the same year that Fletcher Prouty had joined the service. Fleming was solely responsible for drafting the document that would serve as the blueprint for William Donovan's Office of Strategic Services, the prototype for the CIA If one wants, they can find all sort of correspondences and associations connecting both Fleming and Hubbard to "The Room" of Vincent Astor, and while they are interesting, it leaves one like a cat chasing their tail. One can only see magical sympathies, and while many of the connections are entirely plausible if not obvious, it only amounts to a trail of intrigue and nothing too concrete. This is why I stated that magick is often not exactly on the money. None of this matters, however, if you eventually hit the jackpot.

With regard to my own personal research, Fleming initially caught my attention after Al Bielek told me personally that Fleming had unexpectedly died shortly after announcing to Ivan T. Sanderson, a famous naturalist and British intelligence agent, that he was going to fly to New Jersey and brief him on the Philadelphia Experiment (see Appendix C for a further explanation). Sanderson, a favorite on Johnny Carson's *Tonight Show* and on the paranormal radio show of Long John Nebel, coined the term *cryptozoology* and was part of the crowd that circulated around The Room. Fleming never made it to New Jersey because he died on August 12th, 1964, the anniversary of the Philadelphia Experiment. Fleming and Sanderson were definitely well acquainted with each other and both went to Eton College around the same time period. Sanderson, by the way, while engaging in undercover operations in the Caribbean, used a top smuggler to captain his ship.

With regard to Fleming, the implication was that he was getting too big for his britches and thought he had enough clout to get away with talking about the Philadelphia Experiment, something a previous researcher, Morris Jessup, had allegedly and most probably been killed over. The idea of Fleming spilling the beans reminds me of Nibs Hubbard telling bizarre tales of his father. It is not unlike children who will tell a visitor a family secret like where his parents keep a secret stash of cash or other valuables.

In my attempt to connect Fleming and Hubbard, I discovered that the famous science fiction writer, Robert Heinlein, who was also a retired Naval officer, wanted to serve in World War II but was rejected due to not passing his physical. Heinlein's desire to serve, compounded with his expertise in engineering and physics, caused the Navy to employ him in a top secret capacity at the Philadelphia Naval Yard. There, he was assigned to developing radar and high pressure suits. His house became known as a flop house for science fiction writers during this period as he was holding think-tank sessions with them at the behest of the Government. Besides holding think-tank sessions, Heinlein also employed some of them at the naval yard, including Isaac Asimov and L. Sprague de Camp. During an interview, Asimov acknowledged that he had met Hubbard at the Philadelphia Yard although that was not his first meeting with him. Hubbard, who was already in the Navy at that time, was a part of the think-tank sessions.

There is no direct evidence to indicate that any of these science fiction icons, including Hubbard, were directly involved in the Philadelphia Experiment. Heinlein, however, would be the most likely suspect because he was working on radar and the pressure suits he designed could be construed as being invented to protect the sailors involved in the Philadelphia Experiment. What Heinlein worked on remained classified for decades, and although some have claimed he spilled all the beans, claiming you have spilled the beans does not mean that you have. If he did have anything to do with the Philadelphia Experiment, he did not indicate it. Also keep in mind that the security around that project was especially high. In any case, we can only speculate. What is significant is how much these science fiction authors, especially Heinlein, were involved in top secret activities.

What I also learned from my research into this Fleming-Hubbard lead was how incestuous the science fiction authors and their publishers were with the Department of War Information, a propaganda machine in and of itself; and further, how the Department of War Information set the tone for the type of literature that was to be produced for the pulp magazines that Hubbard wrote for. When Hubbard began his pulp writing, he was already a veteran of the Montana National Guard and the U.S. Marine Corps Reserve. His entire youth up to that point was a military life that was heavily influenced by his father's role in the U.S. Navy. It was not as if he appeared out of the blue to become a writer of pulp fiction.

With regard to my dream, the connection with Ian Fleming was far more interesting, even if it did not lead directly to Hubbard for the time being. A short time after the dream, I received a mysterious package in the mail with no letter or return address indicating who had sent it. It was like the delivery of an unsolicited and unexpected cut-up. All I knew was that it was sent from overseas. The package contained a book entitled *OP J.B.* by Christopher Creighton, a.k.a. John Ainsworth-Davis, the English "nephew" of Joachim von Ribbentrop, the German Foreign Minister during's Hitler's regime. *OP J.B.* was never published in the United States and it is no longer in print due to security issues, but you can but it online. Loaded with intrigue, it climaxes with Creighton and Ian Fleming, who used the code name James Bond, sneaking their way into Germany wearing Nazi uniforms in the last days of World War II and facilitating the escape of Martin Bormann, Hitler's secretary who also served as the head of the Nazi Party. What Bormann had to offer the Allies was the fact that he was a signatory on the Nazi's Swiss bank accounts. Bormann's role as the Nazi's chief financial kingpin was ferreted out by Fleming on a trip to Switzerland. Fleming, who had been an international banker prior to the war and knew the Swiss system and its people, met with the Swiss Finance Minister; and by using firm politeness with the potential of Allied wrath, was able to wiggle out the information of who was signatory on the secret Nazi accounts in Switzerland. The specifics of whatever were worked out is not mentioned. Most of the money, if not all of it, was placed into the hands of Desmond Morton and William Donovan, two Roman Catholics whose loyalties belonged to the Vatican and Knights of Malta.

Creighton and Fleming were able to make "diplomatic" contact with the bunker via Joachim von Ribbentrop, a man Creighton knew well when he was young. Although Creighton referred to von Ribbentrop as his uncle, I do not recall whether he was a blood relative or not. I think he was. In any event, von Ribbentrop was an intriguing worldly character who had once lived in the United States and was eventually posted as Ambassador to the Court of St. James. Eventually, he served as the Foreign Minister of

Germany. It was in von Ribbentrop's personal home (in Germany) that meetings were held that would eventually lead to Hitler taking power as Chancellor of Germany.

As intriguing as these other characters and their historical impact are, I am focusing at Ian Fleming here. *OP J.B.* was short for *Operation James Bond*. In his later years, Fleming would never admit that the name for his spy hero was derived from anything significant. He did, however, as did Churchill, give Creighton permission to tell his story after a certain amount of time had passed. I studied quite a bit about Ian Fleming, but what is most significant with regard to the occult matrix we are working with is that he was a close friend and associate of Aleister Crowley and had engaged in occult operations with him against the Germans, all being run out of Navy Intelligence or whatever secret unit he was operating out of.

Previously, Fleming had arranged for Crowley to cast a persuasive horoscope for Rudolph Hess which would be clandestinely slipped to him. In addition to this, Crowley performed a ritual in the Ashdown Forest with several others which included a dummy plane flying to England. When Hess flew to England and was held prisoner, Fleming wanted Crowley to interview Hess, but if we are to believe common history, this request was denied. Instead, a much more sinister character than Crowley was chosen to interview Hess, and that was Donald Ewing Cameron, a notorious psychiatrist whose exploits are well documented and who subsequently executed the MK-Ultra program, at the behest of Allen Dulles, the OSS operations chief in Switzerland who was instrumental in the repatriation of Nazi scientists during Operation Paperclip.

Fleming was fluent in German, having attended the University of Munich when Hess's mentor, Karl Haushofer, was a professor at the university. Crowley, who knew Haushofer personally, was also in Munich at this time. It is quite possible they all knew each other and that Crowley even met Fleming during this time period. Although Crowley proved himself to be an English patriot throughout the years, acting as a spy on their behalf, it is quite possible that, if it is indeed true that Crowley was denied access to Hess, it was for the very reason that "The Great Beast" was viewed as a wild card. Hess and Crowley were both very close to the Haushofers (including Karl's son Albrecht) who, while they both eventually fell out of favor with Hitler, still had significant influence at that point, both of whom were highly regarded by Heinrich Himmler.

Donald Ewen Cameron, who became head of the American Psychiatric Association, the World Psychiatric Association, and the Canadian Psychiatric Association, would become a sworn enemy of L. Ron Hubbard. Cameron was quite notorious for his use of lobotomies and a process called psychic driving which included wiping out a person's mind with drugs and then driving in tape recorded messages to program their behavior. It was quite brutal, and the CIA eventually admitted to their complicity with him.

The veil of secrecy around these colorful and intriguing characters will remain mysterious, but the fact that my dream led me to look in this direction turned up information on Robert Heinlein that was new to me.

Routinely heralded and promoted as the "Dean of Science Fiction", Heinlein worked hand-in-glove with John W. Campbell, the editor of *Astounding Science Fiction* and several other pulp publications. Campbell, in turn, worked hand-in-glove with executives and/or owners who served in the Office of War Information. It was Campbell who introduced Hubbard to Heinlein, both of whom remained on cordial terms to the end of their years.

Heinlein was a graduate of the Naval Academy. After leaving the Navy for health reasons, he became very interested in politics and became involved in the movement to elect Upton Sinclair as Governor of California. After failing at getting himself elected to the California State Assembly, he found success as a writer. His scientific mind was highly regarded by both John W. Campbell as well as the military. Heinlein's gig at the Philadelphia Naval Yard was only natural as was his think-tank of science fiction writers.

What I found most intriguing about Heinlein, however, was not only that he had lived at 8777 Lookout Mountain Road but that Hubbard used

```
                        4 Dec. 45

    To:         The Chief of Naval Personnel
                Attn. Transportation Division.

    Subj:       Transportation of dependents, change of
                address on.

         1.     It is requested that the mailing address
    on a transportation claim submitted in August 1945
    be changed.

         2.     The claim requested reimbursement for
    transportation for my wife and children from
    Portland, Ore., the embarkation port of the U.S.S.
    Algol (AKA54) to which I was then attached, to my
    home in New York City.

         3.     The mailing address on subject claim
    is no longer my address and mail going to me at
    that address has been lost.  I would like
    further correspondence or payment to be sent
    to:
                Lt. L. R. Hubbard USNR
                8777 Lookout Mt. Ave.
                Hollywood, 46, Calif.

         4.     Please advise if the check has already
    been sent so that I can either trace it or request
    that it be re-issued.  The time elapsed leads me to
    believe that the check has been lost.

                    Lt.   L. Ron Hubbard USNR 113392
```

THE ABOVE CAPTION READS AS FOLLOWS:
LOOKOUT MOUNTAIN PARK, BETWEEN THE CITY AND THE SEA
HOME OFFICE, 1103 STORY BUILDING, LOS ANGELES, CAL.

this for his own address as per two naval documents. This actually confirmed what amounted to a rumor I had heard since my first year in Scientology: Heinlein and Hubbard were roommates. The only evidence I had come across up to that point was that Heinlein had used his home in Philadelphia as a flop house for science fiction writers during his think-tank sessions.

While this was clearly Hubbard's address prior to his moving in with Jack Parsons, there are other peculiar convergences with regard to this location. One is that, long before the area became populated, a pictorial rendition of Lookout Mountain was submitted to the U.S Post Office by Jack Parsons for the purposes of it being used as a post card to be published by the Government. Parsons' proposal was rejected. The only reason I can imagine that Jack Parsons would have had a fascination with such a location is that mountain tops are used for magick and are always sacred to shamans. Not only would Heinlein later move to the area but it would later be used by the U.S. Army Signal Corps. to establish the First Motion Picture Unit, a top secret installation that began during World War II to literally co-opt Hollywood and turn it into a propaganda machine. It is quite ironic, however, especially if we consider magical sympathies, that Parsons placed his paw-print on the area before either Heinlein or the military moved in.

The First Motion Picture Unit is a fascinating story in and of itself, and if it were not for the dream with Ingo, I would not have come across it. The most conspicuous aspect of the unit was the secrecy surrounding it. In fact, its existence was not made public until the 1990s, over two decades after it had ceased to function. The history of the unit is filled with colorful characters. Walt Disney, Ronald Reagan and Jimmy Stewart also served the First Motion Picture Unit, the latter starring in a very successful movie that was designed to recruit fighter pilots. Most Hollywood executives were co-opted into the military to serve the unit, including Jack Warner of Warner Brothers who was made a captain in the Armed Forces and ordered to use his producing skills to create war propaganda films. This covert alliance

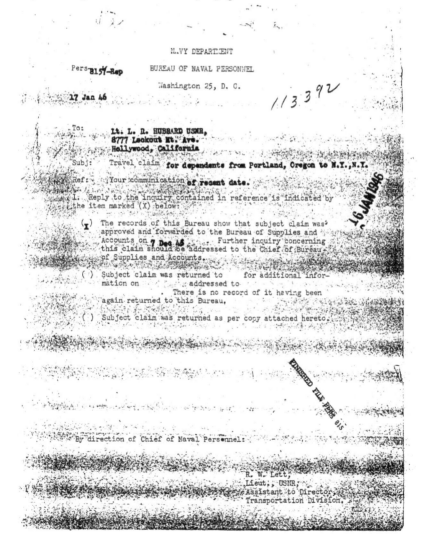

with Hollywood also explains so much of the propaganda films that were released in the Fifties, many of which concerned flying saucers and aliens.

While all different types of military films and photography were produced out of the First Motion Picture Unit and its subsidiaries, its work on chronicling the atomic bomb was probably its highest security function as well as being the most emotionally challenging to the staff. Other challenges included the processing and editing of footage from the German concentration camps.

In the final analysis, it is difficult to overestimate the influence of the First Motion Picture Unit as it actually created the images which were to pervade the collective consciousness of American civilization from World War II and beyond. While the pedestrian history of the unit does not include the use of subliminals, one has to consider the possibility. It should also be acknowledged that this general area, known as Laurel Canyon, has been the subject of different books, citing the area as the home of many movie and rock stars who were up to their necks in drugs, other illegal behavior and under the influence of the military and/or mind control. This is also the general neighborhood of the infamous "Manson Murders", also known as the Tate-LaBianca Murders.

While Hubbard's association with this environment is vague, Heinlein became very involved, his most celebrated contribution being the screen writing of a ground-breaking movie entitled *Destination Moon*. This was literally the first serious modern movie about shooting men into space, and Heinlein also served as a technical consultant with regard to the scientific plausibility of the technology depicted. Any way you look at it, Heinlein was an insider when it came to the most sensitive aspects of military technology.

Having previously written the screenplay for *The Secret of Treasure Island*, Hubbard had already been ingratiated into Hollywood as a screen writer, and while his primary association with Lookout Mountain seems to be as a temporary resident, we cannot dismiss that his friends and associates were involved at the highest levels of the defense of the United States.

Some people who have studied these connections are often too quick to make conclusions and assertions about Hubbard's various roles. This is a mistake. The fact that he was close to these people is enough to assume that he was in the fray. Others try to assert that he was just a chronic wannabe braggart and hanger-on who was ready and willing to impose himself on most anyone he could. This is also short-sighted. All we really know is that he was conversant and friendly with people who were involved in and at the top of the heap when it came to highly classified work. It is therefore of no surprise that he would become acquainted with Jack Parsons, the man who knew more about rocket propulsion than anyone else.

One of the most legendary estates in this area was Mulholland Farm, the home of Erroll Flynn. About fifteen miles to the west was a genuine Nazi stronghold known as Murphy's Ranch. It was operated by the Silver Legion of America of "Silver Shirts", a white supremacist group and was meant to serve as a German headquarters when and if they won the war. Although the Silver Shirts were arrested and evicted the day after the Pearl Harbor bombings, there are reports that it remained operational, at least to some degree, until 1945. The rationale for such is that it is better to have your enemy operating in full sight where he can be monitored to some degree.

There are those who believe that the German Minister of Propaganda, Josef Goebbels, survived the bunker, came to America and worked on the propaganda machine that operated out of Lookout Mountain and became Project Mockingbird. While it did hit its stride two years after the supposed death of Goebbels, it operated in the same vein. The military recognized Goebbels as a very effective propaganda minister, just as they view the Nazi rocket experts to be superior scientists. They also used crack intelligence officer Reinhard Gehlen to establish the Central Intelligence Agency.

Although it was years after Jack Parsons put his paw-print on Lookout Mountain, the Nazis had also put a paw-print of their own. While Hubbard's own involvement with this area seems minimal, he was not absent from the scene or the circumstances surrounding Lookout Mountain. This not only applies to his military career but also with regard to his magical association.

*FIRST MOTION PICTURE UNIT AT **8935** WONDERLAND AVENUE*

```
                    U. S. NAVAL POWDER FACTORY
                       INDIAN HEAD, MD.

                       25 March 1941


To Whom It May Concern:

              This is to certify that I have personally
known Mr. L. Ron Hubbard for the past twenty years. I
have been associated with him as a boy growing up and
observed him closely.

              I have found him to be of excellent character,
honest, ambitious and always very anxious to improve him-
self to better enable him to become a more useful citizen.
His specialty is the writing of fiction stories and I
understand he has made a very good success in his present
profession.

              He has also done considerable work in the
exploring line and holds two masters licenses in sail and
motor vessels. He recently made a survey of British Columbia
and Alaska. He has also piloted in the harbors of the
Caribbean Sea.

              I do not hesitate to recommend him to anyone
needing the services of a man with his qualifications.


                              W. E. McCain,
                         Commander, (SC) U. S. Navy
```

LETTER OF RECOMMENDATION

The above letter clearly alludes to Hubbard's cozy association with the Navy before his enlistment, but he is also being recommended to the powder factory at Indian Head which was very much concerned with rocket propellants. Although this was before the war, it suggests the plausability that his eventual association with Jack Parsons might indeed have been inspired by the Navy. It was initially the Navy that enlisted Parsons to develop JATOs or "Jet Assisted Take Off" rockets to be used on air craft carriers, a famous test having taken place on August 12, 1943 off the coast of Norfork, Virginia with Jack Parsons in attendance.

— CHAPTER FIFTEEN —

THE ANCHLUSS

> "The same individual that transmitted the various Magick tech to Adolf Hitler as a young man also transmitted them to Dad. And like Dad, Hitler, when he came to power, promptly had his teachers and the occult field in general wiped out."
> — L Ron Hubbard Jr.

On April 26, 1940, a census official by the name of Arthur Harrell rang the bell at 8777 Lookout Mountain, and according to his report, the woman who answered the door identified herself as Sigred Heinlein and stated that she had a husband, Richard Heinlein, and a four-year-old son named Rolf. According to the report, Richard and Sigred were naturalized citizens who had been born in Germany. Richard worked in motion pictures and made $4,200 a year.

At face value, this sober report in the census files suggests that there was a deep German connection to the facility at Lookout Mountain and that Robert Heinlein was in the middle of it, and quite ostensibly, was a German double-agent. Robert and his wife, Leslyn, are on record as having owned the house on Lookout Mountain since 1935.

While this entry has intrigued and puzzled Heinlein's fans, most conclude that it was a prank he played. As Heinlein had a sardonic personality, at least from time to time, I do not believe this is a far-fetched conclusion. If we assume that is the case, there is great irony at work here, although the prank, at least according to the report, was from a woman, not Heinlein himself. The census was taken prior to Operation Paperclip and even before the U.S. had entered the war. Falsely identifying yourself as a German at that point in history was not a very wise thing to do as war drums were already beating. If it was a prank, it is like joking with someone not to go to a particular restaurant because they might choke; and then, upon going to the restaurant, another customer is witnessed to be choking on his food.

As was said earlier, magick is not always precisely on the money. It is, however, frequently in the neighborhood. Although he is primarily regarded as a science fiction writer and scientist, Heinlein was also a magician. How much of a magician we can argue about. His role in such a capacity was extensively chronicled in the fringe publication *Green Egg*, a magazine put out by the Church of All Worlds, an organization which was inspired by an institution of the same name in Heinlein's book *Stranger in a Strange Land*. I originally learned about Heinlein's interest in magick directly from Marjorie Cameron who referred me to the article in *Green Egg*. She said that she did not care for Heinlein and referred to him as a cad. Cameron also stated that what he learned about magick was from Jack (Parsons).

Although Heinlein inspired both the hippie movement of the Sixties and the Church of All Worlds, he was off-putting to hippies and would disappoint them when he would show up to lectures in a business suit. His old friend from the Philadelphia Naval Yard, L. Sprague de Camp, denied that Heinlein ever knew Parsons. This, of course, is ridiculous. Besides that, de Camp also boldly stated that there was no such thing as the Philadelphia Experiment. Heinlein's third and last wife, Virginia, also denied that he had anything to do with magick or that he ever knew Parsons. This is also a ridiculous comment.

Heinlein's own letters show that he was openly polyamorous and that he even shared his second wife with L. Ron Hubbard. To whatever degree he was serious about magick, his book *Stranger in a Strange Land* is constructed entirely around the theme of Aleister Crowley's *The Book of the Law*.

Before and after World War II, there have been distinct but enigmatic associations if not outright collaboration between various factions of Americans and Germans. Charles Lindbergh is probably the most obvious, but there has always been a hidden hand providing liaisons of comfort between the two nations, even when they were open enemies. For example, William Donovan, who headed the Office of Strategic Services or OSS was originally an attorney for I.G. Farben, the German conglomerate that had orchestrated so much intrigue and war mongering, including manufacturing gas used for the gas chambers. Entire books have been written about this.

In the background of these shadowy connections were also common interests, and these included rocketry. According to Heinlein historian Michael Patterson, Jack Parsons caught Heinlein's attention after a November 1939 *LA Times* article appeared about Parsons, Frank Molina and Ed Forman. This article resulted after Parsons had a paper on powder rocket fuels published in *Astronautics*. Both Heinlein and Parsons were members of the American Rocket Society. They are believed to have met at the Los Angeles Science Fantasy Club.

To understand the background of the Germanic influence on rocketry and how it influenced Jack Parsons and his eventual association with Heinlein, it is important to mention that Jack was an avid reader as a young man and was a complete fan of the pulps and the science fiction of Jules Verne. A somewhat detailed description of how to mix powders to build a rocket is included in Verne's book *From the Earth to the Moon* and this not only inspired Jack to build his first rockets, it offered hard data on how to proceed.*

---

*Jules Verne's information on rocketry was a direct result of him moving to Transylvania as a result of marrying a woman from that locale. This time period in his life inspired his famous novel, *Castle in the Carpathians*. What is less known about Verne's inspiration for his writing on the practical applications of rocket powder is that there is a rather sizable and mostly hidden tradition of rocketry in Transylvania that goes back at least six *(continued on next page)*

Facilitated by Jack's grandfather covering the costs, Parsons used to telephone Werner von Braun in Germany and have long talks with him about rocketry. Both parties were truly inspired by each other's work. These connections began in the 1930s, well before World War II began. After von Braun was repatriated to the United States and was heralded for his work with the space program, he gave due credit to Jack Parsons for enabling the technology of solid fuel rockets to take shape. When it came to rocket technology, the connection between Germany and America was quite strong, but as was said previously, it was not the only connection between the two countries.

If we consider the quotation from Nibs at the beginning of this chapter, it suggests that his father was inspired by the same source as Hitler. The magick Nibs is alluding to is something referred to as *Vril*, a word and concept that was popularized in Lord Bulwer-Lytton's *The Coming Race*. There are so many misconceptions about *Vril*, what it means, where the term originated and how it parlayed into the Nazi mystique, that it is understandable that Nibs or anyone else who has superficially studied the subject will come up with erroneous conclusions. While it is true that a parchment with the word or letters *VRIHL* was discovered on Crowley's body when he died and that Bulwer-Lytton studied under Alphonse Constant, a.k.a. Eliphas Levi (whom Crowley alleged was his earlier incarnation), there is no direct historical evidence of Hubbard being involved in this train of thought or initiation. *Vril* is actually a Tibetan word or concept that, like the concept of the Chinese term *chi*, the Indian word *prana* or Wilhelm Reich's *orgone*, represents life force. It can be dressed up with lots of different systems and regalia. Bulwer-Lytton, who garnished considerable praise as an author in his day, described *vril* as representing "mesmerism, electro-biology, or odic forces, etc.", further stating that the concept can be applied scientifically through vril conductors and can exercise influence over minds, animals and vegetables.

Between his own identification with Crowley's work and the Excalibur incident, Hubbard had quite enough horse power of his own. He did not need to be initiated into the Vril to become an inspirational leader. The association of vril with mesmerism, however, brings up a very relevant point. All religious and cult leaders exude charisma, a term which also applies to political leaders or leaders of any type. Charisma is actually animal magnetism and it represents genuine life force and the power associated with such. The fact that people are motivated into action by charismatic

---

(continued from last page) hundred years, and we are talking about real rockets, not fireworks and the like. In the Transylvanian city of Sibiu, which contains a huge German settlement, there is a five-hundred year old text that describes multi-stage rockets. These pages are currently available in a museum and you can also find a video or two on the subject on the internet. Other manuscripts on the subject have been removed from public inspection. Sibiu is also the hometown of Hermann Oberth, known as the Father of Modern Rocketry who inspired and tutored Werner von Braun before being repatriated to the U.S. as part of Project Paperclip.

people is in and of itself valid testimony to this idea. Just as magnetic force represents moving objects in space so does charisma literally move people to do things. It represents the exercise of power and the ability thereof.

Anton Mesmer, from whom the term *mesmerism* was named, was known for his ability to heal, but he also developed a scandalous reputation as his magnetic healings often penetrated the private zones of his patients, most of whom were women. While it is obvious that such a skill can be misused, it should be pointed out that charisma and magnetic sexuality go hand-in-hand. This has to do with the fact that sexual energy is the energy of creation, and when one is creating change in a particular condition, one is indulging in the energy of creation. They run parallel to each other.

It should also be pointed out that Hubbard, who was known to be a skilled hypnotist, is often accused of having hypnotized his flock and that Scientology is nothing but a hypnotic suggestion. If you study the subject of hypnosis, you will discover that it originated as a branch of Mesmerism. It is basically about being able to harness and control life force, and it is generally applied to the prospect of being able to influence individuals. This influence can reach across many levels.

When it comes to the Nazis, the concept of the vril converged on them from at least three different sources. First was their association with and what some might call an infiltration from Tibet. Second was the Vril Society itself which was instigated by Karl Haushofer who was also initiated at a Tibetan lama himself. This involved female mediums who channeled technical details of how to build flying craft. Third was *The Coming Race* which was really nothing more than a popular book presented as fiction. It was neither crucial nor pivotal to what was really going on with the Nazi flying craft.

Perhaps the most relevant point about the vril is that it not only represents power, but represents applied power, and by that, it is meant that this power is extended into technology and the like. If you study the legends of Atlantis, you will read that their air ships were powered by vril. This has everything to do with harnessing energy. At the same time, it also applies to being able to mobilize a civilization or group of people. The prospect of raw life force powering a flying craft or any kind of technological device will sound corny to many people, and I would agree that many descriptions of the past have indeed been corny in the extreme, however, this is the very essence of where artificial intelligence leads the human race. The more electronic circuits are conducive to human thinking, the more powerful and easy will be the ability to mobilize technological devices.

Tibet is the oldest culture on the planet. Its deepest and truest heritage is not open to inspection nor is it represented in it titulary rulers with whom people commonly identify with. There is evidence that they guided the Germans with their early television technology. In this guise, however, it is not in the context of sending an engineer from SONY or G.E. to tell them how to wire their circuits. It is more like influence and guidance from another plane of existence. In this context, at least with regard to technology, it is as if the Germans were taking on the role of familiars (in the context of a magician using a cat or other animal to act as their familiar) with the Tibetan lamas serving as the magician and calling the shots.

All of this is vague and can be frustrating to the "serious researcher". Magick, however, is vague and obfuscated by its very nature. What is most authentic about the Tibetan-Nazi paradigm is that what started as a mere legend has grown longer and firmer teeth as the decades roll along. One of the first persons to mention the concept of the vril in the United States was Willy Ley, a man who stands out in both German and American rocketry. He also appears in L. Ron Hubbard's life in a conspicuous manner.

As was the case with Werner von Braun, Willy Ley's interest in rocketry was ignited when he read Hermann Obert's book *Die Rakete zu den Planetenräumen* (*The Rocket into Interplanetary Space*). Ley's greatest contribution was his ability to break down Obert's technically presented information and create a popular forum by writing articles for a broader audience. This contributed to a fad of rocket adulation in Germany. During this period he became a colleague of both Obert and von Braun. He also corresponded with Jack Parsons. Popular history tells a story of Ley being repulsed by Hitler's regime and has him escaping to America via England as early as 1935. Upon entering the United States, he is almost immediately ingratiated into both the science fiction and scientific communities.

Most of Ley's work demonstrates him to be a government propaganda tool who speaks under the guise of a reasonable scientist who is only interested in hard cold facts. Accordingly, Ley ripped the Nazis as being infatuated with pseudo-science, asserting that the Nazis got their idea for the vril from Lord Bulwer-Lytton's *The Coming Race*. Despite the German's clear superiority when it came to different fields of science, there was a preoccupation with portraying them as fools who believed in pseudoscience. Much of the so-called pseudoscience is deliberately misconstrued information that twists the underlying narrative of the core science overlays it with ludicrous presentations of ideas like "fire and ice" and the like.

In 1952, shortly after the country was in an uproar over the flying saucers that had buzzed the White House, Willy Ley appeared on national television on *Longines Chronoscope*, acting as an expert on UFOs, and claiming that all but 15% conform to nature or other reasonable explanations. Not once does he mention or bring up the proposition of the actual vril craft that the Nazis had built during the Thirties and into the Forties. The fact that he continued his close relationship with von Braun and Obert after they had been repatriated to the United States suggests that Ley was deliberately misinforming the public and that his original disaffection with the Nazis was a ploy for propaganda purposes and was done to ingratiate himself into American rocketry and the powers surrounding it.

Where Hubbard fits into the picture is at a heralded meeting that took place at Johnny Arwine's apartment in New York that included Ley, Heinlein, and John W. Campbell. While much has been made of this meeting, even to the point of suggesting it was a top secret briefing by Ley, it only shows that Hubbard swam in certain circles that involved people who were involved in highly classified work. Ley and Heinlein were involved in a rocket club going back to the Thirties.

Johnny Arwine was a classmate of Heinlein's at the Naval Academy and was a professional writer as well. Heinlein made an interesting reference to Hubbard in a letter to Arwine dated 28 January 1945, a year before the Babalon Working. Reminding him of the "red-headed boy" at their 1940 dinner party, Heinlein stated that Hubbard was now headed his way as an MG (Military Government) officer and further stated that Hubbard was "our kind of people in every possible way...and his evaluations match ours."

Although Heinlein is specifically vague on this last point, he once again alludes to this peculiar status in a letter to another Annapolis classmate named Cal Laning in a November 1945 letter. Asking Laning to reconsider his negative opinion formed earlier of Arwine, Heinlein tells him to trust Arwine, stating that Arwine's "evaluations are almost identical" to his, although Arwine didn't occupy Laning's "unencroachably senior position in the circle of our trusted and intimate friends."

It is not known whether Hubbard was meant to be included in this circle of trust and intimate friends, but it is certainly possible. What is more interesting is that, in the same letter, Heinlein mentions that his house guests included L. Ron Hubbard and Henry Sang, his boss at the Philadelphia Naval Yard. Who Henry Sang is, I have not been able to determine, but if he was Heinlein's boss in Philadelphia, his security clearance would have to have been out the roof. Hubbard would move in with Parsons within a month.

Heinlein further states Arwine and Hubbard had "whipped up a plan to organize all the scientists for the purpose of channelizing some of the rational thought for this crisis" and had "organized Cal Tech already". This, of course, was after the initial atomic tests and Japan had been bombed. Additionally, he mentions his intentions to stay in California and write articles that "propagandize for what I believe is sanity, to wit, the creation of a world state to insure peace in the atomic age". At the very least, Hubbard, Arwine and Heinlein were in cahoots on the subject of neutralizing the atomic madness pervading the world at that time. Hubbard made very specific reference to Johnny Arwine and their efforts to calm down the atomic scientists at Cal Tech. After this, Hubbard turned his attention on Jack Parsons. Whether or not he was sent in as an agent, courtesy of Robert Heinlein, is debatable. All we know is that he was focusing on a man who was already under staunch security surveillance from the Government. If Hubbard was not a spy, he was certainly hovering around the most sensitive security domains of the Federal Government. While I have brought the German rocket connection to view and have previous alluded to the intelligence, scientific, and propaganda connections to the Americans, there is another major connection between the two nations and that is magick.

Aleister Crowley was initiated into the OTO or Ordo Templi Orientis, which originated out of Germany, by Theodore Reuss, a native German who was kicked out of England for being a Prussian spy. Crowley's successor as Outer Head of the OTO was another German, Karl Germer, a military intelligence officer who was put in a concentration camp for being associated with Crowley. In what was rather unusual, he was released from that concentration camp and came to America where he was the OTO's representative. Jack Parsons, when he was acting master of the Agape Lodge in Pasadena, answered directly to Karl Germer.

While the German connection is definitely present and Hubbard was in its orbit, they are not as connected as Nibs suggests. Nibs is a complex character and his history as a witness is not reliable. In return for money, he would participate in a article slamming his father. Afterwards, he would be approached by the Guardian's Office from Scientology and sign a document recanting his statements but also receiving money for it. He played both sides against the middle. Both in his diatribes to the press and in his personal letters to his father, Nibs always had a certain regard for the technical procedures of Scientology. He used it to his own advantage.

If we trace back the common denominator with regard to the German connection, we can revisit the fact that Ian Fleming, Aleister Crowley, and Karl Haushofer were all in Munich at the same time. It is, after all, Ian Fleming that started me on this entire thread. Besides an interest in Germany, Fleming and Crowley did share a common interest and that was the man who originally used the designation 007: John Dee, the court astrologer of Queen Elizabeth I. Dee's work was also a focus of Jack Parsons and L. Ron Hubbard when they engaged in the Babalon Working.

While these various factors are all interesting in their own right, they represent the shadows of L. Ron Hubbard's past. These particular shadows are only one aspect of the occult matrix underlying Scientology. We will now examine what sprouted from these early adventures of L. Ron Hubbard.

THE ABYSS

"There are two aspects of individual harmony: the harmony between body and soul, and the harmony between individuals. All the tragedy in the world, in the individual and in the multitude, comes from lack of harmony. And harmony is best given by producing harmony in one's own life."
— Hazrat Inayat Khan, Sufi Mystic

In the next few chapters, I will give you a blueprint with regard to how Hubbard's system worked and also why it was successful to the degree that it was. In addition to that, I will also demonstrate how this system was an extension of his own mind. Before I isolate those factors precisely, however, I will describe the introductory aspects to Scientology's "Bridge to Freedom" which fit precisely into Hubbard's schematic of how the human mind functions.

The lower levels of Scientology are the beginning of what L. Ron Hubbard referred to as "The Bridge", a reference to the "Bridge to Freedom," a term which, more or less, originated from a quotation in his popular book *Dianetics: The Modern Science of Mental Health*. At the end of that book, Hubbard had offered his techniques which, ostensibly, were designed to help Mankind reach a higher plateau of existence. They were, however, far from perfect by his own admission, and he implored others to "help build a better bridge".

The idea of such a bridge, however, is neither unique or unprecedented in the annals of Mankind. While Hubbard would readily and easily agree with such a statement, he would have clearly told you at the time he created his bridge to freedom that no one else was facilitating such a bridge. Before I go into the discussion of the beginning stages of the Scientology bridge, it is important to give some historical context that is little known and also jibes with some of the other themes in this book.

Over a decade after imploring others to build a better bridge, Hubbard himself identified the latest version of his bridge as a metaphor for crossing what occultists refer to as crossing the Abyss. Crowley did not think it was easy to describe the Abyss; but according to him, it could be explained as the gap or chasm between the phenomenal world (that which is perceived by the senses) and that nuomenal world (that which is perceived by the mind or considered purely mental or intellectual). Crowley described everything in this realm as being insane delusions and this was because elements of the Abyss were not grounded to (spiritual) reality or any laws or principles. Hubbard was simpler and more expository in his explanation, stating that crossing the Abyss was representative of man moving to a higher or more beneficial state of existence than he had been experiencing. While Crowley's techniques were more wild and open-ended, Hubbard's were, by comparison, more refined and user-friendly. The whole benefit of such an endeavor would be, ideally, to achieve a harmony between your own existential mental state and that of the physical universe (as you perceive it).

As I already stated, however, the idea of such a metaphorical bridge existed long before Crowley or Hubbard. One of the earliest and most obscure references to such a metaphor was adopted by the Jain religion. Although it is a religion that is overlooked, its roots go back well before Hinduism and the Vedas. Most relevant to the subject at hand, *Jain* is a word derived from the Sanskrit *jina* which means victor but particularly in the context of "crossing over life's stream of rebirths through an ethical and spiritual life". However you want to word it and what system you want to apply, this is the fundamental predicament of a spirit finding reconciliation with the universe around him.

With regard to the concept of the Abyss, the etymology of that word is derived from the concept of chaos. Chaos, of course, is the antithesis of harmony. The Christian idea of hell evolved out of earlier paradigms associated with chaos or the Abyss.

When it comes to the extensive fallout surrounding Scientology, there is no better comparison than the idea of purgatory, and this applies whether it be in the Christian sense or otherwise. Purgatory is a region of consciousness where one is subject to pain, suffering or even torture until one's sins can be purged. Only then is one's soul cleansed whereupon one achieves the harmony of heaven. Such a scenario requires an assessment or hearing of one's misdeeds so that one can do the work that is required to cleanse one's soul. The process of Scientology auditing, as laid out by Hubbard, was designed to make such an assessment; hence the term *audit* as defined earlier. His procedures, however, were not concerned with admitting one to the heavenly realm but rather to relieving the suffering that an individual might be suffering from in present time. The idea of Life Repair, as it was called, is not much different from the concept of purgatory save that the latter was a more absolute concept. All of the suffering and howling you hear from people who have found themselves on the wrong side of life that are attributable to their experiences in Scientology are instances that require relief. They are caught up in the cycle of consequences and punishment. All such people are in need of, if not already engaged in, repairing their life.

While the main approach to attracting people to Scientology was by introducing to them how to repair their life, the initial approach was typically a surface approach, primarily trying to make the prospect reach an understanding of how Scientology procedures could help them. Serious life repair almost always took place within the confines of a formal series of auditing sessions, the entirety of which was dedicated to discovering and addressing areas in the person's life where they were suffering. These areas were referred to as rudiments which are foundational components of happy living.

A rudiment is essentially a requisite to what might be considered a normal or regular flow of life or consciousness. Rudiments include having proper food and rest as well as not being under the influence of drugs, alcohol or other foreign or toxic substances. Other rudiments include not having upsets, problems or being preoccupied with guilt stemming from discreditable acts that one feels remorse about. All of these rudiments have to be addressed before one can get at the core issue concerning a patient or preclear, let alone the more core issues of life itself (as was discussed in previous chapters). In order that you better understand, I will give some specific examples of how and why such rudiments might be necessary.

If one is preoccupied with upsets, such as from a person who is hounding them in their house or work environment, they are not going to be in much of a mood to look inward. Such will fixate their attention. One could also be upset about the way life is treating them. Such upsets could have to do with the opposite sex, not getting promoted at work or most anything else you can imagine. The basic resolution for such is to first isolate the upset and then get the person to talk about it. This would often resolve the issue. If not, one would look for earlier similar upsets and so on. If required, one could go far deeper. In fact, the template for repairing a life as per Scientology procedures would be to do a rather in depth interview with the person and get them to discuss their life. This is like the fishing example I gave at the beginning of the book. One will see all sorts of emotional responses in the expressions of the person, almost all of which will reveal themselves quite articulately on the Scientology e-meter. One goes after the biggest or most reactive fish and addresses that issue. Above and beyond regular communication, there were all sorts of prepared lists and techniques to address the nature of the upset and the emotional buttons or triggers associated with the upset at hand. This would enable the person to see his situation from many different angles, and it would usually result in a lot of happy laughter and the dissolution of the upset as a pressing issue. This type of auditing was a lot of fun to administer because you would really be helping the individual.

In the case of a problem, we are talking about something that is really weighing on the mind of an individual. It might be that they are past due on their rent. Perhaps it is an issue that they have to take up with a colleague, and they do not know how to approach it. A problem has more to do with not understanding how to solve it than it does being upset about it. The approach for such was first and foremost the same as dealing with an upset: communicating about it. Once again, if this did not solve the situation, one would seek out an earlier similar problem. There were also other approaches, but problems are generally resolvable with just ordinary communication.

The realm of guilt is perhaps the most tricky, at least for two reasons. First, the person might not have an easy time fessing up to one's misdeeds. He or she might be embarrassed or cautious about revealing such to another. Second, the person might not actually be aware that certain actions they are doing are actually affecting themselves or others in a negative manner. To give you an example of how this applies, imagine someone involved in a relationship where they are using their partner for either sex or money and are not being honest; or, perhaps a person is stealing from their employer. Such circumstances do not bode well for the psychology of the individual as he or she cannot feel too good about themselves. This will undermine any serious enhancement they might hope to achieve, especially if you consider the prospect of crossing the Abyss. Such issues also resolve with communication, but it generally requires isolating the exact time, place, form and event as well as the various parties who might know about it or almost found out about it. In most cases, coming clean does not require one to go to the person who was wronged and "fess up", unless it is a really heinous act. It might be best to surreptitiously return the merchandise or equipment you stole from your employer and then recommending an inventory system to him in order that such might not happen. Correcting such a behavior pattern could even result in a promotion.

While it is not quite fair to say that such rudiments represent the entirety of psychological dysfunction in individuals, they certainly represent the bulk of people's issues. In Scientology, addressing these rudiments was a prerequisite to any normal auditing session, but there is a much grander aspect to them. Before we discuss that, however, it is very important to point out that former Scientologists who are disgruntled over their experiences would not argue with me that these rudiments as described above are a hallmark of Scientology procedures. In fact, such disgruntled people are indeed suffering from that very same phenomena: upsets, problems or discreditable acts (such also applies if others are creating such acts against you). The fact that their problems have not been resolved with Scientology techniques is not a fault of the techniques but rather an outside force that negates such resolution.

The grander aspect of the rudiments I referred to above has to do with the core aspects of human experience as it relates to the structural function of the mind. One can clear up the rudiments that are impinging upon a person with regard to his ordinary everyday experience, but these events are really only the tip of the iceberg with regard to what is buried deep in the mind; and further, what these daily upsets are resting upon. If you were to probe into the average human mind and evaluate all of the difficult experiences of an individual, you would find it literally loaded with submerged upsets, problems and discreditable acts. Such also applies to people in their environment who are experiencing the same. All of these issues concerning rudiments can trigger back and forth between individuals and can apply to entire groups. For example, if you are surrounded by or were surrounded by people committing crimes, it can register considerable emotional trauma and charge in an individual. So, the grander scheme of approaching the mind in Scientology was to address such rudiments collectively, each general area at a time. This was the foundation of the Gradation and Awareness Chart, Hubbard's scheme for enabling people to cross the Abyss. I will elaborate further to make it clear.

After one completed Life Repair as per above, an entire level or set of auditing procedures was designed to enhance a person's ability to recall experiences from his past. These were fairly extensive and were designed to make his experiences more available. This is like making it easier to get the fish to bite. This level was referred to as ARC Straightwire,* the name being based upon the idea of creating a "straightwire" to one's past through one's addressing the person's feelings of affinity, reality and communication as applied to different images across the stream of time.

The next level was dedicated to communication. In regular psychotherapy, communication is the general approach utilized to help an individual. Scientology is no different except that its techniques are far more disciplined. Communication is broken down into its fundamental components. This level was referred to as Grade Zero. As you know, society is littered with people who do not communicate properly or say what is on their mind. This ranges from the strong silent type to the embittered and resentful person. Various processes were devised, not only for "running out" bad experiences with such people but to rehabilitate one's own enthusiasm for communicating with the environment. Once one had attained Grade 0, one was deemed not only to be able to communicate with the environment but to be able to talk intimately to the auditor about one's problems. If you cannot talk about an issue, you are not going to be able to address the issue, let alone deal with it. On a grander scale, communicating with one's environment can run very deep. An idolized character like Jesus was not only known for his ability to communicate with Rabbinic scholars at a level which superceded their intellectual scholarship, but for his rapport with animals and children. Communication reaches far beyond the verbal aspects and applies to your own ability to perceive the subtle factors of living.

---

* ARC or A-R-C is an acronym for the words *Affinity, Reality,* and *Communication*. Together, these three words define the component parts of the phenomenon known as understanding. A-R-C was explained in metaphorical terms as the "A-R-C Triangle" because each component works in tandem with the others. If one increases the affinity for a person, the reality and communication will also increase. Likewise, if another point is addressed, the other two will increase. This triangle was used across the board in Scientology to reach an understanding about anything that was perplexing.

When Grade 0 was completed, one moved on to Grade I which addressed problems. A problem is defined as an "intention-counter-intention". Again, various procedures were devised to deal with anything and everything that could be considered a mental problem. All problems eventually resolve under the microscope of communication. This is what scientific analysis and study are all about. When one communicates and addresses the constituent elements of mental problems and debris, they respond just like problems in chemistry, physics and technology: perplexing situations generally find a way of resolving themselves. There were many processes directed at solving problems, attacking the very nature of problems from a multitude of angles or approaches. Perhaps you will get the idea of how malleable problems are if you get the idea of a process (a repetitive question or series of such questions) where you repetitively ask a person to "Create an unsolvable problem". Such a question, if asked under the right circumstances, gets a person to participate in creating problems on an imaginary level that will, if done creatively and long enough, will get the person to get in touch with and see the automatic mental machinery he has been engaging in to create problems in his own life. One can address it from another approach by having them "create solutions" or repetitively creating different solutions to an unsolvable problem.

Beyond problems is Grade II which deals with discreditable acts. This not only includes your own discreditable acts but those done to you and those done by others to others. So much of the Christian faith, particularly Catholicism, is based utterly upon the phenomenon of sin and salvation. This grade refers to the entire phenomena of human experience that revolves around the subject of guilt. Although there is no official etymology for the word guilt, it is phonetically expressive of gold as in the Hebrew word *gelt* which refers to gold coins. As guilt has everything to do with owing or paying a debt, the concept of gold fits in very nicely. The entire proposition of guilt includes the idea that you have to compensate for the bad acts that you have committed. One of the trickiest aspects of guilt is not so much the offense one has committed but rather the emotions associated with it. For example, if you have done something wrong or at least think you have, you can create great havoc for yourself by feeling more guilty than you should. Environments are sometimes prone to people who are ready to lay guilt on to you for the slightest offense or perhaps even if you have done nothing at all. Catholic schools, particularly of the past, were notorious for treating the students as sinners. Guilt is often a sucker's game, but this is not an excuse to overlook your own misgivings. It is, however, wise to look with a jaundice eye at anyone who is ready to scold you simply because they are predisposed to do such. It is also wise to consider the fact that there are many people who prey on people's guilt. You see this on television commercials that will plead for you to help with certain causes while, at the same time, the bulk of the money taken in by such pleas does not serve the cause purported. When such factors were completely addressed in an individual, all emotional charge would dissipate and the preclear would be a "Relief Release". I must say, however, that despite the upside potential of what I have laid out here, I seldom saw people in Scientology who were really at peace with this grade. This was not the fault of the materials but rather people's inability to unstick themselves from this pervasive phenomena.

The next level, Grade III, deals with upsets of the past, the techniques used probing more deeply into upsets than those previously described. The procedures are built around the foundation of the A-R-C Triangle (see footnote on page 151). The other side of the A-R-C Triangle was the A-R-C Break which refers to a sudden sundering or cutting of any one of the points of the A-R-C Triangle. For example, when someone you care about or admire unexpectedly tells you to get lost, it upsets you and dissipates all three points of the triangle. You often have no reality on what they are even upset about. Sudden and unexpected changes in one's life also create ARC Breaks. In my personal experience, Grade III was the most fun because it put me in a state of mind where I was able to accept anything that might be presented to me. It increases your confidence and ability in dealing with unpredictable factors. Probing deeply into the human mind and its potential or capacity to adapt to change, Grade III was referred to as a "Freedom Release" because you were free from the upsets of the past and ready to do new things.

Whether or not you agree with the workability of the system I have described thus far, it is hard to disagree that it lays out a very idealistic template for fixing one's life. In fact, you might be wondering why everyone does not just study and follow these procedures and become inordinately happy or at least considerably more so. If only it were so!

It should be pointed out that these procedures, as well as all of the procedures in Dianetics and Scientology, are nothing different than a playbook such as is used in professional or college football. A football playbook will contain literally hundreds of plays, all of which require a somewhat precise if not complicated understanding as well as considerable drilling and practice. In actual game conditions, however, a football team only uses a handful or up to a dozen of plays in a game, perhaps two or three dozen at the most. Most of the plays are not used at all. Whether or not a team is successful depends not only upon the understanding and execution of the play at hand but also that it is used at the right time and place. Having a playbook does not guarantee you a victory. At the very best, the procedures of Scientology are nothing more than a metaphorical playbook. Just as a football team has an opponent who also has a similar playbook, so does the environment present challenges when it comes to attempting to implement such an idealistic template. Any scientific experiment requires controlled conditions. To try and implement such procedures requires considerable control. If the control administered works out, everyone is happy. If the justification for such control exceeds the purpose of what it was originally intended for, you have a justification for control which has the potential to be dangerous, ludicrous, and even downright insane. If you are trying to relieve the insanity of a group of people, let alone the entire human race, it should not surprise anyone that you are going to encounter considerable opposition. Such negative attitudes and potentials lead us right into Grade IV.

Grade IV enters new territory that is not normally considered to be part of the ordinary rudiments. It is structured around the concept of making oneself right and others wrong, such being based upon old inapplicable ideas or experiences that are irrelevant to the time and place of the current environment. One acquires experiences in life where one suffers defeat or humility. The mind seeks to compensate for such a defeat by adopting an identity of behavior that will protect the organism. You could say that this represents a very deeply imbedded defense mechanism. In Scientology technicalese, such a mechanism is defined as a "Service Facsimile".

In Scientology, a facsimile refers to a mental image picture of an incident on the time track. A service facsimile is called such because the preclear uses this particular facsimile to "service" him in reactive efforts to survive. For example, a kid is drowning while his dad is on the beach and does not see his own child's desperate pleas for help. A female swimmer sees the kid and performs a rescue. The child, who is partly unconscious, made a picture of the entire scene in his head and remembers silently cursing his father for not seeing his desperate pleas for help. Forever after, the kid reactively deems that fathers are no good and subconsciously fosters poor relations with anyone who is deemed to be a father figure. In this respect, the person is using an incident to "serve" him by "protecting" him from fathers. It has no rationale basis, but these reactions are common place in the everyday world. Service facsimiles are most pronounced when people make other people wrong. Grade IV addressed not only your own service facsimiles which you use to make others wrong but also those which others use to make you wrong. It addressed others making others wrong, too. Political arguments often get tied up in meaningless arguments of the respective parties based upon service facsimiles that have no rationale basis.

Service facsimiles also include people who become psychologically addicted to illnesses or other conditions as an excuse not to work. Such people cultivate a victim mentality so that they can get sympathy. Sometimes these people will make the environment wrong as opposed to an individual or a set of individuals in it. Some people even precipitate accidents so that they do not have to work for the rest of their lives. This is the work of a reactive service facsimile which actually serves to limit the potential reach of the person using it.

A service facsimile is not considered to be an ordinary rudiment because it is deeply imbedded within the psychological structure of the individual, and it is not readily accessible to his waking consciousness. It is therefore not addressed as such until one gets to this particular level. The so called "fishing" on this level requires considerably more precision by the counselor than the earlier levels. And if you do not come up with a very big fish on this level, you have skimped it and not really accomplished anything. The upside to this level, if it is done properly, is that it releases you from the habitual thinking patterns of the past. Such mechanisms are extremely limiting to your thinking. For example, if one had a service facsimile run on them from their parents, teachers or peers telling them they would never amount to anything, they might find themselves with a predisposition to only take menial jobs. Upon discovering the unconscious mechanisms that were at work in their lives, such a person could experience a resurgence of self-confidence and proceed to live their life in an entirely new direction.

Many people are content to go along in life and are pretty much happy to try and maintain the status quo. If one, however, has the desire, means and persistence to do some "deep sea fishing", they might view a totally new horizon that might lead in an infinitude of new directions. Everything becomes new, fun and exciting and is the opposite of trite and hackneyed.

The beauty of Grade IV is that it gives you the ability to do new things. When one gets rid of such negative and disabling attitudes, one discovers that he or she can indeed do new things. All of a sudden, the secretary who could not type becomes a lightning fast typist. The ball player who could not hit a curve ball can now master it. The soprano who could not hit the high notes just right can now figure out the exact mechanics of what it takes to do just that. The man who is all thumbs around the house can now do minor construction projects. This grade is like a new lease on life.

What I have summarized in this chapter is an overview of the lower levels of Scientology's metaphorical Bridge to Freedom. While I have put a positive spin on these and do not mean to minimize their potential impact upon an individual, their design was in the context of a launching pad. The idea of a Bridge to Freedom was to enable one to take off like a rocket, the analogy of which is particularly significant if you consider the greatest technological contribution of Jack Parsons: the solid fuel rocket.

Before Jack Parsons came along, rocket technology was based upon liquid fuels which burned rapidly, fostering unstable conditions that resulted in many failures and explosions. After watching roofers tar a roof, Parsons realized that he could create a long slow burn by using a solid fuel like tar. Accordingly, he coated the inside of the rocket with fuel tar in the shape of a pentagram, and this is what enabled Mankind to reach the moon. Based upon what you have read so far, I hope you have some sympathy for the idea of how Hubbard persuaded people that they could "shoot the moon" and metaphorically or quite literally go into orbit. The only hope to do so, however, is if one's progress through these levels is like a long slow burn of a solid fuel rocket. Without a strong foundation of truly knowing yourself, you can expect an aborted rocket launch. If you look at all of the fallout from Scientology, every single instance had unresolved issues no different than what might fit into one of the categories of the foregoing examples of rudiments. The basics of life are the basics of life. It does not matter whether you are categorizing them with Scientology or some other system.

Many ardent critics of Scientology have conceded that the lower levels as described herein are positive. It is the upper side of the bridge that they are highly critical about as well as Hubbard's motives for creating it. Before I address that area, however, I am going to address another essential part of the lower bridge that was, in fact, the basis for the idea of a bridge: Dianetics.

DIANETICS AND KARMA

"The true sign of intelligence is not knowledge but imagination."
— Albert Einstein

The subject of Dianetics is based entirely upon the precept that it is possible to alleviate mental trauma and psychosomatic ills by addressing the original experience of such and reliving or re-experiencing what was first encountered until the affliction is vanquished. I do not think it can be stated more simply. The word *Dianetics* originally was stated by Hubbard to mean "through the mind", however, Church publications later changed it to mean "through the spirit" in order to appease potential Government scrutiny and associate such therapy as religious counseling as opposed to "psychological" counseling.

Although Hubbard created his own nomenclature for the subject and frequently changed and updated the techniques of Dianetics, the essential ingredient of what was taking place was that it was designed to put a person in a mental frame of reference whereby he could re-experience and review his past and come to some sort of physical, energetic or mental reconciliation with his traumatic experiences.

Since it first appeared in the world, Dianetics has been virulently attacked as being unscientific and of having no real value to therapists. Many ex-Scientologists, of whom most if not all have been mistreated, are quick to attack Dianetics as unscientific. This deserves some practical sense commentary, particularly if you are to understand L. Ron Hubbard and the paradigm he worked in.

It is challenging if not impossible to confine the humanities to a quantitative analysis of any kind. The fields of psychology and psychiatry, which have been around far longer than Dianetics, do not pretend to have achieved a complete scientific understanding of Mankind. As I stated earlier, Hubbard used a rule of thumb in his assessments, all of it based upon observation and experience. The fields of psychology and psychiatry use their own rules of thumb, once again based upon observation and experience. What is particularly relevant about the Dianetics movement was that it was wildly popular and driven by public interest. Further, it put practical therapy in the hands of the individual without having to go through an authority or "priesthood". Whatever progress the aforementioned fields might have asserted, none of their endeavors caught the public's imagination like Dianetics did. Exciting the imagination of people is, of course, a very different prospect than delivering a workable therapy. In many respects, however, this was the first time many people were led to believe there might be a way to resolve their own mental issues. On the positive side, there were also many of us who used Dianetics to our own advantage and were more than happy with the benefits. Dianetics, like any subject, is nothing more than a body of data than one reads and applies intelligently or otherwise. As it deals with the inner essence of the mind, the entire subject can be viewed as a double-edged sword. One of the principles of Dianetics included the proposition that a crazy or aberrated mind would actively seek to avoid the resolution of its own aberrated condition. When you are dealing with the proposition that a large amount of people have experienced failure with the subject, it should be recognized that the principles of Dianetics would suggest that such a situation would be a victory for the aberrated minds of the people involved as opposed to the therapy itself.

Perhaps the most ironic data to turn up on the subject of Dianetics concerns a recent study of Post Traumatic Stress Syndrome (PTSD) done by Richard Graya and Frank Bourkea. In what was hailed as a tremendous breakthrough, they were dramatically changing the lives of people through a procedure known as RTM or Reconsolidation of Traumatic Memories whereby wounded vets were being helped at a 90% effective rate towards eliminating debilitating nightmares, flashbacks, and other anxious elements of PTSD. High rates of success were cited in fewer than six sessions. The techniques included reminding the patient of the traumatic event, re-experiencing it and retelling it. This would arouse somatic sensations which would eventually resolve if the mental images of the trauma were replayed. As needed, the "movie" of the trauma would be re-run and re-experienced until it dissipated.

All in all, the procedures are so similar to Dianetics protocol that the only real difference is semantics. For anyone who was familiar with actual Dianetic procedures (without prejudiced indoctrination and free from fixed ideas), it would be a relative breeze to oversee such an operation and to also interact with the results presented, continuing to modify the techniques in conjunction with patient response. Hubbard continuously modified his techniques. The reason for such is that you are dealing with live energy, a commodity that is continuously changing and is prone to be unpredictable from time to time.

There is, however, a major divergence between RTM techniques and what Dianetic therapy eventually embraced. I am referring to the concept of past lives. Originally, Dianetics only dealt with the human organism from the early conception state to the grown up human body. It did not deal with past lives whatsoever. Not too many years after *Dianetics: The Modern Science of Mental Health* was written and had become a mass movement, Hubbard alienated a significant part of his audience when he reported that people were not really getting rid of all their psychosomatic ills unless they addressed the issue of past lives. It later became a staple of Dianetic therapy as it was found that people did not recover without addressing trauma associated with previous existences.

Whether or not you or I accept the prospect of past lives, it is a very old idea that did not originate with Hubbard. What is considerably more relevant is that addressing past lives, or any other type of life, gives the opportunity for an individual to address what Jung termed the collective unconscious; and more importantly, the trauma residing in the collective unconscious. In this context, we are extending our view from the individual to the bigger picture of humanity. The human race has experienced many collective traumas, many of them associated with the experience of mass genocide. Such is a pall of darkness that casts a shadow upon the DNA of every living human being. While Hubbard did attempt to address the collective issue, it is too complicated to address at this juncture. In the final analysis, however, what the masses have either experienced or perpetrated with their own interpretation of the tools of Dianetics and Scientology has been viewed by many to have added to the collective trauma as opposed to relieving it.

There are currently thousands of people who either obsess or remain overly preoccupied with their misadventures with Dianetics and Scientology. Much of this consternation is similar if not identical to PTSD. In the context of Dianetics, one would simply address the traumatic experience in therapy and be done with it. However, when you identify, correctly or incorrectly, the therapy with the trauma, you have what amounts to a virtually unsolvable issue, particularly when the actual therapy required is so akin to the therapy you are inclined to despise. This is part of the conundrum Dr. Margaret Singer spoke of when she mentioned that Hubbard's techniques were not only more sophisticated than those used in North Korea and Communist China but that he took the "art of control and persuasion" to an entirely new level. Hubbard once wrote words to the effect that the ultimate charge (emotional trauma) would be to reach for that which cannot be reached or to withdraw from that which cannot be withdrawn from.

To be truthful and objective, it is critical to realize that some people had positive experiences with Dianetics and Scientology and others had negative ones. You can say the same thing about jobs, medicine, sports, and a host of other subjects. To understand the psychology of L. Ron Hubbard, however, it is important to recognize that he created a system whereby one could, under the rights conditions and if they were lucky enough, experience incredible relief with a resurgence of enthusiasm making for a better quality of life. This is what made him an idolized character who was often put on a pedestal. There is, however, more to explain about the procedures of Dianetics, particularly as it was designed to affect the thinking processes of the human mind.

Before one would receive Dianetic auditing, they were interviewed and asked a series of questions about their life but with particular regard to their unwanted attitudes, emotions, sensations and pains. Answers to such were monitored with the Scientology e-meter which would register the most reactive or emotionally charged issues. One would first address the most highly charged issue as such was the most available "fish" that was ready to bite. As one would relieve an individual's burdens, it was not uncommon for them to be able to reach deeper and deeper into their own mind.

If you stop and think about it, what else does the human mind have ailing it other than negative or unwanted attitudes, emotions, sensation and pains? If you think about it a little deeper, you might figure out that there is a virtual fail-safe rhetoric built into the theory of Dianetics. If someone is telling you that it does not work or is highly critical of the subject, they are obviously operating with a very strong attitude or emotion that might well be based upon some sort of emotional pain that is buried. In other words, they are talking out of their own attitudes, emotions, sensations and pains.

Such a critic, however, might aptly and cleverly point out that there is something else indeed that might ail the human mind and that would be illogic. It should be noted that the entire proposition of Dianetics is based upon the observation that the minds of individuals are generally loaded with illogic, the source of it being identified as the reactive mind and all of the unconscious processes associated with such. Even so, it is quite fair to say that the subject of Scientology, particularly when you consider the movement and people involved, is replete with illogical characteristics. This goes back to what I said in the beginning of the book with regard to Scientology and insanity going hand-in-hand. Under the most positive of circumstances, Dianetics and Scientology could address and vanquish particular instances of insanity. Because its stated goal was to conquer the world's insanity, it was taking on the collective insanity of the people of earth and therefore vulnerable to absorb such and become insane in and of itself.

While there is no question that Scientology contains many ideas that are completely out-of-synch with society or the status quo human experience, or perhaps just plain crazy, it is important to point out that within its own core structure, there was an argument or methodology appealing to one's saner instincts. I will give an example.

There are some if not many who believe that Hubbard was using his knowledge of hypnosis to sway thousands of people to become his followers and do his bidding; and further, that the entirety of Scientology was structured so as to induce a mass hypnosis upon the unwitting. At the same time, you could find him very aggressively asserting to anyone who was interested in listening to him that a being actually creates his emotions. A hypnotized person is dependent upon someone else dictating their emotions. If you are creating your own emotions, you are not about to let anyone dictate how you should feel.

People will also vehemently point out that Scientology utilized contradictions so as to induce cognitive dissonance whereby an individual is forced to reconcile two opposite notions in such a manner that renders him analytically dysfunctional. In actuality, Scientology represented a plethora of information. Some information applied to certain situations and other information applied to others. It was a very pick and choose philosophy; and in this respect, afforded itself the potential for containing a saving grace. To the degree that people did not find themselves empowered to the point where they felt they could pick and choose, their power of choice had deteriorated to the point where they viewed themselves as relative slaves to their circumstances. This has everything to do with personal power, an aspect that will be addressed later on in this text.

As it was constructed, Dianetics provided a template whereby one could address every single Pain, Sensation, Emotion or Attitude (collectively referred to by the acronym PSEA) that could be mustered up from their own mind. The techniques provided either a means or potential for eradicating such, providing it was indeed psychosomatic in nature. Once again, this was all about fishing. One would also examine each PSEA from four different perspectives, referred to as flows in Scientology parlance. Flow One = A PSEA caused by another. Flow Two = A PSEA caused by yourself to another. Flow Three = A PSEA caused by others to others. Flow Zero = A PSEA caused by yourself to yourself (self-generated).

I will refer back to the playbook analogy I used in the last chapter. Dianetics offered a playbook for ridding yourself of your mental afflictions. It was, however, no guarantee. In this respect, it is similar to the justice system. While the justice system provides a potential or opportunity for justice, it most certainly does not guarantee it. Such is not only dependent upon the laws themselves but upon the players involved.

So it is that if you had issues about being bullied, pushed around or otherwise impinged upon, you had the opportunity to examine your prior existence and get to the bottom of your own self-generated issues as well as the core cause of issues that had been inflicted by others. In the end, such a self-examination and resolution amounts to a contract you make with yourself. Did you really fully examine your own issues; and further, did you assert to yourself that you had resolved them when you really had not? I have brought this point up because, in my own experience, I could clearly see that engaging in such self-examination actually prevented me from going through the severe trouble that I witnessed others enduring. All of this is akin to the Law of Karma. The Wheel of Life is a series of events based upon cause and effect. When you have an opportunity to change your circumstances to your own advantage, you take it. All of this, however, was complicated by the fact that people were too often disingenuous with regard to what they did. If they were not purposefully disingenuous, they were unfortunate to the degree that they were not predisposed, encouraged or apt enough to fish deeper. It is also possible that fate did not provide them with the proper opportunity to facilitate a positive experience. In the final analysis, however, you have to take responsibility for what you experience in life.

You are probably familiar with the old proverb that it is far more beneficial to teach a man to fish rather than to fish for him. There is also the infrastructure of the boat you are fishing on to consider and that includes the fishing poles and other equipment as well as the mechanical and other components of the boat. As a movement and discipline, Scientologists often found themselves caught up in the infrastructure as well as the various problems associated with it and the efforts to correct them. The real object, however, is for the individual to dig deep into his own mind and address the malfunctions. This, however, requires a safe platform to fish from. The safety and sturdiness of the boat was a big issue in this analogy, and Hubbard found himself dealing with that as well.

Earlier, I alluded to the idea that there are certain outside influences that undermine the prospect of solving the world's problems by repairing its "out-rudiments". Hubbard discovered that such influences could be reduced to evil intentions. After all, if you can make everyone happy by solving their problems, upsets and absolving their discreditable acts, what else is there to deal with? We are also given an example of such in the paradigm presented in the *New Testament* wherein you have the messiah healing people, forgiving their sins, and creating a fervent hope and enthusiasm in the minds of his followers. All of this potential for joy butts up against the infrastructure of the existing status quo which makes it a priority to extinguish the source of this new enthusiasm. The story abounds with evil intentions; and further, so does the history of Christianity itself. Christianity, however, does not have an exclusive market when it comes to either encountering or perpetrating evil intentions. This represents the story of Earth.

In 1972, the same year I boarded the *Apollo*, Hubbard was working on Expanded Dianetics, a further development of Dianetics which utilized more precise diagnostic techniques to dig yet deeper into one's mind and locate evil intentions. The procedures were amongst the most sophisticated and complex auditing techniques he had ever devised. The evil intentions located, by the way, were not necessarily those of the preclears themselves. They were often the intentions of someone else the preclear had encountered and was influenced or overwhelmed by. So, if evil is the impediment to resolving the fundamental problems of life, i.e. rudiments, one might readily conclude that everything had been accounted for. This is wishful thinking indeed.

There were at least two major issues as to why Expanded Dianetics was not implemented to the point where it might affect such. First, it required tremendous resources to implement such as well as to apply the techniques effectively. By resources, I do not mean money as much as providing the platform to audit people on this level. It requires a tremendous amount of time, energy and personnel to learn these techniques, all at the expense of compromising the functional operations of the existing organization. In addition to that, it requires considerable attention to supervise and correct what is being done. To get at the core evil intentions in people, it requires a lot of time invested in digging them out. Some ex-Scientologists, however, are very critical of the prospect of rooting out such evil intentions, claiming it makes the person docile and unwilling to fight back against oppression. This is hardly the case, at least if one does the actual work. If one truly gets at the root cause, and this is up to the individual doing a real inventory of his or her mind, it is then a moot point. He or she will no longer experience it. It is also relevant to point out that a fundamental reason Hubbard developed Expanded Dianetics was due to the staff being generally robotic. In Scientology parlance, a robotic person is someone who must have orders or instructions to operate because he is afraid to take responsibility for his own actions. This mind-set is based upon the evil intentions of himself or others that he was unable to deal with. It is the opposite of initiative.

The second reason that Expanded Dianetics was not implemented was due to the fact that Hubbard had the government of France mustering up evil intentions against him. When Expanded Dianetics was being developed, the *Apollo* was spending much of its time in Morocco, a former French protectorate who was still very much subject to the watchful eye and political influence of various intelligence agencies ranging from the French and the Mossad to the CIA. Soon after those of us aboard the *Apollo* had entertained the princess of Morocco and her entourage as ostentatiously and lavishly as possible, Hubbard left the ship so as to be less visible. Whereas he had been actively involved with the technical departments on a daily basis, his move to a villa near Tangier made his technical participation a non-priority. For the most part, the development and implementation of Expanded Dianetics ceased.

One can be cynical and state that Hubbard's own evil was catching up with him. Even without being cynical, one can still make the argument. The pressure he was under caused him to flee Morocco and hide undercover in New York City in late 1972. When he returned to the *Apollo* in 1973, he suffered a motorcycle accident and was known to be insufferable in his demeanor. When we consider the bigger picture of evil, there is great irony at work here. Many people consider Hubbard to have been a horribly evil character; yet he was intensely preoccupied with addressing and alleviating the fallout that people suffer from as a result of their own encounters with evil intent. As this narrative progresses, you will better understand how intertwined the subject of evil and karma are when we consider the legacy of L. Ron Hubbard.

You have now read a short summary of Dianetics and its derivative, Expanded Dianetics, both of which were designed as pieces of L. Ron Hubbard's bridge across the Abyss. We will next look at the template upon which his idea of a bridge was based.

— CHAPTER EIGHTEEN —

BLUEPRINT TO HEAVEN

"The ideas of economists and political philosophers, both when they are right and when they are wrong, are more powerful than is commonly understood. Indeed, the world is ruled by little else. Practical men, who believe themselves to be quite exempt from any intellectual influences, are usually slaves of some defunct economist."
— John Maynard Keynes

I left the Dianetics and Scientology movement in 1983, well before L. Ron Hubbard passed from this world. It was very clear to me that I had reached the peak of whatever I could achieve in that organization. I was not unhappy at all with myself or what I had accomplished, all of which has to do with the fishing metaphor. I had fished and found whatever I could find and was very happy about it. There is, however, another aspect to discuss and that is the economics of "fishing". It is my hope that this can answer people's questions and dissipate the endless curiosity that surrounds the name of L. Ron Hubbard and his movement. So far, all the vilification has not put an end to that. More relevantly perhaps, I want to give you an idea of how Hubbard's mind worked; in other words, the overall blueprint upon which he operated to excite and sway his thousands of followers.

It is also important to mention that this blueprint applies directly to his method for what was earlier termed "crossing the Abyss". Once again, Crowley referred to the Abyss as the gap or chasm between the phenomenal world (that which is perceived by the senses) and the nuomenal world (that which is perceived by the mind or considered purely mental or intellectual). Crowley described everything in this realm as being insane delusions and this was because elements of the Abyss are not grounded to (spiritual) reality or to any laws or principles. To Hubbard, crossing the Abyss was representative of man moving to a higher or more beneficial state of existence.

Everyone who ever entered the Scientology movement or the Sea Organization itself came into the foray in their own specific way and at a particular and unique moment in time with regard to the goings-on in the organization. No two people had the same experience. There were always changes in the different procedures and curriculums. These variances could result in good fortune or misfortune, all dependent upon countless factors.

When I entered the Sea Organization, I was assigned to study what was a study course called the *Sea Org Member Hat*, an assortment of reading materials and tape recorded lectures, most of them by Hubbard, which were designed to explain the operating principles of the Sea Organization and how to fulfill one's own role in the organization. One of the first issues on this course was designed to give you an overall approach as to how to deal with the new life you had chosen. Titled *The Ultimate Analysis*, it was listed as "confidential", and upon reading it, I felt I was being let in on a big secret. I find it ironic that, many years later, I would discover that many former and old time Sea Org members either did not remember this issue nor was it part of their study materials. I found it very helpful.

Basically, this "secret" gave a very brief overview of what was known in Scientology as an "org board" or organizing board. This was no secret at all because everyone in Scientology was familiar with the concept of an org board, a big chart that was prominent in any Scientology organization which showed a diagram of the organization's administrative structure. What was "secret" was that this organizational structure could also be used in one's own personal life, job or endeavors to sort out any problems one might encounter. What is more relevant to our discussion is that the foundational structure to the org board, which I am about to share, was the key to how Hubbard's mind worked. It not only was his operating basis for all Scientology organizations, it was the foundational structure for his spiritual procedures or technology which could, if applied intelligently and correctly, enable one to cross the Abyss. With reference to the fishing analogy, it represented the foundational principles by which one could build a boat, pilot it, find fishing spots and then fish. All of this was based upon a scale of awareness characteristics as follows.

21 SOURCE
20 EXISTENCE
19 CONDITIONS
18 REALIZATION
17 CLEARING
16 PURPOSES
15 ABILITY
14 CORRECTION
13 RESULT
12 PRODUCTION
11 ACTIVITY
10 PREDICTION
9 BODY
8 ADJUSTMENT
7 ENERGY
6 ENLIGHTENMENT
5 UNDERSTANDING
4 ORIENTATION

3 PERCEPTION
2 COMMUNICATION
1 RECOGNITION
−1 HELP
−2 HOPE

LOWER AWARENESS LEVELS
FROM HUMAN TO MATERIALITY

−3 DEMAND FOR IMPROVEMENT
−4 NEED OF CHANGE
−5 FEAR OF WORSENING
−6 EFFECT
−7 RUIN
−8 DESPAIR
−9 SUFFERING
−10 NUMBNESS
−11 INTROVERSION
−12 DISASTER
−13 INACTUALITY
−14 DELUSION
−15 HYSTERIA
−16 SHOCK
−17 CATATONIA
−18 OBLIVION
−19 DETACHMENT
−20 DUALITY
−21 SECRECY
−22 HALLUCINATION
−23 SADISM
−24 MASOCHISM
−25 ELATION
−26 GLEE
−27 FIXIDITY
−28 EROSION
−29 DISPERSAL
−30 DISASSOCIATION
−31 CRIMINALITY
−32 UNCAUSING
−33 DISCONNECTION
−34 UNEXISTENCE

To the casual or barely interested observer, these awareness characteristics might just seem like a bunch of ink splattered on a page. To Hubbard, these were the keys to thinking and organizing and were a tool he used on a routine basis and in his day to day life. These were also used as the basis for what he called the various levels that one could achieve with Scientology training and processing.

All of this is based upon the idea that life flows or spirals and that it does so in a particular rhythm and pattern; and further, that this spiral of life flows upwards or downwards. If you review the negative awareness characteristics and compare them to much of what has been written about Scientology in the press and also featured in mainstream media and on various internet forums, you might conclude that many of its current and former members and/or adherents have descended into the lower realms of these awareness characteristics. For example, there are plenty of tales of sadism, delusion, suffering and so on. Such human tragedy, as it has been expressed, is more akin to hell than purgatory, particularly when the individual concerned has not been able to move on and continues to remain engrossed in or obsessed about their experiences without actually purging it from their soul. This phenomena is precisely what Aleister Crowley referred to as insane delusions.

Whether or not you like Hubbard's template for crossing the Abyss or whether or not his techniques are beneficial, these awareness characteristics are the foundation upon which he worked. It was his life blood. If you look at the item on the top of the scale, you will notice that the item is "source" and this refers to the foundation, cause or creative element of existence. In other words, if you could or would cross the Abyss, you would arrive at a point where you were in a zone where you are cognizant of creating your own existence and are operating in synchronization with your own determinism. An exalted example of this is what athletes describe as being in the "zone" where they experience success at an abnormal level and feel they are creating it. It is like a batter in baseball who suddenly cannot strike out and hits the ball well every time. In its essence, the foundation of Hubbard's system is hard to argue with as regards the desirability of the stated goal. The fact that so many people associate or identify with the negative awareness characteristics as listed above is another issue.

In terms of proselytizing, the strategy of Scientology was analogous to watching near-dead bodies floating belly-up along the Ganges River, all of them falling in the range from *EFFECT* to *NUMBNESS*, and dragging them out of the river. Patching them up and giving them some nourishment, particularly in the form of live attention and compassion, they are resuscitated to the point where they recognize *NEED OF CHANGE* whereupon one points to a golden road, paved with good intentions, leading to a resplendent ashram in the distance. This gives *HOPE* and is a place where they can receive *HELP*.

It is important to point out at this juncture that, in the ordinary course of human experience, it is quite common that those who aspire to achieve transcendent awareness via such an idealized institution such as a glorified ashram or any similar temple-prone establishment often find themselves reaching the top of the pyramid only to discover that the guru in charge is a vampire dedicated to sucking the life blood out of their followers. It does not matter whether it is Indian, Tibetan, Christian or some other idealized form of spirituality. This is too often the case. The problem in such instances is that the aspirant is seeking something that he considers to be outside of himself. When the vampire becomes recognized, one either learns their lesson or, if too weak to reverse their trajectory, one becomes consumed. In any case, one has arrived at RECOGNITION.

Scientologists, ex-Scientologists and non-Scientologists alike often think that Scientology is based upon the proposition that if one receives processing, which is nothing more than a series of questions or commands on a particular subject or area of interest, that one is supposed to obtain an exalted state of awareness as a result. While there is some degree of accuracy in this statement, this concept is too often reduced to the lowest common denominator.

Asking a series of questions to an individual or giving them directions does not guarantee anything. First, an individual has to be engaged in the process so as to communicate with the psychological or spiritual factors residing within his own consciousness or inner being and become immersed in the various components that make up and influence one's soul. If this does not take place, nothing will happen. The issue at hand is that if a person is going to cross the Abyss, at least with regard to the aforementioned template, one does not only have to be mentally and emotionally engaged in the process, they have to become awake and aware. If the process is working, one is moving up the scale from RECOGNITION and is indulging in COMMUNICATION with the factors within their own mind. In other words, they are getting fish to bite. This increases PERCEPTION of what is in the ocean and one experiences ORIENTATION into a whole new undersea world.

It is possible to take each one of these positive awareness characteristics and to lay them out and explain them vis a vis the various processes of Dianetics and Scientology. In fact, the aforementioned Classification, Gradation and Awareness Chart chart does this exactly. If not always the case, it is typical that the budding Scientologist will look at this chart with both inspiration and awe. It is a map meant to represent their full human potential.

An important aspect of these awareness characteristics is too often overlooked and not understood, and that is the fact that both Scientologists and their critics often view these levels or grades on this chart as being permanent or solid states of attainment. This rigid view leads to much misunderstanding and heartbreak.

From experience, I can tell you that it is quite possible to benefit from these so-called levels to the point where one has achieved a relative degree of permanent stability. This is parallel to what is sometimes referred to in psychology as emotional equilibrium. In instances where one loses their emotional equilibrium, this factor can indeed be addressed if either the counselor or subject is so keen of mind to make sure that it is addressed. The heartbreak factor, however, has to do with the fact that the heartbroken person has not recognized that the Gradation Chart in and of itself, to a marked degree, is an arbitrary template designed to coincide with the various awareness characteristics mentioned above. It is like a guide to the ocean and the undersea world where one fishes for different types of sea life.

It is for this reason that the Gradation Chart was subject to being changed. The map is not the territory and there are times when different techniques or map routes were either discovered or deemed to be effective. The dynamics of life are neither sterile nor still, and any structured system has to be flexible to absorb the changes, variations and nuances that are a staple of living and breathing organisms and the ecostructures that they create.

In fact, people can also get stuck on the proposition that each one of these awareness characteristics have to be slavishly recognized and processed step by step. While there is merit in paying attention to them in an orderly sequence, life often moves unpredictably, not unlike a gopher popping up its head through different holes on a golf course. First, the gopher pops up on the 5th hole, then the 9th, and then the 1st. One has to deal with the moment and the immediacy of what is in front of them.

The usefulness of this is that you yourself can look over this entire list of awareness characteristics and see if any of them light up for you. Their main use, however, was that if one was stuck in a particular area of one's life, one can use the list as a guide to maneuver one's next and proper course of action.

In the mid Sixties, Hubbard took all of the processes and different technical procedures from the previous years and aligned them all generally along these awareness characteristics. Keep in mind, the entire purpose was to catapult one to an improved or higher state of awareness. From Crowley's perspective, this endeavor amounts to reconciling harmony between the components of one's mind with the sensory or physical world. In either case, emotional equilibrium is essential.

Once Hubbard created the Grade Chart, he used these awareness characteristics to create an organizational system that would support the facilitation of enabling individuals to cross the Abyss, the analogy of which he referred to as the Bridge to Freedom. This organizational system was referred to as the Organizing Board or Org Board. Any organization can plot all of its functions and personnel in a diagrammatic schematic that lists duties with reference to these awareness characteristics. As I do not want to risk either boring my reading audience nor myself, I am not going to go into a deep discussion on the Scientology Org Board. If you are interested, there is plenty of supplementary reading you can do on the internet. I want to stress certain key aspects of it.

According to Hubbard's idea, everyone entered the org at a different point and evolved through the various awareness characteristics, each one being designated as a department. In other words, one's endeavors as either a staff member or individual would cause them to cycle through these various awareness characteristics. Many staff members, if not most, tended to gravitate to a particular area of the Org Board and remain their because it suited their own predispositions and life skills.

As this book is based upon the principle of a cut-up, I only want to emphasize certain key aspects with regard to the concept of the Org Board, and this has to do with the auditing process. The only reason the Org Board was even devised was due to the fact that there was an auditing process.

Each one of these awareness characteristics was used to designate a particular department. For example, ORIENTATION was the awareness characteristic for the Department of Promotion which would send out literature designed to entice one to come into the organization by touting all of the potential benefits one could achieve from auditing. The nature of promotion is to oversell or at least put the most positive light on something. Without going into all the details, a public person would arrive at the Department of Income (*ENERGY*) and contribute money and end up in the Department of Technical Services (*PREDICTION*) where they would be scheduled and prepared for either training (*ACTIVITY*) or processing (*PRODUCTION*). It is in the Department of Processing where one would receive auditing and all of the wonderful things attributed to it. As neither the people nor the experiences in life are perfect, there would inevitably be failure or what Hubbard described metaphorically as flat ball bearings on a production line. Therefore, one had a Qualifications Division designed to examine the validity of the auditing or training that had been administered (*RESULT*). This was the Department of Validity. Additionally, there was a Department of Correction (*CORRECTION*) to fix the problem and also a Department of Enhancement (*ABILITY*), to polish off the "ball bearing".

I mention these things because it is necessary to give you an understanding of what could, would, and did transpire but it also gives you a clue to Hubbard's modus operandi. In other words, Hubbard would promote the hell out of what he would refer to as 100% Standard Tech, referring to the technology of auditing. In practice, however, it was imperfect or vulnerable to people making mistakes, sometimes very stupid mistakes. Therefore, a stringent control system was devised to detect and correct the mistakes. Whatever you think of Hubbard or his procedures, this a very laudable idea because you do not find any such mechanism in psychiatry, medicine or dentistry. While there are organized entities to complain to in these fields, none of them have an in-house independent team of people prepared to detect and correct the many mistakes that are made in these fields on a routine basis.

Keep in mind that this corrective modality is nothing more than a natural function of life. Mistakes are going to occur in any field of endeavor and they are going to stand out like a sore thumb. In fact, Hubbard said that this aspect of qualifications (*RESULT, CORRECTION, ABILITY*) was the entire key as to why civilizations would eventually fail and not be able to maintain themselves. A Qualifications Division, he thought, was the only way to buck this trend.

As good or as ideal as this might sound, it completely depends upon having a system that is workable. If the system it is based upon is faulty or if the personnel do not understand the workability of the system, it is going to fail. Aside from this aspect, the normal course of life will tell us that not all people who flow through the organization are going to be metaphorically analogous to either ball bearings or flat ball bearings. Some are going to have a rank odor and be instilled with dangerous microbes, incendiary devices or other malevolent aspects. And in some cases, the personnel of the organization itself will be similarly malevolent, either by happenstance, infiltration or perhaps even by universal design. Such cases are not correctable in the normal course events and end up in the legal arena. On a Scientology Org Board, the Legal Section was under the Department of the Controller (EXISTENCE) which was represented by the Guardian's Office. With regard to the fishing metaphor, the duty of the Guardian's Office was to make sure the boat was secure and to protect it from any eventualities that would make it sink. This included outside interference, encumbrances or sabotage.

Within this organizational structure, there was an umbrella of protection and control over the entire panorama of auditing. First, preclears were not allowed to talk to one another about their own cases. If they had something they wanted to bring up, they were to report it verbally to an "examiner" in the Department of Validity (RESULT) and it would be put in their case folder for a case supervisor to review. This was protective in the sense that people would not judge themselves against the progress of others. It was controlling to the degree that no would have a general idea of what was going on. If, however, you were a counselor or worked in the technical or qualifications divisions, you had a very good idea of what was going on with preclears. The Guardian's Office served as an even sterner aspect of protection and control, but they did not frequently enter the fold save for extreme circumstances.

I mention this aspect of protection and control because this is a feature that the Independent Scientology movement cannot hope to include in any of their activities. The Independent Scientology movement, which sometimes describes itself by different names, consists of people who practice Scientology outside of and independent of the legally recognized Church of Scientology. One of the main problems such practitioners encounter, and some are not necessarily aware of it, is that their preclears will often change auditors and complain about the various practitioners. In other words, they do not like the services they receive from one auditor and then go to another and so on. Scientology, as devised in Hubbard's mind, was never meant to be practiced this way as the lack of central control would result in too many variables. It makes it impossible to monitor or effectively ensure results. With so many different factions, it also make it impossible to determine that they are all performing "standard Scientology" with a positive result.

It is important to recognize that Hubbard's creative imperative was crystallized in the aforementioned Excalibur Incident which offered a smorgasbord of solutions for that which had ever puzzled the mind of man. Whether or not you buy into it or are inspired by it, it is a very broad sweeping statement. The fact that he was able to bring it into fruition to the degree he did is rather amazing. His messianic inclination, which was incredibly strong, mandated that a solution for one man was far from adequate. His technology and organization were shooting for the stars, and this meant saving the planet, universal salvation or whatever else you want to call it. While independent practitioners are indeed capable of achieving positive results, their activities can never be more than a shadow of Hubbard's dream.

It was stated earlier that even many critics do not disparage the lower levels of Scientology; but rather, it is the upper levels of Scientology that they feel amount to brainwashing or occult indoctrination. I will therefore now address this subject.

During my early days at the Mission of Davis, a chiropractor I knew brought two of his acquaintances to meet the Executive Director of the mission. They were a man and woman, both dressed professionally and in contrast to the typical crowd that frequented the mission, most of whom looked "hippie-esque". This doctor told me that these two people were under the impression that the lower levels of Scientology were acceptable but that the levels from "Power" (Grade V) on up were brainwashing.

Power was the level above the lower grades (Grades 0-IV) and the materials were confidential. Nowadays, anyone can find them on the internet, and it has been my impression that much of the confusion about brainwashing at this level has to do with the first of the Power Processes, listed below.

>Tell me a source.
>Tell me about it.
>Tell me a no source.
>Tell me about it.

This was considered to be a very deep process that could last for hours upon hours and was designed to bring about a state of mind in an individual whereby they were mentally in concert with the causation of events. In other words, they could distinguish the source of where events emanate from. This might sound rather simplistic unless you either realize or understand that people in general can demonstrate that they are very confused about what goes on in their day to day life and the society around them. Although the prospect of God is neither necessarily emphasized or non-emphasized in such a process, I am sure that you can readily recall witnessing various people incorrectly attribute causation to God or spiritual forces when, according to your own views, it is obviously not the case. When you can readily and clearly see the source of events or problems in your life, it makes life much easier to negotiate. Seeing the source of events or effects is what makes science a workable endeavor. This is just one example of why Scientology was considered to exemplify the science of life. With regard to this "Power Process", however, I am not trying to make you understand the whole subject of Power Processing but rather give you an understanding of how this level could be construed as brainwashing.

One of the problems of human beings in general, and those who played the game of Scientology are certainly no exception, is the propensity for reducing things to the lowest common denominator. In the ancient art of alchemy, the principle was to transmute lead or base metals into gold. This was a metaphor for taking the base elements of life and transmuting them into a noble reference frame.

When I first saw the Power Process listed above, I immediately thought to myself, "Oh my God, people are going to confuse 'source' with Ron".

The reason I would think such a thought is that Hubbard was constantly promoted and referred to as "Source", an appellation that was often written below his name on Org Boards. The reason for this is that L. Ron Hubbard was the source of Scientology technology and was the entire reason for the goings-on in an organization. Accordingly, he was revered and acknowledged as such. In their own minds, people would hold such reverence to Hubbard that it completely distorted their views of objective reality.

Even when I was steeped in the Scientology movement, I might sometimes make a smart-ass remark such as, "That was before Ron invented toothpaste," and a fellow Sea Org member might respond something on the order of, "Did Ron invent toothpaste?"

You might think I am exaggerating, but I am not. In those days, I could get very weary of people's self-generated misassessments of reality, and I was trying to break them out of their stupor. I was not making fun of Hubbard but rather the errant thinking of my colleagues. And so it is that parishioners who had been exposed to the very dominating organizational presence of L.

Ron Hubbard and his legacy were prone to adopting a submissive mind-set. This is my explanation for why someone might think the Power Processes were a form of brainwashing.

The *Holy Bible* teaches one to be discerning and the example I have offered is the exact opposite of discernment. I would, however, be the first one to tell you that I would expect people to twist and reverse the meaning of such so as to suit their own mind-set, purpose or errant thinking patterns.

If I have given you a strong impression of how something can be so twisted and turned into a deviant thought pattern, you might be interested to know that the deeper I got into Scientology, the more I witnessed and realized how twisted human beings could be in their thinking. I am not talking about mass murderers here or even major or minor criminals but rather common and ordinary human beings that might be quite likable. If you are dealing with status quo subjects such as sports, the weather or the Sunday picnic, everything is copacetic with such people. When you move into the realm of the deepest recesses of the human mind, and these were most definitely the target of L. Ron Hubbard and his upper level Scientology processes, do not expect tranquility, applause or smiling cooperation from the various forces, factors or demons who might regulate or hold watch over such domains. As the lower levels or grades of Scientology primarily deal with the ordinary aspects of existence such as upsets, problems and routine misbehavior, these matters are mostly routine, and this is why the lower levels are hailed as benign. All bets are off, however, when we move "up the Bridge" and across the Abyss. Below are the "insane delusions", demons, or deep sea creatures that are waiting to devour the unwitting aspirant. In such a paradigm, it should not be surprising that people might go quite mad. And if one is offering a service to help people cross such a chasm, the guardians had better be present, attentive and effective. If they are not, they might as well be pushing people into the fiery pits of hell.

Without further discussing the upper levels at this point, it is vital to realize that whatever is described or promoted to be the final destination, the description, particularly as it has been idealized in various religions, is not the actual territory. Whereas Scientology has promoted Total Freedom, Christians have offered Heaven and Asians have advocated Nirvana and Satori, it is the reality of the individual that becomes the prime qualifier in such matters. If we consider the Abyss to be the gap or chasm between the phenomenal world and the nuomenal world, the only realistic solution to this paradigm is to seek harmony between these two regions. It does not matter how many separately designated states of awareness, diplomas or trophies one has obtained. What any conscious entity desires is a comfortable interface between one's mental, spiritual and physical state and that of the outside or external world/universe.

There are many people who have run afoul of Scientology or continually broadcast negativity regarding the subject. The same applies to various religious cults as well. Such people are serving the role of either the demons or prey of the Abyss, voraciously striving to consume or be consumed through the fiery energy that is generated by the lack of harmony between the phenomenal and nuomenal worlds.

With regard to the Scientology Org Board being the ultimate analysis by which one could map out one's life, one was expected to spiral up to a higher level and eventually arrive at "source". This was not meant to be L. Ron Hubbard but rather a return to the source of your own being or YOU. One is never done. Life continues. The whole idea is to continually work in harmony with the various factors of life and improve. This is the closest one can get to an idealized concept such as heaven. It is an old saw that the journey to heaven is equal to the destination. There is also a quotation from the *Tao te Ching*:

The journey of a million miles begins with the first step.

The Org Board was Hubbard's own blueprint. The awareness characteristics were the backbone by which one could gauge one's progress, both individually and organizationally. Whether or not it appeals to you or not is not the point. It is the foundation of how his mind worked and the tool he used to build his organizations. He was seeking a universal harmony that is well beyond the aspirations of the ordinary human being. Such was his choice.

Aleister Crowley taught that "every man and woman is a star" and that one must find their own orbit. Nature provides an orbit for each star. A clash proves that one or the other has strayed from his course.

While Hubbard sought a huge and glorified orbit, most of us are more comfortable in a much more modest role. It is all a matter of our personal choice; and most of all, it is a matter of discovering our role in the world and what we are here to accomplish while on this Earth. That is primarily what you need to concern yourself with.

For those of us who want to purse the ocean's depths, this is nothing more than wanting to achieve, through the process of discovery, harmony with the deeper mysteries of life.

ECLIPSE OF THE SOUL

"A lot of philosophers have said this many, many times, but the truth of the matter is that all the happiness you will ever find lies in you."
— L. Ron Hubbard

As I already alluded to, there were countless people who became involved in Scientology and each one had a different experience. The same could be said about life in general or the many different pursuits that living offers. I have observed that how well one fares in such endeavors is primarily dependent upon three factors: intelligence, access and fate or fortune. Once can have intelligence, but to the degree one does not have access to information or is deceived so as not to receive information, one's intelligence becomes neutralized. If one has complete access to government or corporate secrets or secrets of any kind, one can still prosper in spite of limited intelligence. Fortune can also put one in a position where they can prosper without either intelligence or particularly good access. To the ancients, the idea of fortune was considered to be such an important staple of life that this concept was embodied in the goddess Fortuna, the daughter of Jupiter, who could whimsically decree wealth or starvation on someone in the blink of an eye.

There is also a fourth factor that has the potential to regulate these three factors and that is choice. The word *choice* derives from Middle English *chois* which derives from the Old French *choisir:* to perceive or choose, specifically referring to the action of selecting or the power of choosing. When you exercise choice, you are exercising power. The idea of selection also applies to the concept of random selection with regard to the evolution of life. Sometimes fate selects us and sometimes we select our fate.

If a person has a robotic mind-set or attitude towards life, they will live in a state of expectancy or simply accept what the "master" or the environment hands out. Such people take for granted what is presented to them by life and if they question it, it is with too weak of a volition to do anything about it. Some choices are easy and others are hard. It is sometimes the exercising of the most challenging or difficult choices that are the most rewarding.

When we consider the upper levels of Scientology, we are moving beyond the realm of ordinary upsets, problems and errant behavior, and there are some profound considerations that one needs to address. Between the aforementioned rudiments of life and the upper levels is the realm of power as touched upon in the last chapter. Simply defined, power is "the capacity to do work". For an individual, one has to take stock of who they themselves are and what is their role in the world. Crowley described this function as finding one's orbit in the scheme of life. It is no secret to anyone that power is a very loaded subject when it comes to both social and individual psychosis. We have all seen, heard or read about people who were mad with power.

It therefore becomes paramount that if one is going to participate in the arena of life in a way that in meaningful for the individual, they should take an inventory of who they are and that would include what is inside of themselves. The first key, however, is recognizing that you have power. How much power, however, is the key question. In actuality, you do not need any more power (or money for that matter) other than what is required to negotiate and get through your own personal life and living out the role that you are designed to play in this life.

While the upper or confidential levels of Scientology begin with power, they quickly move on to the proposition that an individual has an assortment of identities and goals buried deep within his mind; and further, that these identities and goals could be at odds with each other, thus wreaking havoc in the day-to-day living of the person concerned.

Keep in mind here that Scientology put forth the proposition that one had a relatively unlimited series of past lives. L. Ron Hubbard stated that the greater percentage of the world, and he was referring to Asia, has always accepted this idea, and it is primarily the Western world which has neglected this aspect.

All of this amounts to the prospect that a person is lost in the stream of life as a result of not having found his true orbit. While there is no question that there are certain people who are quite content with the role they have either carved out in life or have otherwise arrived at, there have always been a host of people who have sought a deeper meaning to their life or their role in it.

In the 1960s, it was very common for Scientologists to plot out and wrestle with numerous if not relatively endless lists of goals as well as the identities that went along with them. For example, the goal of winning a war might be attached to the identity of a general, a soldier or some political figure. One would also seek out opponents to such goals such as a priest, monk or other religious figure who might oppose war. On the endless track of time, it was considered that a person had an endless series of goals and opposition goals, combined with their respective identities, all of which had accumulated huge amount of emotional charge which had been impacted upon an individual and squashed him into the confusion of his current existence.

All of this sounds like a bloody mess, and one might wonder why one would even want to take on such a monumental and perhaps even dubious task. There is only one rational answer. If one was indeed mentally, spiritually and emotionally impacted, the examination and consequent release of the huge amount of emotional charge connected with such could result in a significant if not miraculous resurgence of energy and buoyancy of spirit in an individual. And I should add here that it was routine for people to feel huge and impactful emotional resurgences during auditing. In other words, they felt as if they had unburdened a millennium's worth of trauma. It was not just robotic thinking patterns that attracted people to and kept them involved in Scientology. There were, more often than not, tremendous "ah-ha" moments or great relief experienced by reason of their involvement.

When we look beyond the upsets and problems of life, however, there is a new horizon. One does not just want to be repairing emotional upsets the rest of their existence. If you think about it, what else is inside of an individual besides his or her goals? The entire prospect is rather elementary, but the whole idea at work in Scientology was that experiences over a virtual infinitude of lives had resulted in too many goals at cross purposes to each other. The idea of an endless wheel of lives is not at all knew to humanity as it is a basis of ancient religions such as Hinduism and also embraced by the more recent Buddhism. In the past, people were preoccupied with relieving themselves from suffering by getting off the endless Wheel of Life, sometimes thought of as the Wheel of Suffering. There is also the concept of the Kalachakra or Wheel of Time. All of these are steeped in Maya, the world of illusion.

Hubbard was operating from a modern day reference point and while a certain amount of homage was paid to the past, everything you encountered in Scientology was pretty much "in your face" and you simply dealt with it, poorly or otherwise. The more you learned about the subject, the more it was to your own advantage, at least as far as trying to figure out what was most relevant within your own mind, and that includes your own ambitions.

When we consider trying to sort out the various goals inside one's head, it is a very simple proposition if we can just pick one or a few and live out our lives in a humble and uncomplicated fashion. In Scientology, however, one was invited to embrace the entire gamut of failed purposes and goals of the past. Above and beyond one's individuality, one was also invited to take on the collective insanity of humanity.

I should add in here that the only reason one might be encouraged to engage in such is that a brightly colored map was laid out that offered hope, a purpose and an argument that was, for some, reasonable or easy to buy into. As the map is not the territory, it is far more important to examine the territory. If you do not, the map can become an icon of belief, tending towards superstition and delusions.

If the prospect of sorting out a series of multiple lives does not sound complex enough, the entire proposition at hand was yet more complicated and sinister beyond belief, the reason being that such goals were further impacted by electrical implants that inserted false goals and programs on top of the multitude of goals already acquired. It is obvious that any being subjected to such was experiencing the negative awareness characteristics listed in the previous chapter. You can take your pick.

It is my opinion that what I have described might seem extremely daunting and overwhelming. This is why these were referred to as upper levels. It required an extreme amount of prerequisites and auditing before you could even begin to consider approaching such. Such prerequisites, however, could often be compromised due to various human factors, all of which were destructive to both the individuals involved and the organization itself. Just because there are rules does not mean that they will be followed or enforced.

A novice to this subject might really wonder if any of this is worth pursuing because, if it is not crazy, it is certainly daunting. Before I make a particular point, I want to harken back to the idea of crossing the Abyss and to remind you that it represents an individual's gap or chasm between the phenomenal world (that which is perceived by the senses) and that nuomenal world (that which is perceived by the mind or considered purely mental or intellectual). Also, in the previous chapter, I likened L. Ron Hubbard's gradation chart as a "Blueprint to Heaven". Do consider that the phonetics of the word *heaven* are only a step away from the word "even". You could easily say that the concept of heaven itself is tantamount to a balancing or evenness between the inner world and the outer world. In other words, crossing the Abyss is nothing more than evening out the aforementioned gap. When one is having to deal with "insane delusions" of any kind, they are better off taking a step back and paying more attention to the phenomenal or outer world. This is the case for many ex-Scientologists who found themselves struggling with their own inner world to the point where it was no longer agreeable, desirable or possible for them to continue the pursuit of any such idea.

Such struggles and the failure to deal with them represent an eclipse of the soul, and this is important to mention because there is no question that many if not multitudes of Scientologists have felt betrayed and befuddled by the upper levels of Scientology. Such a state of mind is analogous to believing in the captain of the fishing boat who is continuously taking you to fishing spots where there are either little or even no fish at all; and even to the point where one cannot sustain themselves mentally, emotionally or physically. Worse yet perhaps, one is being forced or persuaded to submerge into the depths of the ocean, as if scuba diving, and being terrified by the monsters of the deep. Such are indeed comparable if not identical to Crowley's "insane delusions" of the Abyss.

If we are either brave, foolish, impassioned or otherwise persuaded to cross the Abyss or the virtual equivalent thereof, the only thing inhibiting us is that which is already inside of oneself. When we consider the "insane delusions" of the Abyss, we can only deal with what is inside of us, and this also includes anything deeply imbedded within the experiential predisposition of our genetic structure.

Finding one's own role in their life can be challenging enough, but if you consider the prospect of either a multitude or virtually infinite series of lifetimes, each with their own specific goals and agendas, it is like a snake trying to find its way through a complex labyrinth that is timeless, formless and infinite in its nature.

If we once again consider the people who have spent countless years and finances pursuing such a dream in Scientology, many readily acknowledge that they suffer from PTSD or Post Traumatic Stress Disorder. This creates an impossible impasse, at least as far as pursuing any such destination as suggested here. One would not only be embracing the proposition of dueling the entities or guardians associated with the "insane delusions" of the Abyss but would be simultaneously dealing with the stress related trauma of their immediate environment that is presently being forced upon them.

All of this tells you that the territory being aspired to is neither for neophytes or casual arm chair observers. Do understand, however, we are no longer talking about Scientology itself but rather the territory it sought to exploit or tame. For the individual, this is the territory within their own mind. We are bridging into the world of the unknown or the occult. Occultists would refer to people undertaking such a venture as either an apprentice or an adept. I would also offer to you the prospect that many apprentices in the occult world do not follow warnings or advice and mess themselves up.

Scientology offered the proposition that one could unsnarl all of the failed purposes and unrealized goals of the past and achieve harmony in what amounted to a restful separation from the illusions associated with the physical plane and recognize and preserve one's spiritual identity so as to live in a peaceful state of existence. This is an approximation of the state of Clear.

Beyond Clear were the OT (Operating Thetan) levels which included the most controversial aspect of Scientology. One can consult more expanded explanations or definitions for these terms, but I am only offering a cut-up so as to offer certain understandings. Some might coherently argue that these upper levels are the least useful, hardest to understand, most nutty and most apt to be understood on a faith basis. This might well be true for many, but I would add that anyone engaging in a faith-based mentality, either as a student or critical spectator, is not going to understand the upper levels or the true nature of the positive or negative attributes that are associated with them.

If you are trying to catch fish and just rely on faith, your chances of success are limited. Rather, it is wiser to understand the migration and behavior patterns of fish and where the reefs are that provide their food supply. There is also the matter of weather and how all of this relates to the time of year and the characteristics of different aspects of life in the sea.

Considerable public ridicule has been leveled at Scientology because of the so-called belief in Xemu (also spelled and referred to as Zenu), the dictator of the "Galactic Confederacy" who 75 million years ago brought billions of souls to Earth seeking to solve over-population problems. Stacking them in boxes around volcanoes, they were obliterated with hydrogen bombs. Such explosions caused the thetans (spirits) to become stuck to one another, sometimes in a whole cluster, all of it based upon the picture of the collision. Rising from the volcanoes, the thetans were collected by an electronic ribbon whereupon they were implanted extensively and violently, resulting in amnesia and identity confusion that, you might say, runs into the deepest corridors of the soul. In essence, this series of incidents could best be described as the deepest form of PTSD imaginable. When we think back to Dr. Margaret Singer's statement that Hubbard took the "art of control and persuasion" to an entirely new level, it should not surprise anyone at all that the "territory" he was dealing with would exude and mimic what she said. It is therefore easy to conclude that if you think Hubbard's discoveries and iterations as per the above are completely nonsensical, his power of persuasion and suggestion was so great that he was as powerful and perhaps as guilty as the implanters he was describing.

A major problem with this proposition, however, is that Hubbard was never associated with performing electric shock or other violent techniques that he described. One can only say that the suggestion of such, and perhaps his charisma, was powerful enough to send endless amounts of people to engage in a journey of madness for fear that, if they did not, they might suffer. Such persuasion is not much different than a preacher paralyzing and hypnotizing his congregation with tales of fire, brimstone and endless suffering. But if Margaret Singer's statement is even close to accurate, Hubbard was much more effective than even the most diabolical preacher. This would put Hubbard in a class by himself.

I can tell you quite honestly and accurately, however, that Hubbard would say that the very idea of such forceful implantation is more powerful than the implantation itself. In other words, ideas (or postulates) are the root of everything. Further, that anyone bringing up such a horrendous subject is prone to being identified with the subject itself, even to the point of being a perpetrator of what one is trying to vanquish. This is akin to transference in Freudian psychology. In other words, if one is undergoing therapy and there is some form of super hostile energy being stirred up in one's psyche, there is the potential for the patient to identify the person stirring it up (the therapist) as the perpetrator.

I cannot reiterate enough how important it is to take stock of the fact that we are talking about "territory" here. The map Hubbard laid out might be far too sloppy and abstract for the taste of some, but it is the territory that matters, not the map. The territory will be even better understood if we consider the context of Crowley's description of the Abyss and what an aspirant might be trying to achieve. The following is from Crowley's *Little Essays Toward Truth*:

> "This doctrine is extremely difficult to explain; but it corresponds more or less to the gap in thought between the Real, which is ideal, and the Unreal, which is actual. In the Abyss all things exist, indeed, at least in posse, but are without any possible meaning; for they lack the substratum of spiritual Reality. They are appearances without Law. They are thus Insane Delusions.
> Now the Abyss being thus the great storehouse of Phenomena, it is the source of all impressions."

People are often quick to happily dismiss Hubbard's iterations as insane delusions. They are certainly challenging to process; but then, they were designed only to be processed if one was extensively prepared to deal with the concomitant phenomena. One can gain a better appreciation if we consider Crowley. His system also recognized and warned that the Abyss is guarded by a demon named Choronzon who, in essence, represents those aspects of the aspirant, inclusive of his ego and its personas, that would block or inhibit them from entering the Divine. If we want, we can argue about whether Hubbard was absorbed by Choronzon himself, but this is not so important in the greater scheme of things. It is most certain that many aspirants have identified Hubbard with the equivalent of Choronzon, even if they have no familiarity with the term. What is important is the territory one is trying to traverse in order to achieve what one is trying to achieve.

The Divine one is trying to enter in Crowley's system is referred to as the City of the Pyramids. This is achieved first by attaining knowledge of and conversation with one's HGA or Holy Guardian Angel. Choronzon will do everything it can to entrap one in one's ego; and it is not until one can shed one's deepest identity with the earth plane that one can enter the City of the Pyramids. There is much more detail you can read if you wish, but it must be realized that just as Hubbard's map is only a map so is Crowley's map only a map. It is not the territory. That is something each individual will have to either figure out or experience for themselves.

It is not well understood or accepted but Hubbard wrote his technical and administrative materials in a trance-like state. It was not a full blown trance because he could easily be interrupted. I learned this from his personal steward who one time asked him what was in the bottom drawer of his desk. He opened it to show her several policies and bulletins that were incomplete because he had lost the "trance" and could not complete them.

Hubbard is known to have communicated to his Holy Guardian Angel, and it is not at all far-reaching to consider that it was his HGA that directed him to the idea of processing body thetans; and further, that this was equivalent to an occult adept wrestling with Choronzon. In other words, the body thetans are what inhibited Hubbard from a higher state of awareness if not the Divine itself. This is only a comparison, but it will help you better understand the territory itself that is at stake in these matters. It is also easy to identify Hubbard's mental escapades with the Insane Delusions of the Abyss.

It is important to note that Hubbard instructed students processing these materials to locate body thetans or a group of them by finding an area of pressure in the body or by getting a significant indication on an e-meter. This, in essence, is getting a fish to bite. Pulling the fish in, however, requires a certain amount of skill. In the end, one is trying to achieve a balance between the nuomenal world and the outer world. Balance is the key, and you can be damn sure that far too many aspirants, whether it be in Scientology or in occult magical studies, are too often prone to conduct themselves in a way that is either imbalanced or extremely imbalanced.

If one is undertaking a great adventure, such as you might see in an Indiana Jones movie or the like, there is always the archetypal struggle of the protagonist walking amongst the relics of the dead in order to find the Holy Grail or whatever miraculous object is being pursued. This not only includes formidable tests and challenges for an individual aspirant but also the voracious and mad pursuits of factions trying to possess it. To put it succinctly and bluntly, the concept of the holiest symbol of the Most High is surrounded by energies and dangers that are chaotic, murderous, wrathful and psychotic by their very nature. Keep in mind that the many movies made about this and other holy objects are often based upon complete fiction and serve only as a metaphor; but keep in mind, the map is not the territory.

When undertaking such an adventure as is described herein, it is indeed possible if not likely to experience an eclipse of the soul. It is also possible for the soul to be devoured. If it is neither eclipsed or devoured, however, there is the prospect that one will reach the light at the end of the tunnel and achieve a balance between the phenomenal and nuomenal worlds.

I think the best way to convey such a pursuit, especially as it regards the mystery of L. Ron Hubbard, is with a metaphorical story of inspired fiction; and this is the province of the next chapter.

UNDER THE MOONLIGHT

"Poetry is the journal of the sea animal living on land, wanting to fly in the air. Poetry is a search for syllables to shoot at the barriers of the unknown and the unknowable. Poetry is a phantom script telling how rainbows are made and why they go away."
— Carl Sandburg, from The Atlantic, March 1923

After shutting down the engine on my fishing boat for the evening, I went out on the deck, sat back on a lounge chair and looked at the beautiful crescent moon. I could barely hear the slight ripple of the calm ocean around me as I looked over the sizable fleet of other boats, each with a captain and a host of anglers, all of them currently asleep, all of whom spent their days fishing, each seeking to discover the mysteries of their own soul. I soon fell asleep under the yellow light of the shining moon.

As I dreamt, a small schooner with a single pilot approached. It was Ron, dressed like an alchemist with a conical wizard's cap.

"Hello!" he said in his most welcoming voice, as he gestured for me to come aboard.

I put the chaffing gear between the two vessels as he tied them together.

"What are you doing here?" I asked.

"How would you like an adventure?" he asked. "Things look rather tame around here."

"Everyone's catching fish," I responded. "Their all finding out about themselves, thanks to you."

"Yeah," he said, "but there's so much more out there. People could fascinate themselves forever by looking into tiny soul worlds with their tiny little games, but we have to consider the collective."

"You mean there's fish out there that are universal, tied to everyone's consciousness?" I asked.

"That's right, but they're not exactly fish. You'll see. Come along."

We untied the boats, and we set sail on his schooner for sights unknown. After about ten minutes, Ron pointed to mountainous islands in the distance.

"Right there!" he said. "There are volcanoes there."

Before I knew it, we were headed down a narrowing sea passage between two huge volcanoes that were sputtering black smoke. As the passage became narrower, I saw several vessels that had crashed and then bodies and skeletons strewn along the banks and shore line. It was a very grim scene against a very beautiful tropical backdrop. Ron pointed to the bodies.

"Casualties," he said. "Most are not ready for this."

Suddenly, I felt the speed of a particle of some sort create a whooshing sound across my face.

"Duck!" said Ron.

As I did, the banks of the sea passage were becoming narrower and narrower. Painted natives with masks appeared on both sides of the banks. They had blow darts and were shooting vigorously at us.

"What the hell is this?" I asked Ron.

"They are the Tcho Tcho. They attach spirits to the tip of their blow darts and try to land them in your body so to control you, mostly through your dreams," said Ron.

Several of the darts were landing on both of us. They were impossible to avoid as we were both in the open part of the schooner. I covered myself as best I could with a couple of loose life jackets and went to the side where I was only vulnerable to one side of the vicious attack.

Trying to get away from the onslaught, Ron stumbled and fell to the deck. As he did so, I saw a man in satanic garb emerge from the noisy natives. As he chucked a spear and hit Ron in the back, the natives started celebrating and jumping for joy. As the life went out of Ron, I could see that only a few Tcho Tcho were still throwing spears. I jumped overboard and swam underneath the water for a good twenty yards. Taking air, I went back under and kept swimming. Finally out of the range of the Tcho Tcho, I could hear them celebrating but it was more distant. They had hit their target. I saw a loose log and grabbed it, floating along with the current of this narrow sea passage. The narrowest part was between two large volcanoes which began to erupt with red fire.

Floating at a rapid pace with the current, I came to a broad archway connecting the two volcano mountains, and it was entirely aflame with red fire. Below the archway was a great heptagon with the letters B-A-B-A-L-O-N in the vertexes. Above the archway, I could see a red image of Marjorie Cameron.

As the narrows began to broaden, I was moving out to sea but was still being carried by a well moving current. On the other side of the narrows were pyramids of all shapes and sizes, and I realized that I was in the City of the Pyramids.

As the current began to wane, I saw an island in the distance. Before I could consider the challenge of reaching the island, I could see a man rapidly paddling a canoe. He was thin and sinewy and very direct in his motions. His hair was dark and his features were slightly Asian.

The man pointed for me to enter the canoe, offering his arm to pull me up, an action which he performed easily with one motion. As soon as I was situated in the canoe, he began paddling with strong swift motions that were calculated for maximum traction between the water and the paddle.

Although he moved swiftly, the island still looked quite distant. I relaxed. The crescent moon had waxed a bit and I enjoyed the light shining over the dark blue sky. As I watched the stars, the man continued to paddle but then began to slow down, growing older in a time lapse sequence until finally appearing with a long white beard and white hair falling down to his shoulders.

Shortly after this transformation had taken place, we were at the island. I could see four women waiting for us, distinctly Asian and in their twenties.

The old man got out of the canoe and made a motion to the young women. As I got out of the canoe myself, the women rushed to me and began treating the numerous wounds I had suffered from the Tcho Tcho. I was surprised, however, because my mind had been suspended by the whole experience, and I had completely forgotten that I had sustained any injuries at all.

Quick and expert in their actions, they placed me on a cotton cot, first putting a salve on my many wounds before placing needles into each wound and setting them afire.

"We heal the wound and purge the spirit out," said one of the women who appeared to be the leader. "My name is Miso. You will rest here for a short while."

One of the women placed a cup of tea before me and helped me drink it.

"Just relax," I heard her say.

Certain areas of my body began to get very hot, and then I felt energy rushing through different channels. I felt like getting up because a strong amount of energy began to overwhelm me. Before I could get up, Miso gently pushed me back down to the cot.

"Rest," she said, directing me to stay prone.

Each of the women picked up the a corner of the cot as they effortlessly took me down a path illuminated with colorful Chinese lanterns. Miso addressed me as they continued to move at a steady but comfortable pace.

"We are taking you to the Jade Palace where we will finish your healing."

"What did I do to receive such incredible generosity?" I asked.

"Oh," said the women behind me and to my right, who appeared to be the youngest. "We love your writing. Your books have given us much joy. You touch our heart!"

As pleasant as it was to hear this, it was a bit nonsensical, but it was life itself flowing positive energy at me. One has to be open to positive channels of life no matter how surprising or off the wall they might seem.

As the ladies continued their steady movement, I was not really relaxed enough to look around too much. The lantern path eventually led to a very wide road of whitish-gray bricks. In the distance was a radiant and pulsating orb fluctuating between a deep emerald and light green color. As we stuck to the side of the wide road, we passed a multitude of martial artists, all of them vigorously engaged in showing off their skills.

"What is this?" I asked.

"These are martial artists," replied Miso. "You will notice that the closer we get to the Emerald Gate, the more competent they are. They are all striving to enter the Emerald Gate and pass on through to Shambhala."

"Shambhala?" I asked.

"Yes. That is beyond the Emerald Gate," she said. "Those martial artists who are qualified will be allowed in. Once there, we will teach them how to fight without using force."

"Fighting without fighting?" I asked.

"Yes," answered Miso. "You will see. First though, we have to take care of you."

When we got to the end of the brick road, there were armored martial guards. Beyond them was a field of grass. The guards let us pass, and once we got to the lawn, the women began a steady trot until we came before the Emerald Gate, beyond which was the large pulsating green sphere.

Going through the gate, we were absorbed by the energy of the pulsating sphere and I felt a temporary "rush" or "whoosh" until we soon found ourselves walking again in what seemed to be the opposite direction. On the "other side" of the green pulsating sphere, there was a similar road to the one that was now behind us, but this one was green and made of stones of green jade shaped like bricks.

"We are now in Shambhala," said Miso.

Everything seemed so relaxed, and I completely lost any focus or reference to the injuries I had sustained. I felt as if I did not have a care in the world: past, present or future.

Before us stood the incredible Jade Palace, an awesome structure that was so beautiful that it would be impossible to describe justly. Ascending the steps to the palace, the doors opened of their own accord, but before we actually entered, Miso spoke.

"We will enter the stairwell to the left," she said, pointing to a descending spiral staircase made of jade. "The temple is straight ahead, but we will enter that later. First, you will go to the healing sanctuary where we will complete your healing."

I was led into a pentagonal shaped room about the size of a large bedroom. The walls were like screens, but they were screens that appeared "alive" with each wall of the pentagon featuring a different element of the five Chinese elements: fire, earth, metal, water, and wood. Each wall gave different versions of each element. While the wall for fire included a rendition of exploding sun spots or moving lava, the wall for water featured the ocean, a waterfall or even a sprinkler effect. There was no limit to the variations, but they were a constant presence. The ceiling overhead looked like a pure blue sky which could also vary, ranging from a sunset or sunrise to a night sky with stars.

"It is important for you to see the five elements in their manifestation because they all manifest in your body in a cyclic fashion," said Miso. "Each one of these flow through the different vessels and meridians in the body. We are going to address the places where the darts hit your body and clear the energy.

"The idea of Hubbard's that thetans inhabit your body is not new," continued Miso. "It is an old Taoist doctrine that just as the planet Earth has people on it so do our bodies have 'people' in it. We mimic Mother Earth."

As she spoke, the projections on the screens turned to specific meridians in the body, each screen showing different aspects of the meridian, including the inward chemistry but also the colors and afflictions associated with blockages in particular meridians.

"We have to clear out the energy in all of the meridians so that the chi flows. Unblock the life force! It does not matter what you call it, and do not think that spirits do not invade and inhabit bodies, especially when one is sick. Some prey off disease."

Miso and the ladies continued to work on me, but now it was more precise and intense. I could feel rushes of energy throughout my body as I felt old situations or encumbrances leaving me. After about an hour of this, I felt good and totally relaxed.

"You are done!" said Miso. "At least for now. You will rest for a while, and then we will take you to the palace."

They brought me tea, and I rested, sleeping for what seemed like hours. I was told not to worry about the time. This was Shambhala, and I could relax forever if needed.

When I was rested, the women came in on cue, and I was given a green robe to put on and escorted to the palace. The inside of the palace was beautiful and included columns of green jade and architecture that was based primarily on themes from Taoist alchemy and the animals of the Chinese zodiac. The jade exuded a very beautiful energy that made the entire palace seem as if it were itself alive.

Inside the palace, there were two large thrones of Jade with light green pillows, and there I saw Quan Yin, the Goddess of Mercy and Compassion. Next to her, and sitting in the other large throne, which was a little smaller and slightly behind the larger one, was the old man who had brought me here. This, I was told, was Lao-tse.

"We are the daughters of Quan Yin and Lao-tse," said Miso. "We are all immortals, and we offer you this time because you are a part of us. You will always have a part of us with you for your name has been placed with us in heaven. You can return here forever when your work on Earth is done."

"This sounds very encouraging," I said.

"But you still have things to learn," said Miso. "Watch!"

Miso pointed to the doors of the palace which were now open. Five of the best martial artists walked inside until they stood before Quan Yin.

"Come!" said Quan Yin, gently gesturing for the martial artists to come forward.

Quan Yin placed her hand on the upper chest of one of the martial artists. "Try to move me," she said.

As soon as the martial artist moved, he flew backwards, stumbling and falling down until he was twenty feet behind everyone. After demonstrating this to each one, she called them back.

This time, she took the first martial artist and placed his hands on her chest and said, "Push me!"

The same thing happened. Each one took their turn and fell backwards.

"This is what you will learn," said Miso in a soft voice, almost whispering into my ear. "These martial artists are all the best, but now they have to learn to fight without physical action and without muscle. They will learn to use energy, and this is what I will teach you. Come. We will return to the healing temple."

Miso took me by the hand and led me back to the pentagonal shaped room. When we entered, the screens in the room were showing different geometric shapes, but they were all represented in the different elements of wood, fire, earth, metal and water.

"First," she said, "we will clean your energy field. It starts with scanning."

The room became completely dark.

"Scan down," she said.

A purple light came down in the darkness and scanned down my entire body. It moved very slowly.

"All the blockages in the meridians are in the energetic field which is senior to the meridians. To get the energy flowing, we need to unblock the dross. The dross is not just invading beings or demons but energies of all sorts, and that includes what they call in the West to be a grigori, an assemblage of energy and beings that is gathered together, often by conjuration, for a specific purpose. Most people are affected by these."

The purple light moved slowly down my body, penetrating what would have otherwise been imaginary realms; but as it moved down my body, I felt considerable releases of energy. When the light got to the bottom, it began again from the top.

"This is something you will need to practice when you return to Earth," said Miso. "It is a continual process."

After several runs through with the purple light, the lights turned on and Miso wanted me to push her like Quan Yin had done with the martial artists. I now found I could push her without doing anything. The energy would flow through my body, but it was not as strong as Quan Yin had demonstrated.

"That is good!" she said. "Now we will engage in another procedure which will make your energy yet stronger."

As the lights became dark again, the outlined template of a human body appeared in front of me. The outline was in purple. When the shape was completed, an upside down pyramid appeared around the groin area. Next, a small fire appeared within the bottom section of the pyramid.

"Now," said Miso, "step into the outline. Step into the fire and feel it cook. You are going to cook the chi."

As the outline and the fire appeared as a hologram, it was not frightening at all. I stepped into the holographic fire and began to feel it.

"Increase your breathing with long slow breaths," she said. "Then you will fan the flames and increase the heat. The concentrated energy will spread through your body. Feel the energy and feel the increase."

This felt incredible as energy was moving into my body in a way that I had never felt before, making me aware of areas of my body that I had not felt previously.

"Very good," she said. "Now step back."

As I did, I could see the template where I had been standing except that it was now burning like a very strong fire. The template itself, however, began to change. Where there had been one outline of an upside down pyramid in the groin area, there was now a second one, right side up, on top of it. The tip of that pyramid reached up to the solar plexus. Above the second was a third pyramid, upside down, the base of the pyramid reaching the clavicle or collar bone, the heart being approximately where the King's Chamber of the Great Pyramid would be. Above this third pyramid was a fourth pyramid, right side up with the top reaching the crown of the head. Above that was a fifth pyramid, upside down, reaching out to the universe.

Gradually, the roaring fire in the bottom pyramid made its way upward until all the pyramids were a roaring fire. The fire then subdued, gradually, as if controlled by a rheostat or dimmer switch. Different states of fire were represented, increasing and decreasing. The fire then disappeared entirely, but the template of the body and the pyramids remained.

"Now step into it," said Miso. "I want you to visualize the fire at the bottom pyramid by creating it. With each breath, you are giving oxygen to the fire and increasing the flames. As you continue the breathing, cultivate the fire and let it rise upwards to fill the other pyramids. Let the energy flow out of your body and treat it like a fire of purification. In real life, you will want to regulate this energy. Too much fire can be regulated by water. You want to have the right amount of fire. This is an art you must learn to perfect by cultivating and refining."

Everything turned back to complete darkness. I was full of energy and felt euphoric yet completely still and composed.

"This is the true City of the Pyramids," said Miso. "It is described by Aleister Crowley, but he did not explain it in the sense of the pyramidal energy structures within the human body. When you cross the Abyss, you can only do so by accessing and energizing the pyramids within. It is not some mystical area on the astral plane or elsewhere. It is inside of you."

Miso then led me by the hand out of the room and then back towards the palace itself. As we entered the palace, Quan Yin and Lao-tse were in their thrones, but the martial artists were gone.

"Where did everyone go?" I asked.

"They will be tested some more, and if their attitudes are correct, they will be introduced to the healing temple below."

"And then what will their fate be?"

"If they pass the tests and go through the temple, they will probably be assigned to monasteries on the borders of Shambhala. Here they can and will serve a great purpose."

Before I could say anything further, we now stood before Quan Yin who rose and put her hands around me, scrutinizing my energy field.

"He is done!" were the only words spoken by Quan Yin.

As soon as Quan Yin made her statement, Lao-tse got up and silently walked out a back entrance.

"Come," said Miso. "It is time for your return."

As we walked back to the beach where I had arrived, I was not sure what I was supposed to do.

"I am not quite sure why I was brought here in the first place or even why I am going back. Can you explain?"

"Your name was put in Heaven. You have been afforded a great honor and also a great teaching, but you have more work to do. People pass to and from here routinely, each one having a different path and destiny. You will return here once your work is done."

Although I did not know specifics, I realized that I had no sensible choice other than to follow the path afforded to me.

"You have gifts," she continued, "and you can share them with others. What you have experienced in the healing temple is something that will not feel the same when you return to Earth. It is something you will have to work towards in order to achieve the feeling you had here. It can take people several lifetimes to get to that temple and can take several more to maintain that state on your own. You have been given a taste of the true City of the Pyramids so that you will know how to work your way back and make it your permanent abode. I will be waiting for you!"

When we reached the boat, Lao-tse was waiting for me. I waved goodbye to Miso, and we proceeded towards the ocean. As Lao-tse paddled, he began to transform into a younger man again, and I now fully understood, in a matter of fact way, that he and his daughters were immortals. He was taking me to my destiny.

The return journey was much faster than the original one. In fact, the experience was as if it was speeded up as things began to blur like a time lapse photo. Before too long, we were moving amongst the many fishing boats. Once here, Lao-tse began to transform back onto the older version of himself. Most of the boats were empty and some had sleeping or unconscious people sprawled across the decks, none of them being awake. Each one of the boats that we passed had a sign that said, "Under New Management".

When we got back to my boat, Ron's schooner was moored to it. I went aboard the schooner and went inside of the cabin. Inside, I saw Ron's body slumped over on a desk. There were open bottles of pink and grey pills. He was clearly dead, but he had his hand on a wooden box with my name on it.

Opening the box, I saw a parchment bag, an old-fashioned skeleton key, and a small parchment with three words on it: *RESULT, CORRECTION* and *ABILITY*. The parchment bag had my initials on it and contained several gold coins which I knew were for me.

When I had finished with the box, I was surprised to see that Lao-tse had entered the cabin and was facing me.

"You're still here!" I said to him.

"I have more work to do. You go back to your boat and rest. I will awake you in the morning."

I went to bed and had a dream where I was inside a very small cozy house. There was a warm fire in the fireplace and the windows were frosty. Through different windows, I could see Aleister Crowley, Jack Parsons, and L. Ron Hubbard looking in. They were in the cold and were looking for the door but could not find it. Turning around, I saw Marjorie Cameron standing in front of the fireplace.

"They cannot come in," she said. "Like the inventor, the magician does not always get to enjoy his invention or reap the full benefits of it. It is the same for artists when their work sells for millions after they die."

It was a short dream; and when I woke up, it was still dark. I went up on the deck and saw Ron's schooner lit up in flames. Lao-tse was on his way back to my boat, paddling away from the flames. When he arrived, he spoke.

"Get your box and come," he said, motioning towards the boat.

I quickly retrieved the box and got in the canoe. As I did, Lao-tse began to paddle towards a distant shore that was in the opposite direction of where we had entered Shambhala.

"What happened?" I asked.

"Purification," Lao-tse replied. "The phoenix rises from the ashes."

"Where are we going now?"

"To return you to the Earth. You have work to do."

The canoe soon came to a placid shore, and Lao-tse motioned for me to get out.

"I'll see you when you are ready to return."

It was dawn as I got out of the canoe, and the sky was turning a lighter shade of blue. As I began walking on the shore, I heard Lao-tse clap his hands, and I turned around. He was pointing to the sky where the flames of Ron's schooner were transforming into ashes that looked like a phoenix flying away.

"All things come to their natural end," I said.

"And now it is your new beginning," he said.

I walked towards the jungle beyond the beach. When I reached it, I turned around and saw Lao-tse in the distance. He looked like a small spot in the ocean, and I watched him until he disappeared.

THE CITY OF THE PYRAMIDS

"I live in my dreams — that's what you sense. Other people live in dreams, but not in their own. That's the difference."
— Hermann Hesse

There are different motivations I had for writing this book. Ever since I got involved with Scientology, five decades ago, I have noticed observations and conclusions about Hubbard that were either errant, judgmental or based upon incomplete data. This, however, is not meant to suggest that certain criticisms against him are in error. While many such criticisms do fit into the above categories, there are also others that, while arguably true, do not come close to giving a complete picture of the man and his work. One can spend far too much time either correcting or criticizing the criticizers.

Perhaps the most constructive insight I can offer concerns the often made assertion that Hubbard either stole, acquired or otherwise misappropriated Scientology from other sources; and, in particular, from Aleister Crowley.

While many people are either familiar with Scientology and L. Ron Hubbard, including those involved with it, there are extremely few of them who have any real experience or involvement with occult orders or the actual players in that realm. The problem in this situation is that occult orders have an outer shell, such as that which is found in books and articles, but there is also an inner shell which is reserved for practitioners and insiders. Sometimes insiders will become disaffected and share secrets, most of which reveal the personal foibles of the members of the occult order, particularly the leaders. What gets lost is any core of meaning and original intent that might have been put into the occult system that is supposed, under ideal circumstances, to enlighten the individual. Too often, the members become bait for either the ill-intentioned leaders of such an order or an entity that it is feeding.

Whether it be Scientology or the occult, there is no question that aspirants can end up serving as bait who end up getting burned. The other side of the coin is that one has to pay for their own ignorance. Sometimes this comes in the form of paying for one's initiation and sometimes it can cost someone far more dearly, even their life. People who have lost vast amounts of money or portions of their life have paid dearly for whatever knowledge they might have learned, even if that knowledge is to stay away.

When it comes to Scientology and the occult tradition of Aleister Crowley, there are obvious similarities, but the practices of each are so drastically different that it is hard to compare the two. Crowley's initiation fees were like chump change compared to donations required of Scientologists. On the other hand, Scientologists receive much more personal attention with regard to their individual problems than would members of an occult organization like the Ordo Templi Orientis or OTO.

There is, however, a common denominator, and that is that both are advocating the proposition of crossing the Abyss as has already been described. In Crowley's system, one takes the Oath of the Abyss, a solemn vow amounting to a pact with oneself that one will treat whatever pops up in their life as an expression of the Divine. What too often gets missed in this scenario is that the aspirant takes the oath far too seriously and to the point where his filter or interface with the universe becomes compromised and illogical. The same thing could, did and does happen with Scientology.

The key in all of this, as was said previously, is to find a balance between the nuomenal and phenomenal worlds. This cannot be emphasized enough. This has everything to do with emotional intelligence.

When I was involved with Scientology, I often saw people get very excited, enthused or "blown out". There is, of course, nothing wrong with that in and of itself. The nature of Scientology is that it can get you to look at situations, including the apparatus inside of your mind, and kindle a fire of inspiration that is beyond anything you might have ever felt before. Such an experience of enlightenment or whatever else you might want to call it was enough to completely sell a person on the path he was pursuing and the system that instigated the revelation. What I noticed at that time was that people too often grasped at or experienced such inspiration in a way that can best be described as manic. In other words, they felt the "mania" of a purpose and all the excitable or nervous energy associated with such. The problem was that it was not always easy for them to temper it, contour it and integrate it into the routine of their life. This amounts to channeling your deepest inspiration into the pragmatism of your daily surroundings. Such an idea is not much different than finding a career that you truly love.

Previously, I wrote of the importance of intelligence, access and fate. Emotional intelligence would come under the heading of intelligence, and it is an aspect that cannot be over emphasized. It is easy or tempting to write an essay or even a book on emotions and how they relate to intelligence, but this is something one has to figure out for themselves. People who "believe" often abandon intelligence or logic by reason of emotion. The whole point is that one needs to seek a balance between emotions and intelligence. They are supposed to work together, and it is up to the individual to figure this out.

Scientology contains hundred upon hundreds of processes or procedures designed to release the traumas of the past. There are also procedures to bring one out of the past so that one can focus on the present. Being in the present is key to everything because it represents a balance between the past and the future. It is also a place where you can center your emotions. To the degree that one can maintain one's attention in the present, one will not be confused by either the past or the future. While simply stated, this is a huge key to everything.

Without putting on robes, mustering up the accoutrement of the occult and formally taking the Oath of the Abyss, one can accomplish the most incredible feat for oneself by simply realizing that they are indeed in the present and treating each occurrence, communication or manifestation as an inspirational message. I am not talking about going to extremes and treating a paperclip as a divinely inspired manifestation of God. What I am talking about, however, is taking the mundane aspects of your life and potentially upgrading anything and everything in it.

For example, you notice that your car has not been washed for too long. Instead of being lazy and dismissing such, you make an effort to clean it, including the inside. Although its a small act, it will bring good fortune, even if small, for it is a positive act and will gate in new experiences. It applies to the kitchen as well. If you've been in a rut as far as what you eat, change the pattern. I could go on and on. There are so many small things in life that people put off or dismiss responsibility for. By building upon such a pattern of change, one can become a dictator over one's own life and take charge of present time. In other words, all you ever need is right in front of you or around the next corner. And if you become too excited about the next big deal or the next big party, just focus on spending your time preparing for such. I think people often have more fun preparing for an activity, such as Christmas, than they do during the actual happening. In any event, you can always find a creative outlet in your day to day life that will enhance it. This might also include avoiding people who are downers.

If one chooses to become more ambitious, one can make a "to do" list of everything one wants to accomplish, including study courses or engaging in procedures that delve deeper into different areas. Such an endeavor is a very similar but much less intense approach to what was said earlier about seeking out one's goals. While such an approach can be overly dramatic, there are other ways to address one's personal desires. Insisting upon balance makes it a lot easier and more fun. There is no question, however, that some people will want to take grand excursions that will lead them to the edge of the cliff if not entirely off of it. Both Hubbard and Crowley, and you could also add Parsons into the mix, were taking on the mantle of humanity and the cosmic riddle that accompanies life on Earth. The balancing or interaction between the nuomenal and phenomenal worlds take on a much bigger scope when we consider the exploits of these various characters and what they were bringing to the table for consideration.

When we consider the bigger scope, an excellent metaphor is the long standing oral and written tradition, if is not indeed reasonably accurate history, recognizing the pyramids of Egypt as the last outpost of Atlantis, a monument to an ancient time when the veil between the "worlds" was thin. By "worlds" I am referring to the doctrine that there are other planes of existence than the physical plane, something the ancients referred to as the celestial realm. This corresponds, at least in part, to what more contemporary sources refer to as the etheric world, such as has long been expounded upon in occult doctrine, where the constituency of what one experiences in terms of sensory experience, whether it be ghost-like bodies or objects, is much more flexible in terms of responding to the thinking process of an individual. In other words, it is a paradigm of experience such as you experience in the world of a lucid dream where you are more god-like in your influence of the characters and circumstances around you. So it is that Atlantis is cited as a world where magicians had will power and technology to match it. The fall of Atlantis is deemed to be a time when the veils between these worlds closed and magical skill became rarified and predominantly subordinate to the laws of Newtonian physics.

The Pharaoh, a kingly attribute recognized in both the cultures of Atlantis and Egypt, served as the interlocutor between worlds. His job was to balance heaven and Earth. The word *pharaoh* is defined in different ways, but it basically refers to "fire" in the "Great House" or pyramid.* One could attribute all the ills of civilization and life on Earth to the fact that there is no active Pharaoh doing his job nor is there a capstone on the Great Pyramid wherein he could do his most exalted work in order to balance heaven and Earth.

While all of this might sound lofty and exalted, the architecture of the Great Pyramid clearly symbolizes the extant hierarchy of Earth's power structure. First, consider that the 32 degrees of Scottish Freemasonry are based upon 32 chambers within the Great Pyramid where initiation rites took place. Further, that Scotland got its name when the Celtic leader Niul (or Nile, meaning blue) married Scota, the daughter of the Pharaoh of Egypt.

It is relevant to point out that Aleister Crowley mentioned in his commentaries that when he once visited a Masonic lodge how shocked he was at

---

* The word Pharaoh itself means "Great House". Analyzing the etymology, the word "great" is derived from the Greek *magos* and the Persian *maz*, meaning "magic". "House" is derived from Indo-European "skeu" or "keu" meaning "to hide". Translated, the word *Pharaoh* means "magic hiding place". The *phar* in *Pharos*, the lighthouse near Alexandria, is equivalent to the *pyr* in *pyramid* which means "fire". This also relates to the divine spark in the capstone of the Great Pyramid which is also equivalent to the *shekinah glory* associated with the Ark of the Covenant. It should also be mentioned that, according to the *Bible*, the architecture of the Holy of Holies is such that the capstone of the Great Pyramid would fit snugly inside of it, thus suggesting that the Shekinah Glory itself would equate to the fire of the Pharaoh.

The analagous role of the Pharaoh runs deeper still when we consider that the "Great House" was symbolized by a pentagon, thus associating it with the magical formula of pentagrammaton or the Hebrew letters *yod-he-shin-van-he*, later transliterated into *Yeshua* and *Jesus*. [For a more through explanation, read *The Montauk Book of the Living* by Peter Moon.]

the emptiness of it. He was not referring to an absence of bodies or furniture but rather any spark of living knowledge of the traditions it was supposed to embody. Hence, do not expect Scientology organizations or secret societies to be much different. As one of my friends who delved deeply into the occult once said to me, "One cannot expect to become much more than middle management in such organizations."

Also consider that while the Great Pyramid features depictions of virtually every characteristic or habit of Egyptian life at the time of its construction, it features none of its builders or even why it was built. This information was deliberately left secret as sacred knowledge for the elite or priestly caste. When we consider life on Earth, this feature of the Great Pyramid is an apt analogy for both the political and spiritual predicament of Mankind. You have an "organism" with a lot of tentacles operating without a head. This is symbolized by the missing capstone. So it is, however, that secret societies run around with pieces of the great secret or bigger picture, too often beset by characteristics that might best be analogous to the seven deadly sins.

Into the architecture of the Great Pyramid we have Aleister Crowley inserting himself by having sex with his wife, Rose Kelly, in the King's Chamber, later resulting in the transmission of *The Book of the Law*, a work which was deeply influential upon both Jack Parsons and L. Ron Hubbard. Here we are talking about a territory — the pyramid — which is also a map, but it is far more than just a map. It is an energetic resonator and transceiver. A pyramid amplifies energies, and it can also act as a receiver or transmitter. Do you get the idea of what is happening in this scenario?

We are talking about a Moon Child. I will explain further.

Regardless of the actual mechanics of how the pyramid was built, the builder, according to Egyptian mythology, was THOTH or Tahuti (derived from the pronunciation of *Te-He-O-Te-He*, the Greek word *Thoth* serving as an acronym), the ibis-headed secretary of the gods who also served as the god of sex magick. What does this reference to sex magick tell us about the builder?

The identification of Tahuti as the god of sex magick suggests that the Great Pyramid itself is tied to the process of procreation which, in its most exalted form, would be the ultimate Moon Child, identifiable as the Pharaoh or Christ, who would serve as the ultimate balancing factor between the celestial and earthly realms.

The schematic and legacy of the Great Pyramid gives insight into the common interpretation of Freemasonry's "secret word": *mahabone*, interpreted as "what, the builder?" Tahuti or Thoth is the builder of the Great Pyramid who calculatingly built 32 chambers or degrees of initiation.

To refer back to the prospect of the Great Pyramid as a template or reference point with regard to procreation, this was manifested by Aleister Crowley when he transmitted *The Book of the Law* from April 8-10, 1904. Although

Crowley was completely perplexed by this communication from Aiwass, the entity he identified as the originator of the text, and never claimed to understand what he deemed to be his most important work, he spent much of his life preoccupied with what he had transmitted. As the book itself explained, there would be someone else who would come along later and discover the "Key of it all". The following is from *The Book of the Law* (see page 276 for handwritten version with the "line drawn"):

> "This book shall be translated into all tongues: but always with the original in the writing of the Beast; for in the chance shape of the letters and their position to one another: in these are mysteries that no Beast shall divine. Let him not seek to try: but one cometh after him, whence I say not, who shall discover the Key of it all. Then this line drawn is a key: then this circle squared in its failure is a key also. And Abrahadabra. It shall be his child and that strangely. Let him not seek after this; for thereby alone can he fall from it."

According to Nibs (L. Ron Hubbard Jr.), his father identified himself as the one who had indeed discovered the Key. While Hubbard was a truly incredible character and made some unprecedented headway in his own right, he did not understand the specifics of the key. There is no question, however, that he was riding the energy of Crowley who was, in turn, imbued with the transmission of the book.

As I have written about in a previous book of mine, *The Montauk Book of the Living*, I met a former member of the OTO who had broken the code. Although he was kicked out of the OTO, his scholarship on this point was absolutely brilliant. While I am not going to go into the details of it in this work, it revealed that "this line drawn" referred to the letters "I try to shape a Beast"; and further, that codes within the text revealed the basic schematic for DNA and how it relates to the basic schematic for the Tree of Life upon which the Holy Kabbala is based.* In other words, Crowley's iterations during the transmission of *The Book of the Law* were revealing the scientific structure of DNA before DNA was even discovered in the scientific world.

While I think many people would be quick to judge Crowley's incursion into the King's Chamber so as to have sex with his wife as an effort to prank the gods or to desecrate the Great Pyramid itself, he was much more astute and generally well-informed than his critics. We have to consider, however, whether the pyramid was working him rather than the other way around. In this case, we do not have an instance of the specifics of DNA being coded in the hieroglyphics or structure of the pyramid itself; rather, it is associated with an energy or entity that is connected to the pyramid.

---

* See Appendix B for a further explanation of *The Book of the Law*.

THE CITY OF THE PYRAMIDS 201

So, it is no surprise that Tahuti, designated as the builder of the Great Pyramid, is also recognized as the god of sex magick. The analogy with regard to the Moon Child, however, runs far deeper. I am referring to various associations between the Great Pyramid and the life of Christ as has been depicted in the *New Testament*. In other words, there have been copious efforts to demonstrate how various angles and units of measurements within the Great Pyramid point directly to the life of Christ as described in the *Bible*. You can look these references up for yourself if you wish, but there is a much more important and relevant factor with regard to the veracity of these associations, something that is likely to be missed by most people.

I am not suggesting that such correspondences prove that the *New Testament* and/or the life of Jesus is true; rather, I am suggesting that such literature derives from a chain of scribes who had been initiated in one of the various traditions I have alluded to with regard to the Great Pyramid and were contouring what they wrote to the political and/or spiritual environment of the times. In other words, "The Greatest Story Ever Told" is the Great Pyramid itself, and everything else is a knock off. This only applies, however, if you can understand the entire story and all of its components. While this scenario only alludes to the *New Testament* rather than verifying it in any detail, it does refer to the role of a Christ or what can best be termed an immaculate Moon Child. Refer back to the line from *The Book of the Law*: *"then this circle squared in its failure is a key also"*.

As covered in *the Montauk Book of the Living*, the "circle squared" refers to the fact that the base of the Great Pyramid is a square whose perimeter is equal to the circumference of a circle with a radius equal to the height of the Great Pyramid. The dimensions of the Great Pyramid are as follows:

> Height = 481 feet
> Base = 755 feet (some say 755.5 or 756)
> Perimeter = 3,020 feet (755x4)

We then get a circumference that equals 3,020.68 feet which is virtually the same as the 3,020 feet of the perimeter of the base. The radius is then derived from a circle that looks something like the following which is only an approximation and not drawn precisely to scale:

Based upon this depiction, the comparative size of the Great Pyramid would look as follows. The square below is the base of the Great Pyramid. The circumference of the circle below is based upon the aforementioned instructions. The triangle represents the height of the Great Pyramid.

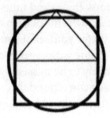

This demonstrates how small the height of the Great Pyramid is in relation to its base, and it is all very nice except for one very key point. These measurements are all done taking into account an imaginary capstone. The real capstone was removed long ago. Therefore, all attempts to square the circle are futile because the "height" of the Great Pyramid has been compromised due to the missing capstone. This "failure of the circle squared" is a particular reference to a level of Freemasonry. Crowley would have known this reference very well. In other words, the additional key he refers to besides "the key of it all" is a reference to the missing capstone of the Great Pyramid. This equates to Christ as the "rejected stone".

Once again, we have the Great Pyramid "talking" and telling a story of itself and the macrocosm.

The Great Pyramid, with its capstone in place, represents a fully functioning template of universal mechanics and the role of humanity within it. The Christ or Pharaoh function represents the balance between the nuomenal and phenomenal worlds. Note, however, this paradigm also applies to everyone on an individual basis. This is why I offered the analogy to the City of the Pyramids in the previous chapter. The body is based upon pyramidal structures.

The analogous City of the Pyramids that Crowley alludes to with regard to crossing the abyss also applies on a collective basis, but that should not require further explanation at this point. Just like Hubbard's bridge to freedom, these are maps. What I have written here is for the purpose of giving you a better idea of the territory. There are a lot of maps. Some of them are not so good. You will only learn and come to know the territory by investigating and experiencing it on your own.

QUALIFICATIONS

"The only person that is qualified for miracles is the person that has been qualified in the real life."
— Sunday Adelaja

In his own mind, L. Ron Hubbard never believed that he was merely operating a cult or a scam. He believed he was a whirlwind of power having an impact on the planet as had not been seen in the entire history of the universe. Due to the explosive impact of what he had created and the relentless immediacy to implement his wisdom, he commented, in his own words, that there would be considerable collateral damage. While you can question his relative impact, you cannot question that there has been considerable collateral damage.

Hubbard's solution to these problems was delineated in his organizational scheme with what was called the Qualifications Division. The awareness characters for this part of the organization were *RESULT, CORRECTION* and *ABILITY*. I emphasized these in a previous chapter for a couple of reasons. The first reason is that Hubbard considered that the entire reason why civilizations of the past had failed was due to their omission of this function. In other words, there was no function within their cultures by which to monitor and correct themselves. To him, it was the key to everything. The second reason I emphasize it is that I was comprehensively schooled in these aspects of Scientology. Most were not.

Earlier, I mentioned the importance of three factors: intelligence, access and fortune. My fortune was that I would be meticulously disciplined with regard to assessing the value or result of an action or endeavor, correcting it if necessary, and then observing or experiencing the consequent ability or success concomitant with it. To be a bit more clear, I was given extensive counseling sessions, at two different times during my Sea Org career, wherein I was exhaustively coached to give and view correct and incorrect examples of what might be termed a correct product or result and how to correct such. None of this was coercive in the least. It was educational, and it had a tremendous upside with regard to putting one in a mind-set where one did not have to accept, put up with or endure inferior results. This also meant that one could recognize collateral damage and fix it.

This sounds like an ideal situation, and it is, providing that the assembly line you are working with is workable and has integrity. It becomes an impossible situation to deal with, however, in the event that politics undermine the integrity of the assembly line.

Besides having extensive experience in Qual, as we called it, I also had extensive experience dealing with Hubbard's personal communications as well as his management directives. Unlike most of the common staff and management staff, I was also given routine briefings on his personal views and what problems he was having with organizations. With regard to the activities of the Guardian's Office, the organization which infiltrated the IRS and performed other "dirty tricks", I was only given the most general briefings and did not receive too many details, all of which would have been on a need-to-know basis. In the long run, all of this access worked to my advantage. When people did wrong actions and got bad results, whether it was in management, public relations or technical procedures, it was glaringly obvious. It was not so glaringly obvious to others, and this includes many intelligent and long time Sea Org veterans, some of them remaining for years after it became evident to me that the organization had lost any semblance of integrity. There were also many other Sea Org veterans who did indeed see the writing on the wall and departed. We all had different sets of circumstances and different orientations.

Let us next look at the definition of the word *qualify*:

qualify
1. To make competent or eligible for an office, position, or task.
2. To declare competent or capable, as to practice a profession; certify.
3. To render deserving of a descriptor by having or enumerating certain necessary characteristics.

The word *qualify* has everything to do with passing a test. Everyone, however, is familiar with the person with a diploma or otherwise heralded reputation who cannot actually perform in the workplace or some other area of earthly endeavor. In Scientology, like most everywhere else, human beings will lie, steal and cheat to obtain status without merit. This has everything to do with the human condition. When we take away the veil of illusion and position one's progress in life vis a vis the Abyss, we are dealing with a situation where you cannot fake it. The universe itself will judge you on your own merits. If you are adrift at sea, you cannot fake your seamanship skills.

It is the same in the martial arts. Originally, one "achieved" a black belt by doing so much work or combat in the dojo[*] that one's belt was blackened with dirt. It was not something one was given in an awards ceremony after going through arbitrarily assigned gradations of accomplishments signified by different colored belts. Thus, an experienced street fighter is going to have a distinct advantage to someone who has "earned" a black belt in a dojo without

---

[*] *Dojo* is a Japanese word which refers to a location where martial arts are practiced. It derives from *do* (*Dao* or *Tao*) and *jo* (work) which means "where the Tao is practiced" or where one "works with the *Tao*".

having engaged in a real fight. We are talking about negotiating territory, and when we are talking about Scientology and Hubbard, we have to address the underlying occult matrix and the various and assorted accoutrements that either influence or befuddle the human mind. The same situation applies in occult orders where people get very hung up, petty, and miss the forest for the trees with regard to titles and status. It means nothing unless you can actually walk the walk.

Hubbard himself had little regard for diplomas and certifications unless he issued them himself; but even then, he took them with a grain of salt. The reason for this is that he viewed the world as a broken and degraded world that was dedicated to self-destruction by reason of massive implantation that humanity has suffered as a whole. The real test in life is whether or not you can perform.

All of this begs the question of whether or not Hubbard was qualified to do what he did. The mainstream response of most anyone would be, "No, of course he was not." He is often criticized for not having a degree in psychology, psychiatry or any of the sciences. It is important to keep in mind, as I said earlier in this book, that you are not going to find anyone qualified in these fields who could do what Hubbard has done in terms of creating such a huge organization and an intelligence agency larger than most countries. Further, it was all self-generated. Just as Hubbard created and delineated designations with diplomas, so did he create his own status as the Founder of Scientology and the Commodore of the Sea Organization.

The most fundamental aspect of all this, particularly from the approach I have taken in this book, is what are his qualifications with regard to the occult? While he had no formally known or recognized designation in occult orders, his qualifications can best be realized by what Jack Parsons wrote about him in a letter to Crowley:

> "I deduced that he is in direct touch with some higher intelligence. He is the most Thelemic person I have ever met and is in complete accord with our own principles."

In other words, Hubbard was a natural Thelemite, at least as far as Parsons was concerned. That means he was a person who was not only in touch with a higher intelligence (his Holy Guardian Angel) but was exercising his own will. Without judging this as good or bad, it certainly puts him in a category where he is extremely different than the average individual, particularly with regard to the time period he lived in. It takes one to know one, and Hubbard was extraordinarily comfortable with the magical accoutrements that Parsons surrounded himself with as well as the magick he practiced. These are not the type of waters an average person will swim in.

In a future book, I hope to go further into Hubbard's genetics and why he would be predisposed to such a life of magick and messiahship. Upon information and belief, Hubbard was an aborted messiah. In other words, he had some characteristics of a messiah, but there is also the prospect of an "aborted messiah" or one that did not fully develop. Further, I believe his entire genetic line represents a wild maverick or mutation on the wheel of life (like "0" or "00" on a roulette wheel) and that he is the mutation of the mutation. This statement, by the way, is not meant to diminish him or his work in any way. I say it to help better explain who he is and what he represents.

In the final analysis, Hubbard is qualified by life itself. One can safely say that because life presents itself without certificates. It is just life, and it appears any old way it wants to appear. If you are confronted by an animal in the wild that you have never heard of and do not recognize, you deal with it and recognize it for what it is and not by the fact that it does not appear in text books on zoology. In the traditional Cabalistic Tree of Life, such an aspect is relegated to The Fool, an archetype that derives from Kether, the Hebrew designation for the Most High (the original source of all). On the opposite side of The Fool is The Magician, also deriving directly from Kether. These two aspects of the Tree are the most befuddling to man, especially when he is trying to reconcile himself with the Creator. If you can truly respect and understand these concepts, Hubbard is much less mysterious, but he is still mysterious, a principle that he understood and deliberately capitalized on.

With regard to his own personal qualifications, a fair amount of accusations have been directed at him for plagiarizing or misappropriating materials from others, some even stating that he never did anything original. Former Scientologists can be very snarky about this. While it is fruitless to pursue all of these claims, it is noteworthy that such criticisms are something like spraying a hose at an elephant. Whatever Hubbard did or did not do correctly, he was a potent force that generated considerable power and influence over people's minds. The structure that he created ignited hope and enthusiasm to the point where thousands upon thousands of people were willing to completely change their lifestyle to embrace Scientology. None of the contributions of the people who were allegedly ripped off, no matter how great their contribution, would have ever been heard of otherwise. This is something on the order of giving a set of lyrics to a famous musician and then being surprised and dumbfounded when you hear it on the radio with no acknowledgement of yourself. While this is not fair, it happens all the time. And most of those lyricists might not have had their lyrics heard in any other way. But whether or not the accusations against Hubbard are accurate, there is another factor at work that is much more relevant.

There were a considerable number of high profile Scientologists over the years who were very successful in promoting Scientology and getting people to experience the lower levels of the bridge. They were very popular and also effective at applying Scientology, particularly at the lower levels, and also establishing excellent public relations with the general public. For all of their skills and knowledge, which was usually considerable, none of them were capable of creating a mass movement to the extent that Hubbard did. In other words, they were reliant on Hubbard's writings and methods to be successful. And consequently, when they were cut off by Hubbard of the Church, they were either broken or greatly reduced in their capacity to attract and maintain a large following. What I say here is not intended to diminish such people in any way. They were indeed incredibly knowledgeable and skilled. The point is that Hubbard was the main spark. And beyond the spark, there was an incredible power that most definitely eluded those who tried to either follow in his wake or co-opt his legacy. Hubbard held the reins to the entire movement, and he also designed it that way. If he did not, however, it is quite possible that the organization would have not grown to the extent that it did.

In spite of his voracious and at times ruthless efforts that precipitated collateral damage along the way, he was very mindful of this process and was keen to make an effort to correct the various discombobulations that occurred along the way. He viewed his work as the most dynamic impact the world had ever known, not unlike a comet that was so huge that it might change the orbit of an entire planet. As a result, he acknowledged that there would be damages to people who were either in the way or could not absorb the impact. Consequently, he gave instructions and remedies to pick people up, dust them off and put them back on a path to happiness. This was one of the many duties of the Qualifications Division. While this was a laudable idea, it did not work so well in the final analysis.

Is it too late to pick up the pieces? Certainly not in any pragmatic and immediate sense, and here I am referring to the collective or big picture. The real issue at hand, if we consider the "territory" is to find a balance between the nuomenal and phenomenal worlds, both as individuals as well as the collective. Whatever broad-based positive applications are contained within the legacy of Scientology, it requires far more time and effort than the public generally has at its disposal. It requires a sequestered or even cultish framework to make any sort of serious impact. In my opinion, any broad-based effort to identify and utilize anything valuable with regard to Scientology procedures and reach large numbers of humanity would have to come out of the world of artificial intelligence, something that might happen well after the Scientologists of today are long since gone.

With regard to Hubbard himself, no matter how much he and his work are vilified, his name and that of Scientology continue to intrigue people, and I do not see any signs of it letting up. He has had his life scrutinized like no other, and people continue to try and dig up little pieces of it, often in an effort to explain him. No matter how much is discovered, the name of L. Ron Hubbard cannot be put to rest. Per his own writings, if you want something to disappear, you have to view it from all possible vantage points. If we heed the statement from Jack Parsons that you cannot begin to evaluate a person's contributions until 100-150 years after his death, Hubbard's legacy cannot be adequately assessed until the turn of the next century, and it won't be until 2034 that we begin to get a clue.

When we get back to the proposition of the "territory", there is a very relevant aspect I want to share which was a staple of L. Ron Hubbard and Scientology, and particularly so in the daily toil of the Qualifications Division. That was the discipline of clearing words, called Word Clearing, which involved studying the full definition of words, including the etymologies. I spent so many hours clearing words and helping others clear words that the experience was invaluable in terms of learning a new subject, particularly difficult ones. It is incredibly helpful with esoteric subjects such as the occult.

As was said earlier, the underpinnings of the occult and asserting one's will by casting spells is done via what is called *grimoire*, a French word meaning "grammar" which refers to the proper alignment of words or letters, all of which can be re presented by symbols, so as to cast a "spell" in order to achieve a result. These were often put together in a book which was referred to as a *grimoire*, but the word itself applies to structuring words and letters.

Studying the etymology of words undercuts the process of words because one is dealing with the actual source or thought that the verbalization or inscription is intended to express. If you take this a step further and think of it as a wave form, it points to how powerful radio waves can be in terms of transmitting ideas or what is referred to as "intelligent information" that turn into radio or television broadcasts. When you examine the etymology of a word or a series of words, you are, in fact, doing a "cut-up" as was described by William Burroughs and Brion Gysin. This applies to the phonetics of a word as well. Brion Gysin said, "Rub out the word". This strips down the shell of what is surrounding the underlying essence of what is being communicated.

Occult magicians are very precise and particular when it comes to magical practices, even to the point of being dogmatic. There is an understandable reason for this, and it is not any different from a chemist, a physicist, or an engineer following precise laws and procedures to produce a specific result in a scientific reference frame. In this respect, scientists and magicians can be very rigid. While such rigidity in a scientist is completely understandable, the magician is also dealing with similar issues.

In magick, you are dealing with a hierarchy of forces that regulate the ordained structure of the universe. For example, if you invoke forces to tear down an entire ecosystem, population or other huge enterprise, you are going to have to answer to those forces that are keeping them in place. This might result in some very curious and animated "eyeballs" giving you more attention than you thought possible and certainly more than you would ever want.

When you genuinely "cut up" the magical intonations of magicians and their various iterations, you are moving into the quantum realm. This can perhaps be best understood with reference to what is called Quantum Electrodynamics. Q.E.D., as it is called, is a theory describing how light and matter interact and bridges or harmonizes quantum mechanics with Einstein's Theory of Special Relativity. Breaking down physical matter into subatomic particles shares a deep sympathy with the cut-up method. Just as you are tapping into the essence of meaning when you cut up words or letters so are you tapping into the essence of matter when you cut it up. It should be noted, however, that the latter also includes the scrutiny of the aforementioned hierarchy.

While there are various ways to engage or enter into the magical realm, it is as easy as cutting up the various grimoire or other writing you encounter. The reason for this is that you are literally penetrating the frequencies (intelligent information) that are behind the words. This literally places you in the quantum realm. Keep in mind that the entire proposition of quantum physics is based upon the proposition that a particle can be a wave and vice versa; and further, that either will or can repeatedly appear and disappear; and further still, that they can participate in other systems (such as different realities or universes) during the time they are not "here" in our universe. In other words, when a particle or wave has disappeared in our world, it is serving a function in another world or has the potential to do so.

Keeping in mind that there are various levels of penetration, anyone can enter the most rudimentary level of this quantum realm by simply going inside of your mind and deciding to change the frequency of a regular routine or habit that you have mentally subscribed to. For example, suppose you get up every morning and habitually pour water or coffee into the same cup. Now, just decide to simply change that habit. Maybe you will use a different cup. Maybe you will drink tea instead. In any event, you have changed the frequency connected to the routine.

Changing a simple habit or even making a major life adjustment in this context is really not such a big deal. When you begin to cut up grimoire or the major work of a magician, however, you are moving into a deeper realm where you are going to get "eyeballed" to some extent. Just as the structure and laws of the physical universe are maintained in a relative status quo, so is the relative framework of the quantum realm. Hierarchies are in place as well as old energies, entities or egregore that might have a score to settle with you or other unfinished business.

Whether it be called Dianetic reverie, hypnotic regression, meditation, or any other number of names, anyone can move into this realm with varying degrees of depth and penetration. It is a world of frequencies, energies, vectors, intentions and various forces. In fact, this realm features everything that the human mind can conjure up and it rides hand-in-hand with one's imagination and the creative process. There were literally hundreds upon hundreds of different processes in Dianetics and Scientology that were designed specifically to deal with this realm and the challenges one could face. While much of it has to do with the aforesaid rudiments (upsets and problems, etc.), there are a host of other approaches to smooth out this realm. If these process were intelligently applied, they could work wonders for the individual. If not intelligently applied, nothing might happen or worse.

As was stated earlier, people could experience something along the order of a miracle and become way too excited to the point of imbalance. While there were also techniques to deal with this, it cannot be over emphasized that balance is the key issue at hand, at least if we are taking into consideration the relationship between the nuomenal and phenomenal worlds.

To harken back to the doctrine of "Nothing is true. Everything is permitted", we are dealing with the prospect that the quantum world contains all possibilities. We are steered into our own experiences based upon a host of factors which include but are not limited to our decisions, our past, our observations, our perceptions, our interests, our susceptibility to the inducement or directions of others, and so on. Such an environment also includes the potential for unlimited power such as you might see in a super hero, an idealized martial artist or as discussed in some of L. Ron Hubbard's earliest books on the infinite capabilities of thetans.

As a creative writer and explorer, Hubbard was prone to dive into the quantum field without much consideration for explaining himself or contextualizing it. It was not a major concern to him nor to many Scientologists. Such a disposition leaves one open to being interpreted as nuts. I would also add that there is a considerably high percentage of the population who is similarly inclined not to discriminate when it comes to delineating the quantum world from hard based reality. This is where "fiction" is contradicted by fact. This mind-set applies equally to other religions as well, Christianity being a prime example. Distinguishing the two references frames is important, at least if you want to be understood. It is important not to diminish either reference frame or how they might influence each other in the general stream of consciousness and life experience.

The grand interface between these two worlds, at least in its most perfected form, is the Moon Child. It is important to remember that Jack Parsons was using L. Ron Hubbard as his familiar in order to manifest such. As Dianetics and Scientology came soon afterwards, it is both tempting and easy to speculate that they were positioned to serve the original magician: Jack Parsons.

ON THE RADAR

"I SING the Body electric
The armies of those I love engirth me, and I engirth them;
They will not let me off till I go with them, respond to them,
And discorrupt them, and charge them full with the charge of the Soul."
— Walt Whitman, Leaves of Grass

Perhaps the greatest incongruity with regards to the claim that L. Ron Hubbard ripped off everything he developed concerns his writings about electronics being used to influence, capture, and implant spiritual beings.

Specifically, Hubbard stated that a spiritual being or "thetan" has no mass, no wavelength, no energy, etc. but that he emulates such in order to interact with the universes of matter, energy, space and time. In order to interact with the universe, a being has to convince himself that he is mass and energy in order to interface with or negotiate the territory. It is somewhat similar to putting on a virtual reality helmet.

Hubbard also defined electronics as a "lower and cruder manifestation of the same order of actuality as thought". In other words, one is a harmonic resonance of the other. As there is a sympathetic relationship between the two, it would stand to reason that one could influence the other. We readily see this in the case of electric shock therapy.

There are different accounts in his writings of electronic incidents, and these include many specific descriptions. Most of these are rather abstract accounts of thetans in space. He states that MEST beings would routinely use electronics in order to capture and degrade spiritual beings to the point where they would think they were simply meat bodies and nothing more. In this regard, it is a technique for brainwashing.

Whether or not any of this is true is secondary to the question: where on Earth did these ideas come from? While the general idea was not necessarily unprecedented, his emphasis on it was, and he did not hold back on his mentations. The way he went into detail was if he was relaying information from a master text on the subject. At the same time, he wrote as if he had direct knowledge of such. The question must be repeated: where did these ideas come from?

It is very tempting for Scientologists to assume that he figured this out from his investigations into the whole track, all of which could either include his own meanderings or what turned up in the auditing sessions of other people. Besides his taped lectures, many of his theories and techniques were in the books *Scientology 8-80* and *Scientology 8-8008*.

Conventional research has now long established that radio waves can influence human behavior, but this is a far cry from documenting that the same can be said for "thetans" or the specific electronic assaults that they might have suffered. There are, however, countless instances of ghost hunters establishing scenarios where ghosts or other beings can be identified in the context of electromagnetic phenomena.

The idea of there being a deep relationship between electronics and human beings was presented to me very early on in my Scientology adventures. Hubbard clearly stated that his writings were meant to stimulate the mind in order to conjure up residual energy that could be audited out. To "audit out" or to "run out" means to process an idea, feeling, pain, etc. until it would dissipate, erase or no longer impinge upon the individual. One is essentially using the same or a very similar faculty one uses when imagining something. On a personal level, I found that if I had headaches or other pains that would not resolve so easily by processing usual incidents in my memory, addressing the issue from the prospect of electronics being used upon my mind, body and soul could lead to a resolution of the issue.

It is very important at this point to address the subject of force and particularly how it relates to the function of the mind. Scientology and Hubbard are sometimes if not often accused of exerting mental force upon people, all of which can be called mind control. Without singling out Scientologists, many people are mentally weak. Peer pressure is only one such example. There are all sorts of incidents in life where people are either hesitant or afraid to speak up about something they do not like, all of which comes down to an issue of force. Electronics represents a very potent form of force in the physical universe, a cattle prod being only one example.

People who cannot stand up for themselves are succumbing to force on the mental level. While there might not be actual electronics involved, we have all seen domineering people use body language in such a way that is energetic in nature and mimics electronics. This might include "shooting vectors" out of the eyes or pointing a finger in a way that can be very introverting. If people who are mentally weak can be made to confront energy on the mental level, they will find it easier to negotiate actual situations in their life. This is only one example of what processing electronic incidents might offer. The idea of a civilization of free thetans being attracted and trapped magnetically and then being implanted forcefully is another issue. In Scientology, the entire civilization on Earth was viewed as a victim of such activity; and most specifically, it was implanted to forget.

To get back to my original question, I found it noteworthy that Hubbard was involved with and had an understanding of radar while it was in its relative infancy. Please refer to the letter about Hubbard from Jimmy Britton to the Secretary of the Navy on the next two pages.

Alaska Radio & Service Co., Inc.

JAMES A. BRITTON
PRESIDENT

R. W. BRITTON
VICE-PRES.

KGBU
"The Voice of Alaska"

880 KILOCYCLES
1000 WATTS
BROADCASTING STUDIO
KETCHIKAN, ALASKA

March 15, 1941

The Honorable Frank Knox
Secretary of the Navy,
Washington, D.C.

Dear Sir;

Until a year ago I did not have the pleasure of knowing L. Ron Hubbard except through his stories and articles on many subjects. Last spring, however, I had the pleasure of meeting him on his arrival in Alaska with the Alaskan Radio-Experimental Expedition and, for the ensuing ten months, had the pleasure of being with him often.

His versatility and ability seem to be boundless for, in the process of exploring the world for story material, he has become a sailor of great skill, a fact which is verified by the repute in which Alaskans now hold him. Sailing a large vessel in these tide-bedeviled waters where the channels are torturously enclosed by reefs is a feat not lightly to be regarded and yet Captain Hubbard brought his ship through thousands of miles of such waters without mishap, despite storms and fogs, both of which were unusually heavy last year.

The log of his Alaskan saga, just concluded, reads most excitingly for he had not been in Alaskan waters a week before he detected, with his radio navigational instruments, a source of interference which had remained a mystery to the engineers of the Signal Corps, the Coast Guard and myself. Working with the FBI's Mr. Naughton, Captain Hubbard was instrumental in bringing to justice a German saboteur who had devised it to be in his power to cut off Alaska from communication with the United States in time of war through the sabotage of Signal Corps signals. The Coast Guard and the FBI must both have a report of this. Other events of similarly adventurous nature distinguished Captain Hubbard in the eyes of Alaskans.

However, Captain Hubbard's principle value must not be considered to lie in his marine abilities for he has, as I had occasion to discover, a proper claim to his reputation as a writer.

Alaska Radio & Service Co., Inc.

JAMES A. BRITTON
PRESIDENT

A. W. BRITTON
VICE-PRES.

K G B U

"The Voice of Alaska"

900 KILOCYCLES
1000 WATTS

BROADCASTING STUDIOS
KETCHIKAN, ALASKA

-2-
The Honorable Frank Knox

During the early part of his life he must have had considerable training in radio work for he knows much about radio stations. Nearly every traveler and explorer who comes through Ketchikan pretends to a knowledge of programs but Captain Hubbard is the first for whose help I am grateful. He was on the air here many times, both by remote and in the studio, and his material was so well organized and his voice so peculiarly adapted to radio that he commanded great interest in our listeners who are spread all through Alaska and Northern Canada.

He seems to have great organizational ability for, at my request during several stays in port here, he undertook to rework the operation of the station and created for us a new system of programs which we will continue to use for a longtime to come.

In line with his writing he is a good professional photographer for some of the pictures he took in Alaska are still on display here at the local photographic shop. I have also seen his work in the National Geographic Magazine and in that high standard of photographic excellence, THE SPORTSMAN PILOT.

He has a very sunny and pleasant disposition and was much in the graces of his crews. He made many friends here in Alaska who will remember him for a long time to come.

I do not hesitate to recommend him without reserve as a man of intelligence, courage and good breeding as well as one of the most versatile personalities I have ever known. And I say this as one who has been in constant touch with celebrities both in the United States and the North for twenty years.

Sincerely,

Jimmy Britton

This letter not only suggests that Hubbard was well versed in radar but that he had enough expertise to be considered an expert in the subject. This was, however, prior to him receiving his naval commission in 1941.

While the gushing letter (see Chapter 13) Hubbard received from Ian MacBean, the highly placed MI6 agent he hung out with in China during his formative years, is a clear indication that he was chummy with top levels of British Intelligence, his experience in radar is a second one. The British were early pioneers when it came to radar, and their knowledge of this subject accelerated greatly when they defended themselves against the Germans in the 1939 Battle of Britain.

Anyone who is a serious professional in radar is predisposed to seeing all of the subtle and not so subtle effects it can have on human behavior. As radar was already a weapon of war, do not think for a minute that this aspect would have gone unnoticed by the British war machine or any of the other players on the world stage. Secrecy in such matters is paramount and so is being secret about the secret.

Other than Ron's nondescript service in the Montana National Guard (October 19, 1927 to October 28, 1928)* and the 20th Regiment of the Marine Corps Reserve (May 1930 to October 22, 1931), both terms of which had ended, there is no ostensible explanation for him to have been briefed on military secrets. While he had nautical adventures during the Thirties, none of these necessitated learning about radar. How he acquired such knowledge remains a mystery, but the letter from Jimmy Britton indicates that he was unusually adept for a non-military person. The fact that he came from a military family, however, as well as his seemingly innocuous service in the Guard and Reserve Corps, offers a strange window of opportunity, particularly when it is coupled with his mysterious friendship with the British agent Ian MacBean.

We are offered some insight into this mystery when we consider an article featured in *Stories in the News* by June Allen entitled *L. Ron Hubbard's Alaska Adventure — His Long Winter in Ketchikan*.** While this article is a puff piece which is primarily aimed at writing an anecdote about one more famous person that passed through Ketchikan, it also sheds further light on this data trail. Note the following excerpt from the article.

---

* There are various discrepancies in the dates given for Hubbard's service in the Montana National Guard, but they all agree on 1927 and/or 1928. The oddest aspect, however, is that he seems to have completed his service while in the Orient in 1928. The dates I have given above were provided by R.A. Derr, Special Assistant for Officer Correspondence by direction of the Commander, Naval Military Personnel Command.

** Ketchikan is a small fishing village on the southern panhandle of Alaska and has served as a sort of central relay point for those taking excursion into the panhandle. Consequently, several celebrities have passed through there, and the small city (currently about 8,000 people) is eager to publicize their colorful history.

"Years later Hubbard grandiosely dubbed his unanticipated Ketchikan stay as just one leg of an 'Alaskan Radio Experimental Expedition.' Hubbard wrote several rather romanticized and semi-fictionalized accounts of these far north experiences; he also elaborated on the reasons for the Alaskan 'expedition.' Among other things, he had an interest in what today is called "white noise," the suspicious static that so annoyed radio listeners. On a more noble level, the Alaska experiment, he said, was to 'augment his knowledge of more cultures - the Tlingit, the Haida and the Aleut Indians of Alaska' — an ethnological study with emphasis on the universal Great Flood myth."

To add context to what Hubbard was doing in Alaska, it is important to offer a quote from General Billy Mitchell, an early advocate of military air power who is often credited as the father of the modern Air Force.

"I believe that in the future, whoever holds Alaska will hold the world. I think it is the most important strategic place in the world."

Ever since Commander Perry invaded Japan in 1853, the United States has maintained a very aggressive posture towards that country in an effort to assert and maintain their own interests in Asia. After having their oil supply cut off more than once and enduring Jack London's rhetoric about genocide being a solution to the Yellow Peril, Japan viewed that the control of the Aleutians would prevent an attack from the Americans. On the other hand, the Americans knew very well that they had aroused a previously sleeping giant and feared that the Aleutians could be used to carry out an aerial attack on West Coast cities. These were key points of military strategy well before the Germans invaded Poland and World War II began. Billy Mitchell had offered his warning about the Aleutians in 1935.

Ketchikan and the surrounding area was the first line of defense against a possible invasion of the Aleutians, an event which was realized in 1942 when the Japanese actually occupied the islands. It was prudent for someone, if not Hubbard himself, to explore the entire area with radio direction finding equipment and to map out the location for future military operations.

Hubbard's equipment for the radio direction finding was provided by the Cape Cod Instrument Company. This fact and several others suggest he was deeply tied to Vincent Astor, the most pivotal character on the map with regard to U.S. Naval Intelligence.

Astor, an avid sailor and explorer, grew up next to Franklin Roosevelt and the two were fast friends. As the war approached, and well before the

Pearl Harbor incident, Roosevelt selected Commander Astor, U.S. Naval Reserve, to be his Area Controller for the New York area with his direct orders being given by Naval Intelligence. By this time, Astor had already been patrolling the Pacific and other areas to make full reports on the capabilities of potential adversaries as well as mapping their coast lines. He used instrumentation from the Cape Cod Instrument Company, and due to the nature of his interests in protecting the country and spying on countries, there is no question that he himself would have been on the cutting edge of radar technology. His international connections, especially with the British, were extensive. Astor was also incredibly rich, and he provided a home for "Intrepid", the moniker for another high powered industrialist, William Stephenson, a key figure in British Intelligence who would set up the OSS in America. Astor assembled a rogue's gallery of power players and spies known as "The Room", and besides those affiliated with the Allies, he cultivated Germans and Russians to occupy the building, plus anyone else who was deemed a potential rival.

Hubbard was extremely proud of his membership in the Explorer's Club, an exclusive New York City society, many of whom served the needs of The Room, the Explorer's Club flag serving as an ideal front for conducting espionage. While these connections remain obscure to a certain degree, they run deep and are intriguing. To go into them any further, however, requires an entire study in itself. It should be noted that some people take great umbrage over the proposition that Hubbard was seriously involved in any Naval Intelligence operations, the reason being that it does not show up in his military records. It is, however, well documented that Vincent Astor did not operate within the military proper. His formal assignment under U.S. Naval Intelligence came directly from the White House and this was in 1941, eight months before Pearl Harbor. This information itself was classified for many years. All I am trying to do in this narrative is to provide the reader with the fact that there was a window of opportunity for Hubbard to have learned cutting edge information on radar.

It is also highly ironic if not a meaningful coincidence that Hubbard applied for his commission in the Navy only one month after Astor officially assumed and acknowledged his role as Area Controller after receiving orders from the White House to take instructions from Naval Intelligence. Upon receiving his commission, Hubbard applied to serve in Naval Intelligence.

Another ironic if not meaningful coincidence concerns June Allen's statement in her article that he had an interest in "white noise" which she described as "suspicious static that so annoyed radio listeners". White noise is a phenomenon that is usually underestimated and frequently misunderstood, one of the reasons being is that it is defined in different ways, but we will explore that in the next chapter.

By the time Hubbard joined the Navy, he had lived an awful lot of life. He had obtained a "License to Master of Steam and Motor Vessels", a "License to Master of Sail Vessels, Any Ocean", he was a pilot, a self-styled adventurer who had traveled extensively in the Far East, and he had also conducted sea faring expeditions which included a mineral survey Puerto Rico, a motion picture expedition to the Caribbean, and the Alaskan expedition. This was all in addition to his flirtation with the human mind at St. Elizabeth's, the first-hand knowledge he learned from Commander Thompson, and his adventures as a profession writer of westerns, fantasy, and science fiction.

Most people of his day were neither so adventurous nor multi-faceted. Just this small description is enough to tell you that there is no way he could have subjected himself to the so-called normal life to which so many aspired to during a time of national depression: a secure nine-to-five job and a secure foothold in society. Whatever you might think of him, this was most certainly not his cup of tea.

Whatever L. Ron Hubbard learned as a result of these adventures and whatever his precise or imprecise role in the intelligence world might have been, all of it set the stage for his seminal emergence in what many occultists have referred to as the greatest magical act of the Twentieth Century: the Babalon Working.

Regardless of what people might think of him, he was a player on the world stage like no other. People have tried to dig up every little detail of his life they can find. Sometimes this is done with an agenda to make him look better or worse than he actually was. Other times, people are just curious. When these efforts are not a rush to judgment in order to assert "the truth" about him, they are an effort to discover a truth about this man that eludes their grasp.

All of us who experienced L. Ron Hubbard each did it in a different way. Some of us got to work in a close-up capacity while others knew him only by his reputation and the techniques he offered. You might even say that he was on our respective radars.

When I left Scientology in 1983, almost three years before Hubbard passed away, I was very self-contained and happy inside. I thought I would live out my life peacefully and fade into old age, spiritually content and comfortable with the proposition I would pass from this world, never to incarnate again, emerging into eternal peace.

As life would evolve, I was in for some major surprises.

WHITE NOISE

"If you want to find the secrets of the universe, think in terms of energy, frequency and vibration."
— Nikola Tesla

As I alluded to previously, I felt I was in a very balanced state of equilibrium after leaving Scientology in 1983 and moving back to the regular world. There was, however, a period of adjustment before I felt so much peace. That adjustment had everything to do with finding my economic balance in the world around me. The internal peace was a result of all the inner work I had done. Everyone, of course, will have different inner experiences and while one can find commonalities at times, these can vary drastically from individual to individual. I would not find my place in the world and hit my stride until seven years after leaving the Sea Organization.

I had engaged in different businesses, but the details are not so important. What is important is that each and every business I engaged in, and especially my years in Scientology, served as perfect prerequisites for what would become my future career: a writer and publisher.

While pursuing my regular business of design and advertising, I learned of an inventor who needed help marketing his inventions. I was told that his inventions were superior to other products on the market but that he needed help. Consequently, I arranged to introduce myself to this man. His name was Preston Nichols, and he would change my life forever. The day was November 7, 1990, and it is a day that I will never forget.

I was told that I could meet Preston at an evening meeting of the Long Island Chapter of the U.S. Psychotronics Association or U.S.P.A. Although I did not know it at the time, a Scientologist by the name of Ingo Swann had been credited with coining the word *psychotronics*, a subject which studies how electronics interfaces with the mind, body, and spirit of human beings.

The first thing I noticed upon meeting Preston was unmistakable. He was not in his body. While this might sound strange or highly subjective, such an observation is commonplace to a Scientology auditor who has audited thousands of hours. Completely aside from this, he was unlike any other person that I have ever met. My experiences in Scientology not only came in very handy, there was no way that I would have been in a position to either understand or work with him had I not had such training.

Although I did not know it at the time, Preston was an expert on the subject of white noise, but we will get into that in just a bit. Most relevant to this narrative was that Preston was on a panel that night which featured a group of people talking about upcoming Earth changes. He told me that I would have to wait until the break to speak to him.

Most of what Preston talked about that night to a small room full of interested people concerned the Philadelphia Experiment and the Montauk Project, two secret projects of the Government, the latter of which sought to influence the mind of individuals with electronics or electromagnetic waves in order to control mental phenomena, including time itself.*

What we know of the Philadelphia Experiment is a mixture of legend, history and science with a lot of hyperbole thrown in. It has been the subject of different books. As far as the technical end of it, no one was more familiar with it at that time than Preston Nichols. Although none of this could be printed during the time he was alive, he worked at Airborn Instruments Laboratory (AIL), a major defense contractor on Long Island. When he worked for AIL, he was assigned to read a rather involved technical report on the Philadelphians Experiment, and it was something he would never talk about publicly nor privately due to a non-disclosure agreement he had signed. As far as I was able to determine, the reason he was assigned to read this report and given the security clearance to do so was that he worked on highly classified projects regarding stealth aircraft. Although the public is told that stealth technology mainly concerned absorbing radar waves with a reduced cross section and a certain type of paint, Preston always said that there is a level of stealth technology that enables a craft to actually disappear from sight. The Philadelphia Experiment was relevant to this effort because that involved making a ship appear invisible to radar.

What I learned from Preston is that white noise is an impulse at every frequency at the same time. When you are tuning your FM radio dial, the noise you hear between stations is white noise.** It can be thought of as a sudden burst at every frequency or a bunch of impulses thrown together. White noise, however, is much more than that, it being a somewhat elusive term for science

---

* The Philadelphia Experiment occurred in 1943 when the Navy was conducting experiments to make a ship appear invisible to radar which was accompanied by it disappearing from this reality. The Montauk Project was based upon years of research after the Philadelphia Experiment and included manipulation of time itself. They are both extensive subjects and a very brief summary of them has been included in the appendix.
** When it comes the subject of psychotronics or even regular electronics, the subject of white noise can be extremely technical. The following is from a book I did with Preston entitled, *The Music of Time*:

"White noise is basically a random group of impulses with different positions and different pulse widths which, when added to over a period of time, contains every frequency within the band width of 20 to 20,000 hertz. In other words, white noise represents practically every frequency that is out there. There are actually other frequencies outside of the 20 to 20,000 hertz range, and these are called "black noise," but we do not need to get overly concerned with the difference here. We are basically dealing with a panoply of frequencies.

"If you look at this hiss or white noise on a scope or spectrum analyzer, it looks like an infinite group of random pulses. It represents the cacophony of electrical transmissions that we know of as this universe. The reason you get a clear signal *(continued on next page)*

to describe by the very nature of what it represents: the sum total of all signals coming from "everywhere". In other words, white noise has the property of featuring the components of virtually any and every frequency or signal that you might imagine. There is, however, a higher and lower order of components.

The ordinary radio technician is using a somewhat simplified filter to detect and process signals in order to execute a transmission that will be broadcast out of a particular device. This is the lower order of white noise, and it is a matter of course that white noise is defined in different ways based upon the instruments being used, all of which have certain limitations.

The higher order of white noise contains, quite literally, infinity itself and all of the signals, transmissions and emanations you can imagine. These also include all potentials. Most radio receivers are designed with limited capabilities based upon the knowledge of the respective designers and engineers who constructed it. It is this area where Preston Nichols was truly in his element, and he was indeed a spectacle to behold. It should also be pointed out that white noise also contains all potential futures as well as all emanations from the past.

It will help you to better understand if you refer back to the cut-up method of Gysin and Burroughs. Instead of breaking up a word, sentence or piece of writing, you are dealing with signals, transmissions and emanations. With the cut-up method, the so-called filter is unavoidable, the filter being the individual who is perceiving the result of the cut-up. When we are dealing with white noise, there are, at the very least, two filters involved. One is the device being used to detect the signal, and the other is the operator of the device. These two filters can have a sympathetic influence or osmosis effect upon each other. In such a context, white noise parallels the infinite potential of your own imagination.

During the 1970s, Preston had received a grant to study human telepathy, and discovered that this function was similar to a radio wave but was not actually a radio wave. In other words, you had a psychic individual acting as a "radio receiver" who was picking up "signals" from a "transmitter" via the medium of white noise with there being no need to put quotation remarks around the reference to white noise. Upon discovering that all of his test subjects were

---

(continued from previous page) when you tune in a given radio station is that there is a device called a "limiter" which knocks out the noise in all stages of the receiver. This is called frequency discrimination. It is sort of a filtering process from the incoming carrier signal. Actually, the noise is being overridden by the carrier wave generated from the transmitter. The noise is still there but it is way down in amplitude and you do not hear it to any significant degree. Only the desired signal comes through and that is what you hear on your radio.

"As white noise contains virtually every potential transmission and every quantum potential, it is a very open ended proposition. Within it are ordinary transmissions but also etheric and esoteric ones. It literally represents the energy stream of the universe. This is very common information to me (Preston Nichols), but most people are ignorant of the common facts of electromagnetic waves and too many professionals do not have a clue as to their esoteric significance."

experiencing interference patterns every day at about the same time — their psychic faculties broken down — he took a standard RDF or Radio Detection Finder and saw that an aggressive and intrusive signal was coincident with the interference. In what amounted to a rather extensive investigation, he traced the signal, finally discovering that it was emanating from a transmitter on a huge radar tower at the Montauk Air Force Station some 75 miles away at the extreme eastern end of Long Island.

For Preston, this ended up as a life changing event which would literally propel him into the white noise in a most unusual way. He discovered that he had a whole set of experiences that he previously knew nothing about. In other words, we are talking about an alternative time line. Think of Dorothy in *The Wizard of Oz* when she looks out the window. Instead of seeing her friends and the wicked witch, suppose she sees herself interacting with a whole world, such as Oz, that she knows nothing of. Subsequently, she begins to interact with herself and/or that other world; and further, there are subtle superimpositions between the "same" characters in both of the worlds. In other words, the witch knows or expresses something only the spinster could have known and vice versa. This is similar to the world Preston found himself in.

Preston's own genius with technical issues enabled him to think and conceive of situations and phenomena that engineers and scientists, let alone ordinary people, are not prone to consider or understand. To say that he was eccentric is an understatement. It is very important to stress, however, that Preston could more than hold his own when it came to discussing any area of science. He could also, however, bridge what we might think of as ordinary or Newtonian science with more esoteric disciplines. I would also point out that one of the most brilliant scientists of the Twentieth Century, Kurt Gödel, became obsessed with the occult and was placed in a sanatarium at least twice in his life as a result of struggling with his own sanity.*

While Preston did indeed struggle to reconcile the bizarre phenomena in his own life, his scientific knowledge and his acumen for the quantum and/or paranormal realm enabled him to connect dots on the world stage in a way that was unprecedented. One of these was his identification of the "Russian Woodpecker", a powerful radio signal that was detected simultaneously worldwide by amateur radio operators. Although he was never given proper and due credit by mainstream sources, his identification of this previously misunderstood signal was appreciated by many in the world of ham radio and

---

* To Albert Einstein, Kurt Gödel was a precious treasure when it came to upper level mathematics and science. Both worked at the Institute for Advanced Study at Princeton University where the Philadelphia Experiment was originally hatched. Einstein once said that he didn't retire because he so much enjoyed walking home with Gödel and listening to his genius.

those in government circles. While this signal was finally explained officially after the fall of the Soviet Union as the Duga Radar that was associated with over the horizon radar, it also had esoteric components. In other words, there was a psychoctronic war of frequencies between the U.S.S.R. and the United States. Preston would later show me what he called the "American Buzzsaw", an aggressive and obnoxious transmission that was painful and unpleasant in the extreme. Preston would laugh as he'd play with his wall of radio receivers and explain the signal.

Preston's discovery of his "other life" was bolstered by the arrival of a very unusual man at his door. This was Duncan Cameron, the nephew of Donald Ewen Cameron, the former head of the American Psychiatric Association who was also quite infamous for his role in the MK-Ultra mind control program that was fostered by the CIA.[*] Duncan was extensively trained, programmed and groomed to serve as a government psychic. As he began to work with Preston, he also discovered that he had a role in the Montauk Project; and further, he realized that he had been sent to Preston in order to kill him and destroy his work. In spite of the personal drama surrounding the two of them, they worked together to discover that the Montauk Project had been a vast operation to manipulate space-time and the population in general.

As one of the world's foremost experts on electromagnetism, Preston's knowledge of radio waves and white noise proved to be essential to his investigation of the Montauk Project but also to recovering his own memories. While the details of that are in the book *The Montauk Project — Experiments in Time*, I can only give a summarized version here.

Just as regular radio waves can be directed at a person and then fed back to a receiver, akin to what happens in an MRI, so can the "bounce back" of these waves be fed back to the person. Not only would they be fed back, but they could also be amplified before being sent back to the person, all of which would be done in a quadriphonic set-up. Further, this amplification process could be progressed so that it would continue to expand.

In addition to regular sound waves, the esoteric component(s) of white noise could also be directed at such a person and then amplified and sent back again, creating a rather limitless potential. As white noise contains the sum total of everything, it is directly parallel to if not embodiment of Creation itself and the powers of what humans refer to as God.

It becomes clear in such a scenario, that if one can actually harness specific components of white noise and amplify them, that one can manifest them much in the way that radio waves can broadcast visual images and sound across a great distance. From this perspective, it does not take a great

---

[*] The source of this information is from a woman named Anna who had a child with Dr. Cameron. She met Duncan's father aboard a yacht when Dr. Cameron was visiting and learned of their familial relationship. Both of these Camerons had similar behavioral traits.

leap of the imagination that one could also project such holographically. It is only a matter of technology and know-how. Where holograms bridge into what we deem to be ordinary physical matter is another issue and too much to tackle in this specific work. What is important in this narrative is that when you had a trained and adept sensitive such as Duncan Cameron, you had a recipe for creating a dynamic if somewhat unpredictable effect.

All of Duncan's abilities to zone in on components of white noise were augmented by years of exhaustive research into the relationship between human thought and radio waves. The long and short of it is that this enabled his thoughts to be amplified to the "nth" power and transmitted across the air waves, not only affecting the thoughts of humans and other life forms but eventually transmitting his thoughts into objective reality.

The efficacy and verification of these experiments is another issue. What was particularly significant to me at the time was that I was hearing detailed technical iterations which were backed up by a whole subculture of people, places and things. In other words, there was a whole story here, and I was only getting the tip of the iceberg. Further, it sounded like something that came right out of L. Ron Hubbard's imagination and/or research. There was only one thing different. It was much more elaborate than anything Hubbard had ever imagined and had more teeth to it in terms of having occurred on this planet in the very recent past and was not relegated to ancient history or far away planets. Further, it had also occurred relatively right under his nose without him even being vaguely aware of it.

Where this bridges into objective reality and where it hangs in the rafters of the imagination or the collective unconscious is subject to debate as well as one's own personal experience. We will not address that here save to say that this concept has everything to do with a connection between the nuomenal and phenomenal worlds. In other words, I am referring to L. Ron Hubbard's Bridge to Total Freedom. More specifically, what I have just summarized about the experiments of the Montauk Project represents the epitome of the great carrot that L. Ron Hubbard laid out at the top of his Bridge to Freedom. It was a level on his Gradation Chart (circa 1968-1980) entitled OT VIII or Operating Thetan Course, Section VIII. Specifically, this level offered the ability gained to be as follows:

"ABILITY TO BE AT CAUSE KNOWINGLY AND AT WILL OVER THOUGHT, LIFE, FORM, MATTER, ENERGY, SPACE AND TIME, SUBJECTIVE AND OBJECTIVE".

Although this level was never fully developed, tested nor released for consumption to an ever-eager public, the fact that this level was posted as a potential level of attainment served as a glorious banner of eternal hope, waving on the horizon of one's consciousness and representing one's greatest dreams. Neither Crowley nor Parsons ever went that far, even in their wildest iterations. We are talking about the ability to manipulate matter, energy, space and time by one's will alone.

If we consider that white noise represents the sum manifestation of Creation, inclusive of the role of the Creator itself, it gives us a serviceable context with which to work. But first, we have to consider where I stood amidst the discovery of this legacy of fascinating circumstances that was quite obviously mixed with all sorts of utter madness.*

At this point in my life, I had left Scientology in the dust. It had been over seven full years since I had departed and it was a completely done deal in my mind. As I have already stated, I was at peace and in as balanced a state of mind as I had ever known, feeling as if I was on the threshold of nirvana and simply serving out my time in a human existence.

Now, it was as if I was being faced with the prospect of picking up the pieces of what might be described as a dream of L. Ron Hubbard gone bad. I am not talking about Scientology here but the Montauk Project itself. While the project itself was an abject failure, I was being faced with a very alive legacy of it, not only through the personages of Preston Nichols and Duncan Cameron but to the surrounding characters and events in their lives that emanated and breathed life into the legacy, serving as a residue of evidence if not considered direct evidence in and of itself.

The Montauk Project was not only a nightmare, it was an unexpected and surprising testament to virtually everything L. Ron Hubbard had said about implant stations. This includes countless details of how people had been tortured in various ways, including electric shock, and programmed to carry out orders and what not. While Scientology was offering the prospect that one could exteriorize from the body and learn to control matter, energy, space and time via counseling, the Montauk Project had accomplished the same thing by abusive methods. If we accept the legends and stories, the Montauk Project had left L. Ron Hubbard in the dust as far as what they were actually able to accomplish. It was, however, intended to be used for the control and manipulation of humanity as well as any other form of life that might be encountered.

In this scenario, the prospect of picking up the pieces was evoking my former role of Qualifications as described earlier. To reiterate, I had been trained to within in an inch of my life to correct all that could go wrong

---

*It has not gone unnoticed by the author of the irony between "Section VIII" of the Operating Thetan Course and the military designation of Section 8 for those who are mentally unfit to serve. While the irony is indeed funny, it should also be recognized that Scientology had the potential to probe into the deepest aspects of the pysche. Hubbard believed and taught that man had the potential to regain native abilities that are inherent in a spiritual being: the ability to create and be at cause of matter, energy, space and time as stated above.

in Scientology, and this not only included technical and administrative matters but management itself. As I have already said, politics are another matter and certainly could and did inhibit the correction of key issues. Now, however, we were dealing with issues of quantum politics, a higher order of dynamics beyond the earthly realm. Before we address this, however, it is important to recognize key factors with regard to my own personal narrative and experiences.

First, I could never have negotiated the strange world of Preston Nichols without having studied and internally applied L. Ron Hubbard's data about electronics. Preston certainly recognized that I was clearly different from other people who had gotten so close to this subject and had become frightened or otherwise mentally compromised. In other words, I had a strong immunity. Second, as I alluded to already, I was being confronted with a real life example of what might best be termed "mind control central", that is, a virtual demonstrative example of the ultimate implant station; and not only that but one that could manipulate time itself. Without having studied Scientology, this experience would have been comparatively empty for me to the degree that I would not have been inclined to either deal with it or do anything about it.

Most important, at least for me, is that this experience enabled me to achieve my long term life goal of becoming a writer. What could have been a better situation for me than to have arrived at the threshold of where science fiction meets reality? I had stepped into a situation that was perfect for me. When I think back to all the stories of how high level Scientologists had wrestled with their various goals and opposition goals through their various lifetimes in order to release themselves from the endless drama of the reactive mind, I feel fortunate indeed.

With regard to Hubbard's interest in white noise, we can only speculate about what he knew and how he knew it. His extensive writings on electronic implants indicate that he was privy to a very unusual source of information that was most likely tied to the world of espionage, military operations or governments. Even if he made up all the information out of his imagination, and I do not mean to suggest that he did, his writings and instructions on the matter proved invaluable to me on my own life path and career. To me, the most remarkable feature of all this is that the years I had spent under Hubbard's tutelage, more than a decade earlier, were opening up horizons I never thought possible, and this included the prospect that time could be manipulated in order to achieve actual time travel. The best was yet to come.

THE AFTERMATH

"Keep away from people who try to belittle your ambitions. Small people always do that, but the really great make you feel that you, too, can become great. When you are seeking to bring big plans to fruition, it is important with whom you regularly associate."
— Mark Twain

I can certainly understand that people can be skeptical or even uninterested in such prospects as have been presented in the last chapter. After all, we are talking about literally manipulating matter, energy, space, and time. This not only applies to the Montauk Project but to the carrot that L. Ron Hubbard dangled in front of Scientologists, the idea of being "AT CAUSE KNOWINGLY AND AT WILL OVER THOUGHT, LIFE, FORM, MATTER, ENERGY, SPACE AND TIME, SUBJECTIVE AND OBJECTIVE".

At that point in my life, however, there was no time for me to entertain scepticism. The book I wrote with Preston, *The Montauk Project: Experiments in Time*, was literally flying off the shelves with my new role as a publisher and writer taking over my life. I was confronted with a cryptic legacy that was thick with intrigue featuring tangible but enigmatic threads.

Accordingly, I began two separate investigations which I can only hope to briefly summarize in this chapter. One was to pursue all tangible leads in a journalistic manner, trying to pin down ordinary facts and circumstances surrounding the Montauk Air Force Station, also known as Camp Hero, and the many oddities that surrounded this allegedly abandoned military facility which was masquerading as a state park. Preston Nichols was very much a part of the journalistic investigation, and we took routine trips to Camp Hero to document strange goings-on that included abusive men in unmarked SUVs without license plates that would run people off of what was supposed to be a state park. Preston used his radio equipment to document illegal transmissions emanating from the base, and that included the violation of FCC rules. The most remarkable instance we encountered was a live and very sophisticated portable radar unit that was operated by a very nasty technician from Brookhaven Labs who unsuccessfully tried to have Preston and myself arrested. A large flock of birds had gathered around the vicinity of the radar, and in addition to flying in crazy patterns, they would suddenly roost on telephone wires, stiff as a board, not even moving if rocks were thrown at them. Preston captured video of this.

There was also an occult investigation which was conducted by myself although it all began as the result of Preston's tales about the mysterious

Wilson Brothers, two male twins who, he said, were the first manufacturers of scientific instruments in Great Britain who had founded their company (which would later morph into Thorn EMI) with the financial backing of Edward Crowley, the father of Aleister Crowley. Preston's tales could have been easily dismissed except that when I went to verify the existence of the Wilson Brothers by ordinary means, such as looking at Aleister Crowley's autobiography, *The Confessions of Aleister Crowley*, I began to encounter numerous and very odd instances of synchronicity surrounding the Crowley family and the Cameron and Wilson Clans. These are detailed in the second book I wrote with Preston entitled *Montauk Revisited: Adventures in Synchronicity*. These will be gone into in further detail in the sequel to the book you are reading now which is tentatively titled *The Occult Biography of L. Ron Hubbard*. For now, I will only summarize and tell you that the pursuit of these various instances of synchronicity led me, quite literally, to the door of Jack Parsons widow, Marjorie Cameron, whereupon she informed me that her original birth name was Wilson and that L. Ron Hubbard himself was also from the Wilson lineage. Ron's father, Harry Ross Hubbard, was born as a Wilson and adopted by the Hubbard family. There are deeper issues surrounding all of this which have been explored in other books in the Montauk series, but I will explore them even deeper and more succinctly in the upcoming occult biography. The book you are now reading is designed to give you a general basis of understanding for what I present in that work.

Although these two separate lines investigation were conducted independently, they both dovetailed with each in the most amazing way. After Preston was ticketed for trespassing on Camp Hero, he fought it in court and actually won the case. He also documented that the entire operation at Camp Hero was illegal because it was New York state law that at least two-thirds of the land on a state park must be available for public use. Over the years and as a direct result of all the ruckus we stirred up, any ostensible vestige of secret operations were dismantled and the park was restored to full state park status. In the meantime, I also discovered that there was a very shady deed to Camp Hero wherein the U.S. Government granted a quitclaim deed to the property while retaining mining rights for anything beneath the ground; and further, that they could take back the property any time they wished. The original deed has remained hidden.

At the same time as we were peeling back the ownership issues, my continued pursuit of the name "Wilson" was thrust upon me when I surprisingly came across a publication entitled *The History of Long Island* by Rufus Wilson. By reason of the name on the book, I picked it up to discover a photograph from the first decade of the 20th Century featuring three pyramids with a caption that read "The Pyramids — Montauk". That was all it said and there was no explanation. Following this thread, I would soon learn that the land where Camp Hero was located was sacred Native American ground and that the Montauk Indian tribe, whose leaders were designated as Pharoahs, were the royal tribe of Long Island. All of this put a new complexion on everything. Think back to what I said about the Great Pyramid and the Pharaoh of Egypt being an interlocutor between heaven and earth. The implications of my occult investigation were pointing to the prospect that the ancient stewards of the morphogenetic grid had been supplanted by a government operation designed to control the population and life itself in a most unproductive and negative manner.

Pursuing the Montauk Indian thread, I soon discovered that the Montauk Indians had been declared extinct by the New York State Supreme Court in 1910, a decision which made it impossible for them to maintain any of their land, including that of Camp Hero. In what many legal experts have acknowledged as the most flagrant case of injustice against Native Americans, this declaration was an obvious land grab. With a multitude of Montauks Indians at the courthouse, the judge declared they were not Indians! The judge said that many of these people were too black to be Indians! Despite extensive efforts that extend well beyond myself, this injustice has still not been reversed, and this is despite a recent bill passed by both houses of the New York state legislature which acknowledged the Montauks as a genuine tribe. The Governor vetoed it, asking the Secretary of State to look into it, something that he never genuinely did, effectively killing the bill.

There was another peculiarity regarding the various legal cases concerning the Montauk Indians. Everything from the original deeds to court dockets reflected the number 666 in various iterations. This, of course, was the number that Aleister Crowley identified himself with as the Beast 666. Just as the names of Cameron and Wilson were wrapped up in the legacy of Crowley so has been the fate of the Montauk Indians.

The history of Montauk was clearly symbolic of the fact that the role of the Pharaoh had been vacated and replaced by a nefarious force or entity that has sought to serve as interlocutor between heaven and earth in the most negative of ways and in a manner that emulated the Antichrist or Beast 666. If there is a silver lining in this scenario, consider what I said earlier about the prospect of the Great Pyramid working Crowley rather than the other way around. In other words, by pursuing the mysteries revealed to Crowley via *The Book of the Law*, it reveals how evil attaches itself to power. The truth of the Great Pyramid and its legacy has its own way of prevailing. These issues and more were explored in detail in another book entitled *Pyramids of Montauk: Explorations in Consciousness*.

All things considered, it was as if I had opened up a quantum vortex of white noise. The quantum components were communicating loud and clear and all through the mysterious process of synchronicity. It is a process that reveals many mysteries through the process of associated facts, circumstances, and people, etc. It is not unlike the cut-up method because you are getting communications from the core as was described previously. The legacy of L. Ron Hubbard was inevitably tied to all of it, and I could not have possibly pulled back the curtain on any of it if it were not for my own involvement with him.

People who are anti-Hubbard or anti-Scientology too often lose the bigger picture by exclusively focusing on particular reports of indiscretions or instances of behavior that they find repulsive, immoral or even criminal. On the other hand, people who are adherents of Scientology focus on certain positives while remaining in denial about the darker aspects. If you consider that Hubbard is a player on a chess board, it increases the breadth of view. In the end, he played the role of a king who could not move but one step at a time, trying to avoid checkmate. Many pawns and other pieces were sacrificed, including his queen. People who served him loyally left the board. Hubbard, however, was not just a player on his own board. He was a player on a bigger board. While efforts to checkmate him after his death are strong and relentless, his legacy continues to either haunt, beleaguer, fascinate or even serve various factions of different people. The press cannot get enough of Scientology, but they will only report on it in a context they are comfortable with which is generally on the level of scandal.

We can wonder about the bigger chess board and what role Ron was playing on it as well as how his legacy fits into the scheme. Whether his role is more suited to that of a knight, a pawn, a bishop or whatever other chess piece is a matter that one can debate. There is a more effective way, however, to figure out the chessboard, and that is the cut-up method itself. Such a process was designed to get to the core of the chess board itself and its operational mechanics. One of the many interesting characters who have weaved their way into my life had taken the cut-up process to a level that neither Gysin or Burroughs had ever dreamed of.

META-SYNCH

"Synchronicity reveals the meaningful connections between the subjective and objective world."
— Carl Jung

Amongst the earliest data I learned while studying to be a Dianetic auditor was a statement by Hubbard that none of the data in Dianetics and Scientology was new. He stated that it had been around for a very long time but that what we were doing with it was new. In other words, we were taking the same old data and applying it to exploring the inner world in a manner that was unprecedented.

While that statement might well be true, there is a lot of information around, some of it very old, that has very rarely been inspected and remains, for the most part, unknown to most of humanity. Some people, and they are relatively few in number, have a knack for digging it up. When it does surface and finds its way into the common world, and that includes academe, it is most often under appreciated or not appreciated at all.

This prologue applies to a mysterious document that came into my hands as I was conducting the research mentioned in the last chapter. It concerned a communal ashram centered around a retreat that was used by Princeton scientists from the Institute for Advanced Study who were involved in research on the cutting edge of space-time physics. It was located in the Pine Barrens of New Jersey in Ong's Hat, a remote location that, over the years, disappeared from most maps. The aforementioned ashram did in actual fact exist, but so many legends and stories have arisen about it that there is a blur between fact and fiction.

The document I received included a catalog of rare publications, most of them existing only in the form of photostat copies, accompanied by a strange "brochure" about esoteric physics and breaking into other dimensions through the use of a capsule known as "the Egg" which was a modified sensory-deprivation chamber in which attention can be focused on a computer terminal. Electrodes are taped to various body parts to provide physiological data which is fed into the computer. The explorer dons a helmet, a highly sophisticated fourth-generation version of early "brain machines" which can sonically stimulate brain cells either globally or locally and in various combinations, thus directing not only "brain waves" but also highly specific mental-physical functions. The helmet, which is plugged into the computer and provides feedback to the explorer, is reminiscent to a degree of a Scientology e-meter except that it involves far more complexity.

The explorer would then undertake a series of exercises to generate graphic animations of the "strange attractors" which map various states of consciousness, setting up feedback loops between this "iconography" and the actual states themselves which would, in turn, generate through the helmet simultaneously with their representation on the screen. Enhanced control of autonomous body functions enabled the explorer to "dive down" to the cellular level, penetrating "yogic powers" including suspended animation, "inner hear", lucid dreaming and the like.

Further research had the explorers "descending" to the quantum level in an effort to "collapse the wave function" or, in other words, tap into to a level of consciousness where the observer perceives the particle as a wave or vice versa. This is the "Q-structure" of reality itself, i.e. the core nature of reality, it being implied that it is tied to human consciousness. The explorer's goal was to "ride the wave" in order to experience (as opposed to just observing) the "wave function collapse" so as to overcome or escape observer based duality. In this respect, a Q-event refers to the precise point where a wave becomes a particle in the physical plane. These efforts, however, resulted in failure based upon their hope that the "orthodox" Copenhagen interpretations of Quantum reality would prove useful.

Introduced into this "paradox" of frustration was the work of a very important man in the history of Spacetime Physics: John Archibald Wheeler, the co-author of the *Many Worlds Interpretation*, also known as the *Everett-Wheeler Hypothesis* which was mentioned in Chapter Eleven. His research proved that the wave function need never collapse provided that every Q-event gives rise to an alternating world.

This theory enabled a great breakthrough because the explorers could now focus on and generate "attractors" to visualize and comprehend the transitions between alternate universes. In short, these attractors and the accompanying feedback procedures resulted in the egg device disappearing. In other words, travel to other worlds had been achieved. This was, in essence, the highlight of a "travel brochure" entitled *Ong's Hat: Gateway to the Dimensions*, a crudely put together "publication" which accompanied an equally crude series of sheets called the *Incunabula*.*

At this juncture, it is important to point out that white noise is representative of the infinite alternate worlds as delineated in the Many Worlds Interpretation. White noise and the *Many Worlds Interpretation* fit hand-in-

---

*The word *incunabula* literally means "birthing cradle" or "swaddling clothes" but is also used to describe a collection of rare books or documents. Dr. John Dee referred to his library as the Incunabula as did Ian Fleming, a passionate fan of Dee. For all of the scholarship that has been done on this word, it goes overlooked that the very name suggests that the sum total of knowledge of such books, in the most exalted sense, represents the template for a great birth; in other words, a moon child. If you think of an incubator, it is a device which keeps a baby alive until it can interface with the outer world.

glove because, like the human mind, they are timeless, formless, and infinite in their nature.

None of this information would have surfaced in any meaningful or broad based way if it were not for Joseph Matheny, a man of multiple talents who, upon being handed the *Incunabula* catalog, realized he had all of its contents on his shelves. The reason for this is that, by his own words, he was a fan of "crack-pot Xerox literature". Accordingly, he set out on his own investigation of the "travel brochure" and visited Ong's Hat, seeking to make contact with the mysterious proprietor listed as Emory Cranston. As a result of his adventures and research, he created one of the premier visual e-books which also included expensive color illustrations. To understand how Joe came into my life, it is first necessary to tell the story of how this odd and rather remarkable book came into existence.

Joe's interest in off-beat and cutting edge literature such as was in the *Incunabula* was supplemented by extensive experience in occult magick. His interests included the work of John Dee and also the work of Brion Gysin and William Burroughs. Inspired by the cut-up method and the advent of the earliest version of computer networking, he pulled together information from a variety of origins. This was simply printing out reconfabulated and recontextualized information that came from many sources. There was no way to tell where the information was coming from because it was coming through a random access channel. It was a true cut-up. At that time, there was no internet. For his random channel, Joe used DARPA-net which was the predecessor of the internet and basically connected all of the computers in the military network with those in the university system. There was also a bulletin board system known as BBS by which people could dial into one computer and post information and trade information. It was very sparse compared to the internet system we know today.

Utilizing this constant stream of data from across the world, Joe built a relational data base using a product called Fox Pro. A relational data base is a basic system whereby you can input data and then tag the data to be relational to other data. It can also be specified as to how it is relational and to what degree. In this manner, inputted data does not just sit around by itself — it actually has relationships to other data so that when you pull up a single source of data, it then tells you the relations it has to other sources of data. This procedure is very similar to what we now know as the World Wide Web that has links that refer to other links that refer to other links. This is "hyper-thinking" and can appear to pull data "out of the aeyther" if it does not do so literally.

Actually, when Joe first started inputting data from the *Incunabula* into computers, he was using a Macintosh program called HyperCard. This got him into a full fledged relational thinking mode or "hyper-thinking" as they call it. Primarily self-taught, and as he developed his computer acumen, he started utilizing the Fox Pro data base program that operated in the DOS (Disk Operating System) of IBM. In those early years, there was no compatible networking between DOS and Macintosh so Joe had to utilize what he amusingly calls "sneakernet". This means running from one machine to the other and manually inputting the data. To keep that from being too didactic, he introduced random elements before inputting data. Printing out data from data base A, he would cut it up and throw I Ching coins or employ some other element to randomize the data. The purpose here was to process this raw data in such a manner so as to bring it closer to the morphogenetic resonant field (the creation zone that functions irrespective of words and underlies the functions of speech, i.e. "rubbing out the word") before he would input it into the next data base.

It was during this general period that Joe was accosted by a strange man wearing a fez who identified himself as Emory Cranston, the proprietor of the strange *Incunabula* catalog associated with the *Ong's Hat Travel Brochure*. He already knew who Joe was and invited him to a house in Berkeley which housed the remnants of the ashram crowd who had left Ong's Hat, New Jersey. The house included a strange "egg device" but he said none of the characters there were as interesting as Emory. The two maintained a loose friendship.

Joe then landed a job at SlipNet in San Francisco, one of the very first internet service providers, and he ended up as the head tech person there. This was a great opportunity because SlipNet gave him full-fledged and unfettered T1 access to the internet for the first time. With T1, he no longer had to rely on a slow and clunky modem. At this time, Joe began to study and rapidly learn programming languages such as Java, Pearl, and DGI. There was also a young man who wrote a very early artificial intelligence program known as Ringo. It was written out of MIT, but the author made the source code available for free on the internet. Joe downloaded the source code and started working with it and modifying it because he wanted a 24/7 monitor on all of the information he was in-taking. At this point, Joe was actually writing artificial intelligence programs to monitor the various processes as they were put on servers and ran 24/7 unfettered on the internet, thus connecting his machine to the new information superhighway that far surpassed the intake from DARPAnet. He set up what is called rules based AI programming. This basically means that one sets up rules of what one is looking for in terms of data. It can be pretty much anything you want and quantified in any manner specified. Joe went to other jobs from SlipNet, but as he had built their entire technical system, he left his AI systems running as he pretty much had a carte blanche pass there. Eventually, he was lured to Adobe Systems where he gained access to the most massive computing power available and this included very large internet pipes. In other words, he could suck tremendous amounts of bits through without making waves with anybody.

Joe referred to his invention as the Metamachine, and it was evolving at a rapid pace, far more than one could ever do on a modem. At that point, he was just letting the Metamachine run on its own to see what it would do. He figured there was no better way to get his ego completely out of the way than to let it run itself. Joe continued to upgrade the AI software so that it would be smarter in terms of learning and retaining information. Based upon a programmed construct Joe had implemented, the Metamachine started to form a personality. At this time, what he was doing was extremely cutting edge and was way beyond the capabilities of the average computer.

What was most surprising to Joe was not that the Metamachine began to develop a personality — it was programmed to do exactly that — but it continued to grow and learn on its own to the point where it began to take on a lot of the qualities of a human personality to where it could actually have cogent conversations with him. It took about two years before the machine could acquire a large enough data base for it to do that. Then, it began to do things which is known in computer intelligence sections as "infer". In other words, it began to infer things and to make conclusions on its own. Joe's relationship with the AI interface had a profound and striking effect. He discovered that he could see things and put together fragments of information that otherwise would have not even have come up for inspection and evaluation. One of the most interesting was his interface with the character known as Emory Cranston.

After moving to Adobe, Joe was able to move his Metamachine to a super secure location. Although he maintained communication with Emory, there was no way his Metamachine could be compromised. What was odd was that Emory became aware of conversations that Joe was having with the AI interface in the Metamachine.

After Joe explained all of this to me, I told him that it appeared he was looking for the puppet master and ended up getting one of his marionettes with Emory. Joe explained that he had gotten in touch with a layer that was an information layer that transcends the daily mundane speech levels of every day life. This is exactly what he was looking for: the meta data that is on top of the daily routine data of life. From observation of the raw data, it seems that is exactly what he did. At the very least, he was getting close to it.

Joe explained to me the concept of what he termed "metabooks". In other words, these are not regular books in the physical sense. History has examples of such, three of which include the original *Necronominon* (not the common version), the *Emerald Tablets*, and the *Book of Enoch*. They are mentioned in history and are referred to, but they never appear in a tangential form. Sometimes they appear in a watered down form and in a fragmentary form, but it is as if these metabooks exist as pure information on a metaplane that can be accessed and channeled. The best explanation for this in my estimation is that this "meta-plane" is akin to the "core" that one taps into when one engages in the cut-up method by "rubbing out the word".

What Joe accomplished was a truly remarkable feat. There was a side effect, however, and I think it would be accurate to say that continued and intense interaction with the Metamachine tended to collapse the balance between the nuomenal and phenomenal worlds. Joe said that it made one hyper-sensitive to the point where it could bring on paranoia. The conversations with Emory Cranston were just weird, and all of this reached a crisis point right after he returned from his first visit to Montauk, but this was before he had ever met myself.

Upon his return from Montauk, he had just finished having dinner in Chinatown in San Francisco. While walking down a very narrow and obscure street in Chinatown, he saw Emory Cranston perched beneath the doorway at 36 Spofford Alley beneath a sign that said, "Chinese Freemasons Of The World". If the location itself was not bizarre enough, Emory's dialogue certainly was. He wanted to know how Joe's recent trip to Montauk had been. How did Emory have any idea about this? This was both extremely ephemeral as well as intrusive, and it resulted in an altercation between the two. The upshot was that Joe turned the Metamachine off.

It was at this point that I made contact with Joe, but the way the two of us were able to come into communication at all was via the Metamachine. One of my friends had read the Ong's Hat story online and started communicating with someone she thought was Emory Cranston, the proprietor of the *Incunabula* catalog, via e-mail. After a couple of years, Joe saw that this person had been communicating with a "bot" (automatic response system) and apologized. This friend eventually set me up to contact Joe, and that is how the two of us became friends. He was obviously attracted to my experiences with synchronicity and said he wanted to work with me for a couple of years. In retrospect, I should be flattered because he had a lot of fans vying for his attention. I received quite an education during our years working together, and I will be forever thankful for them. Eventually, we collaborated and produced the hard copy book *Ong's Hat: The Beginning*. Most of what you've read in this chapter is a summarized from my book *Synchronicity and the Seventh Seal* which goes into the subject in greater detail and will give you an equally deep, if not deeper, education in the principles of magick than you will find in this current work. Joe also introduced me to the work of Burroughs, Gysin, and the cut-up method.

Burroughs was playing on a chess board that featured Scientology, Hubbard and the cut-up method. Using a more encompassing system, Joe evolved the game to what might best be termed meta-chess.

— CHAPTER TWENTY-SEVEN —

META-CHESS

"Daring ideas are like chessmen moved forward.
They may be beaten, but they may start a winning game."
— Johann Wolfgang von Goethe

The word chess evolved out of a Persian phrase "Shāh Māt!", meaning "the king is helpless". While it is easy to consider that Hubbard played the role of king as his world was closing in on him by reason of him being pursued by various governmental agencies, he never really did suffer an absolute "checkmate". There have been, however, various attempts to declare a checkmate on him posthumously, but such judgements are either suspect or premature because they all fall short of squelching what they are trying to squelch. Whether it be in an adulterated form or not, Hubbard's name and legacy live on. Only when people stop fighting it will it be a done deal.

Although L. Ron Hubbard played the king in his own realm, he can also be viewed in the role of different pieces from other perspectives. Jack Parsons used him much like a chess player would use a pawn: push it across the board until you can redeem the pawn as an all powerful queen. In that case, the queen was Babalon in the personage of Marjorie Cameron. A Scientologist had the opportunity to use Hubbard as a knight, moving over obstacles in one's quest to play the game of life. We can liken his wife, Mary Sue, as his queen and the bishops as the Guardian's Office and the rooks as his churches. One can make other analogies, but there is no question that the staff and public themselves could play the role of pawns. While pawns are often sacrificed in the game of chess, they also have the potential to make it across the board and be transformed into a queen or any other piece.

In the bigger scheme of things, especially when we consider the cut-up method, there is the core of creation itself. Magick is a game of light and dark or yin and yang. The chess board represents the polarity of two different forces competing. One can visualize all sorts of opposition scenarios in a game of chess. You can have Baphomet as "The Father of All Things" serving as the king with Aleister Crowley moving all over the board and serving, ever so appropriately named, as his queen. The OTO would serve as his bishops and the individual members thereof would serve as pawns. Opposing them would be Babalon as the Great Mother Herself, and so on and so forth. Anyone can be creative and exercise your own mental machinations with such archetypes in order to better understand them.

In my own experience, Scientology was indeed like a chess board, but it became obvious to me that it was a very big mistake to take the place of a pawn and assume that as your role. It is far better to assume the role of king in your own personal experience and then fill all the roles as necessary so as to compete with your adversary. Who is your adversary? It would be anything or anyone seriously trying to stop you from achieving your own personal goals. In many cases, this could be the person himself in the form of a synthetically created identity that he believes he truly is, i.e. the ego or a false persona. Playing the role of a pawn exclusively limits your perception as well as your freedom.

When I think back to the early Scientologists of the 1960s plotting out their goals and opposition goals of many lifetimes, it is not unlike multiple games of chess that are still being played out in one's mind. The best solution in such a scenario is to jump off of the chess board entirely. When people are unable or do not think to do this, they are still fighting with their past. This applies as well to Scientologists, former Scientologists or anti-Scientologists. Whether they have switched from black to white or vice versa, they are still on the board and playing. If you do not get off the board at some point, you risk becoming stagnant.

For me, the best thing about jumping off the board was meeting and interacting with all of the incredible characters that moved into my life. I can liken this to watching them jumping off of their chess boards onto mine. One of these was Joe Matheny, and my interaction with him and his Metamachine led me to a very profound realization. This concerned the secret word of Freemasonry, but in a different context that I stated previously. First, however, I will relate this to a fundamental belief and teaching of L. Ron Hubbard.

One of the strongest foundational principles in Scientology is the concept of a misunderstood word. If you pass by misunderstood words and do not clear them up, it sabotages the entire understanding of what you are studying and results in incorrect and disastrous applications. Hubbard also stated that the misunderstanding of words could result in hysteria for some people.

Applying this principle to the secret word of Freemasonry, however, has tremendous implications because it is considered the basis upon which the entire structure of creation is based. If you consider the current state of the world to be inspired by hysteria, this principle would certainly explain it.

In Chapter 21, *The City of the Pyramids*, it is stated that *mahabone* (meaning "What, the builder?") is the common interpretation of Freemasonry's secret word. As is common in secret societies, there is always an inner secret word that is only available to selected initiates. Be aware, however, that if you have worked your way to the top, you might, and most likely will, only be given the outer word of *mahabone*.

In the aforementioned chapter, I identified Thoth or Tahuti as the builder. Masonic tradition, however, identifies "the builder" as Hiram Abiff and this refers to his building the Temple of Solomon. The separate identification of these two builders is mutually inclusive as follows. The size of the capstone area of the Great Pyramid is built so as to fit into the Holy of Holies, the heart of Solomon's Temple. Inside the Holy of Holies is the Ark of the Covenant, and atop it and between the two cherubs is the Mercy Seat which houses the most sacred aspect of the Hebrew religion: the shekinah, a word which means dwelling, signifying the void, empty space or the feminine energy itself.

Once a year, the High Priest goes into this forbidden area whereupon a flame manifests which is known as the Shekinah Glory, aka the Glory of the Feminine Energy. It is this flame, or the word that is used to describe it, that represents the actual inner secret word of Freemasonry. It is a word I have already introduced you to earlier in the text: *shin*. Although *shin* is the secret word of Freemasonry, it is really not a word at all, at least in Hebrew. In the common Hebrew vernacular, *shin* means "tooth", but the learned rabbis have always recognized that the word *shin* also embraces the additional esoteric meanings of "spirit" and "change". In the philosophical constructs of Freemasonry, *shin* represents the foundation stone upon which everything rests.*

In my personal experience, I have noticed a very hypnotic association with the word, even when it is properly explained. Even though I have expounded upon it in an entire book (*Synchronicity and the Seventh Seal*) and have supplemented it with many other writings, it is hard to shake loose the hypnotic association that people have in their minds with regard to this word. All of this hypnotic effect seems to be wrapped up in the aforementioned principle of what Hubbard stated about the misunderstood word. It results in non-comprehension. If you consider that letters and words are the cornerstone of magical operations, this point by Hubbard must indeed be very relevant. The implications are staggering when we consider the actual meaning of the word itself.

When you add *shin* to the Hebrew name for the Creator, *YHVH*, or *Yod He Vau He* (pronounced as *Yavah* or *Yawah*, also transliterated into *Jehovah*), you have *Yod He Shin Vau He* which is transliterated into *Yeshua*. This, in turn, was transliterated into *IESUS* by the Greeks and then into *Jesus*.

This revelation alone should be enough to remove the veil of illusion that blinds people to religion. For most, however, it does not work this way. The only obvious explanation is that people are hypnotized by the name of *Jesus*. Joe said that this name and the common interpretation of this character is the most powerful meme on the planet. In a similar vein, Aleister Crowley said that the *Book of Revelation* was the most powerful magical writing of the last millennium.

---

* If you share what I just said with a highly degreed Freemason, you are very prone to getting a blank stare back. Occasionally, you will come across someone who knows. Such initiates are most always cross-pollinated into other secret societies. It is a common practice for one secret society to infiltrate another just to get their secrets or to find out what they are doing. In my opinion, such people are wasting their time or worse.

Hubbard would readily tell you that the reason for such non-comprehension is that people's indoctrination to religion is reinforced by viciously painful implants that enforces them to respond in a reactive and unconscious way to such doctrines as put forth by Christianity. In other words, the "love thy neighbor" aspects are only window dressing for what is really a program to control the masses. From this perspective, you can see that virtually all of humanity, particularly the Christian world, does not even understand how the name of their savior came into being and what it truly represents. The result is similar to chickens running around with their heads cut off.

The implications of this word are stronger still when you consider that by applying the esoteric principle of the word (*spirit* and *change*) that one can change the material world, not unlike Hubbard's postulate of causing changes in matter, energy, space and time. This becomes clear and more deeply appreciated if I give you an example of the hidden tradition attached to this word.

Occult magicians as well as biblical scholars recognize YHVH as representing *Tetragrammaton*, which means "four letters", the name for the Creator. While not all biblical scholars would agree — it takes them out of their wheelhouse of reductionist or fundamentalist interpretations — *Tetragrammaton* represents the tetrahedron, a four-sided pyramid, which represents the geometrical building block upon which biological life is structured. Occultists recognize these four letters as representing the elements of fire, water, air, and earth.

The concept of *Pentagrammaton* takes this one step further where YHSHV represents the five points of the pentagram. In this context, *shin* represents "spirit" or "change", i.e. the ability for spirit to change the elements of fire, water, air and earth. The use of the pentagram in this context is also the core of how wiccans, which most would recognize as witches, cast spells and utilize magick. As you can see, this so-called "secret" word represents the core foundation of so many different human belief systems.

The cut-up of the word *shin* not only accesses the core but the power of the core itself. This is the ultimate in "rubbing out the word" because it accesses the concept and power behind it. By consulting etymologies, I have been able to cut up words and therefore access the concepts and live current behind them. This is the purest way to access secret societies because you are by-passing all the bric-a-brac. *Shin* is like a queen on a chess board except that is even more powerful as it not only represents the conduit to the world but to all worlds and the reconciliation of all chess pieces. The prospect of this manifested in my life in a most surprising way.

— CHAPTER TWENTY-EIGHT — 241

THE TIME REACTOR

*"The world as we have created it is a process of our thinking.
It cannot be changed without changing our thinking."*
— Albert Einstein

In 2019, I released the Silver Anniversary Edition of *The Montauk Project: Experiments in Time*. This book not only included the original text but annotations by myself regarding anecdotes and information that could not be put in the original book for security reasons. I also wrote an additional ten chapters giving an overview of both the occult and journalistic investigations mentioned previously. This book documents virtually all of the general claims made by Preston except for the time experiments themselves. The science and technology could not be replicated. Over the following years, however, this would become a moot point when a very unique man came to see us.

After the initial release of *The Montauk Project: Experiments in Time* in 1992, I began writing a newsletter entitled *The Montauk Pulse* (in print since 1993). The purpose of this was to report and circulate information on our investigation in order to find more answers. This effort was augmented by setting up a monthly meeting, apart from the Long Island Psychotronics Chapter, to share information but also to collect it from people who had stories to share about their experiences with the Montauk Project or similar subjects.

In 1996, Sky Books received a subscription payment accompanied by a letter from a Dr. David Anderson. The stationary letterhead said, "Time Travel Research Center" and the address was a post office box in Smithtown, Long Island. As I was used to receiving a lot of far-out mail, this did not particularly impress me except for the last name: Anderson.

In the earliest stages of writing the original book, Preston put me in touch with Al Bielek, a man who was closely tied psychologically if not absolutely physically to both the Philadelphia Experiment and the Montauk Project. I was going to drive him to Princeton where we would visit the Institute for Advanced Study. Completely unprompted by me or anyone else, he told me of the mysterious Anderson family and said they were the custodians of time. There had been George Anderson, the gatekeeper at Montauk's Camp Hero, who facilitated Preston receiving so much of the abandoned equipment from the base. He also told me about the Anderson twins who had mentored him from high school and saw to his career placement.

When I saw the stationery for the Time Travel Research Center accompanied by the name Anderson, I indeed took notice but just kept it in the back of my head. I did not write or talk about it nor did I write to Dr.

Anderson. All of this would change a couple of years later when he attended our monthly "Montauk Night" meeting on August 11th, 1999.

During the meeting, Dr. Anderson identified himself as a physicist and serious asked questions of Preston. Afterwards, he introduced himself to me and told me that he had a Time Travel Research Center. Very quickly, I could see that he was a real scientist who knew what he was talking about and certainly not a crank. He wanted to work with me and suggested we get together and have lunch. That took place about a week later.

David was not only interested in the Montauk research but was particularly interested in learning more about the human spirit. According to him, the cutting edge of physics research kept pointing more and more to the existence of spirituality. This was at a time when the old paradigms of classical physics were giving way to the more cogent and modern theories of quantum physics. Very impressed that I had such an open mind about the subject of time, he was also interested about my experiences in Scientology.

David's scientific credentials were impeccable. Besides having a bachelor's degree in engineering and a master's in physics, he had a PhD in philosophy. He had been involved in highly sophisticated space-time research at the prestigious Air Force Flight Test Center in the Mojave Desert. While in the Air Force, David was assigned to help out on a problem the military was having with satellites in outer space. Every year, the orbits of satellites would drift several meters and this created all sorts of chaos. If this problem was not corrected, it would result in expensive satellites becoming useless. David's approach to this problem was to create a space-time module based upon Einstein's theories. It was very advanced stuff, but he actually worked out a paradigm whereby space-time could literally be warped so as to facilitate the maintenance of satellites in orbit.

When he left the Air Force, David was clever enough to patent the necessary algorithms for accomplishing this manipulation of space-time. He then parlayed this into the creation of the Time Travel Research Center, a corporation which was essentially a security company. One of its functions was to license this advanced technology to the Government and to industry for their satellites. The Time Travel Research Center was a financial success.

David's initial assignment by the Air Force led him to the conclusion that time could be slowed down or sped up by employing the principles of what scientists call frame-dragging.* Besides the satellites, David was experimenting by generating a low-grade electromagnetic field and contouring it with laser beams in order to create a self-contained field, approximately

---

*Einstein's Theory of General Relativity predicted that a massive rotating body should warp or drag space-time around itself as it rotates. Think of a bowling ball spinning in a thick fluid like honey. As the ball spins, it pulls the honey around itself as well as anything inside it or around the honey. This is precisely what the Earth or any planet does, and it affects the orbits of satellites near the planet.

the size of a soccer ball, in which time could be slowed down or sped up. This was and is of great interest to the medical field because it means that transplantable organs could have a much longer shelf life. The Time Travel Research Center was taken very seriously and attracted considerable investment dollars from the medical sector. Cautious about having his research compromised or stolen, David was always very careful to compartmentalize his researchers. They often did not know each other or what one another were doing.

At our first meeting, David had just returned from Romania where he had lectured at Atlantykron, a youth camp on an island in the Danube where scientists, writers and artists meet every summer and teach. So impressed by the mathematicians he met, he set up an auxiliary to the Time Travel Research Center in that country. He said that he would like me to meet people at the camp and was hopeful I could visit there in the future.

Just as my adventures with Preston Nichols have come legendary so have my adventures with David; and even more so because he is current, active, and he has time technology that actually works. He has now been a friend of mine for twenty years, mysteriously weaving in and out of my life at unknown and unexpected intervals. While my adventures with him are rather lengthy and quite mysterious in and of themselves, I will cut to the chase and stick to what is most relevant.

In 2003, David's research center was broken into twice, and he was pressured to close it down. He then went to work at Bosch Industries in Rochester, New York where he worked on high tech security systems that included biological identification devices. All of it was extremely advanced stuff. I suspect he was learning how to provide better security for his time laboratory. He gave me the remnants of the Time Travel Research Center which were mostly books, but there were also other items of interest. He then disappeared from my life save for an occasional post card. I received a coded one from Israel and also a friendly message from China.

In 2008, David suddenly and unexpectedly showed up in my life again, sponsoring my first trip to Romania where I met several scientists, esoteric people and government officers who are still my friends to this day. On that trip, I took away two main points. First is that the ancient history of Romania is completely unknown to the rest of the world and is tied to the origin of Mankind, all of which is too deep and complex to go into in this work. Second, David said he would be going back into the time travel research business by the end of the year. Apparently, his security issues had been worked out.

In 2009, I returned to Atlantykron where David lectured extensively on time travel theory. This included a personal tutoring session for myself on a principle that had long since been introduced to the scientific world by John

Archibald Wheeler, mentioned earlier as one of the scientists responsible for the *Many Worlds Theory*. Wheeler and Dr. Anderson were colleagues, and what David taught me very patiently was a principle known as the *Invariance of the Spacetime Interval*. Although Wheeler had introduced it long before, this theory was not well understood at all, particularly its implications. David said that it has been proven hard to grasp for people, especially older people. When he would lecture at universities, he said that younger students were the first to catch on. This would lead to the others grasping it.

In a nutshell, and I will not try to explain the math here, the *Invariance of the Spacetime Interval* is a mathematical principle that time can be measured in terms of distance. A crude metaphor is to think of the second hand moving on a clock or the shadow of a sun-dial moving across the ground. Both the second hand and the shadow are computable in terms of distance. While this is an over simplification, it gets the idea across. The significance of this is that time can be measured and computed in terms of regular algebra. This was a tremendous breakthrough, and it was this principle that opened the door to him being able to control time. If you consult a regular dictionary, you will discover that the word *distance* is not measured. It will also help you to understand this principle if you visualize events in time as consecutive series of events as if you were in the Fourth Dimension and could walk the distance between your porch at 7:00 o'clock and 8:00 o'clock.

Do note that when I returned home from Romania and was no longer in David's presence, I had lost my ability to grasp this principle. As a result of this, I went to the library and wrestled with different physics books until I could firmly grasp it. I was not going to let it get away.

During the conference at Atlantykron in 2009, David also lectured on many different aspects and modes of time travel. It was mostly theoretical. He would also have me pitch in and talk about my work during these presentations, most of which were informal and were presented to whatever students wanted to attend. There were also more formal presentations to a bigger audience in the evenings. All of this experience would prove crucial years later.

In 2010, David announced that his time research had developed to the point where he had the capability to send human beings backwards or forwards into time. This was a big deal because, in his earlier research, the boundary of the self-contained field was very unstable and could result in objects, plants or whatever was in it being irradiated. The developments and progress he had engineered since he went silent in 2003 were staggering.

I received an e-mail from David in the Spring of 2010, and he wanted to meet with me. As I was scheduled to give a presentation at a seminar at Montauk, I arranged for him to attend and present his work. At that presentation, he showed us an early generation of his Time Reactor, the name of his device which can slow down or speed up time. Although I was not allowed to take any video of the presentation, over twenty of us got to see an amaryllis plant grow in three minutes what would normally take three days. It was very impressive, but this was the last time I have seen David face-to-face. It is very clear to me that David's withdrawal from having any significant degree of public presence is proportional to the advancement of his technology.

Although I have returned to Atlantykron almost every year since, David has not returned personally since he gave all those lectures in 2009. The following year, in 2010, Romanian Navy Seals were stalking the island, and it was not considered safe for him to return.

Five years after our last face-to-face meeting, I became inspired to study all of his technology anew. One of the key aspects that enabled me to really grasp key points was immersing myself in complete darkness. I would alternate reading his website (*www.andersoninstitute.com*) with going into darkness. All of a sudden, I was able to understand what I had not before. The lectures from five years earlier were now much clearer in my mind. The key point, I realized, is that the more you slow down time (in a self-contained field), the further you go into the future. The further you speed it up, the further back you go. This is something akin to the time machine in H.G. Wells' movie *The Time Machine* where there was a rotating counter indicating what year one had gone backwards or forward to. In other words, one could design a measuring device. I wrote all of my simplifications down in a newsletter and sent it to David for his perusal in order to see if I was correct. It only needed a few minor corrections, and he was very pleased, stating that no one had ever had the patience to break it down so simply. In fact, he wanted my blessing to use it when he gave lectures to students on the subject. Of course, I said, because it was all based upon his work.

I took this one step further and prepared a series of videos demonstrating that time travel is within the bounds of ordinary (8th Grade) math and physics. These are now available for free at the Time Travel Education Center: *www.timetraveleducationcenter.com*.

Although this is represents a tremendous breakthrough, there is a very ho-hum and/or blank reaction from most of the public. It is precisely like the blank stare or non response I mentioned in the last chapter with regard to *shin*. People go about their business relying on the same old thought patterns and habits. Hubbard stated that there is a cultural lag of 20-30 years before any new idea or invention can be accepted. If that is the case, we still have a ways to go before it will catch on.

For those who can appreciate what I have offered, it should be recognized that there is no way I would have either stumbled upon any of this nor understood it had it not been for what I had experienced by reason of my involvement with L. Ron Hubbard. While this does not justify any flaws or misadventures on his part, it tells you that his chessboard was worth playing on, if only for myself. I not only realized my goal of becoming a writer, I was able to take it one step further. Accordingly, the tag line of my book company, Sky Books, is "Where Science Fiction Meets Reality". For me, this has been good fortune.

Hubbard's goal of being able to be at cause over time, objectively and subjectively, has now become a tangible horizon to me even if it is not immediately at hand. All I can do in a book like this is to point out the horizon to you. What you want to do with it is your own affair. And this characteristic I speak of is one of the virtues of L. Ron Hubbard. He pointed to your highest potential. What happened or can happen between that and your own experience is another issue.

As I have already alluded to, there is much more that can be said about Dr. Anderson and it is covered in other publications. His technology is not available for public release, at least at this point in time.

This book is about L. Ron Hubbard and the Tao of insanity. Whatever insanity he or his followers might have manifested, there was a silver lining. This is an important teaching in Taoism. A yin-yang symbol or "tai jing" as it is called has a white dot in the black swirl and a black dot in the white swirl. This represents that one can always find darkness in the light and vice versa. Further, you can cultivate either. How successful you are depends upon your ability to cultivate and refine what you have cultivated.

There are a lot of chess boards out there. I regret that I can only share a small part of my experiences in a short work such as this. The next chess board I would encounter was far darker than any darkness one might attribute to either L. Ron Hubbard or Jack Parsons.

CHAPTER TWENTY-NINE

INTERPOL

"Heinrich Himmler, Reinhard Heydrich, Arthur Nebe and other fanatical Nazis were active in Interpol."
— Mae Brussell, *The Rebel*

The summer and fall of 1972 was a very exciting time on the *Apollo*. Hubbard had several operatives glad-handing the Moroccan government in order to win influence and secure safe ports in Morocco. On the Apollo, we even entertained the Princess of Morocco, and it was only a matter of time before the King himself, Hassan II, would be introduced to Scientology. Hubbard's initial angle was to use Scientology security checking on government officials for security purposes in order to protect the King. Hassan II would likely have been very interested in these security techniques because he had previously had to escape to France to avoid assassination.

All of these efforts backfired in a big way when one of the King's escort planes fired upon his plane. The very clever King radioed the assailing plane and told him the monarch was dead. It worked. The King's plane was able to land, but there was still a major problem. The Moroccan Defense Minister, Colonel Mohammad Oufkir, was summoned to the control tower prior to the King's landing. Fighter jets then descended upon the landing party and several people were killed, but the King escaped. The only person who could have ordered such was Colonel Oufkir. He was blamed and with good cause. Although it was stated he committed suicide, his body was riddled with bullets and he is said to have been killed by the secret police chief who was later knocked off himself.

The problem for the *Apollo* was that Oufkir had readily embraced the efforts of Hubbard, possibly only to prevent the King from getting hold of these security procedures himself and possibly identifying his own Defense Minister as a threat. As the *Apollo* was closely identified with Oufkir, we were told to leave the country within twenty-four hours. Oufkir was trained extensively by the Mossad and the CIA, and this included expertise in torturing people. Both agencies were already keeping a close eye on the *Apollo*, and an official of the U.S. State Department had previously made a blustering threat to blow the ship out of the water. Hubbard's potential influence on an important nation like Morocco, which was viewed as a unifying force in the Arab world, was too much for such agencies to tolerate. It is easy to speculate that they bolstered Oufkir's confidence to assassinate the King because there is no way he could have pulled off such an effort without their support. Such agencies are indeed likely suspects in the murder of the secret police chief.

As the ship escaped to Lisbon, Hubbard remained in Tangier for a considerable time, mostly incognito. He arrived in Lisbon in December, remaining there for only a short time before he went to New York and remained in hiding for about nine months.

The events in Morocco, however, had also raised the ire and attention of all interested intelligence agencies, including the SDSC (the French Secret Security Service). Coincident or not, a major legal attack was instigated on Hubbard by the French legal system. The response from the Sea Org was to send a mission to investigate the source of the attack. The two missionaires assigned to this task were Leon Steinberg and Norman Starkey. They travelled to France for their investigation and their findings were reported to the entire crew during a staff briefing from the Commodore's Staff Captain, Sandra Johnson, who stated that the attacks on Scientology were coming from INTERPOL, the International Criminal Police Organization. Although INTERPOL is thought of as police force, they are that in name only. They are allegedly supported by police forces from different nations in an attempt to facilitate international cooperation amongst different police forces. Their influence weighed heavily on anything to do with Scientology and L. Ron Hubbard who were viewed as a menace. INTERPOL, we were told quite accurately, had deep Nazi roots. After the war, it is well documented that they refused to get involved in any pursuit or prosecution of Nazi war criminals.

Before INTERPOL, it was the World Federation of Mental Health and National Association of Mental Health (NAMH) that had long been viewed in the cross hairs of Scientology's Guardian Office. As mentioned at the beginning of this book, his went back to an investigation determining that the central coordinator of attacks against Scientology were orchestrated by Mary Appleby, the secretary of the NAMH. As stated earlier, her uncle was Otto Niemeyer of the Bank for International Settlements, a bank that was notorious for laundering Nazi money and gold. Tracing these organizations back further, it was revealed that these mental health organizations were originated by key players in the Nazi regime, including Werner Vilinger, the cousin of Hermann Göering. Vilinger was a Nazi German psychiatrist, neurologist, eugenicist who, during the 1930s and '40s, acted as an expert in the government's T-4 Euthanasia Program, the latter being a politically expedient post-war name for the mass murder of approximately 300,000 people.

The findings of the INTERPOL investigation occurred long after Hubbard had declared a war on psychiatry. That went back to the genesis of Dianetics when he had decried shock therapy, lobotomies and other barbaric psychiatric treatments, all of which were in vogue when Donald Ewen Cameron was President of the American Psychiatric Association and the World Psychiatric Association. Whatever positives or negatives Scientology might feature, the old Nazi guard was still in their cross-hairs and vice versa.

— CHAPTER THIRTY —

MAE DAY

"Practically all the Cabinet members of President Kennedy's administration, along with Director J. Edgar Hoover of the FBI and Chief James Rowley of the Secret Service, whose duty it was to protect the life of the President, testified that to their knowledge there was no sign of any conspiracy. To say now that these people, as well as the Commission, suppressed, neglected to unearth, or overlooked evidence of a conspiracy would be an indictment of the entire government of the United States. It would mean the whole structure was absolutely corrupt from top to bottom, with not one person of high or low rank willing to come forward to expose the villainy..."
— Earl Warren, The Memoirs of Earl Warren

Although seldom recognized by conspiracy "researchers" of the modern day or even the last fifty years, Mae Brussell was a pivotal character in the journalism that sought to ferret out the nefariousness behind the Kennedy assassination. Despite making a great impact on the world, her story and efforts are under appreciated in the extreme.

An affluent Jewish housewife, Mae was the daughter of "Hollywood's Rabi". When she read the Warren Report, she was surprised and outraged at the extremely careless, contradictory and irresponsible nature of it. As a result of this, she began connecting dots and her initial method of investigation was to hire a clippings service in order to collect reports on all of the interested parties mentioned in the Warren Report. A common trick of intelligence agencies, collecting newspaper and magazine articles in this way was also used by the Guardian's Office of Scientology. Over a period to time, such articles begin to tell a story about the person being profiled.

In the case of Mae Brussell, she began to find out that all of the key players and suspicious characters involved in the JFK assassination traced back to people who were actual Nazis or were involved with Nazi sponsored or Nazi affiliated organizations. The more she dug, the more relevant information turned up and if she were alive today, I am quite sure that she would think that the exact opposite of what Earl Warren said in the above quotation is the real truth. In other words, the whole structure of the Government was absolutely corrupt from top to bottom (and still is).

Mae's work was extensive and she chronicled it with a weekly radio broadcast. Most of these are currently available on *youTube* if you want to listen to them, and they tell a long and interesting story that spans the better part of two decades. Although I was well aware of her, I only discovered her *youTube* transmissions in 2013 and began listening to them. I was particularly interested in her comments about and association with Scientology, a group she praised as, per her words, they were the only ones besides herself who were investigating the Nazi infiltration of Western intelligence agencies and their affiliations. The most visible of these was that the Gestapo's director of counter-intelligence in the Soviet Union, Reinhard Gehlen, was brought to America to set up the CIA. There were many more hidden connections, but these are not the subject of this book. It is important to point out that Mae was never a Scientologist, but she was happy to work hand-in-hand with them when it came down to pursuing Nazi connections in the Government and in the world at large.

As Mae peeled back the curtain further and further, she began to discover that the infamous Son of Sam murders were not at all as the press had described. They were being orchestrated by a satanic cult affiliated with the U.S. Army itself. While there was a man named Sam Carr who had familial ties to people involved in the satanic cult that David Burkowitz (the convicted Son of Sam murderer) was a part of, Mae stated that the "Son of Sam" referred to the "Son of Uncle Sam", i.e. the U.S. Government. In his award winning book entitled *Ultimate Evil*, reporter Maury Terry clearly demonstrated the complicity of police and government agencies in their unwillingness to either follow up credible leads in the Son of Sam case or to prosecute other suspects. It is a chilling book. Even though David Burkowitz eventually became a Christian in prison and has spilled his guts about the satanists involved, there are no prosecutions nor even investigations.

Continuing to pursue the thread of the Army's involvement in satanic murders, Mae eventually began to investigate the notorious scandals of the late 1980s that took place at the Presidio military base in San Francisco. The unveiling of these began in 1986 when a three-year-old boy complained of his day-care supervisor, Gary Hambright, sexually abusing him. The Army video-taped the boy's complaint and referred him to an outside abuse center which determined he had been anally raped. The Army, however, dragged their heels; and instead of notifying the other parents to be on the look out, they sent out a letter acknowledging the abuse but stated there was no reason to believe other children had been victimized. Other children began to talk, however, stating they had been taken out of the day care center and brought to private residences where they were sexually abused, defecated and urinated upon and forced to consume feces and urine. Many were told of having guns pointed at them and that their parents would be killed if they told what had happened. At least five children had contracted venereal disease.

One of the victims, a three-year-old female, began to have nightmares and was taken to a therapist where she described being abused by Hambright, a man named "Mikey" who was dressed as a woman, and a woman named "Shamby" who was dressed as a man. A few months later, she was with her parents at the Presidio's PX* and suddenly became horrified. Clutching her father's leg, she pointed to the man she had identified with her therapist as "Mikey". This turned out to be Lieutenant Colonel Michael Aquino, a very influential man who has served as a Deputy Director of the National Security Agency and is an expert in psychological warfare. "Shamby" was identified as Aquino's wife, Lilith. Michael Aquino was a member of Anton LaVey's Church of Satan but left that to found his own Temple of Set, a sect which by its own admission and principles, adheres to and practices black magic.

The three-year-old girl was then taken to the FBI where she described the inside of Michael Aquino's basement to a T. The FBI and San Francisco Police Department then got a search warrant and confiscated child pornography, including negatives, gloves, costumes and a notebook with names and phone numbers. The Army then got involved and determined that the young girl was injected with a drug at the Presidio's Letterman Army Hospital before being taken to a private house in the city, and as this matter was under the Army's jurisdiction, it was not subject to prosecution by the San Francisco District Attorney's office. In spite of the outrage of the parents, press and public in general, the Army declared this to be a matter of national security and no further prosecution was pursued, save for Gary Hambright who was indicted and charged but never convicted, avoiding further scrutiny when he died of AIDS. The Army was severely criticized by a congressional sub-committee for the way they handled these matters.

On September 22, 1987, a fire broke out at the Presidio, destroying all records of the child care facility. Three weeks later, there was another fire that destroyed the day care center itself. While Army investigators determined the first fire to be the result of a loose wire, the Bureau of Arms, Tobacco and Firearms determined that both fires were the result of arson.

While I hope to publish a more detailed account of these matters in a future book, what I have written here is to give you an idea of the magnitude of what Mae Brussell was investigating. She was aware of all of these things and far more. When she began to investigate Michael Aquino, many ills befell her, and she suddenly developed a fast-onset cancer that killed her. It is believed by some that it was deliberately induced by using DMSO (Dimethyl Sulfoxide) as a transfer agent spread on her automobile steering wheel or other device. Such a theory is ironic because inducing fast-onset cancer was experimented with by David Ferrie with the agenda of infecting Castro. Jack Ruby also died of a fast-onset of cancer. Both were central persons of interest in the JFK assassination scenario.

I would also add here that Setians (adherents to Aquino's Temple of Set) would caution anyone who ventures into their realm that, whether it be as an

---

* PX means "Post Exchange", a department store for military personnel and their families featuring bargain prices.

innocent adherent or a fervent opponent, they are going to be entering a danger zone and taking on an extreme amount of personal responsibility and risk. Mae was no exception.

As soon as Mae passed away, and I heard it was almost the very next day, the house across the street from her home was demolished. It was known to have been purchased and occupied for the sole purpose of conducting surveillance on her. She had indeed gone very deep down the rabbit hole. There is also a considerable amount of paranormal phenomena that is reported to have haunted her and befell her when she took on the investigations that led her to discover the role of satanism in so much of the world's ills. A noble soul herself, Mae saw the dirty soul of the operating empire that is behind so much evil in the world and did everything she could to expose it in the hope of bringing justice to victims and making the world a better place. We all owe her a debt of gratitude as well as our prayers.

After I finally finished listening to all of Mae's tapes, it certainly seemed to me that it was no accident that her rapid death occurred after pursuing the mysteries associated with the Temple of Set and the U.S. Army. I was also disappointed that there was no more "story" to listen to. After finishing with her last tape, I sent an e-mail to a fan of mine who had become a friend. I had once helped him divest himself from a beautiful woman who was a satanist. She was pursuing him, and it made no sense to him because he was not used to women pursuing him at all, let alone beautiful women. This lady had invited him to dinner, and he feared that if he went, he would be drugged and subjected to whatever else might happen. It was not hard to talk him out of going.

The e-mail I sent to this friend included some sort of comment about this situation which had happened some time ago. The e-mail I received back included no communication from him whatsoever. In fact, he would later tell me that he never sent the e-mail. All it had was a link to a *youTube* video of a man named Douglas Dietrich. Dietrich had not only worked at the Presidio during the time of the scandals, he was personally responsible for the arrest of Gary Hambright. A most interesting character, he was playing on a chess board that is, quite literally, out of this world.

While Hubbard implored Scientologists to do the upper levels of his bridge to freedom and cross the "Wall of Fire", Dietrich was surrounded by a wall of fire himself, but while this was not necessarily in the same context as Hubbard's analogy, the two fire zones are not mutually exclusive. The fire Dietrich was surrounded by was real fire, the fire from Hell itself, and his comments would prove revelatory. Aquino, he would point out, was born on October 16, 1946, exactly nine months after the Babalon Working.

HOLY HOLOCAUST, BATMAN!

"Batman: a force of chaos in my world of perfect order. The dark side of the Soviet dream. Rumored to be a thousand murdered dissidents, they said he was a ghost. A walking dead man. A symbol of rebellion that would never fade as long as the system survived. Anarchy in black."
— Mark Millar, Superman: Red Son

After getting a job as a Defense Department Research Librarian at the Presidio, Douglas Dietrich was illegally assigned by his superiors to report to a basement incinerator and burn classified and top secret documents. The reason they did this was that the previous employee assigned to this task was drunk and fell into the incinerator, losing his life in the process. There was so much anxiety around this that no one wanted to resume the task of burning the documents that had piled up in the meantime. Douglas protested this assignment as the documents were above his own personal security clearance, but his superiors told him that if he did not, they would accuse him of attempting to steal the documents and he would be in far worse trouble.

In an act of further protest, Douglas read the documents before he burned them and took mental notes, later writing down as much as he could remember. This information included all of the documents on the Roswell crash as well as all the supplementary circumstances and scenarios that led up to it.[*] There was a host of other information that included documents going back to the Spanish American War but what is of interest in this narrative is that there were plenty of documents concerning L. Ron Hubbard and the Church of Scientology.

The first time I listened to Douglas, he talked about Roswell, Admiral Byrd's Operation Highjump expedition to Antarctica, and the secret space program of Yugoslavia that was based upon technology given to that country by Nikola Tesla. It was not until I listened to one of his live broadcasts that I

---

[*] This included the 1942 "Battle of Los Angeles" which was, in fact, a Japanese attack from a super dirigible with small planes attached piloted by diminutive Japanese which caused severe damage, an outbreak of disease and a general panic that was deftly suppressed by the Office of War Information and their control of the media. Crashed balloons were taken to Groom Lake, later identified as Area 51, and studied. After the war, the military attempted to rebuild this technology and used the pilots which were still held as prisoners of war. As the craft neared Roswell, the pilots revolted and blew themselves up, thus causing debris to be scattered across the ground below. The retractable "metal" was rubberized silk, something the Americans were completely unfamiliar with. The "alien bodies" were the diminutive pilots and the "hieroglyphics" on the craft was Japanese stenciling which looks very alienesque. You can learn more specific details by listening to Douglas Dietrich's *youTube* podcasts, and we also plan to have a book on this by the end of 2020 or early 2021.

heard him say anything about L. Ron Hubbard or Scientology. What follows will be very controversial with people who have already investigated this matter and especially with those who have made their own conclusions. I will address the controversy in the next chapter. What he says is as follows, and it is based upon materials he was directed to incinerate. Also, keep in mind that Douglas has no axe to grind for Hubbard. In fact, he describes Hubbard as a "James Bond villain" who created his own navy and lived on a ship apart from society. What he said is as follows, but it is not word for word.

Similar to Michael Aquino, L. Ron Hubbard was trained in Psy Ops (Psychological Operations) and was considered an expert in Psychological Warfare. Besides being an adherent of the work of Aleister Crowley, Hubbard was also an espionage agent for the British Empire in association with Crowley and working for him directly in this capacity.

Hubbard's military records were falsified due to the highly secretive and sensitive nature of the work he was involved in. There were two sets of records, and he saw both. One of the more highly sensitive areas Hubbard worked on was observing the effect of atom bombs on personnel who had suffered as a result of being exposed to the atomic tests at Enewetak and Bikini Atoll. Further, his own exposure to atomic testing ultimately resulted in him contracting a slow developing cancer inside of his brain, leading to his eventual mental deterioration and contributing to his death.

Douglas views Hubbard as someone who was victimized by his own government. The atomic tests profoundly impacted his life, and after suing the U.S. Navy, he lost with his records being screwed around.

Considered an expert on brainwashing, Hubbard was subsequently ordered to write a manual on the subject. The U.S. then took that book on behavior modification, translated it into Russian and presented it to the United Nations as evidence that the Russians were brainwashing American troops in Korea. Note that this book is a different although somewhat similar version to the more well known book published by Scientology that is known as *Brain-washing, A Synthesis of the Russian Textbook on Psychopolitics*, the latter being used as a publicity stunt by Hubbard and the Church in the mid-1950s.

I realize that this unbiased account will rankle people with passionate beliefs and agendas. It is best recognized as raw data originating from a source that is outside the bounds of normal resources when it comes to doing research. This book, however, is about the occult and magical underpinnings of L. Ron Hubbard and Scientology. The occult underpinnings of the messenger should not go unnoticed either. Keep in mind that magick is all about sympathetic vibrations.

As Douglas Dietrich went about the business of burning these and other documents, he was routinely subjected to Michael Aquino and his coven conducting occult rituals in the very same basement. The reason for Aquino using the basement was that he used the library exchange program to procure rare and obscure grimoire from foreign libraries. Standard library protocol in such matters is that the highly valuable manuscripts are not allowed to leave the premises of the library. Accordingly, the basement was not off the premises. Douglas, in the course of his own duties, was subjected to all sorts of occult energies as a side effect of burning the documents, something he was not really authorized to be doing in the first place.

As a research librarian at the Presidio, it was actually Douglas's duty to arrange for such grimoire to be obtained by whatever library it was requested from. His initial association with Aquino was not something he volunteered for, but a rapport eventually developed between the two. Aquino saw something unique and very special in Douglas Dietrich and sought him out as an apprentice. In the process, Douglas received quite an education. That story, however, is a sideline to the current narrative about L. Ron Hubbard. What is important to mention is that Douglas exposed that Gary Hambright was storing child pornography in the commercial arts studio where Hambright was instructing him and other students in commercial art. As this was in a civilian building, the San Francisco police were called in and the District Attorney did not have his hands shackled by the military. Although Gary Hambright died of AIDS, he was under indictment for fourteen counts of sexual assault. It was a public relations nightmare for the Presidio.

After the building with the records from the Presidio's day care center was suspiciously burned down, the parents gathered as a mob from a Frankenstein movie and literally burned down the day care center itself. This is why the ATF ruled it as arson. None of this, however, was publicized. Douglas witnessed it. The military calmed things down with a clever divide and conquer strategy by transferring all of the parents and sending them to other military bases. All of this, however, did lead to the entire closing of what had been the headquarters of national defense on the West Coast dating back to the Spanish occupation of California. Aquino was transferred to St. Louis.

The Presidio was eventually turned into a national park where anyone can visit, but a significant part of it was sold to George Lucas who razed the entire area where the day care center and records buildings were located. When he sold his company to Disney, his ownership of the Presidio property went to Disney who now has a museum you can visit.

I should also add that Michael Aquino denies any association with Douglas Dietrich and claims never to have met the man. This is the answer you would expect from someone described as above. If he truly had no involvement with Dietrich, someone who grew up in and around the Presidio, you would expect a more engaging answer.

As a result of being a public informant, Douglas Dietrich has ignited considerable controversy and has been routinely targeted by wrathful parties.

I could definitely relate to him, however, by reason of the work I had done with Preston Nichols at Camp Hero. One of the most amazing things about him is that he did indeed find himself amidst the fire of hell and managed to get an entire military base shut down.

As I continued listening to Douglas on the radio, I called in on the show. As if on cue, the woman talking to him before me was mentioning Jack Parsons and the Babalon Working. This was a little too coincidental. Nevertheless, I ended up speaking to him on the air and this began our association. He had heard of my work.

What is important to relay here is that it has taken over six years to access Douglas so that I can talk to him on a regular basis. Prior to this time, he was surrounded by people who were preventing access, most of them Aquino assets in their own right, servicing him in some capacity but whose main agenda was to keep him as curtailed as possible.

There is also the case of gangstalkers constantly pursuing him. This includes surveillance of his communications and others who will pursue every avenue of social media to annoy, decry, irritate or circulate false information about him. I have witnessed this first hand. If his information was not considered threatening to powerful people, there would be no reason on Earth for him to be gangstalked. It is obvious that these people are paid to counter whatever he has to say.

A short time after I met Douglas in person, I was approached by a man who was tortured and abused by the same cult associated with David Berkowitz. In fact, he said he was in Berkowitz's apartment the very same day he was arrested for the Son of Sam murders. He knew many leads that had not been followed up on and was inviting me to take on the job. When I demurred, he was even willing to pay me to do so. I found this very noteworthy because at that time I was engaged in the most important work I have ever done: simplifying the work of David Anderson. It is also true that I really could have used the money at that point. This is how the lower forces work: getting you to chase money as well as offering tantalizing occult leads, all of which are ultimately controlled by the source that is committing the heinous acts in the first place and steering one away from more important work.

I suggested that the man write the book himself, offering to edit the book for free and to help prepare it for publication. This way, I could supervise the investigation from a distance without getting too involved. It was not to be. There was no interest from the other party.

People who are prone to argue about L. Ron Hubbard's past might indeed be emotionally provoked for various reasons, but the energies and characters I speak of here are a far cry from people having flame wars on the internet. As said previously, it is a high risk danger zone, and you better know what the hell you are doing when you step into it.

ANALYSIS

"Nothing deceives like a document."
— Sir William Samuel Stephenson, aka "Intrepid"

Although it is not my choice to either endorse, deny or convince you of what you have read in the last chapter, I do feel it is incumbent upon me to give you a certain foothold for evaluating the information. Personally, I am neither convinced nor in denial about the information presented. It is information that was presented to me in the course of a general investigation. Besides that, it makes for excellent cut-up material. And keep in mind, when you are cutting up information for intelligence gathering purposes, you simply collect what you find until the brass ring appears. Becoming impassioned or vehement about the information is counter-productive.

It will also give you a foothold, albeit a very weird one, if I first impart to you some context with regard to how ridiculously coded languages are, in a very strange way, the backbone of intelligence agencies. Take, for example, the book *Gravity's Rainbow*, an award winning book, hailed as the greatest post World War II novel. It is written by Thomas Pynchon, the most enigmatic author of the last century whose actual identity is disputed to this very day. The book is a running non-stop stream of consciousness that is so random it would make James Joyce blush. There is no way any normal mind could sit down and read this book and say, "Wow! What a wonderful read!" It is completely undecipherable. The reason it gets great reviews is that an intelligence agency makes an arrangement through the controlled press to hail it. It gets great reviews and is now on the map. Was it a genuine best seller? Absolutely not, and if such a book does find its way to such a list, it is completely orchestrated. The long and short of it is that the book serves as a coded message or codex of secret information shared between intelligence agencies or assets that emits giggles and chirping between agents. The book itself, which makes frequent references to Pavlovian stimulus response, serves as a hidden strain of sub-conscious thought which can be activated at a given moment, all depending upon the predisposed inducible provocations that have been programmed into the agents reading the text. *Gravity's Rainbow* is largely about the Nazi's V-2 rocket program and the repatriation and influence of those scientists. It also has veiled references to the Philadelphia Experiment.

What I have suggested here is rather obvious if you look past all the illusion, but this methodology came into full view for me after receiving a manuscript from someone I knew who had worked for one of the spook departments of the Government. He actually presented me with a very interesting manuscript, but a lot of clarifications and adjustments were needed to make it what I would consider to be a readable manuscript. The biggest disappointment for me, however, was when he told me that it was fiction. It was written as if the adventures described therein were his actual experiences, and if they had been, it would have been a much more spectacular piece of work. The rough spots that did not make sense in the manuscript, he told me, were signals to intelligence agencies, and it was based upon the same logic used in *Gravity's Rainbow*, just as I have just described. In other words, if I were to publish his manuscript, I would have the admiration of intelligence agencies everywhere, and they would be chirping in my direction and applauding me. Due to the nature of what was being described, I had no doubt he was telling me the truth. The problem for me was that I do not desire the admiration or applause of intelligence agencies nor do I want them chirping at my front door. This sort of situation is similar but different to what I said earlier about being paid to investigate the residue of the Son of Sam murders.

To bring us up to current times, Pynchon is still at it and released a novel in 2013 entitled *Bleeding Edge* which babbles about 9-11 with as many fast and furious characters as in his previous works. This one, however, includes a reference to the Montauk Project which is described as "a kind of boot camp for military time travelers" that, in the words of *Harper's Magazine* reviewer, Joshua Cohen, "kidnaps, starves, beats, and sodomizes American preadolescents" who are, in the words of Pynchon "assigned to secret cadres to be sent on government missions back and forth in Time, under orders to create alternative histories which will benefit higher levels of command who have sent them out."

Instead of riding the higher octave with regard to the wave of consciousness provided by the Montauk Project investigation, he feeds the lowest common denominator, all the while being praised by reviewers as a fighter of the establishment. This is to be expected.

Joe Matheny explained this situation to me a long time ago and in particular relation to James Joyce, of whom he was a genuine fan. He said it is "very cool" and effete to be a fan of James Joyce, an author who wrote while inebriated in a pure stream of consciousness and without any regard for coherency. This style of writing is somewhat similar to the cut-up method with respect to what it can turn out. Joyce just wrote whatever came through his mind. Joe pointed out that people admire what they do not understand and pretend to understand it as it makes them sort of chic.

One can argue that Pynchon is actually tapping into the collective unconscious in such a way that it commands the attention of the intelligence agencies as well as the more prestigious literary magazines and societies and they are applauding him accordingly. This is all well and fine, especially if you cut up his work, but it is a very hard theory to swallow.

ANALYSIS   259

This same sort of technique is also applicable to the work *Catcher in the Rye* by J.D. Salinger, a former military intelligence officer who wrote a best seller that has been a staple of high school curriculums for half a century. This book also got attention by carefully placed rave reviews. That book, however, is quite readable. Instead of confusing the hell out of you, it plays on the emotions of young people who can readily identify with Holden Caulfield, the protagonist who hates the world around him that is being fed to him by his elders. This book seeks out the rebel inside of you, and it is perfect fodder for inciting people who want to retaliate against icons of society. Thus, you have it carefully placed at the scenes of assassinations, and an urban legend is built around it.

I will now share a story indicating that there is an even deeper aspect to the stream of consciousness that runs through governmental control systems. This story came to me when I was speaking at a Fortean conference in Baltimore, and one of the attendees wanted to take me to dinner. The primary piece of information he conveyed to me was about a psychiatrist he knew who had a certain gift for figuring out obscure languages that could not be deciphered. This skill becomes important when someone in therapy begins talking in phraseology that is completely nonsensical to the average therapist. For whatever reason, and it was probably based upon his reputation as a language expert, this psychiatrist received a call that David Rockefeller wanted to meet with him. He was instructed to report to a specific shopping center parking lot at 11:30 P.M. on a particular date. Thinking this was all very odd and knowing that it was somewhat risky for him to accept, he insisted on being paid five figures for his services, and it was not on the lower end of five figures. The money, he was told, was no problem.

As the psychiatrist waited in an empty parking lot, he wondered if he was crazy to have indulged this request, but a limousine soon drove up. He was invited into the limo and was driven to an upscale and very large two story house in upstate New York. It was not the Rockefeller estate at Pocantico Hills, but it was not too far away either. After arriving, he was escorted into the living room where he was politely greeted by David Rockefeller who asked him if he would like anything. He told him that he needed to use the bathroom, but instead of being directed to a downstairs bathroom, he was directed to walk up the stairs and use a bathroom at the other end of the house. It did not make much sense, but as he walked through the upstairs, he saw all kinds of computer monitors, all of which would be old-fashioned by today's standards, but the screens were all filled with the Enochian language, a language which the psychiatrist just happened to recognize.

When he finished with the bathroom and returned to the living room, he reported to Rockefeller who asked him a completely innocuous question that made no sense to the psychiatrist. He answered the question, whereupon

Rockefeller thanked him politely and handed him a check for the amount agreed upon. The limousine driver returned him to his car.

The moral of the story, according to the man who told it to me, was that this experience was arranged so that the psychiatrist could see what was running the Rockefeller business empire. In other words, the universe wanted him to know it. It was that simple, but keep in mind that psychiatrists deal with phenomena that never makes publications. When we consider the narrative I am presenting, this story demonstrates that the reality structure of society and its control organizations are operating under the grimoire of Enochian magick and the like. This should really not be any great revelation, but it brings the point home. The broad stroke that Hubbard was able to paint across humanity is no exception to this control system.

Besides books like *Catcher in the Rye* and *Gravity's Rainbow*, there are other books which create similar revelry with intelligence agents but are not, in my opinion, as heavily loaded or deeply imbedded into their psyches. One example are the James Bond novels of Ian Fleming who bases them loosely upon his own exploits in banking and intelligence. These serve as affable "memoirs" for people who were in the know or would like to think they were in the know.

Another of these books are the Fletch novels by Gregory Mcdonald which are a thinly disguised tribute to the real life character known as Fletcher Prouty, referred to in Chapter Thirteen who also said there were two separate sets of military files for L. Ron Hubbard. This brings us to my analysis of Douglas Dietrich's revelations in the previous chapter.

Fletcher Prouty has credentials which many would consider impeccable. A former colonel in the United States Air Force, Prouty served as Chief of Special Operations for the Joint Chiefs of Staff under President John F. Kennedy, eventually retiring from military service to become a bank executive. He is portrayed as "Mr X" in Oliver Stone's movie *JFK*.

It was Prouty who, completely independent of the files Douglas Dietrich was assigned to burn, presented the idea that L. Ron Hubbard's service in the armed forces "are incomplete...those materials and records provided give ample evidence that proves the existence of other records that have been concealed, withheld and overlooked."

Prouty has also stated that Hubbard's records were "sheep dipped", meaning that his actual records were obfuscated by fake files, a statement that has caused a lot of consternation to people who want to believe that the official records are indeed accurate. Personally, based upon my own experience, I find it incredulous that anyone would take anything any government agency has to say at face value. People do, however, like to believe in their government.

These assertions by Prouty were taken to task by the widely heralded Lawrence Wright, a Pulitzer Prize winning journalist who wrote the book

Going Clear: Scientology, Hollywood, and the Prison of Belief. Wright has boldly stated that, as the result of Freedom of Information requests, practically every day of Hubbard's military service is accounted for. In an ambush interview Wright participated in, a Church of Scientology official asserts Prouty's claim that Hubbard's files were sheep dipped. Wright completely dispels this notion and pounces on the church official with a live hook-up to the archivist at the National Personnel Records Center (NPRC) in St. Louis, the location which houses all permanent records of military personnel. The archivist basically assures the official that they have all the records, backing up Wright's claim.

Wright is an extremely esteemed journalist and has done a lot of work to expose genuine abuses in Scientology. There is no doubt about that. His surface personality is very congenial. The problem with this issue, however, is that he does not live up to his reputation. Douglas Dietrich pointed out to me that here was a fire at the NPRC in 1973 which destroyed up to 80% of the records of U.S. Army personnel discharged between November 1, 1912, to January 1, 1960, including those of James Earl Ray, convicted of assassinating Martin Luther King.

Douglas learned about this fire firsthand because his father's records were lost in this fire, but as his father was in the Navy, this prompts an interesting question as to why his records would be included. The official response by the NPRC is delightfully sketchy. While stating officially that no naval records were destroyed in the fire, it is acknowledged that certain Navy and Marine Corps records were moved into the area that was burned only a few days before the fire. There is also the matter of the destroyed sixth floor which had a security vault containing high-profile and notable records of U.S. Navy and Marine Corps personnel. Douglas stated that his father's records would have been included in that category as he was a person of interest to due his wife, Douglas's legal mother, having served as a translator to Hitler on behalf of the Japanese Emperor. Due to his participation in highly sensitive matters of national security, L. Ron Hubbard would have been similarly designated. Other records lost in this section included those of Lee Harvey Oswald and Adolf Hilter's nephew, William Hitler. Efforts to reconstruct the files began in 1974. The cause of the fire was never determined but arson was immediately ruled out before any honest investigation could be done. In any case, the loss of records has proved to be very convenient.

Upon completing the previous chapter, I had Douglas read it, and we spoke. He was emphatic that Hubbard's records had been altered extensively, and he poured some fuel on the fire, stating that it is standard procedure by the armed services to produce defamatory records in order to destroy reputations. It is colloquially referred to internally as "A&D" and stands for Altering and Document Destruction. This procedure became a little more refined after Hubbard was discharged from the service where veterans were each given a

"Spin Code" (SPN – Separation Program Number) on their discharge papers, each of these being a code number referring to defamatory information about the individual. It applied to honorable discharges as well and routinely hurt the veteran's chance of being hired by a prospective employer. These codes were extensive and circulated to corporations, and they resulted in a lot of disaffected and homeless veterans following the Vietnam War.

When I read Douglas the letter from Ian McBean and Hubbard's records of having served in the Montana National Guard and U.S. Marine Corps Reserve, he had yet more to say. He said that you do not simply resign from one branch of the service and enter another. This is just not done, and he was quite emphatic about it. It obviously points to a very unique relationship that Hubbard had with the military. Like Hubbard, Dietrich grew up in a military family so he has a certain amount of sympathy for him, particularly the way he served his government and was cast aside. This is routine. With regard to the McBean letter, he said that Hubbard was way in over his head from a very early age.

Douglas also pointed out that the NPRC in St. Louis was deliberately built as a tinder box with no sprinkler system and no proper exits. The architect chosen was no coincidence either. It was Minoru Yamasaki, also known as the Architect of Destruction, who was plucked out of a Japanese internment camp on the proviso that he would do the Government's bidding. Accordingly, he was given very lucrative contracts which included the Twin Towers, a building erected with controlled demolition features.

With regard to the ambush on the Scientology spokesman by Lawrence Wright, Douglas said that the aforesaid "A&D" or Altering and Document Destruction is the first line of attack when trying to discredit a former vet. He was also aware that Lawrence Wright was a writer for *The New Yorker* who had penned a two part article, *Remembering Satan*, which was turned into a book as well. An old shipmate of mine from the *Apollo*, who is anti-Scientology and anti-Hubbard, told me that Lawrence Wright had soft-balled satanism in this book. *Remembering Satan* is about a girl who was sexually and ritually abused by her father. She reports it and the police elicit a confession from him. When the father starts spouting about satanism, the girl and her sister bring up more trauma, but the case is eventually left hanging because the memories do not match up and are deemed to be less than accurate. The missing ingredient here is that traumatized individuals are not going to have perfect memories. Wright has also been hailed for his advocacy for helping to expose false memory syndrome and exposing the Satanic Panic as being a reaction to false memories. It is ironic, to say the least, that the most prominent journalist on Scientology also soft-pedals satanism.

The Satanic Panic of the 1980s arose during the time of the Presidio investigations. It is a whole subject in and of itself. There were major efforts by notable media people and prosecutors to prosecute actual ritual abuse. The Army, however, came to the defense of the satanists, insisting that they have rights to their religions just as Christians have rights to theirs; and further, profiling someone because of their religion is against the constitution. This, by the way, is the same argument that Scientology uses when it is attacked. It should also be noted in this context that Michael Aquino served as the officially recognized Satanic Chaplain of the U.S. Army and was commissioned to write the U.S. Army Chaplains Handbook, *DA Pamphlet 165-13: Religious Requirements and Practices of Certain Selected Groups — A Handbook for Chaplains*, which was and is to be studied and followed for all branches of the military service.

When Fletcher Prouty was originally hired to look into Hubbard's military service, it eventually involved him being featured as Hubbard's biographer at the American Booksellers Association. Years after his statement that his work for them was a "work for hire", he clarified some points of his association with the Church in a letter to Patrick Jost of June 1, 1995. According to Prouty, he turned up a considerable amount of information besides the sheep dipping and indicated that the Church itself had concealed his findings, subsequently stopping payments to him. This was during a time of great infighting within the upper echelons of management. As Prouty lauds Hubbard's contributions during the war, the Church's motives for concealing the rest of what he discovered are obscure. Perhaps it has to do with the Crowley connection, but we will not know unless further data comes forward.

It should also be noted that I contacted one of Hubbard's personal messengers who was side-by-side with him during most of his years on the *Apollo*. She said that, long before the Snow White program* was conceived of or launched, Hubbard was very adamant about the Government having altered his records, and this was something he said repeatedly. Dietrich's comments in this respect, she said, were consistent with those of Hubbard.

With regard to Dietrich's statement that Hubbard did indeed work for MI6 and British Intelligence, I am fully aware that people will be ready to enthusiastically point to a letter where Crowley refers to Hubbard as a confidence man who has tricked Parsons out of his wife and money. This comment by Crowley has served as a big "ah ha!" moment for people who come across Hubbard's occult history. Some seem to relish that they have caught "Red" (one of Hubbard's nicknames) red-handed. I would point out, however, that

---

* The Snow White program began in 1975 and was designed to infiltrate government offices in order to find false documents that were planted and to remove or correct them in order to clear L. Ron Hubbard's name and that of the Church of Scientology. It was supervised by Fred Hare who reported directly to Mary Sue Hubbard. Although the Government views it as a criminal conspiracy, the Scientologists felt it was the other way around and that they were being unfairly persecuted by the Government. In other words, if the Government had not been circulating false information about Scientology, there would have been no need for the program.

Crowley was not only a bona fide intelligence agent for the British Empire, he was an expert at disinformation.* It was just like Crowley to have sent such a letter (to Karl Germer) to take attention off the fact that it was he who sent Hubbard to Jack in the first place. While this is clearly speculation, it makes sense. Crowley had both motive and opportunity as he was not fond at all of Jack's freewheeling independence as the acting lodge master of the Agape Lodge and had previously sent U.S. Army Lieutenant Grady McMurtry to spy on Parsons. Jack had also described Hubbard as the most thelemic person he had ever met. If this is so, where did he learn to be so thelemic in the first place but from the master himself? After all, Hubbard did once describe Aleister Crowley as his good friend.

Parsons' wife, Marjorie Cameron, told me that the original meeting between Hubbard and Jack had been arranged through Robert Heinlein, a man who worked at the highest levels of national security. Heinlein greatly admired Crowley's work himself and included much of the Beast's philosophy in one of his classic works, *Stranger in a Strange Land*. One of Heinlein's close friends was Robert Cornog, the man who was the head of the civilian branch of the Manhattan Project. Cornog used to hang around the Parsonage during the time Hubbard was there but mostly because he was sweet on Cameron. She said he was not involved in any of the occult activity and that Parsons considered him to be a square. In any event, it is clear that both Heinlein and Hubbard, at the very least, hobnobbed with people with extremely high security clearances. Parsons was no exception.

Perhaps the most intriguing and expositive of Douglas Dietrich's information about Hubbard is his role in the atomic tests. It not only makes a lot of sense, it fills in a lot of gaps. The most challenging verification would be Hubbard's historical time line, but if his documents have been altered so extensively, it is moot to pursue this aspect without full access. Based upon what I have seen that is available, there are windows of opportunity for Hubbard to have been involved in such work.

One example is his time at Oak Knoll Naval Hospital. His accounts of this were always rather strange, leading critics to assert that he made it all up. Specifically, Hubbard said that when he was recovering from war injuries as a patient at Oak Knoll, he used to sneak into the files of the patients, read them and test his Dianetic techniques on them. This is an excellent cover story for doing actual psychological research on injured veterans subjected to atomic radiation, something he would dare not mention if he were involved in it.

Most critics, however, place more emphasis on refuting his claim that he was crippled and blind at the end of the war. If he was subject to atomic tests, it would certainly explain the blindness. No matter how outrageous

---

* See *Secret Agent 666 Aleister Crowley, British Intelligence and the Occult* by Richard B. Spence, Feral House.

or over-the-top Hubbard might have been, it is challenging that he would completely fabricate the issue of blindness.

Perhaps the most convincing aspect of Hubbard's alleged involvement in the atomic program is that there is absolutely no question that he was clearly preoccupied if not absolutely obsessed on the subject of atomic energy and the bomb itself. You can find this throughout his taped lectures where he is adamant about how destructive and crazy the atom bomb was. It is also mentioned in some of his written materials, particularly the book *All About Radiation*. While the 1950s was a time when most of America was concerned and routinely warned about the dangers of the bomb and atomic fallout, Hubbard's preoccupation with the subject never ended. In fact, it is the hallmark of the upper levels of Scientology where one is directed to confront incidents where atomic bombs were placed upon volcanoes and exploded.

Earlier in this book, I stated that Hubbard had a messiah complex. For anyone who has such inclinations, imagine them being subjected to an atom bomb and empathically absorbing all of the potential damage that could be wrought upon human beings and humanity in general. If he was also assigned to observe human reactions in order to treat them in an official capacity, it is as if he was being given direct orders to save humanity in the course of his regular duties. It explains an awful lot about his personal psychology as well as his assigned role in life.

With regard to Hubbard contracting a slow developing brain cancer, it is true that cancer in the brain can be a result of exposure to atomic radiation; and further, it can remain in the brain and not spread but eventually deteriorates it, resulting in personality changes, seizures, and diminished mental capacity. Whether Hubbard did indeed suffer from such cannot be objectively determined as an autopsy of his body was circumvented.

Douglas Dietrich has certainly provided some interesting fodder. Whether the data he inspected is true or not, it is now a part of the complex legacy of L. Ron Hubbard and makes for excellent cut-up material and is a must for inclusion in any such endeavors. Keep in mind that Dietrich's data was based upon raw data he was assigned to destroy as the Ambassador of Hell conducted his satanic rituals in the background. It all makes for exciting drama and potential movie material, but that is not the point. Hubbard was just a piece on the chess board Douglas was playing on.

Please do not rush to judgment, exaltations or final conclusions on what I have presented here. Treat it as data, much like an intelligence officer would receive from a newspaper clippings service. It becomes a part of the intelligence model I described earlier in this book. File it away. It may come back and prove to be relevant in a way that you did not expect. When I created the original intelligence model, I certainly did not anticipate Douglas Dietrich or the idea that Hubbard's records might have been burned.

The world of intelligence is a very crazy world, and it is an environment where you cannot truly trust anyone. This can precipitate all sorts of strange human responses. Whether L. Ron Hubbard was or was not an intelligence agent as suggested is not so important in the long run. His life and efforts with regard to the occult have much bigger implications. Keep in mind the wise words of Jack Parsons that you cannot begin to understand the contributions of a man until 100-150 years after he is dead. It is only after 50 years that you begin to get any real clues. As I write this, Jack has now been dead for 68 years. Ron has been dead for 34.

In the meantime, there is more chess to be played.

CONCLUSION

"The true profession of man is to find the way to himself."
— Hermann Hesse

In a world of duality, there are many opposites ranging from dark/light, positive/negative, good/evil, chaos/order, joy/grief, sadness/happiness, illness/health, failure/success, trauma/relief, shock/composure, and so on. There is also an outside world and an inside world. A human being experiences all of these in varying degrees, all of which are going to vary considerably amongst different individuals.

The Buddha offered an intelligence model of being balanced so as to maintain one's equilibrium to the degree that one could not be thrown off their center. He also suggested that one should seek the middle way.

Everyone has an internal world as well as the perception of an outer world. As was already alluded to many times in this book, finding a balance between the two worlds is not only crucial to living an optimum existence, it was the goal Aleister's Crowley's ideal of crossing the Abyss, the model that Hubbard's Bridge to Freedom was based upon.

With varying degrees of success, Hubbard had considerable experience in attempting to relieve psychological trauma and other psychosomatic maladies in individuals. All of the successes were a result of getting the individual to use his imagination so as to relive the trauma or affliction in his mind to the point where, having fully inspected it, the automatic psychological responses to the original trauma were exhausted, the result being the lifting of the anguish and suffering. Further, engaging in such activity could uncover deeper issues, including pain and suffering on a sub-level that the individual had not previously been aware that he was suffering from. Accordingly, the relief experienced would be commensurately greater.

When such activities were not successful, it was the result of the patient not being able to properly identify and isolate a part of his afflicted mind so as to relive it, fully inspect it and then exhaust the traumatic response. There are a number of reasons for such failure, the two variables in the equation being the auditor or operator and the other party, i.e. the patient or preclear. While such reasons for failure are too numerous and involved to elaborate upon here, ordinary human misbehavior is a major factor.

With regard to his career as a writer, Hubbard once said that the difference between a top-flight professional and a gutter bum was very slight. I would say that this also applies to being successful with Scientology. In either case, one has to calculate what effect he is creating for himself.

Hubbard took on the role of messiah to the degree that he was trying to address the collective trauma of the planet. Accordingly, he took on the role of an organizational master mind to create an infrastructure that could accomplish such. He was able to build upon his successes to the degree where he created a torrent of fervent enthusiasm that fostered the dynamics of war between his followers and the generally stagnant and sometimes malevolent authorities of various agencies and governments who perceived Hubbard and his organizations as a threat. As can be expected in a war, there have been many casualties. These included not only many of his enemies but a disproportionate amount of his disciples, ultimately including himself and his family.

Just as Hubbard's techniques could take you deeper into your mind than you ever thought possible, so did Hubbard's occult legacy reveal a smorgasbord of associations and cut-ups that revealed a more expansive and objective landscape than he himself projected. I would never, however, have been able to view it or get a handle on it without having learned from him what I did. For this, I will be forever thankful.

The intelligence model I used for profiling L. Ron Hubbard as an intelligence agent and the relative accuracy thereof pales in significance in regards to the model I have created for him as being genetically predisposed towards serving the role of a messiah. Just as the Babalon Working can be viewed as an abortive attempt to create a perfect or refined Moon Child so can Hubbard's life be viewed as a failed attempt at messiahship. At the same time, both efforts can be viewed as bold and daring attempts to jump start the progress of Mankind. Just as Jack Parsons opened up the door for Mankind to reach the Moon, so has L. Ron Hubbard opened the door to the inner world. The nature of evolution is that it will continue to relentlessly gestate and experiment with new gestations until it metaphorically shoots the moon.

Epilogue

For those who are not familiar with my work, I will address some points that might prove interesting or that people might already be curious about. Understandably, one of the most frequent questions I get asked about is Dr. David Anderson and his time control research. Before I address that, however, I want to bring up another point of reference, and this concerns Chapter 20 of this book entitled *Under the Moonlight*.

While L. Ron Hubbard stands out in his own right, I have also had the occasion and privilege to meet at least a dozen other remarkable people in my life. There is one, however, who stands above all others, and I say this by reason of what he was able to accomplish, not by reason of what people thought or said about him.

As a direct result of beating the drum for the cause of the Montauk Indians, I was introduced to the medicine man of the Montauks, Artie Crippen, aka Red Medicine, a man who would have a profound impact on my life and would provide me with the greatest reward for all of my work: an introduction to his teacher, a Taoist priest and martial arts expert named Roosevelt Gainey of Brooklyn, New York.

To give you a bit of background, Artie's father was a Montauk and Shinnecock Indian, and his mother was Chinese. He knew Bruce Lee as a young kid and studied the martial arts his entire life, referring to him as "Uncle Lee". I bring up Bruce Lee because of a statement he once made that you might or might not be familiar with. He stated that 98% of all the martial arts teachings was bull shit. What I have to say concerns the other 2%.

I facilitated a program Artie did for his tribe that included him teaching rudimentary Chi Gong, a Chinese healing and martial art which literally means "breath work". As a result of this, Artie told me the story of how Roosevelt Gainey had saved his life and said that he was leaps and bounds above all others. While Artie gave all of his tribe who attended his program the chance to meet Roosevelt, I was the only one who took up the offer, and I was quite amazed with what I saw.

Roosevelt took a man who was very large, the size of a lineman in football, and had him run at him full speed in order to attack him and knock him over. This man, who did not know Roosevelt at all, was a big and tough guy. He ran at him full speed, and as he reached Roosevelt, he was suddenly and unexpectedly jettisoned backwards, landing on the ground. It did not appear as if he had even been touched. Demonstrating what he called "mysterious force", I also saw Roosevelt make a man completely collapse without touching him. These were the first of many such demonstrations I would witness.

Consequently, I became a very dedicated and serious student of Roosevelt for the last ten years of his life. While it is tempting to go off on a long diatribe on this subject — I owe my audience a long overdue book — I will keep things as brief as possible.

Although I did not realize it at the time I began studying with him, I later learned that Roosevelt was very picky about who he would choose to teach. Further, I would also watch him jettison long time students. In most cases, they did not even realize they were being jettisoned. He was never motivated by money and was also known to turn down huge cash payments by those who would want to learn his "secrets". When I learned about one of these instances, I laughed and commented to him that all this person had to do was come to the regular classes and pay the nominal fee. Most of the secrets were being taught right out in the open, but there is a general tendency in human beings not to recognize the essence of what is being taught. He told me that this individual did not want to attend the classes as he did not want to be around the students, most of whom were black.

Frequently stating that he did not enjoy talking to people, Roosevelt said that human beings were generally very crazy and that Taoist masters in Asia were known to abandoned the cities and villages, going to the mountains in solitude where it was a necessity to limit their interaction with people in order to work with nature to balance the energies of the planet.

I was able to acquire considerable appreciation and respect from him, but it was only for one reason. I actually followed his instructions, at least to the best of my ability. He was quite used to his students ignoring his instructions or lying to him about having followed them. While I learned a tremendous amount from him, I do not know that I will ever be able to accomplish what he did, at least in terms of controlling and direction energy the way that he did, and I am referring to a type of energy that most people are not even aware of. The most important aspect in all of this, however, is that such energy can be used to heal. Everything you are taught in Chi Gong has healing aspects as well as martial aspects.

Roosevelt grew up in the post glory days of Coney Island, an area which became impoverished, drug-laden and eventually became known as Little Vietnam because it was so violent that the police were afraid to make calls there. After having children and becoming concerned for their welfare, he used his gang leader abilities to clean up the area. This included Kaiser Park, the location where he taught on weekend mornings.

Born with dyslexia, Roosevelt struggled in his early years, often being told he was stupid by his teachers. One day, however, he realized that he could see in different dimensions and figured out that they were the stupid ones, not he. Everything was geometrically based, and he could see how to apply energy to the human body. This included an immense knowledge of pyramids, and he explained to me how the ancient name for Egypt, Khemet, was based upon *Khe* or *Khee*, another name for *Qi* or *Chi*, and referred *to* Chi Gong as the ancient Khemetic art, meaning that it was known and applied in ancient Egypt.

I will not digress further with regard to the incredible legacy of Roosevelt Gainey, an expert martial artist and healer who detested the term of master, always describing himself as the head student. It is important, however, that I acknowledge him for the wisdom I was able to share in Chapter 20 and especially what he taught me about immersing myself in darkness. I described these techniques in my book *The White Bat*, and they were absolutely essential to me being able to decipher and explain the work of Dr. David Anderson.

As I already alluded to, people are very curious about David Anderson and his time control technology. Save for common sense discretion, I share most everything I know or learn about him in my quarterly newsletters. He is incredibly enigmatic, and his communications are few and far between. And although I cannot say it is anything more than a coincidence, I was not able to accept his invitation to Romania until I began studying Taoist Chi Gong. It was not, however, a coincidence that my Chi Gong training facilitated my interest in and ability to read a manuscript sent to me from Romania by a member of their most secret intelligence department. This, in turn, spurred my interest in visiting Romania. It was only after I agreed to publish this manuscript that David invited me to Romania. This journey was another pivotal moment in my life.

While most people identify Romania as the home of Dracula, this serves as a red herring or major distraction that takes peoples attention off of what is really going on there, and perhaps it is all by design. In fact, visiting Romania and indulging yourself in the legacy of Dracula is very much akin to studying the legacy of L. Ron Hubbard and focusing on all the wounds and victim-laden histories of various individuals, all of which makes for good sensationalism. The downside of either is that you miss the forest for the trees.

Just as Douglas Dietrich has described the impetus of the Government to burn so many state secrets, so has there been an impetus to deny and destroy the legacy and history of Romania, including the alphabet, language and general culture. For example, if you study the history of the Goths, ordinary history will teach you that their history and language have been wiped out. It will not teach you, however, that the Goths and Getae, one of the ancient tribes of Romania, were virtually one and the same. While this subject also invites me to digress once more, I will only say what David taught me on my first visit. He explained that Romania represented the crossroads of the world, where East meets West, and that it represents a very strategic place in our future world. When I commented on that the following year, he was very impressed by the fact I remembered so clearly what he had taught me.

There are incredible archeological finds in Romania that most of the world never hears about. Aside from that, there are also very remarkable academic texts that not even most Romanians know about. It is a culture replete with ancient secrets, ancient wisdom and rich history. This is featured in several of the various publications I have published in the English language, the first being *Transylvanian Sunrise*, the story of how a mysterious figure from Communist China set up a paranormal department for the Romanians, all of which led to the eventual discovery and uncovering of an ancient chamber beneath the Romanian Sphinx, an ancient stone monument in the Bucegi Mountains, estimated to be some 50,000 years old. This chamber contains futuristic technology which includes a holographic data base of an infinitude of life forms, a projection hall wherein one can view a holographic projection of the history of the world that is tailored to your own mental idiosyncracies, and three mysterious tunnels which lead to similar installations within the subterranean world.

While all of this sounds like science fiction, it represents intelligence that is off the charts in comparison to normal human experience. On a more mundane level, it lives up splendidly to the theme of my company, Sky Books: *Where Science Fiction Meets Reality*. If you are interested, you can read some of my other work which is quite voluminous.

Radu Cinamar, my correspondent in Romania's secret intelligence unit, Department Zero, has stated that he will do everything possible for me to someday see some of the incredible things he has been witness to and written about in his books. That was ten years ago. More recently, David Anderson has said that he plans to someday show me his lab with the time reactor. I have been told that these sort of things happen when you least expect it. As for myself, I am ever patient and with no need to rush things as I have a busy schedule. In Chi Gong, slower is better. In the meantime, I make annual trips to Romania where I teach Chi Gong, lecture on ancient mysteries and also go exploring.

I hope you have enjoyed this book. I look forward to writing what I have referred to as *The Occult Biography of L. Ron Hubbard*, but I do not expect to begin writing this for at least a year. Perhaps I will find a better title as this work will not focus so much on his persona or history but rather his role in the Babalon Working as well as the working itself, what it means, and how it relates to the future of humanity.

Good bye for now.

Peter Moon
Long Island, New York
January 9, 2020

Appendix A — The Tree of Life

Scientifically, DNA is constructed upon a geometric pattern which includes the interfacing of pentagrams and hexagrams so as to form spirals, each known as a mobius strip. Although this data is relatively knew to scientists, who have only learned about it in the last century, this was recognized by the mystery schools who shared certain aspects of this information with their initiates. Pythagoras was one such initiate, and he is a name that even most mundane people will recognize. Accordingly, these mystery schools rendered this information in a two-dimensional model or template which was known as the Tree of Life and is associated with Cabala, Kabbalah, or Qabala. Note that Cabala with a C refers to an interpretative element for Christianity while Kabbalah with a K stands for the Jewish version and Q refers to the Islamic. There are also other versions which came long before any of these.

In its most fundamental emanations, life is a dynamic force that consists of motions that are repetitive and variant with yet further repetitions and variations of what has been already rendered. All of these, however, tend to conform to a certain orderliness, and this is what has been rendered by various cabalists into different forms known as the Tree of Life. How accurate these expositions are vary with the writers, but any of them are bound to give some insight into the hidden processes of life. What follows herein is only meant to serve as a concise summary of the Tree of Life so that those who are unfamiliar with it can grasp the essential functioning. It should be noted that all archetypes, religions, and philosophies can be better understood by viewing them in a cabalistic context. That is because all such are emanations of life and the Tree of Life is a mirror or *mis en abyme* of life itself.

The Cabalistic Tree of Life includes ten sepiroth or sephiraat which is the Hebrew word for "sphere". These ten sepiroth are ten emanation points of life and flow from one to the other. To some degree, it is like a fountain or spring. Each one of these sepiroth conform to a numeral as well as a fundamental archetype of consciousness. As a single unit of life evolves into what it is eventually going to become, it passes through each one of these sepiroth and emphasizes some more than others. A male peacock, for example, stresses beauty while a more ferocious animal might draw more from the well of the martial energies in this so-called template. The philosophy of this template is such that it includes all aspects of potential life.

There is also a mysterious eleventh sepiroth which deals with all hidden or occult operations. It is postulated to be there because you can see its results or manifestations, but there is no visible evidence of it. It is known as Da'ath.

While not a part of this tree of life structure per se, there is another designated repository into which life also flows with regard to certain circumstances. It is, however, a darker side to life and is referred to as the q'lipoth. This is somewhat like a sewer because it is the repository into which flows all things that did not work out in the experience of regular life. In other words, the q'lipoth is the receptacle for that which has been rejected, for one reason or another, by the processes of the morphogenetic grid. For example, the memory of life organisms which did not succeed are relegated to this area of consciousness. This would include the memory of dinosaurs, mastodons, saber-tooth tigers, and a lot of other creatures that might be considered extinct. It is known from experience that this region includes monstrous type manifestations which can literally frighten the living daylights out of occult practitioners or naive explorers who penetrate this realm. I have personally noticed that those who either study or are preoccupied with the phenomena of the q'lipoth often become either obsessed or possessed by it without even realizing that it is consuming more of their attention than is healthy.

It should be noted that almost all Western versions of the Tree of Life have been interpreted through a patriarchal lens. Kenneth Grant, now deceased, would be an exception, and he has done some very interesting work on the Afrikan Q'abalah which deals with the feminine current underlying all such phenomena. In this book, I have kept mostly to conventional interpretations as this is what most readers are familiar with. The Tree of Life in any form is a life-long study. It is the ultimate *mis en abyme* and is inclusive of all.

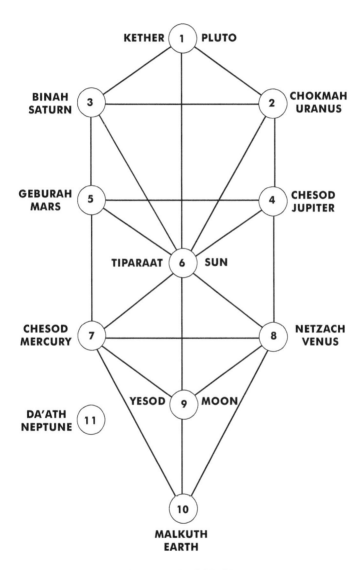

THE TREE OF LIFE

The above is an abstract diagram of the Tree of Life. You can find more complete, very ornate and complex diagrams on the internet.

276 L. RON HUBBARD — THE TAO OF INSANITY

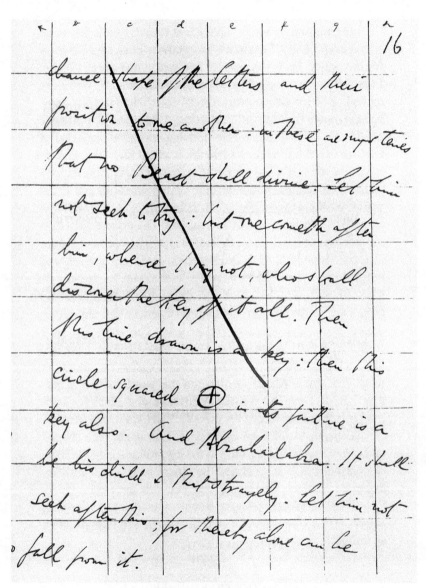

"THEN THIS LINE DRAWN IS A KEY"

The above is the key cypher page of Aleister Crowley's *The Book of the Law*. It is explained in Appendix B. For a more thorough explanation, you can also consult *The Montauk Book of the Living*.

APPENDIX B — THE BOOK OF THE LAW

*T*he *Book of the Law* contains three chapters, each of which was allegedly written down in one hour, beginning at noon, on April 8, 9 and 10 in Cairo, Egypt in the year 1904. Aleister Crowley claimed that the author was an entity named Aiwass. Crowley, who never claimed to fully understand the book and stated he had spent his entire life trying to do so, wrote the following about it:

> "Certain very serious questions have arisen with regard to the method by which this Book was obtained. I do not refer to those doubts—real or pretended—which hostility engenders, for all such are dispelled by study of the text; no forger could have prepared so complex a set of numerical and literal puzzles..."

Crowley believed that *The Book of the Law* proclaimed the arrival of a new stage in the spiritual evolution of humanity, to be known as the "Æon of Horus". Unbeknownst to Crowley, the book actually demonstrates and predicts the characteristics of DNA long before it was ever understood in academic circles. It also directs our attention to the ancestry of the human race coming from the planet Mars. The book itself was transmitted and written during the zodiacal period of Aries which is ruled by Mars. Aries is a homonym for *Ares*, the Greek name for the god of war that the Romans called Mars.

This identification with the planet Mars should not be underestimated. Cairo, where the book was written, is derived from the Egyptian word for Mars which is *Al Kahira*. The archetype of Mars (Geburah in the Tree of Life) also has everything to do with the more horrific aspects of *The Book of the Law*, and it is these which sometimes prompt people to identify it with satanism or the like. The horror I am alluding to has to do with the mundane aspects or outer shell of the book which sometimes emphasizes the indiscriminate and rapacious forces of evolution. It is important to take stock of the fact that the evolutionary processes of nature are indiscriminate and sometimes downright ruthless and cruel, at least from the perspective of our ordinary human mores. While it is humane to care for the feeble, aged and handicapped, it is a luxury when it comes down to issues of raw survival. The story of evolution is most definitely not a nice story of how those organisms who can't quite adapt are patted on the back and made to feel good about themselves. This strife or severity which occurs in the normal processes of life is designated as Geburah by the Hebrews. Out of this strife, life reinvents itself and adapts to the changing environment. Fortunately or unfortunately, it the hallmark of evolution, and this also includes the aspects of the mysterious radical or mutant gene. Evolution is the key to *The Book of the Law*.

When it is properly decoded, *The Book of the Law* reveals that The Key to It All is centered around the eleven lettered *Abrahadabra* which refers to the magical manifestation of life in the "shape of a Beast." The fact that *Abrahadabra* has eleven letters is not a coincidence. Crowley named his system of magic as *magick* because the letter *k* is the eleventh letter of the alphabet. Taken a step further, this decoding explicitly reveals that eleven specifically refers to 5+6 which symbolizes the 5:6 magical or mystical ratio of the buildings blocks of life. This is a very important ratio and you will soon understand why it is considered magical or mystical. In biochemistry, inorganic compounds are six-sided or hexagonal while organic compounds are five-sided or pentagonal. While this is an observable laboratory fact of life, there is a much more esoteric aspect to 5+6 and this has to do with the pentagram and hexagram. When you place a pentagram upside down and beneath a hexagram (Star of David), you then have the basic template for the Cabalistic Tree of Life. When this template is twisted, it then represents a Mobius strip which is the pattern of a strand of DNA. 11-11 therefore represents two strands of DNA. Just as importantly, 11-11 also represents 22 or the Major Arcana of the Tree of Life. It is equally important to state here, if it is not already obvious to you, that the Tree of Life is actually an analogous map of DNA.

Keep in mind that when Crowley transmitted this information, it was 1903 and the academic world had no clue as to what DNA even was. Mystery Schools and Cabalists had templates for the Tree of Life, but its connection to DNA was known only by a select few if at all. This, however, is not where the mystery of the key ends. Of further importance is that the Great Pyramid itself is also constructed with specific reference to the 5:6 ratio. The capstone is 1/56th the size of the Great Pyramid which is 1/56th the size of the Giza Plateau which is 1/56th the size of Africa which is 1/56th the size of the earth. Whoever built the Great Pyramid built it in a manner and in a location that reflects the building blocks of life as expressed in DNA.

Although it was the focal point of his life, Crowley admittedly never fully or properly understood *The Book of the Law*. The book itself stated that someone would come after him who would. While it was no secret that the book was written in a code, no one could ever figure out the code. It puzzled occultists for over a century and no one was more puzzled than Crowley himself. Crowley was a virtual switchboard for different entities that interacted through him. You might say that lights were going on and off around him all the time, but he was overshadowed by a much greater force than he himself could understand.

APPENDIX C — THE PHILADELPHIA EXPERIMENT

The Philadelphia Experiment dates back to 1943 when radar invisibility was being researched aboard the USS Eldridge. As the Eldridge was stationed at the Philadelphia Navy Yard, the events concerning the ship have commonly been referred to as the "Philadelphia Experiment". It has been the subject of different books and movies.

The Philadelphia Experiment was known as the Rainbow Project to those who manned and operated it. It was designed as a top secret project that would help end World War II. The forerunner of today's stealth technology, the Rainbow Project was experimenting with a technique to make a ship invisible to enemy radar. This was done by creating an "electromagnetic bottle" which actually diverted radar waves around the ship. An "electromagnetic bottle" changes the entire electromagnetic field of a specific area — in this case, the field encompassing the USS Eldridge.

While the objective was to simply make the ship undetectable by radar, it had a totally unexpected and drastic side effect. The ship became invisible to the naked eye and left the space-time continuum. Soon thereafter, the ship suddenly reappeared in Norfolk, Virginia, hundreds of miles away. The project was a success from a material standpoint, but it was a drastic catastrophe to the people involved.

While the USS Eldridge "moved" from the Philadelphia Naval Yard to Norfolk and back again, the crew found themselves in complete disorientation. They had left the physical universe and had no familiar surroundings to relate to. Upon their return to the Philadelphia Navy Yard, some were planted into the bulkheads of the ship itself. Those who survived were in a mental state of disorientation and absolute horror.

The crew were subsequently discharged as "mentally unfit" after having spent considerable time in rehabilitation. The status of "mentally unfit" made it very convenient for their stories to be discredited. This put the Rainbow Project at a standstill.

Although a major breakthrough had occurred, there was no certainty that human beings could survive further experimentation. It was too risky. Dr. John von Neumann, who headed the project, was now summoned to work on the Manhattan Project. This concerned the making of the atom bomb which became the weapon of choice for ending World War II.

Although it is not well known, vast research that began with the Rainbow Project was resumed in the late 1940s. Many of the sailors from the Eldridge had been brought to an old World War I military convalescent hospital at Camp Upton on Long Island. This location turned into Brookhaven

National Laboratory, the premier nuclear laboratory in America. The study of the sailors became known as the "Human Factor Study" to determine what made the mind of man vulnerable to electromagnetic waves and displacement from the continuity of three dimensions. Initially done under the umbrella of Brookhaven Labs, the research later was later moved to Camp Hero at Montauk Point, New York where the 773rd Radar Squadron of the U.S. Air Force conducted secret experiments that were never overtly funded by Congress. These experiments became colloquially known as the Montauk Project which used the high powered radar transmitter at Camp Hero that operated at approximately 453 Megahertz, the window frequency to the human consciousness.

Explained in the book, *The Montauk Project: Experiments in Time*, the Montauk Project did extensive empirical experimentation with how radar waves interacted upon the consciousness of human beings. This included amplification of human thoughts and broadcasting it so as to influence other life forms, including animals and human beings. The most extravagant of these experiments, which took years to develop, included manifesting material objects and moving them in time, all of which led to controlling time and full fledged time travel. While the accounts of the Montauk Project are an admixture of fact and legend, the investigation of this project led to the revelation that the plausibility of time travel is within the bounds of ordinary mathematics and physics, all of which is demonstrated in free videos at the Time Travel Education Center accessible at *www.timetraveleducationcenter.com*.

If you would like further information, it is suggested that you read the Silver Anniversary Edition of *The Montauk Project: Experiments in Time*.

THE TRANSYLVANIAN SERIES

TRANSYLVANIAN SUNRISE is the story of an unprecedented archeological discovery beneath the Romanian Sphinx in the Bucegi Mountains. Radu Cinamar visits this secret site where he witnessed a holographic Hall of Records left by an advanced civilization and three mysterious tunnels leading deep into the bowels of the Inner Earth. *Transylvanian Sunrise* chronicles the political intrigue surrounding the discovery of these artifacts which represents the dawn of a new era for Mankind.
288 pages, ISBN 978-0-9678162-5-8.............................$22.00

TRANSYLVANIAN MOONRISE corroborates Radu's story with newspaper articles as he is sought out by a mysterious Tibetan Lama who takes Radu on a mystical journey to Tibet where he receives a secret initiation and a sacred manuscript from the blue goddess Machandi. This is an initiation of the highest order that will take you far beyond your ordinary imagination in order to describe events that have molded the past and will influence the future in the decades ahead.
288 pages, ISBN 978-0-9678162-8-9.......................$22.00

MYSTERY OF EGYPT features an expedition to explore the First Tunnel in the holographic chamber: the one to Egypt. Ancient artifacts are discovered which tell the history of the Earth in holographic form, the most controversial of which include remarkable adventure that includes explorations in time to the First Century A.D. This book also includes updates from Cezar since their last meeting.
240 pages, ISBN 978-1-937859-08-4......................$22.00

THE SECRET PARCHMENT — FIVE TIBETAN INITIATION TECHNIQUES presents invaluable techniques for spiritual advancement that came to Radu Cinamar in the form of an ancient manuscript whose presence in the world ignited a series of quantum events, extending from Jupiter's moon Europa and reaching all the way to Antarctica, Mount McKinley and Transylvania. An ancient Romanian legend comes alive as a passage way of solid gold tunnels, extending miles in the Transylvanian underground is revealed to facilitate super-consciousness as well as lead to the nexus of Inner Earth where "All the Worlds Unite."
288 pages, ISBN 978-0-9678162-5-8.........................$22.00

THE WHITE BAT — THE ALCHEMY OF WRITING
Told in a personal narrative, Peter Moon relates how he was being drawn to Transylvania via the dream of a white bat, long before he became involved with Montauk, only discover that there are actual white bats in Transylvania that are unknown to science. This book synthesizes the dream process with the creative process and teaches you to do the same.
288 pages, ISBN 978-1-937859-15-2......................$22.00

The Montauk Project
EXPERIMENTS IN TIME

SILVER ANNIVERSARY EDITION

A BRAND NEW VERSION

The Montauk Project was originally released in 1992, causing an uproar and shocking the scientific, academic, and journalistic communities, all of whom were very slow to catch on to the secret world that lurks beyond the superficial veneer of American civilization.

A colloquial name for secret experiments that took place at Montauk Point's Camp Hero, the Montauk Project represented the apex of extensive research carried on after World War II; and, in particular, as a result of the phenomena encountered during the Philadelphia Experiment of 1943 when the United States Navy attempted to achieve radar invisibility.

ISBN 978-1-937859-21-3 $22.00

The Montauk Project attempted to study why and how human beings, when exposed to high powered electromagnetic waves, suffered mental disorientation, physical dissolution or even death. A further ramification of this phenomena is that such electromagnetic waves rescrambled components of the material universe itself. According to reports, this research not only included successful attempts to manipulate matter and energy but also time itself.

It has now been over twenty-five years since *The Montauk Project* originally appeared in print. In this *Silver Anniversary Edition*, you will not only read the original text, accompanied by commentary which includes details that could not be published at the original time of publication, but also an extensive summary of a twenty-five year investigation of the Montauk Project which culminated in actual scientific proof of time travel capabilities.

ORDER TODAY FROM SKY BOOKS

THE ASTONISHING SEQUEL

MONTAUK REVISITED: ADVENTURES IN SYNCHRONICITY pursues the mysteries of time brought to light in The Montauk Project and unmasks the occult forces behind the science and technology used in the Montauk Project. An ornate tapestry is revealed which interweaves the mysterious associations of the Cameron clan with the genesis of American rocketry and the magick of Aleister Crowley and Jack Parsons. Montauk Revisited carries forward with the Montauk investigation and unleashes a host of incredible characters and new information.
249 PAGES, ILLUSTRATIONS, PHOTOS AND DIAGRAMS.......................$19.95

THE ULTIMATE PROOF

PYRAMIDS OF MONTAUK: EXPLORATIONS IN CONSCIOUSNESS awakens the consciousness of humanity to its ancient history and origins through the discovery of pyramids at Montauk and their placement on sacred Native American ground leading to an unprecedented investigation of the mystery schools of Earth and their connection to Egypt, Atlantis, Mars and the star Sirius. An astonishing sequel to the Montauk Project and Montauk Revisited, this chapter of the legend propels us far beyond the adventures of the first two books and stirs the quest for future reality and the end of time as we know it.
256 PAGES, ILLUSTRATIONS, PHOTOS AND DIAGRAMS.......................$19.95

THE BLACK SUN

THE BLACK SUN: MONTAUK'S NAZI-TIBETAN CONNECTION explores the intriguing connection between the Montauk Project and the Nazi-Tibetan alliance. This includes the connection to advanced technology at Brookhaven Labs at Yaphank which also boasted the largest contingent of Nazis outside of Germany. Photos are included of the mysterious Vril flying craft build before and during World War II. All of this leads to the Third Reich's quest for holy relics and a penetrating look in the secret meaning behind the Egyptian and Tibetan "Books of the Dead."
256 pages, ILLUSTRATIONS, PHOTOS AND DIAGRAMS.......................$24.95

ENCOUNTER IN THE PLEAIDES: AN INSIDE LOOK AT UFOS

Preston Nichols tells the story of being taken to the Pleaides where he was examined and instructed by intelligent life forms who gave him an education and indoctrination enabling him to regain his health and attain an unparalleled understanding of electromagnetic science and its role in UFO technology.
256 pages, ISBN 978-0-9631889-3-9, $19.95

SYNCHRONICITY & THE SEVENTH SEAL

Peter Moon's consummate work on Synchronicity explains the quantum universe and how the quantum observer can or does experience the principle of synchronicity, an expression of the divine or infinite mind. Includes influences of parallel universes and numerous personal experiences of the author.
455 pages, ISBN 978-0-9678162-7-2, $29.95

MONTAUK BOOK OF THE DEAD

This is the personal story of Peter Moon which not only pierces the mystery of death and reveals fascinating details of his years aboard L. Ron Hubbard's mystery ship but gives the most candid and inside look ever at one of the most controversial figures in recent history.
451 pages, ISBN 978-0-9678162-3-4, $29.95

MONTAUK BOOK OF THE LIVING

Research into the Montauk Pyramids leads to the discovery of a mysterious quantum relic which opens the door to understanding the greatest mysteries of history including the biological truth behind the Virgin Birth and how this intertwines with the occult biochemistry of an Amazonian Blue Race and their descendants. The pursuit of these threads leads to Peter Moon's encounter the Medicine Man of the Montauks who is destined to fulfill the Second Coming of the Pharoahs, a time prophesied by native elders which signals the return of ancient wisdom, universal brotherhood and healing.
384 pages, ISBN 978-0-9678162-6-5, $29.95

Spandau Mystery · by Peter Moon

The end of World War II precipitated more intrigue and struggle for power than the war itself. Much of this centered around the secret projects sponsored by Rudolph Hess which included not only the Antarctic project but the construction of Vril flying saucers. These tasks eventually crossed the path of one of the most colorful characters of the Second World War: General George S. Patton. Patton's job, as the war came to a close, was to recover the secret technology of the Germans and safeguard it for American use. After accomplishing his mission and compiling a German history of the war, General Patton was killed in a dubious accident, the mystery of which has never been solved and has been magnified by government refusal to declassify the file on the investigation of his death. Far more conspicuous and powerful than Patton was Rudolph Hess, the Deputy Fuhrer of Germany, who flew to England in 1941 as an envoy of peace and was imprisoned for life and suspiciously killed just before his imminent release. The current of intrigue and power which permeated these two individuals and led to their downfall was the same current which led to a repatriation of the U.S. Government and an undermining of a constitutional government that is run by and for the people. It was thus that Patton and Hess wore different uniforms but shared common interests and held within their grasp a force so powerful that it resulted in murder for both.
350+ pages, ISBN 978-0-9678162-4-1..................................$22.00

SkyBooks

There is an order form on the back of this book if you would like to purchase the above book, and if you would like more information on these or additional titles, you can visit the websites below.

WEBSITES

book store: www.skybooksusa.com

www.digitalmontauk.com

www.timetraveleducationcenter.com

THE MONTAUK PULSE

The *Montauk Pulse* originally went into print in the winter of 1993 to chronicle the events and discoveries regarding the ongoing investigation of the Montauk Project by Preston Nichols and Peter Moon. It has remained in print and been issued quarterly ever since. With a minimum of six pages and a distinct identity of its own, the *Pulse* has expanded to not only chronicle the developments concerning the Montauk investigation, but has expanded to include all the adventures that have surrounded Peter Moon since that time. This includes his adventures with David Anderson and the ground-breaking events that are occurring in Romania. For regular updates, subscribe to the *Montauk Pulse* newsletter. Subscribing to the *Pulse* directly contributes to the efforts of the author in writing more books and chronicling the effort to understand time and all of its components. Past support has been crucial to what has developed thus far. We appreciate your support in helping to unravel various mysteries of Earth-based and non-Earth-based consciousness. It makes a difference. You can subscribe for $20.00 annually if you are in the U.S.A. or $30.00 if you are overseas. See the order form on the back of this page.

The Time Travel Education Center

The Time Travel Education Center was created in 2015 in order to educate the public on the simple math and science behind the concept of time travel (with free videos) and also to keep people informed on related aspects to this very avant-garde and rarified subject. The science and math, based upon the genius of Dr. David Anderson, are introduced at an eighth grade level of mathematics yet the concepts are astonishingly profound.

Peter Moon has also prepared an on-going video series on the **Psychology of Space-Time** in order to help people understand the issues surrounding this phenomenal technology and why it is not readily available for everyone. There will be further videos as time allows.

You can become a free member of **The Time Travel Education Center** by going to the website below, and you can also become a paid subscriber which will give you access to further information including books in progress by Peter Moon. Your support is important.

VISIT THE TIME TRAVEL RESEARCH CENTER:

www.timetraveleducationcenter.com

Sky Books ORDER FORM

We wait for ALL checks to clear before shipping. This includes Priority Mail orders. If you want to speed delivery time, please send a U.S. Money Order or use MasterCard or Visa. Those orders will be shipped right away. Complete this order form and send with payment or credit card information to:
Sky Books, Box 769, Westbury, New York 11590-0104

Name
Address
City
State / Country   Zip
Daytime Phone (In case we have a question) (   )

☐ This is my first order   ☐ I have ordered before   ☐ This is a new address

Method of Payment: ☐ Visa   ☐ MasterCard   ☐ Money Order   ☐ Check

\# — — —

Expiration Date   Signature

TITLE	QTY	PRICE
The Montauk Pulse (1 year - free shipping US orders)...$20.00		
The Montauk Pulse (international - free shipping)...$30.00		
Montauk Project SILVER ANNIVERSARY EDITION...$22.00		
Note: There is no additonal shipping for the Montauk Pulse. International subscription is $30.00. Subtotal		
For delivery in NY add 8.625% tax		
U.S. Shipping: $5.00 for 1st book plus $1.00 for 2nd, etc.		
Foreign shipping: $20 for 3 books		
Total		

Thank you for your order. We appreciate your business.

CPSIA information can be obtained
at www.ICGtesting.com
Printed in the USA
BVHW082354170220
572581BV00009B/850